THE 100 GREATEST BOXERS OF ALL TIME
BY BERT RANDOLPH SUGAR

A Rutledge Book

BONANZA BOOKS
New York, New York

THIS BOOK IS DEDICATED TO BOXING'S "GREATEST": ITS FANS

Library of Congress Cataloging in Publication Data

Sugar, Bert Randolph.
    The 100 greatest boxers of all time.

    "A Rutledge book."
    1. Boxers (Sports)—Biography. I. Title.
II. Title: One hundred greatest boxers of all time.
GV1131.S84   1984   796.8'3'0922 [B]   84-188224
ISBN 0-517-67246-4

h g f e d c b

Designed by Richard Kubicz and Antonio Grippi

Edited by Hedy Caplan and Jennifer Weis

The author wishes to thank Jimmy Jacobs and Murray Goodman,
who generously opened their archives and donated many
photos, most of which will be seen here for the first time. Thanks
also to John Grasso, who provided the thumbnail sketches of
each fighter's career.

INTRODUCTION

In days of olde, religious contemplatives were wont to argue over minor points of esoterica, like the number of angels on heads of pins, and other such wonderfulnesses. Boxing contemplatives go through the same masturbatory exercises. Only their arguments center around the word "Greatest"—as in who was the "Greatest" this and the "Greatest" that.

Scholars of the religion known as boxing even have their own *sanctum sanctorum* to rival the monastery, that of the public house or pub. There, they congregate to argue the relative merits of their convictions and come prepared to deny those of their brethren.

Thus, it was appropriate that the concept for the book "The 100 Greatest Boxers of All Time" first bestirred itself at one of those so-called ecclesiastical watering holes named O'Reilly's Pub, where I had taken up my Office-in-Exile after being summarily relieved of my duties at *Ring* by my three former partners.

O'Reilly's was a library where I could smoke and drink. It also was a wellspring of opinions, not only those expressed by patrons and barkeeps, but also those framed and hung on the walls surrounding the booths. One of those, which hung just over my hat, read:

"Dear Son,

Just a few lines to let you know that I am still alive. I am writing this slowly because I know that you can't read fast. You won't know the house when you come home, we've moved.

About your father, he has got a lovely new job. He has 500 men under him. He cuts grass at the cemetery. Your sister Mary had a baby this morning. I haven't found out yet whether it's a boy or a girl, so I don't know if you're an aunt or an uncle.

I went to the doctor's on Thursday and your father came with me. The doctor put a small tube in my mouth and told me not to talk for 10 minutes. Your father offered to buy it from him.

Your uncle Patrick drowned last week in a vat of Irish whiskey at the Dublin brewery. Some of his workmates tried to save him, but he fought them off bravely. They cremated him and it took 3 days to put out the fire.

It only rained twice this week: First for 3 days, then for 4. We had a letter from the undertaker. He said if the last payment on your grandmother's plot wasn't paid in 7 days, up she comes.

Your loving Mother.

P.S. I was going to send you 5 pounds, but I have already sealed the envelope.

With solid wisdom like that, O'Reilly's was obviously a place for boxing mavens to congregate and share their views. And several did, including men like Ray Arcel, Barney Nagler, and Jimmy Jacobs, among others, sharing my table and my conversation.

Now, normally, whenever I hear someone utter those magic words, "I remember . . . " I reach for my drink. However, those many friends I shared talk and table with constantly dropped that phrase into their conversation like an olive into a martini and reminisced about the "Greatest." It soon became a war that would never have an armistice and would never end. But, most importantly, it became the seed of an idea for a book, a book on boxing's "Greatest."

I started scribbling the names of those who could be considered under the amorphous title "Greatest" on the placemats at O'Reilly's, constantly adding, deleting and refining my selections as more information and greater insights became available. It soon became apparent that a man's greatness could not necessarily be deciphered by his mere won-lost record, which merely illumined his greatness as smoke defined light in the old movie houses of my youth. In fact, no amount of fistic bookkeeping could account for greatness.

And yet, as I pondered the problem of assembling a group of greats, it occurred to me that the very word "Greatest" takes on an undefined meaning, like water assuming the shape of its carrier. In some, that greatness may be seen in their punching power, in others their defensive skills, in still others a crowd-pleasing style or a determination or a thousand and one other elements that go into building that fragile monument called "Greatest." Granted, no one has ever been overheard saying, "Let's go to the fights to see So-and-So's stamina . . . " but it, too, is one of the many elements that goes into the making of greatness. So, too, is their competition, for every great needs a whetstone to hone his greatness on, or, as Marvelous Marvin Hagler—who unfortunately, through no fault of his own, has never stepped in with the best of his time—said, "If you're going to be the best, you have to fight the best."

Yet another factor in assessing a fighter's greatness is his durability. But not the kind of durability that has a fighter mimicking and mocking his once-greatness with a public epilogue in the ring. Thus, we will not judge the John L. of the tumorous belly casting an image of manly disaster or of Joe Louis of the sagging skin or of Muhammad Ali of the eyes hanging low in their sockets. No, even though each man's body is like a bar of soap, wearing down from repeated usage, we must judge him at his peak, just when the wrapper is taken off. Otherwise, because so many greats and potential greats have ended their careers not with a bang but with an "L" in the record books for a last loss, we would be forced to conclude from the last fight that Alvin Green was better than Ezzard Charles, Trevor Berbick better than Muhammad Ali, Chester Slider better than Henry Armstrong, etc., etc., *ad nauseum*. Each of these men included between these covers must be selected like a properly ripened fruit, at their peak of picking. Not before, and certainly not after. But at that magic moment of greatness.

Next, I ran into the problem of those whose greatness has been marinated by memories, those roses that blossomed once and then faded forever. And yet, many still are cherished by those who relive the indelible memories of their childhood through the exploits of their heroes. For greatness to many means the greatness of the scrapbook sirens of our youth. And, in a manner similar to a concert audience which breaks into applause when a performer who has nothing to do with a song introduces it from the stage, applauding themselves for recognizing the song, nothing more, we tend to applaud those we recognize more than those we don't. Having listened to men of old talk about the good old days as if the clock never moved, and younger men whose world started but a few years ago—and to whom this era will be their "good old days" in just ten years—I have tried to cherish their memories without actually embracing them, applauding their recognition of fighters but accepting them along generational fault lines.

Then there are those traditionalists who believe, as Walt Whitman did, that "No really great song can ever attain full purport till long after the death of its singer . . . " and hold that no career of a boxer can ever be fully assessed until long after that boxer passes from the scene. I cannot accept that, because once their peak has been reached, the rest becomes history and can be assessed.

Now it became time to wrestle with the problem of ascribing varying degrees of greatness to those whom I already had identified as belonging to the specie "Greatest." It was a time-honored problem, one best stated by the late Al Buck, who asked, "If you grow a near-perfect peach, then produce a similar fruit, can you honestly say one is better than the other?"

Already drunk on research after reading and re-reading the moldering yellowed newspapers and clips of bygone eras and as much in a haze as others are on drink, I decided to stir up the research, mix in all the advice, and garnish it with my own gauge to come out with my list of "The 100 Greatest Boxers of All Time."

In an attempt to do so, I took all of the so-called "Greats" and reduced them in my mind's eye, which became a reverse telescopic lens, to the same height, the same weight, and the same ring conditions. Then, I shook them all up in the time warp of my mind so that time was both separated and unified and my thoughts became almost oriental in that the images of the mind truly reflected history. In that manner, those whose deeds could be found only in yellowing pieces of crumbling newspapers were comparable to those as memorable as yesterday's television interview. Hopefully retaining all the essentials and rejecting all the superficialities others found important, I was able to filter them through what Hemingway called my "inbuilt shit detector" and find degrees of greatness.

Truth to tell, it was something I could have arrived at without all of the warm-up gymnastics: that although conditions, equipment, and competition—not to mention styles—change from era to era, there are still individuals who would have been superior no matter when or against whom they competed. And in whatever era they competed.

But even then there is no such thing as objective truth. For one man's objectivity is another's subjectivity, no matter what you call it. Others have tried it before me, using their own built-in gauges and prejudices. When Red Smith, sports' poet laureate, was asked to pick the three greatest fighters for *Argosy Magazine's* "All-Time Poll," he listed Jack Dempsey, Joe Louis, and Sugar Ray Robinson, adding as marginalia, "Muhammad Who?"

Realizing there are almost as many lists as there are so-called experts, I hereby provide you with some that have been drawn up over the years as proof-positive that no two experts see eye-to-eye.

NAT FLEISCHER'S ALL-TIME RANKING OF WORLD BOXERS

HEAVYWEIGHTS: 1—Jack Johnson 2—Jim Jeffries 3—Bob Fitzsimmons 4—Jack Dempsey 5—Jim Corbett 6—Joe Louis MIDDLEWEIGHTS: 1—Stanley Ketchel 2—Tommy Ryan 3—Harry Greb 4—Mickey Walker 5—Frank Klaus 6—Billy Papke LIGHTWEIGHTS: 1—Joe Gans 2—Benny Leonard 3—Owen Moran 4—Freddy Welsh 5—Battling Nelson 6—Tony Canzoneri BANTAMWEIGHTS: 1—George Dixon 2—Pete Herman 3—Kid Williams 4—Joe Lynch 5—Bud Taylor 6—Johnny Coulon LIGHT HEAVYWEIGHTS: 1—Bob Fitzsimmons 2—Kid McCoy 3—Philadelphia Jack O'Brien 4—Tommy Loughran 5—Battling Levinsky 6—Georges Carpentier WELTERWEIGHTS: 1—Joe Walcott 2—Mysterious Billy Smith 3—Jack Britton 4—Ted Kid Lewis 5—Mickey Walker 6—Ray Robinson FEATHERWEIGHTS: 1—Terry McGovern 2—Jem Driscoll 3—Abe Attell 4—Johnny Dundee 5—Johnny Kilbane 6—Kid Chocolate FLYWEIGHTS: 1—Jimmy Wilde 2—Pancho Villa 3—Frankie Genaro 4—Fidel La Barba 5—Benny Lynch 6—Elky Clarke

THE ASSOCIATED PRESS MID-CENTURY POLL, 1950

1. Jack Dempsey: 251 Votes. 2. Joe Louis: 104 Votes. 3. Henry Armstrong: 16 Votes. 4. Gene Tunney: 6 Votes. 5. Benny Leonard: 5 Votes. 6. Jack Johnson: 4 Votes. 7. Jim Jeffries: 2 Votes. 8. Bob Fitzsimmons: 1 Vote. Joe Gans: 1 Vote. Sam Langford: 1 Vote. Sugar Ray Robinson: 1 Vote. Mickey Walker: 1 Vote. *Panel: Associated Press member sports editors.*

ARGOSY MAGAZINE, GREATEST BOXER, 1975

1. Joe Louis: 17 Votes. 2. Sugar Ray Robinson: 14½ Votes. 3. Jack Dempsey: 10 Votes. 4. Muhammad Ali: 7½ Votes. 5. Henry Armstrong: 3 Votes. Willie Pep: 3 Votes. 7. Harry Greb: 2 Votes. Rocky Marciano: 2 Votes. 9. Gene Tunney: 1 Vote. *Blue Ribbon Panel:* Pete Axthelm, Joe Falls, Curt Gowdy, Tom Harmon, Willard Mullin, Bill Schroeder, Red Smith, C. C. Johnson Spink, Bert Randolph Sugar and Maury White.

RING MAGAZINE'S "THE GREATEST FIGHTER EVER" POLL, 1980

1. Sugar Ray Robinson: 221 Votes. 2. Joe Louis: 165 Votes. 3. Henry Armstrong: 150 Votes. 4. Muhammad Ali: 132 Votes. 5. Benny Leonard: 95 Votes. 6. Willie Pep: 94 Votes. 7. Rocky Marciano: 56 Votes. 8. Jack Dempsey: 45 Votes. 9. Roberto Duran: 41 Votes. 10. Jack Johnson: 40 Votes. 11. Carlos Monzon: 38 Votes. 12. Joe Gans: 35 Votes. 13. Stanley Ketchel: 32 Votes. 14. Mickey Walker: 30 Votes. 15. Harry Greb: 29 Votes. 16. Sam Langford: 28 Votes. 17. Sandy Saddler: 21 Votes. 18. Archie Moore: 16 Votes. 19. Gene Tunney: 14 Votes. 20. Tony Canzoneri: 12 Votes. 21. Marcel Cerdan: 11 Votes. Barney Ross: 11 votes. 23. Jimmy Wilde: 10 Votes. Bob Fitzsimmons: 10 Votes. 25. Kid Gavilan: 8 Votes. Billy Conn: 8 Votes. 27. Jake LaMotta: 6 Votes. Abe Attell: 6 Votes. 29. Ezzard Charles: 5 Votes. 30. (Original) Joe Walcott: 4 Votes. 31. Kid Chocolate: 3 Votes. Emile Griffith: 3 Votes. 33. Sugar Ray Leonard: 2 Votes. Jose Napoles: 2 Votes. Jersey Joe Walcott: 2 Votes. 36. Miguel Canto: 1 Vote. James J. Jeffries: 1 Vote. Terry McGovern: 1 vote. *Blue Ribbon Panel:* Pete Axthelm, Freddie Brown, Gil Clancy, Cus D'Amato, Don Dunphy, Eddie Futch, Harry Gibbs, Herbert Goldman, Randy Gordon, Al Goldstein, Billy Graham, Jerry Izenberg, Jim Jacobs, Mike Katz, Jerry Lisker, Tommy Lopez, Nat Loubet, Barney Nagler, Murray Olderman, Pat Putnam, Harold Rosenthal, Art Rust Jr., Ed Schuyler, Bert Randolph Sugar, Bob Waters

Before I release you to start your own arguments with the man standing next to you at the bar, I just want to offer my heartfelt thanks to those who, when I put out my lifeline, always seemed to be there to save me—people like the aforementioned Ray Arcel, Barney Nagler, Jimmy Jacobs; and others, like Murray Goodman, John Grasso, Herbert Goldman, Charlie Spina, Irving Rudd, Ben Sharav, Cus D'Amato, Alec MacKenzie, Randy Gordon, and Al Bachman. Then, there are three special thanks, with oakleaf clusters, to *all* of the people at O'Reilly's, waitresses, bartenders, patrons, and Con O'Reilly, himself, who carried me longer than my mother; my bemused wife, who supported me and even intercepted the reverse-charge phone calls from heavy breathers I would have accepted to break up the monotony; and Richard Kubicz, who is up for sainthood in five churches for having endured me and my seemingly never-ending project.

Now you're ready to go with just two caveats: First of all, I don't seek to convince you, that would just weaken you; I only want to stimulate you, for that's the nature of a bar argument. Secondly, remember the line from the movie "10" rendered by the bartender himself, "I'm opposed to bartenders making value judgments while on duty. . . . "

That's all there is. . . . Now, at the bell, come out of your corners arguing. . . .

BERT RANDOLPH SUGAR, O'REILLY'S PUB, JUNE 7, 1984

THE 100 GREATEST

SUGAR RAY ROBINSON	1	PACKEY McFARLAND	32	TONY ZALE	70
HENRY ARMSTRONG	2	TED KID LEWIS	33	YOUNG GRIFFO	71
HARRY GREB	3	MARCEL CERDAN	34	ALEXIS ARGUELLO	72
JACK DEMPSEY	4	KID CHOCOLATE	35	MAX BAER	73
BENNY LEONARD	5	PASCUAL PEREZ	36	MARVELOUS MARVIN HAGLER	74
JOE LOUIS	6	TOMMY LOUGHRAN	37	BATTLING NELSON	75
MICKEY WALKER	7	JIM DRISCOLL	38	JOE JEANNETTE	76
SAM LANGFORD	8	EMILE GRIFFITH	39	MYSTERIOUS BILLY SMITH	77
TONY CANZONERI	9	KID McCOY	40	WILFREDO GOMEZ	78
MUHAMMAD ALI	10	JIM CORBETT	41	JERSEY JOE WALCOTT	79
JOE GANS	11	BILLY CONN	42	ROCKY GRAZIANO	80
WILLIE PEP	12	JAKE LaMOTTA	43	SONNY LISTON	81
JACK JOHNSON	13	MAXIE ROSENBLOOM	44	HARRY WILLS	82
BARNEY ROSS	14	PANCHO VILLA	45	AD WOLGAST	83
JIMMY WILDE	15	JOSE NAPOLES	46	TOMMY HEARNS	84
GENE TUNNEY	16	SANDY SADDLER	47	MANUEL ORTIZ	85
ROBERTO DURAN	17	FREDDIE WELSH	48	SALVADOR SANCHEZ	86
JOHNNY DUNDEE	18	JOE FRAZIER	49	FIGHTING HARADA	87
ROCKY MARCIANO	19	JOHN L. SULLIVAN	50	WILLIE RITCHIE	88
JOE WALCOTT	20	CARLOS MONZON	51	JAMES J. JEFFRIES	89
STANLEY KETCHEL	21	KID GAVILAN	52	JOHNNY KILBANE	90
JIMMY McLARNIN	22	PETE HERMAN	53	BOB FOSTER	91
ARCHIE MOORE	23	TIGER FLOWERS	54	MIKE GIBBONS	92
TOMMY RYAN	24	BILLY PETROLLE	55	BENNY LYNCH	93
GEORGE DIXON	25	SUGAR RAY LEONARD	56	GEORGE KID LAVIGNE	94
EDER JOFRE	26	NONPAREIL JACK DEMPSEY	57	AARON PRYOR	95
ABE ATTELL	27	DICK TIGER	58	LEW JENKINS	96
JACK BRITTON	28	BEAU JACK	59	CARLOS ORTIZ	97
BOB FITZSIMMONS	29	IKE WILLIAMS	60	JACK DELANEY	98
TERRY McGOVERN	30	PANAMA AL BROWN	61	WILFRED BENITEZ	99
EZZARD CHARLES	31	LARRY HOLMES	62	GENE FULLMER	100
		CARMEN BASILIO	63	MIKE TYSON	
		CHARLEY BURLEY	64		
		PHILADELPHIA JACK O'BRIEN	65		
		PETER JACKSON	66		
		JIMMY BARRY	67		
		CARLOS ZARATE	68		
		GEORGES CARPENTIER	69		

ONE: SUGAR RAY ROBINSON

SUGAR RAY ROBINSON

Any and all descriptions implying greatness can be applied to the man born Walker Smith in Detroit on May 3, 1921, but the one appellation that stuck was first uttered by writer Jack Case, who, while witnessing for the first time a young lanky boxer fighting for the Salem Crescent gym in New York, remarked to the manager of the team, George Gainford, "That's a sweet fighter you've got there." "Sweet as Sugar," replied Gainford for posterity. And so it was that "Sugar" Ray Robinson was born. Robinson came by the other part of his name honestly. Or somewhat honestly. For back in those days when the bootleg circuit—unlicensed fights held in small clubs—held sway, the youngster originally went by his given name, Walker Smith, "Smitty" to his friends. One night "Smitty" borrowed the amateur card of a friend named Ray Robinson and became, from that night on, the man who would go on as Ray Robinson to become "The Greatest Fighter, Pound-for-Pound, in the History of Boxing."

NO SINGLE LABEL FOR ROBINSON IS ADEQUATE. He was boxing's version of Rashomon; everyone saw something different: He could deliver a knockout blow going backward; he was seamless, with no fault lines; his left hand, held always at the ready, was purity in motion; his footwork was superior to any that had been seen in boxing up to that time; his hand speed and leverage were unmatchable; and on and on. There was an unaltered chemistry to Ray Robinson. He was magic; he was Hemingway's "Grace under pressure."

Robinson went unbeaten, untied, and unscored upon in his first forty fights, and it wasn't until his forty-first fight, against Jake LaMotta in Detroit, that he was derailed—losing a ten-round decision. It was a decision he would reverse five times. Robinson went on to become welterweight champ and middleweight champ, losing only to LaMotta in his first 123 fights, in which he managed a total of 78 knockouts.

But while Robinson was the shellac for the rough exterior of the sport, boxing was being run by the IBC and a group of characters to whom legitimate

Sugar Ray regains his middleweight crown for the second time with a second-round knockout of Carl "Bobo" Olson in Chicago, Dec. 9, 1955.

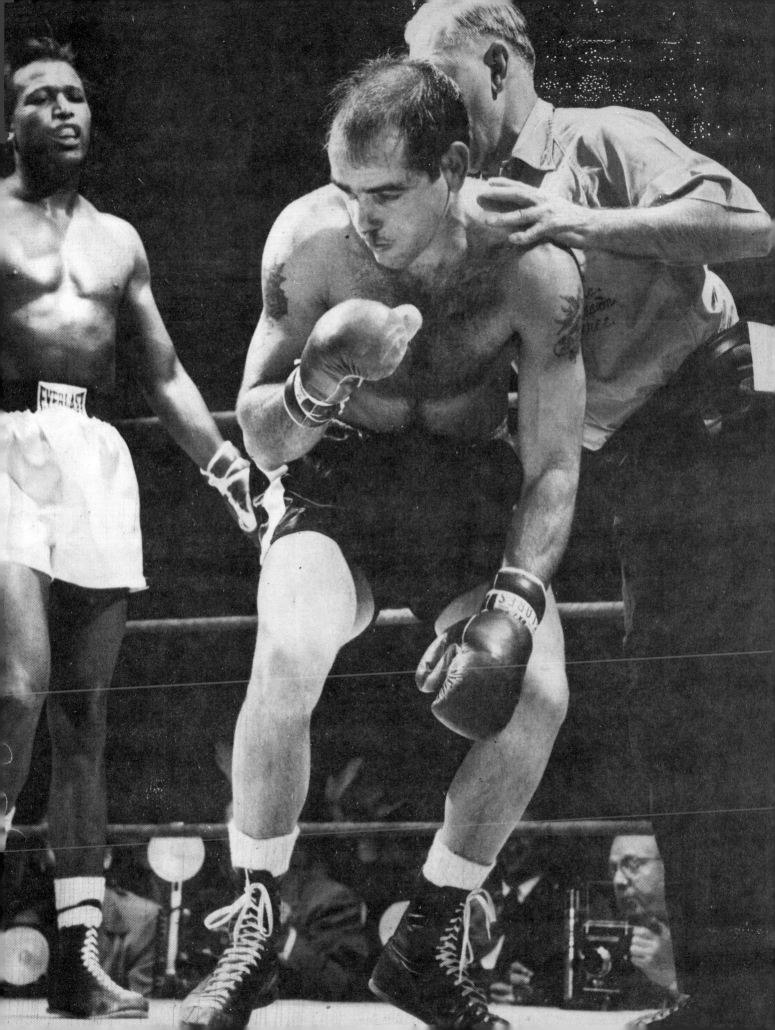

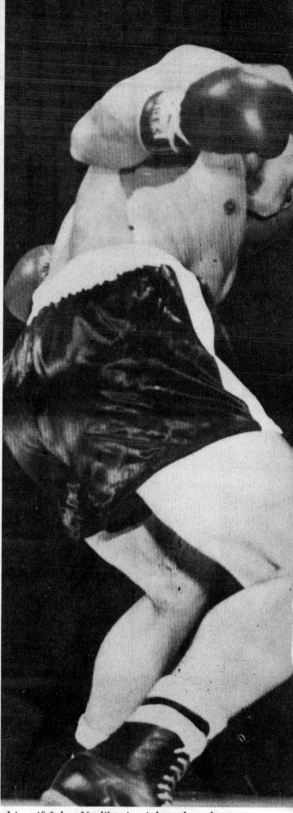

business was only a matter of speech. And when Robinson disobeyed their commands and failed to carry LaMotta in their sixth fight, as he had so many others (writer Barney Nagler once called him "The greatest carrier since Mother Dionne"), he was banished from the States, and had to ply his trade in Europe. He went first class, taking with him an entourage that included two of everything, like Noah, as he toured the continent. On one of his

stops, he left behind the championship in the competent hands of Britisher Randy Turpin, who lost it back to Sugar Ray three months later. It would be the first of four times he would redeem the title he had lent away.

After losing to the heat, and, incidentally Joey Maxim, in a bid for the light heavyweight championship on a night that turned him into a wilted head of lettuce, Robinson retired, due to the lack of opportunity and opponents. But

if John Updike is right when he says, "Retirement is a little like death," Robinson must have died a thousand times only to come back to reclaim his title from Bobo Olson and stage his classic fights with Gene Fullmer and Carmen Basilio in the twilight of his career—proving that the great ones can come back, and back again.

Sugar Ray Robinson was, indeed, the sweetest practitioner of "The Sweet Science."

Born Walker Smith, 5/3/21, Detroit, MI . . . Started boxing as an amateur using given name, later adopted name of a friend and became Ray Robinson . . . As Smith, lost to Pasquale Pesca in preliminary round of bantamweight class of 1938 New York Golden Gloves . . . As Robinson, won 1939 featherweight title by defeating Salem-Crescent A.C. teammate Louis Valentine . . . Won 1940 NYGG lightweight title with 30-second knockout in final round (still an NYGG record). Also won 1939 and 1940 Tournament of Champions and New York-Chicago Intercity Golden Gloves titles . . . First professional bout, 10/4/40 . . . Won first 40 professional bouts (including 7 against future or ex-world champions) . . . Lost to Jake La

Motta, 2/5/43, and won rematch 3 weeks later . . . Did not lose again for next 9 years . . . Won vacant world welterweight title from Tommy Bell, 12/20/46, by decision . . . In first title defense, 6/24/47, knocked out Jimmy Doyle in 8 rounds—Doyle died the following day . . . After 3 more defenses of welterweight crown, won middleweight title from Jake LaMotta, KO 13, 2/14/51 . . . Lost it to Englishman Randy Turpin, 7/10/51, and regained it 2 months later . . . Defended against Bobo Olson and Rocky Graziano . . . Challenged Joey Maxim for light heavyweight title, 5/25/52, but was stopped in fourteenth due to extreme heat . . . Retired to pursue career as a nightclub entertainer . . . Returned to ring, 1/5/55 . . . Won middleweight title from

Bobo Olson, 12/9/55 . . . After successful defense in rematch, fought 8 more title bouts in next 5 years without winning 2 consecutively—lost title to Gene Fullmer, 1/2/57, regained it 3/25/58; lost it to Carmen Basilio, 9/23/57, regained it 3/25/58; lost it to Paul Pender, 1/22/60, and failed in 3 attempts to regain in for sixth time, although in one of these attempts he held Gene Fullmer to a draw . . . Continued boxing until 11/65 . . . Had 45 bouts after age of 40 and 15 of them in final year at age 44 . . . Of 19 career losses, only the first was in a nontitle bout before the age of 40 . . . Elected to the Boxing Hall of Fame, 1967 . . . Complete record: 201 bouts, 174 won, 19 lost, 6 draws, 2 no-contests, 109 knockouts.

Left to right: Sugar Ray decisions Fritzie Zivic in ten rounds: he wins the title for the fourth time vs. Gene Fullmer; he knocks out Randy Turpin.

TWO: HENRY ARMSTRONG

HENRY ARMSTRONG

Henry Armstrong was a physical loan shark, a fighter who adopted General Clausewitz's theory that the winning general is the one who can impose his will upon the enemy. One hundred forty-five times Armstrong imposed his will on his opponents, suffocating them in his swarming style, firing off his punches and then running over them, much like a runaway locomotive, with a ten-ton truck rumbling over their remains for good measure. But the perpetual-motion machine might have been a mere footnote to American boxing history, more a curio than a contribution, had it not been for the fact that one of the members of his managerial brain trust was entertainer Al Jolson. And that Armstrong's greatest year, 1937, was also the year of Joe Louis. Until 1934, Henry Armstrong had been a struggling featherweight, fighting in and around Los Angeles with mixed results against opponents who remain almost as unknown as the soldier under the tombstone in Arlington. During one of the weekly Hollywood Legion fights, in front of a star-studded crowd, Armstrong distinguished himself, scoring a sensational knockout. Two of the stars, Ruby Keeler and Al Jolson, took a liking to the human hurricane and underwrote the purchase of his contract for their friend, Eddie Meade. All of a sudden, his fortunes improved. And so did the caliber of his opponents.

BY 1937, BETTING ON ARMSTRONG WAS like getting money from home without writing. He fought an incredible 27 times that year and won all but one by KO. Together, Armstrong and his manager didn't care what the opposition weighed or what their credentials were. They took on anybody and everybody regardless of race, creed, or weight, fighting featherweights, a few lightweights, and a sprinkling of welterweights as well. But because Joe Louis had just won the heavyweight championship, and because Armstrong never shared Louis' celebrity status, they determined a course of action that would make more money. And, not incidentally, make ring history at the same time.

Armstrong remembered the meeting between Meade, himself, Jolson, and George Raft, another financial backer. "Joe Louis was going to take all the popularity, everything, away from me, from all the fighters, because everyone was saving their money to see Joe Louis fight." That's when someone hit upon the idea that would rival all ideas that emanated from Hollywood in those days, all spelled "colossal," "stupendous," "bigger-than-life." The idea, simply stated, was to go after three titles.

Now Meade started moving Armstrong along in the boxing world willfully, their collective eye on the three brass rings. Armstrong took the first olive out of the jar in October 1937: the featherweight title, beating Petey Sarron in six rounds. With the 126-pound title stashed away, Armstrong turned toward heavier and more lucrative bouts. Fourteen more bouts and 14 more wins followed and then Armstrong was matched to fight the welterweight king, Barney Ross. Despite a 13-pound pull in the weights, the perpetual-motion machine took the fight to Ross and the crown from the gallant warrior, halting his whirlwind attack only long enough to carry Ross through the last 5 rounds. With that title now added to his ever-growing list of crowns, the man who sought more titles than Charlemagne now played the part of the original rubber man and dropped down to the lightweight class to wrest the crown from Lou Ambers in

Right: Hammering Hank knocks out Lew Jenkins in six rounds. Far right: Armstrong decisions lightweight champ Lou Ambers to win third crown.

a brutal fight that had Armstrong swallowing his own blood for the last six rounds in fear the bout would be stopped. Three titles in a little more than nine months; a hat trick that was indeed something "stupendous, colossal, and bigger-than-life." (Armstrong would try for yet another crown, the middleweight title. But, in a fight against Ceferino Garcia, even though Armstrong won handily, the decision came down a draw, one of boxing's little prearrangements that weigh more heavily than any opponent.)

No one who ever saw this fighter known as "Hammerin' Hank" or "Homicide Hank" or "Hurricane Hank" will ever forget him: a nonstop punching machine, his style more rhythmic than

Born Henry Jackson, 12/12/12, in Columbus, MS . . . Eleventh child in family . . . Raised in St. Louis . . . Fought early amateur bouts as "Melody Jackson" . . . First pro bout in Braddock, PA, 7/27/31, knocked out in 3 rounds . . . After winning 6-round decision in second professional bout, moved to Los Angeles and fought as an amateur again . . . Borrowed name of Armstrong from friend Harry Armstrong to cover up previous pro status . . . Lost close decision to Johnny Hines in 1932 Olympic trials . . . Turned pro again shortly afterwards . . . Lost decisions in next 2 bouts—total of 3 losses in first 4 pro bouts . . . Boxed on West Coast and in Mexico 1932–36 . . . After 15 consecutive knockouts in 1937, won world featherweight crown from Petey Sarron by knockout in 6, 10/29/37 . . . Had 11 more knockouts in nontitle bouts for total of 27 consecutive knockouts—tenth best on all-time list . . . Won world welterweight title, 5/31/38, by 15-round decision over Barney Ross despite weighing only 133 1/2 . . . In next bout, 8/17/38, won world lightweight championship in 15 from Lou Ambers . . . Only man ever to hold 3 world titles simultaneously . . . Never defended featherweight title and relinquished it shortly after winning third title . . . Successfully defended welterweight championship 18 times in 2-year span . . . Made 5 defenses in October, 1939 . . . Lost lightweight belt in first defense, 8/22/39, to Ambers . . . Challenged for middleweight title, 3/1/40, and held Ceferino Garcia to 10-round draw . . . Lost welterweight title to Fritzie Zivic, 10/4/40, 15-round decision . . . Failed to regain title in rematch with Zivic, 1/17/41, KO 12 . . . Continued boxing until 1945 . . . Faced 17 champions throughout career and defeated 15 of them . . . Charter member of Boxing Hall of Fame, 1954 . . . Published autobiography in 1956, *Gloves, Glory and God* . . . Became an ordained minister after leaving ring . . . Complete record: 174 bouts, 145 won, 20 lost, 9 draws, 98 knockouts.

headlong, his match-stick legs akimbo, his arms crossed in front of his face, racing the clock with each punch, and each punch punctuated by a grunt. His

likes will never be seen again. The feats of Henry Armstrong are a benchmark against which all future generations will be measured.

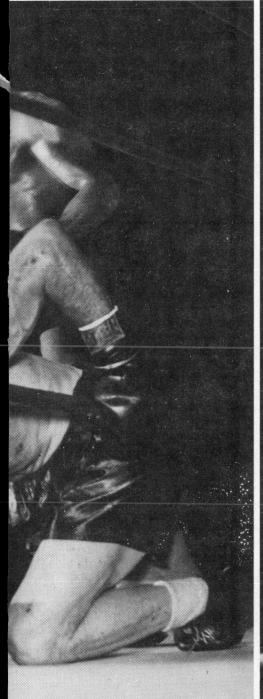

THREE: HARRY GREB

HARRY GREB

Jimmy McLarnin, one of boxing's best, once told an admirer, "If you thought I was great, you should have seen Harry Greb." And Ernest Hemingway once, in the presence of another writer, mentioned the name "Greb." When the writer couldn't place the name, Hemingway shot back a look of disgust and cried, "Imagine anyone not knowing one of our greatest Americans!" Today, there are still a few vestigal reminders of his magnitude captured in yellowing newspaper clips in out-of-date scrapbooks and in the memories of those few eyewitnesses still around who haven't been run over by errant trolley cars. For Harry Greb was a ring marvel, a one-man destroyer who was not only hard to hit, but a fighter who could sustain a destructive fusillade of short-arm blows from all angles.

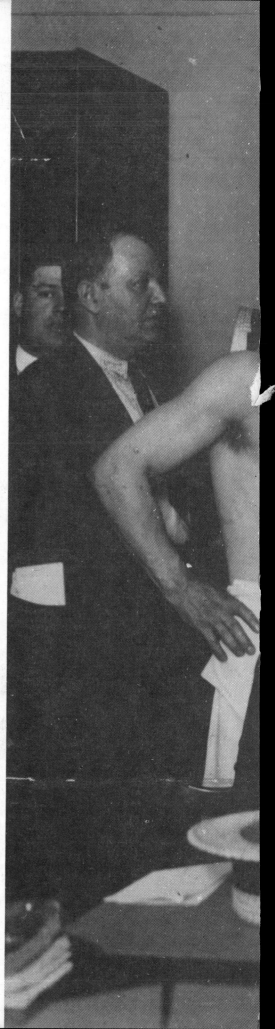

Above: Gene Tunney carries casket of the only man to beat him. Right: Greb (left) in pre-fight physical before defense against Ted Moore in New York.

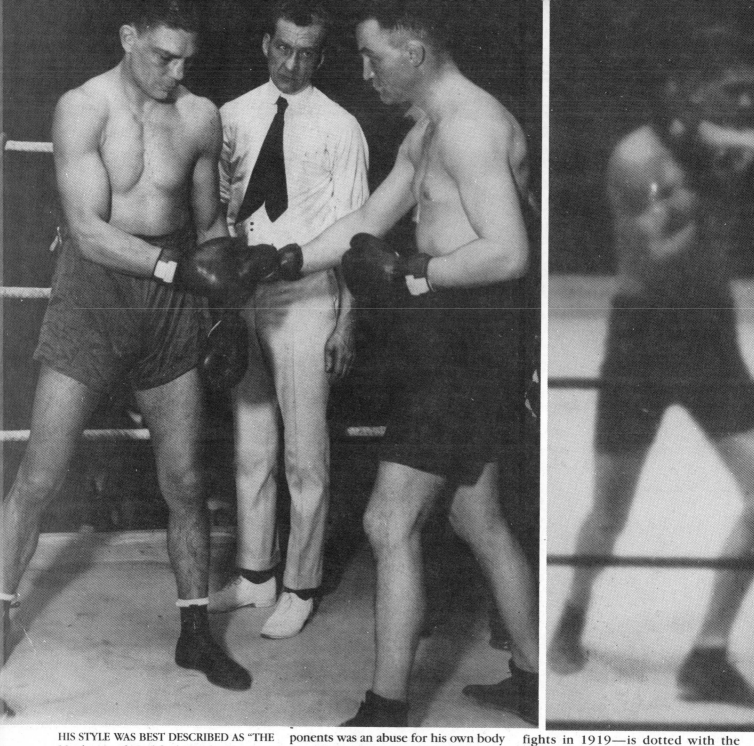

HIS STYLE WAS BEST DESCRIBED AS "THE Manly Art of Modified Murder" by boxing writer W. O. McGeehan, and the faces of his opponents bore mute testimony to his handiwork, all looking like losers in razor blade fights.

The Greb style was dictated by his personal estimate of what the opponent and the referee would hold still for. Somewhat lacking the social amenities of the Queensberry rules, Greb fought as an early-day terrorist, without rules, inhibitions or prisoners taken, his opponents more often than not feeling as if they had to fight him off, rather than actually fight against him.

Combined with his abuse of his op-ponents was an abuse for his own body as well, his one big quarrel with life being the fact that each day contained only 24 hours. Too busy living his next half hour and too busy trying to keep busy to stop anywhere, Greb somehow managed to incorporate more boxing and booze into his 32 years than any 32 men could have done—hardly a testament to the kind of clean living needed to cope with the rugged demands of boxing.

Still, "The Pittsburgh Windmill" fought more recorded fights than all but two boxers in ring history, fighting everyone and everywhere. His 294-bout career—including a record 44 fights in 1919—is dotted with the names of some of the greatest battlers in ring history, including Gene Tunney, Mike McTigue, Tommy Loughran, Mickey Walker, Battling Levinsky, Mike Gibbons, Tiger Flowers, Johnny Wilson, Frank Klaus, Gunboat Smith, Al McCoy, and nearly every one of the near-champions in three weight classes up to the heavyweight division, where he was considered a serious challenger for Jack Dempsey's crown.

Greb's most famous win was his 15-round victory over Gene Tunney for the American Light Heavyweight title. Not only was Greb to do something no other boxer ever would, defeat Tunney,

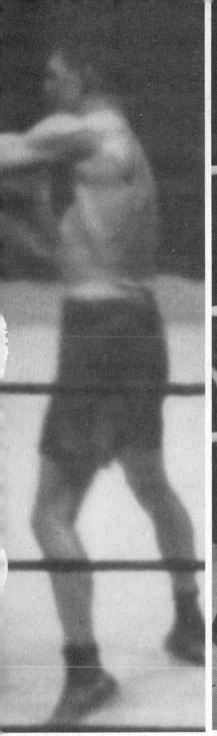

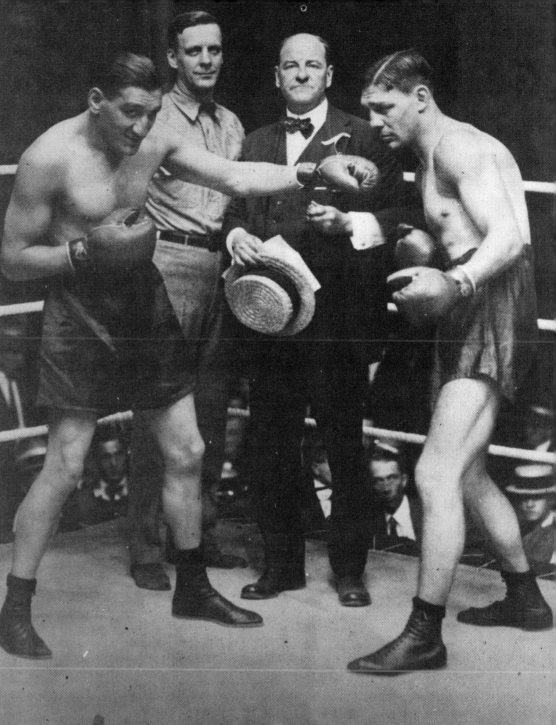

Left to right: Greb (left) before beating Tommy Gibbons; Greb loses rematch to Tunney in 1923; Greb poses with Johnny Wilson before victory.

he inflicted a severe beating on Tunney, one of the worst documented in modern ring annals. Another was his famous handicap match in 1925 with Mickey Walker, a bout which legend would hold continued later that night outside one of New York's speakeasies, a natural battleground for two of boxing's greatest pleasure seekers.

Harry Greb was almost never beaten, except for an early defeat by Joe Chip, his return-bout losses to Tunney, and the end-of-career losses to Tiger Flowers. But his greatest loss came on October 22, 1926, when following an operation for a bone fracture at the top of his nose resulting from an auto acci-

dent, Harry Greb died. It was only then that the doctors discovered how great Harry Greb really was: He had fought the last part of his career with sight in only one eye.

Born Edward Henry Berg, 6/6/94, in Pittsburgh, PA . . . Started as a pro, 1913 . . . Most of career fought during "no-decision era" . . . Knocked out by Joe Chip in 2 rounds in 1913—did not lose again in more than 40 bouts in 2 years . . . Broke arm in second round of bout with Kid Graves, 12/16/15 . . . Did not lose again until 1923 . . . Had more than 200 bouts, 1913–1922, and lost but 2 . . . Became blind in one eye following a bout with Kid Norfolk, 8/29/21—blindness kept secret until his death . . . Won American light heavyweight title from Gene Tunney by 15-round decision, 5/23/22—only loss in Tunney's career . . . Successfully defended title against Tommy Loughran, 1/30/23, W 15 . . . Lost title to Tunney, 2/23/23, 15-round decision . . . Became world middleweight champion, 8/31/23, by defeating Johnny Wilson in 15. Successfully defended title 6 times in next 3 years. Defeated William Bryan Downey, Johnny Wilson, Fay Kaiser, Ted Moore, Mickey Walker, Tony Marullo in title defenses . . . Lost championship to Tiger Flowers, 2/26/26, by 15-round decision . . . Lost rematch with Flowers, 8/19/26, also 15-round decision . . . Both Greb and Flowers died within 15 months of that bout as a result of minor facial operations . . . Bad eye was removed, 9/16/26, although not publicly known . . . In auto accident shortly afterwards; operated on, 10/22/26, to remove fractured bone in nose, fell into coma after the operation and died of heart failure . . . Although only 14-year professional career, recorded impressive totals—44 bouts in 1917 . . . Had more total bouts than Jim Corbett, Jim Jeffries, Gene Tunney, Joe Louis, Rocky Marciano, and Muhammad Ali combined . . . Complete record: 294 bouts, 112 won, 8 lost, 3 draws, 1 no-contest, 170 no-decisions, 47 knockouts.

JACK DEMPSEY

William Harrison "Jack" Dempsey was, purely and simply, the greatest fistic box-office attraction of all time. And, not incidentally, one helluva fighter, to boot. If Dempsey's opponent could walk away from a fight, it was considered a success. Some 60 of them, including those he met in exhibitions, never walked away from the first round, so great was his punch. Dempsey was the perfect picture of the ring warrior. Approaching his opponent with his teeth bared, bobbing and weaving to make his swarthy head with the perpetual five-o'clock shadow harder to hit, his black eyes flashing and his blue-black hair flying, Dempsey took on the look of an avenging angel of death.

HIS AMAZING HAND SPEED AND LETHAL left hook combined with an anything-goes mentality bred of necessity in the mining camps of his youth, making every bout a war with no survivors. He used every possible means at his disposal to win, his definition of survival less a breaking of the rules than a testing of their elasticity—hitting low, after the bell, behind the head, while a man was on the way down, and even while he was on the way up. "Hell," he said, "it's a case of protecting yourself at all times."

But Dempsey never had to: his opponents did. After having spent several years out-boxing the local sheriffs, Dempsey came out of the west with a fearful record, a nickname, "The Manassa Mauler," and a manager named Doc Kearns, who was to play spearcar-

rier to Dempsey's greatness. With an animal instinct, an inner fury, and a lust for battle never before seen, Dempsey blazed a searing path through the heavyweight division. Dispatching contender Fred Fulton in just 18 seconds in July of 1918, Dempsey proved he was no one-fight phenomenon as he followed that up with a 14-second knockout of former "White Hope" claimant Carl Morris. Now all that stood between "The Manassa Mauler" and the heavyweight crown was a small mountain by the name of Jess Willard. But after one puerile jab with the left.

Above, left to right: Dempsey trains for the second Tunney fight; Jack gives Tommy Gibbons a going-over in Shelby; after the famed "Long Count," his last fight.

Born William Harrison Dempsey, 6/24/95, in Manassa, CO . . . First recorded professional bout, 8/17/14 . . . Confusion exists for historians since brother also fought and occasionally used name "Jack Dempsey"—at times Dempsey used name "Kid Blackie" . . . Fought primarily in West, 1914–18, although made brief trip to New York City during June and July, 1916 . . . Knocked out in first round by Fireman Jim Flynn, 2/13/17 . . . Established reputation during tour of country 1918–19 with string of knockout victories . . . Won world heavyweight championship, 7/4/19, with devastating third-round knockout of Jess Willard—7 knockdowns of Willard in the first round—controversy in later years as to whether gloves were "loaded" for that bout . . . First title defense, 9/6/20, against Billy Miske (a former sparring partner who was seriously ill and in financial need) resulted in third-round knockout . . . Next defense, 12/14/20, twelfth-round come-from-behind knockout victory over Bill Brennan . . . "Battle of the Century," 7/2/21, against Georges Carpentier, much-publicized bout that drew boxing's first million-dollar gate, although bout itself was a mismatch—172 pound Carpentier was stopped in fourth . . . After 2-year vacation, won 15-round decision from Tommy Gibbons in Shelby, Mon.—$300,000 guarantee bankrupted town—Gibbons received nothing for his efforts . . . In bout with Argentinian, Luis Angel Firpo, one of boxing's greatest bouts, Dempsey was knocked down twice in first round, Firpo knocked down 7 times in first and twice in second round, last time for a 10-count . . . Boxed only exhibitions, 1923–26 . . . Lost title via 10-round decision to Gene Tunney, 9/23/26, largest paid attendance in history of boxing, 120,757 . . . Defeated Jack Sharkey, 7/21/27, KO 7 . . . Rematch with Tunney, 9/22/27, knocked Tunney down in seventh round, but Tunney, up at count of 9, actually had 14-second rest in a 10-round decision again to Tunney . . . Retired after bout, although continued to box exhibitions . . . Owned Broadway restaurant after retirement . . . Charter inductee to Boxing Hall of Fame, 1954 . . . Died 5/31/83, New York, NY, oldest ex-heavyweight champion at 87 . . . Complete record: 78 bouts, 62 won, 6 lost, 10 draws, 49 knockouts.

Dempsey whipped out his meal ticket, his left hook, and left a dazed Jess Willard on the floor, his jaw shattered in seven places, his dreams of retaining his title just as shattered.

Dempsey would become a legend in his spare time, defending his title but six times in the next seven years. Still, they were almost all classic feats of arms, fights that made ring history in the ring and at the box office, as well.

But Jack Dempsey's place on the boxing landscape cannot be measured by barebones statistics alone. He had fewer fights than Jimmy Braddock, fewer knockouts than Max Baer, and fewer wins than Primo Carnera, three of his successors—in name only. What Dempsey had that no one else had was the ability to capture the imagination of the American sporting public. For he alone spawned "The Golden Age of Sports," becoming the greatest gate attraction of all time, without exception, catnip for the masses who paid millions of Coolidge dollars for the privilege of witnessing this legend in action.

FIVE: BENNY LEONARD

BENNY LEONARD

Benny Leonard was like an artichoke, the more you peeled away, the more you discovered. Leonard was the nearest thing to a perfect fighter boxing has ever seen. He combined the boxing ingenuity of Young Griffo, the masterful technique of James J. Corbett, the pinpoint accuracy of Joe Gans, the punching power of Jack Dempsey, the alertness of Gene Tunney, and the speed of Mike Gibbons. Little wonder boxing experts of his day thought he was a fighter who had to be savored, not taken in gulps. Back when boxing—not to mention the world—was a simpler place, fight clubs in and around New York would provide entertainment in the form of morality plays within the confines of the four ring posts. Invariably, one local favorite from one section would be pitted against the local favorite from another for ethnic or block-bragging rights. And so it came to pass that as one of the enforcers of his street gang, upon whose sloping shoulders it had fallen to avenge all the slings and arrows of outrage visited on them by roving bands of street toughs, Benny Leonard should take his skills into the ring.

IN A DAY AND AGE WHEN NO JEWISH fighter fought under his own name, Benny "Leonard" was born, appropriating the name from the old minstrel performer Eddie Leonard so that his mother wouldn't discover his new calling. He soon became known as "The Ghetto Wizard," and his fight became the fight of the many who identified with him. Budd Schulberg remembers him as "Our champ [who] was doing with his fists what the Adolph Zukors and William Foxes were doing in their studios and in their theatres . . . fighting the united efforts of the *goyim* to keep them in their ghettos."

Those few still remaining who saw Leonard remember him as a picture-book fighter who used what Ray Arcel calls "great mental energy" to move in and out on his opponent, employing his talented left to set up an opponent for the kill, his hands never moving in an ambiguous gesture, his slicked-down, brilliantined hair intact. Practicing what he called the "Art of Self-De-

fense," the master technician put into words his strategy: "To hit and not be hit." And he was to prove it when, after each fight, he would proudly run his hand through his hair and announce, "I never even got my hair mussed."

But there were times when, if his hair wasn't "mussed," at least Leonard was. And then Leonard was at his most impressive, brushing his hair back, hitching up his trunks, and circling his adversary, all the while using his "mental energy." Against Lew Tendler, one of the greatest left handers of all time, Leonard took a powerful left to the body that momentarily paralyzed him, his legs unresponsive to his will. But even though his body was paralyzed, his brain still was capable of working miracles, and Leonard hollered, "C'mon, keep 'em up, keep 'em up!" all the while gesturing that Tendler had hit him low. Tendler paused and started to argue, "That wasn't a low blow, quitchersquawkin'!" but by then it was too late and Leonard took a much-

needed breath and began circling out of trouble, his wits, body, and title together again.

Against Richie Mitchell, Leonard found himself on the canvas with 28 seconds remaining in the first round. Pulling himself semierect and fighting from sheer memory, Leonard possessed enough ring savvy to hold out both hands and motion to Mitchell to "Come on." Mitchell, unsure of his adversary's intent—and not knowing that had Leonard taken one step toward him he would have pitched forward—stood

Born Benjamin Leiner, 4/7/96, in New York, NY . . . Turned pro at age of 15 . . . Stopped on cut in first pro bout by Mickey Finnegan, although in lead at time . . . Leonard claimed victory and early record books erroneously list bout as third-round knockout for Leonard . . . Stopped twice more in first 3 years . . . Fought 154 bouts without a loss over next 9 years—50 knockouts, 6 wins by decision, and 98 no-decision bouts . . . Won world lightweight championship, 5/28/17, by ninth-round knockout of Freddie Welsh . . . 8 successful title defenses: 7/5/20, Charley White, KO 9, 11/26/20, Joe Welling; KO 14; 1/14/21, Ritchie Mitchell, KO 6; 6/6/21, Rocky Kansas ND 12; 2/10/22, Rocky Kansas, W 15; 7/4/22, Rocky Kansas, KO 8; 7/27/22, Lew Tendler, ND 12; 7/23/23, Lew Tendler, W 15 . . . Lost on foul in thirteenth in bid for welterweight title, against Jack Britton, 6/26/22 . . . Retired as champion, 1/15/25 . . . Held title longer than any other lightweight champion—7 years, 7 months, 18 days . . . Made comeback after 7-year layoff—longest layoff of any world champion . . . 18 wins and 1 draw during 2-year comeback before losing to Jimmy McLarnin by sixth-round knockout, 10/7/32 . . . Retired permanently after McLarnin bout . . . Served as lieutenant in U.S. Merchant Marine during World War II . . . Became referee after discharge from service . . . Collapsed and died in ring while refereeing bout at St. Nicholas Arena, New York, NY, 4/18/47 . . . New York State Commission rules changed shortly afterwards so that one referee would not be required to work an entire boxing card without relief . . . Elected to Boxing Hall of Fame, 1955 . . . 1947 Biography by Nat Fleischer, *Leonard the Magnificent* . . . Complete record: 210 bouts, 87 won, 5 lost, 1 draw, 115 no-decisions, 71 knockouts.

his ground, falling for the trickery. Again, the most cerebral fighter in the history of boxing had used his brains to carry the moment, and the fight.

Benny Leonard was also a student of the game. He even studied four-round fighters in the gym. "You can never tell," he once told Ray Arcel—then considerably younger—"when one of those kids might do something by accident that I can use." And another time he was heard to comment, "The toughest fighter to fight is a stupid fighter. When you feint him, he doesn't even know you're doing it."

Although Leonard would retire as the undefeated lightweight champion after holding the crown longer than anyone in history, he would eventually be forced to come back when his stock portfolio became frayed around the edges, compliments of the Crash. Leonard, too, was more than a little frayed around the edges, fading in the worst place, his front, his belly that of an older man, his proud hairline receding almost faster than his skills, with barely enough left to fill out a paint brush. But even though he was eventually forced to retire, this time by Jimmy McLarnin, Benny Leonard will always be remembered as one of boxing's memorable champions, a man about whom Mayor Jimmy Walker said, "He left the ring finer and better than he found it."

Top left: Leonard shakes with Lew Tendler before "the greatest lightweight championship" ever.
Bottom left: Leonard knocks out Charley White in nine rounds in Benton Harbor, Michigan.
Below: Benny and "Momma".

SIX: JOE LOUIS

JOE LOUIS

Joe Louis' exploits are accorded no special place of prominence in *The Ring Record Book*. His 66 bouts are sandwiched between the records of James J. Braddock, the man he succeeded, and Ezzard Charles, the fighter he was succeeded by. Both Braddock and Charles had more professional engagements, as did Johnson, Dempsey, Tunney, Schmeling, Carnera, Baer, and Walcott. And there have been men who had more KOs, Carnera and Charles; a higher percentage of knockouts, Marciano and Foreman; and those who fought longer, Fitzsimmons, Charles, Walcott, and Ali. Even Tommy Burns and Larry Holmes have more consecutive knockouts in defense of their titles than Louis. But no heavyweight champion—and probably no sports figure—ever captured the imagination of the public, fan and nonfan alike, as the smooth, deadly puncher with the purposeful advance who, at his peak, represented the epitome of pugilistic efficiency. And no man was so admired and revered as this son of an Alabama sharecropper, who carried his crown and himself with dignity, carrying the hopes of millions on his sturdy shoulders.

BUT THE MEASURE OF THE UNCOMPLI- cated man they called "The Brown Bomber" cannot be found merely inside the ring. For, in a field devoted to fashioning halos, Joe Louis wore a special nimbus. And wore it with a special dignity.

Joe Louis used his words, as he did his punches, with a commendable economy of effort, saying a surprising number of things, and saying them in a way we all wish we had. There was his evaluation of his country's chances in the global confrontation with the Axis powers: "We'll win 'cause we're on God's side." Dignity. And there was his enunciation of his opponent's chances in the second Conn fight: "He can run, but he can't hide." Honesty.

But Joe Louis' place in the pantheon of greats doesn't rest on his using his words, but on his using his body—and the bodies of his collective, and soon-to-be collected, opponents. He drove Max Baer to the canvas like a nail, straightly driven, his body almost flush to the surface. He hit leading con-

tender Eddie Sims so hard with his first punch that the beclouded Sims walked over to the referee and asked "to take a little walk around the roof." He sent out one single shot that sifted through the supposedly impenetrable network of elbows and arms covering Paolino Uzcudun's face, knocking out his front teeth and knocking out the "Basque Woodchopper" for the first time ever. He destroyed Primo Carnera, shifting his face like pudding and turning the gargantuan's picket-fence smile into that of a hurt, kicked dog with one first-round punch, on his way to hewing him down bit by bit in six rounds. He dropped the human butcher block Tony Galento, with a left hook in the second round of their title fight that was described by humorist Bugs Baer as being "so hard they could have counted him out in the air." And he drove into the Boxing Home for the Bewildered most of his other opponents, who, crediting the growing legend, approached the ring as though it were an abattoir

Louis and Max Schmeling on their way to the weigh-in before their second fight June 22, 1938 in which Louis got revenge in a first-round annihilation.

Joe Louis was accorded a special place as a superhero by enthusiastic reporters, who believed he was the most dependable story in sports, and by the public, who began to view him as invincible. But Max Schmeling, brought out of near-retirement to be yet another sacrificial lamb, derailed the Louis bandwagon, hitting him with a right hand over a lazy left no less than 54 times and finally knocking out the myth in the twelfth. For most fighters it would have been devastating, their utter confidence, which was the essential property for success, receiving an enormous jolt. Usually the entire flashy structure settles as earthward as the fallen fighter. But not in the case of Joe Louis. He would come back within two months to knock out another ex-cham-

pion, Jack Sharkey, and then, almost one year to the day after his destruction at the hands of Schmeling, he would win the heavyweight championship of the world from Jim Braddock.

Louis would go on to avenge his loss to Schmeling with a 124-second anni-hilation that would set back the cause of the Master Race and bring joy to millions of Americans, and then would embark on what was charitably called "The Bum of the Month Campaign," giving everyone a job as a heavyweight challenger, much like the WPA. He was the very symbol of perseverance, plod-ding forward, his imperious mien track-ing down his prey, his indefatigable pa-tience waiting for the chance, always punishing them with his presence. And then, he would pull the trigger, with

the two fastest hands in the history of the heavyweight division moving al-most as if they did what they pleased, with an intelligence all their own in a graceful exercise of power. Finally, when he had hooked his opponent, Louis, the greatest finisher in the his-tory of boxing, would never let him get away—ask Billy Conn for references.

Louis would retire as the undefeated heavyweight champion, after running out of competition, and then come back. But he had emotionally packed it in, fighting only for the benefit of the IRS and the deified memory of his fans, many of whom were to leave Madison Square Garden the night of October 26, 1951, their eyes wet with unshed tears for their hero, who had been beaten by a younger future champion, Rocky Mar-

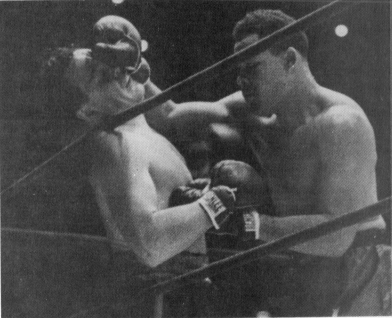

ciano.

In boxing's galaxy, Joe Louis was a star for a longer period of time than most, burning intently, and with dignity. He will be remembered not only as a benchmark for all boxers but as a lighthouse who lit the way for so many.

Clockwise from top left: Louis knocks out Billy Conn, 13th round; Buddy Baer, 1st round; Bib Pastor, 11th round; Jersey Joe Walcott, 11th round; Max Schmeling, 1st round; "Two Ton" Tony Galento, 4th round; Tami Maruiello, 1st round.

Born Joseph Louis Barrow, 5/13/14, in Lafayette AL . . . Raised in Detroit, MI . . . Won National AAU Championship in 1934 as a light heavyweight . . . First pro bout, 7/4/34, won first-round knockout over Jack Kracken . . . All professional bouts throughout career were main events . . . Won first 23 bouts, 19 by knockout, before twelfth-round KO loss to Max Schmeling, 6/19/36 . . . Won world heavyweight championship, 6/22/37, by eighth-round knockout of James J. Braddock . . . In rematch of significant sociological impact, 6/22/38, defeated Schmeling in first-round knockout . . . Won next 2 title defenses by first-round knockout over John Henry Lewis and Jack Roper to become only man ever to win 3 consecutive heavyweight championship bouts by first-round knockout . . . Defended title more frequently than most champions—3 times in 1938, 4 times in 1939, 4 times in 1940 . . . Had "Bum of the Month" tour 12/40–5/41, made 6 title defenses in 6 cities in 6 months against 6 opponents . . . Came from behind to knockout Billy Conn in thirteenth round, 6/18/41 . . . In military service during World War II, title "frozen for duration" of the war . . . Inactive for 4 years, 1942–46 . . . Returned with decisive eighth-round knockout victory over Billy Conn, 6/19/46 . . . Awarded controversial decision over Jersey Joe Walcott, 12/5/47, but scored eleventh-round knockout in rematch, 6/25/48 . . . Retired as champion, 3/1/49 . . . Returned to ring, 9/27/50, against Ezzard Charles (NBA heavyweight champion) for undisputed championship, but lost 15-round decision . . . Won next 8 bouts before being stopped in 8 rounds by Rocky Marciano, 10/26/51 . . . Ended comeback after that loss . . . Held title longer than any world champion of any weight: 11 years, 8 months, 7 days . . . Defended title successfully 25 times and 21 by knockout . . . Ended careers of Paolino Uzcudun (1935), Jack Sharkey (1936), John Henry Lewis (1939), Buddy Baer (1942), and Abe Simon (1942) with knockout victories . . . Known as the "Brown Bomber" . . . Charter inductee to Boxing Hall of Fame, 1954 . . . Died 4/12/81, Las Vegas, NE . . . Complete record: 66 bouts, 63 won, 3 lost, 49 knockouts.

SEVEN: MICKEY WALKER

MICKEY WALKER

"Mickey Walker will best be remembered as the middleweight who had the best left hook and the biggest thirst in the business." So spake Jim Murray, one of sports' most Puckish writers. "If it hadn't been for the one, the thirst, the other, the hook, might have made him the only 155-pound heavyweight champ in modern history," Murray concluded.

Correctly. In that Era of Wonderful Nonsense, when the all-enveloping hand of prohibition was on the land, somehow Mickey Walker slipped through its fingers. Together with his manager, the fun-seeking Doc Kearns—who at the suggestion of Damon Runyon took over the managerial reins of Walker after his first manager-mentor, Jack Bulger, died, thereby becoming, as one writer noted with tongue-in-cheek, "Damon to Walker's Runyon"—The Magnificent Mick made a little cause for celebration go a long way. And in doing so made a small fortune out of a somewhat more substantial one.

BETWEEN DRINKING ENOUGH TO KEEP twenty speakeasies busy, and training for fights by getting the proverbial "shave and a haircut," Walker covered more fistic ground than any man in modern boxing history. His fistic ambitions knowing no weight bounds, he alternately fought elephantine opponents and defended his two titles in his spare time. "Sober or stiff, I belted the guts out of the best of them," Walker boasted.

And he did, too, as he came barreling into an opponent, squinting through arms crossed in front of his face, and ceaselessly hammering enough bruising, bone-crushing left hooks to the body to set their ribs afire. Called "the Toy Bulldog" by Francis Albertanti because of his ferocity and tenacity—and "A Miniature Jack Dempsey" and "A Larger Edition of Terry McGovern" by those with an eye for fistic comparisons—the incomparable Walker looked the part, his puggish nose and accumulating scar tissue over his eyes giving him the droopy-eyed look of a bulldog. But, truth to tell, Walker fought more like a bull terrier than a bulldog. It was almost as if his between-round exhortation from Kearns had

been "Sic 'em" as he attached himself to his opponent and never let go, worrying his opponent as a pit terrier would worry a bone.

But style was hardly the Mickey

Born Edward Patrick Walker, 7/13/01, in Elizabeth, NJ . . . First pro bout, 2/10/19 . . . Fought only in New Jersey for first 2 years . . . During no-decision era, had won only 14 of 41 bouts (but had only lost 2) when he challenged Jack Britton for the welterweight title, 7/18/21. Bout ended with no decision at end of 12 rounds . . . Won world welterweight championship in rematch with Britton, 11/1/22, 15-round decision . . . Defended welterweight title successfully 4 times in 1923–24 . . . Challenged Mike McTigue for light heavyweight crown, 1/7/25, no decision—even though he weighed only 149¾ pounds—lightest man in history to fight for light heavyweight title . . . Later that year (7/2/25), challenged Harry Greb for middleweight title but lost 15-round decision . . . Defended welterweight title twice more in 1925 . . . Lost title in 10-round decision to Pete Latzo, 5/20/26 . . . Won 10-round decision from Theodore "Tiger" Flowers to become world middleweight champion, 12/3/26 . . . Challenged Tommy Loughran for light heavyweight title, 3/28/29, but lost 10-round decision . . . Relinquished middleweight crown, 6/19/31, after 3 successful defenses: 6/30/27, Tommy Milligan, knockout-10; 6/21/28, Ace Hudkins, won-10; 10/29/29, Ace Hudkins, won-10 . . . Moved into heavyweight ranks and fought 15-round draw with Jack Sharkey, 7/22/31 . . . Stopped in 8 rounds by Max Schmeling, 9/26/32 . . . Made third unsuccessful bid for light heavyweight title, 11/3/33, losing 15-round decision to Maxie Rosenbloom . . . Defeated Rosenbloom in 10-round nontitle rematch, 5/8/34 . . . Faced 13 world champions throughout career—had 17 world title bouts but won only 8 of them . . . Retired after 12/1/35 loss to Eric Seelig . . . Made 1-bout comeback in 1939 . . . Known as the "Toy Bulldog" . . . Elected to Boxing Hall of Fame, 1955 . . . Died 4/28/81, Freehold, NJ . . . Complete record: 163 bouts, 94 won, 19 lost, 4 draws, 1 no-contest, 45 no-decisions, 61 knockouts.

Walker story. For the man who loved fast fights, fast women, and sloe gin—even lacing his corner bottle with gin during his fight for the middleweight title—was also one of the most courageous men ever to step foot into the ring. A half-pint who fought on sheer guts, Walker fought them all: welter-weights, middleweights, light heavy-weights, and heavyweights.

After winning the welterweight and middleweight crowns, Walker stepped up to challenge for the light heavy-weight championship no less than three times. Then, renouncing his middleweight title, this 5-foot, 7-inch warrior, following the going theory in pugilistic economics that the bigger the weight, the bigger the purse, entered the heavyweight tournament to decide the successor to Gene Tunney—a tournament that was so crowded it began to take on the look of the start of the Boston Marathon. Giving away big odds in weight, height, and reach, the bulldog-tough Walker met them all, beating such top-notchers as Paolino Uzcudun, K.O. Christner, King Levinsky, Johnny Risko, and Jimmy Maloney and fighting a draw with future heavyweight champ Jack Sharkey in a fight many ringsiders thought he deserved to win.

Below, left to right: "The Toy Bulldog" draws with Natie Brown; Walker weighs in for fight with Jack Sharkey. Walker knocks out Max Schmeling in 1932.

The smallest man this side of Charlie Mitchell to ever contend for heavyweight honors finally came a cropper gainst Max Schmeling, who battered him so unmercifully that even the ASPCA would have intervened had not Doc Kearns, in an uncharacteristic move for a man pictured as the only living heart donor, signaled for the referee to stop the fight after the eighth round. But even then the courage of Walker was evident as Kearns soothed him with, "I guess this was one we couldn't win."

"Speak for yourself," snarled "The Toy Bulldog," spitting blood. "You were the one who threw in the sponge . . . not me."

Through it all, this man with the happy-go-lucky attitude, the smile on his playful Irish face, and the penchant for attempting seemingly impossible odds, will forever be known as boxing's version of "The Happy Warrior".

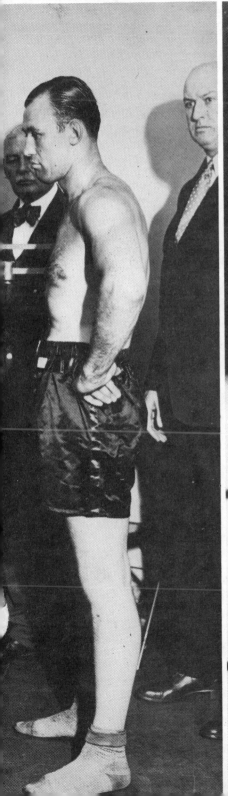

EIGHT: SAM LANGFORD

SAM LANGFORD

Had there but been an investiture, Sam Langford would have been crowned heavyweight champion by acclamation. He was that good. But in a day and age when boxing's blacks were relegated to the back of the bus and forced to fight on the Chitlin' Circuit because white fighters could hide behind the color line and refuse to fight them, Langford instead faced the blackest fighters and the blackest future in boxing. Starting as a featherweight, Langford worked his way through boxing's weight classes fighting everyone who would cup an ear to his challenge. Throughout 21 years, he fought—and beat—such greats as Joe Gans, Young Peter Jackson, Fireman Jim Flynn, Jim Barry, and Joe Walcott. But it was those he didn't fight who better tell the story of Sam Langford.

FOR JACK JOHNSON WOULD NEVER ANswer the challenges of "The Boston Tar Baby" once he had won the crown, having been hard-pressed to stay the distance against Langford's slashing blows in an earlier encounter. And even in the twilight of his career, when his eyes were so bad he could scarcely see his own hands in front of his face, Langford was turned down by Dempsey.

Time and again, Langford, proverbial hat in hand, would call on Doc Kearns, Dempsey's manager, seeking a match with the then-heavyweight champion.

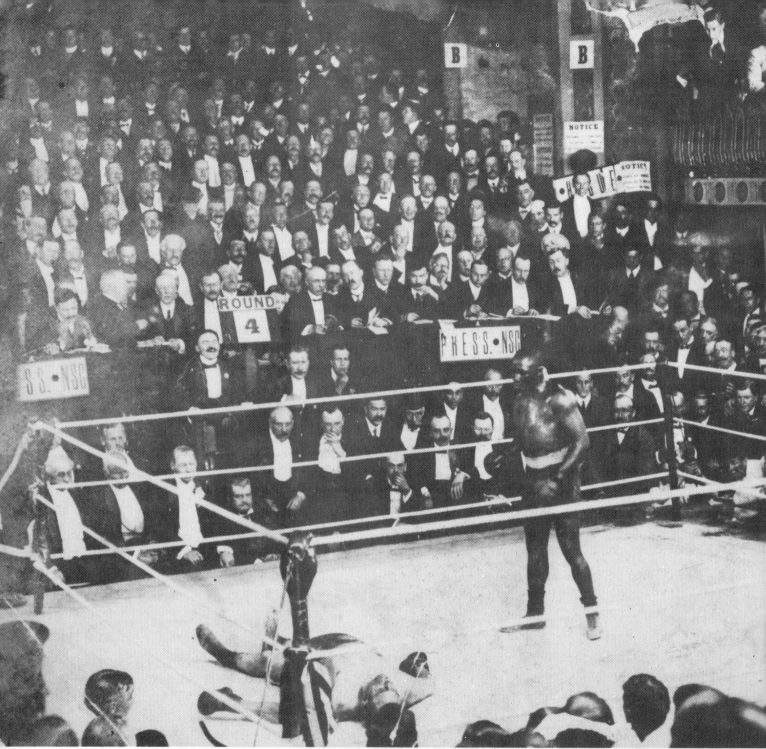

But always Kearns would reply, "Sam, I'm looking for something easier."

Anything was easier than "The Boston Tar Baby." Short and squat in build, Langford continually pressed up against the numbers of his opponents, landing short, vicious punches to the body, the head, or any place available to what he called "his referees."

For Langford carried his own referees, not in the literal, but in the figurative sense. Once, when scheduled to fight at London's famed National Sport-

Left: Langford knocks out Iron Hague at National Sporting Club, London, 1909. Bottom: "Old Tham" squares off with "Fireman" Jim Flynn before knocking out the "White Hope," 1910.

Born 2/12/80 in Weymouth, Nova Scotia, Canada, (3/4/83 has also been reported as birth date) . . . First recorded bouts in 1902 . . . Fought early bouts in hometown of Boston, known as "Boston Tar Baby" . . . Possibly the greatest boxer to never receive a chance at a world title . . . Opportunities limited by career and lifestyle of Jack Johnson . . . Lost to Johnson, 4/26/06, 15-round decision, avoided by Johnson during Johnson's reign as champion . . . Fought 75 bouts against just 5 opponents: faced Henry Wills 23 times (2 won, 6 lost, 15 no-decisions); faced Sam McVey 15 times (4 won, 2 lost, 4 draws, 5 no-decisions); Joe Jeanette 14 times (4 won, 3 lost, 2 draws, 5 no-decisions); Jim Barry 12 times (6 won, 6 no-decisions); Jeff Clarke, 11 times (3 won, 1 lost, 2 draws, 5 no-decisions) . . . Twice knocked out The Dixie Kid: 9/28/09, 5 rounds and 1/10/10, 3 rounds . . . Boxed 6-round no-decision bout with Stanley Ketchel, 4/27/10, while Ketchel was middleweight champion . . . Knocked out Philadelphia Jack O'Brien, 8/15/11, in 5 rounds, while O'Brien claimed light heavyweight title . . . Fought in all classes from lightweight to heavyweight . . . Fought in Australia, 1911–13, won Australian heavyweight championship from Sam McVey, 4/3/12 . . . Probably fought over 300 bouts although only 252 recorded . . . In all-time top-ten list with 102 knockouts recorded . . . Elected to Boxing Hall of Fame, 1955 . . . Died, 1/12/56, Cambridge, MA . . . Complete record: 254 bouts, 139 won, 25 lost, 31 draws, 58 no-decisions, 1 no-contest, 102 knockouts.

your own referee in the ring." Unmoved, Langford merely lifted his right hand and said, "Ah carries mah own referee. He goes into the ring with me whenever ah fights. Here he is," and menacingly waved his "old Betsy" under the nose of the by-now thoroughly chastened ring official.

But it wasn't only ring officials the man who called himself "jus' plain Sam" chastened. He also threw fear into opponents as well, calling his shots like an early-day Muhammad Ali. Once he noticed one of the seconds of his opponents slicing up oranges while awaiting the call to action. "What you doin' with all them oranges?" Sam shouted over to the second. "I'm slicing them up for my man to suck on between rounds," came the answer. "Man, you ain't gonna need them oranges," promised Sam and he went out to dispatch his opponent in one short round. Another time one of his opponent's seconds was screaming for his man to do something or other to Langford and that he would tell him what to do when he came by that way again. Langford merely looked down disdainfully and said, "Man, he ain't coming back there again," and, sure enough, cold-cocked him one punch later.

Sam Langford could call every shot, except his shot at the heavyweight title. And so he remained a nonchampion, perhaps the greatest nonchampion, in the history of boxing.

ing Club, the club manager asked Langford why he "had not brought up the subject of a referee." He went on to explain, "All the other American boxers who have appeared here have been interested in the choice of a referee, yet you have not even mentioned the subject." Langford just looked at the official and said, "Ah carries mah own referee." "Tut, tut," the official is reported to have replied, "That will never do. The Club always appoints the referee. We positively cannot permit you to put

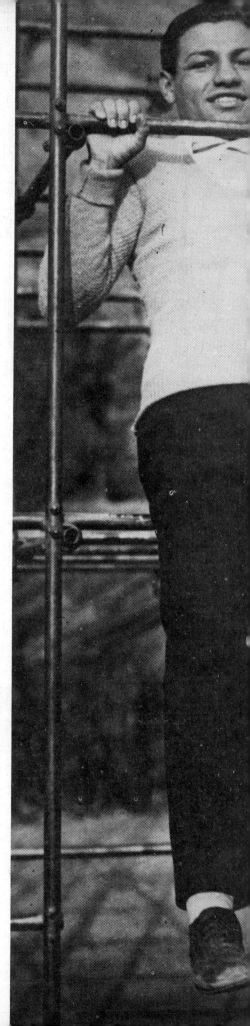

NINE: TONY CANZONERI

TONY CANZONERI

His nickname was the diminutive "Canzi," short for Canzoneri. But other than his size, nothing else was small about Tony Canzoneri, a shooting star of unforgettable magnitude. Possessed of the hands of an artisan, not the laborer's hands of his Italian forebears, "Canzi" was a puncher who could punch and a boxer who could box, one of the greatest combination ringmen of all time. With inexhaustible energy, Canzoneri would tirelessly pressure his opponent, ready to drop in his deadly right with such precision that one writer said of his power punch, "If you crossed him, he would dot your eyes," or swing his low-held lethal left with bludgeoning effect. Canzi's foes usually took on the look of a boilerplate, bearing hundreds of hammer marks and rivets put into place by this miniature boilermaker who came complete with a cast-iron jaw. And yet, this man who was built like a fireplug and fought like a one-man house afire blazing brilliantly against any extinguisher had one major flaw: cockiness.

MOST BOXER-PUNCHERS PLAY POINT-counterpoint, boxing the punchers and punching the boxers. Not Canzi, so pouter-pigeon proud of his skills that he would try to beat his foes at their own game. And sometimes lose.

But losses were few and far between for this naturally talented warrior. Especially at the beginning of his career, which started, fittingly enough, with the first knockout ever scored in the then old-new Madison Square Garden. The first rough draft of his greatness came less than two years after he turned pro when the young 18-year-old was matched against one of the toughest fighters around, Bud Taylor, for a version of the vacant bantamweight title—and a $4,000 belt. It would be nice to note that Canzi took chance by the throat and beat Taylor. But truth to tell, the fight went to a 10-round draw, the title remaining vacant and the belt remaining in the hands of the promoter. Rematched two months later, Canzoneri gave a good accounting of himself; unfortunately, it was not good enough and the experienced Taylor got the decision—"which," one writer

noted, "in many quarters was considered a gift."

Exactly 4 months later came the fight that began the Canzoneri legend: his 15-round demolition of that aging idol, Johnny Dundee, for the vacant featherweight crown. But even though Canzoneri had combined his fire, stamina, and agility with a small sprig of compassion, the cheers that night were still reserved for the fallen hero of Italian fight fans for over a decade, Dundee, whose name rebounded from the rafters of the Garden for almost an hour after the fight.

Popularity is glory's small change. And while Canzi could win the glory, the popularity still eluded him, as it did the night, some three years later, when he beat the dashing Cuban, Kid Chocolate in 15 rounds, and found himself the target of small change—together with catcalls, jeers, cigar butts, and assorted debris. More than somewhat at a loss to explain his unpopularity, Canzoneri in a choked voice said, "I don't know why they did that to me. I tried to make the fight and I won. . . . Some nights you just can't please 'em." But two years

Opposite top: Canzoneri wins title from Jack "Kid" Berg April 24, 1931.
Opposite bottom: He overcomes overhead mike and Jimmy McLarnin in 1936.

later Canzi was able to "please 'em" when he knocked the Havana Bon Bon kicking in two rounds. For a full five minutes the gallery gods on the Forty-ninth street side of the Garden reacted with an ear-splitting roar, shouting and stamping for their new idol. Canzoneri stood there mid-ring, backlit by spots, soaking it all in, saying over and over again, "I made them like me. . . ."

By now the man who was part Alamo and part buzzsaw was thought to have little or no future, only a recycled past, as he proved by rewinning the same lightweight championship he had won five years earlier from Al Singer with

Left to right: "Canzi" successfully defends lightweight title against Billy Petrolle, 1932. Beats Benny Bass, 1928. Meets Kid Chocolate, retaining junior welterweight title, 1931.

one deadly accurate left hook in 66 seconds, just enough time to say "China Chin." But if lasting fame comes only after retirement, Canzi was in no hurry for it and wanted to fight the man-tiger known as Jimmy McLarnin "before I get out of boxing," because, as he put it, "of the danger attached to it." And so, on the night of May 8, 1936, Canzoneri met McLarnin in a fight no one will ever forget. For, after the two greats had received their final instructions, Canzi headed back to his corner as he had thousands of times before. Only this time he walked directly into the public address mike dangling in the air a second too long. Canzoneri staggered to his corner, his forehead cut open and blood flowing like an unchecked red river. Administered to by his corner as best they could, and still unsure of his whereabouts, Canzoneri turned to fight the deadliest puncher this side of the Garden microphone. For one round he was hammered around the ring by McLarnin. But in the second round, his head finally clear of the mike-induced fog, Canzoneri caught McLarnin with one of his still dynamite-laden right hands and won the next nine rounds—and the decision—going away. That was Tony Canzoneri at his best.

Winding down with the inevitability of gradualness, Canzoneri continued fighting anyone and everyone down the long, hard highway that serves as the path for most over-the-hill fighters. But he would not give in to time any more than he would give in to his opponents, his iron will matching his iron chin. Finally, looking like a grandfather and fighting like a godfather, Canzoneri was brought back to the Garden one last time, to face a swashbuckling left-hooker from Brownsville named Al "Bummy" Davis. In just three rounds, Davis did something no one else had; he knocked out the great Tony Canzoneri. The sentimentalists, with tears in their eyes, booed Davis and cheered their hero. For Tony Canzoneri *was* "The Noblest Roman of them All," and one of the greatest heroes in the long history of boxing.

orn 11/6/08, in Slidell, LA . . . Raised in New York City . . . New York State amateur champion, 1924 . . . Started as a pro, 1925 . . . Challenged Bud Taylor twice, unsuccessfully, for NBA world bantamweight title: 10-round draw, 3/26/27; 10-round loss, 6/24/27 . . . Would have been youngest champion had he won—only 18 years and 4 months . . . Won world featherweight championship from Benny Bass, 2/10/28, by 15-round decision—only 19 years and 3 months old—youngest featherweight champ ever and sixth youngest champion of all time . . . Lost title to Andre Routis in first defense, 9/28/28 . . . Challenged Sammy Mandall, 8/2/29, for lightweight title, lost 10-round decision . . . Knocked out Al Singer in 1:06 of first round to win lightweight crown, 11/14/30, fastest knockout in lightweight title bout . . . Defeated Jack Kid Berg, 4/24/31 by third-round knockout to win junior welterweight title to became second man to win 3 world championships . . . Lost rematch to Jadick, 7/18/32, also 10-round decision . . . Regained junior welter title from Battling Shaw, 5/21/33 . . . Lost both lightweight and junior welterweight titles in 10-round decision to Barney Ross, 6/23/33 . . . Lost 15-round rematch to Ross, 9/12/33, for titles . . . Rewon lightweight crown in bout with Lou Ambers for vacant title, 5/10/35, lost it to Ambers 9/3/36, both bouts 15-round decisions . . . Lost rematch to Ambers, 5/7/37, in attempt to regain crown . . . Fought 21 world championship bouts—won titles in 5, lost titles in 4, defended successfully in 6, and made 6 unsuccessful bids for titles . . . Record in championship bouts: 11 won, 10 lost . . . Fought 36 bouts with 18 world champions and defeated 15 of them—overall record of 22–12–2 in bouts with champions . . . Last bout, 11/1/39 . . . Owned Broadway restaurant and appeared as actor in motion pictures . . . Elected to Boxing Hall of Fame, 1956 . . . Died 12/9/59, New York City . . . Complete record: 176 bouts, 139 won, 24 lost, 10 draws, 3 no-decisions, 44 knockouts.

TEN: MUHAMMAD ALI

MUHAMMAD ALI

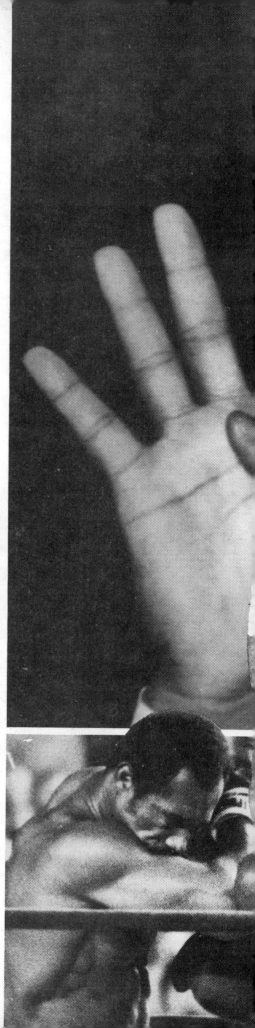

Part showman, part promoter, and all champion, Muhammad Ali was boxing's version of the Pied Piper, always heading up his own parade with a band of admirers in his wake as he rolled through the sixties and the seventies. Coming on the scene when the heavyweight championship—if not all of boxing—was just a rumor, this man-boy who answered to the name Cassius Marcellus Clay for the first part of his life, proved that charm travels as far as talent, as he became the most celebrated and flamboyant figure in the world of sports in a period of merely three years. Clay-Ali strutted with the air of a carnival midway and considered fame his due so much so that he took a sword and dubbed his own shoulders "The Greatest," a title many of his followers were willing to concede to him after he had twice destroyed a supposedly invincible Sonny Liston.

Above: The "Anchor Punch" fells Liston. Right: Ali wins rubber match against Norton. Far right: The "Rumble in the Jungle" against Foreman.

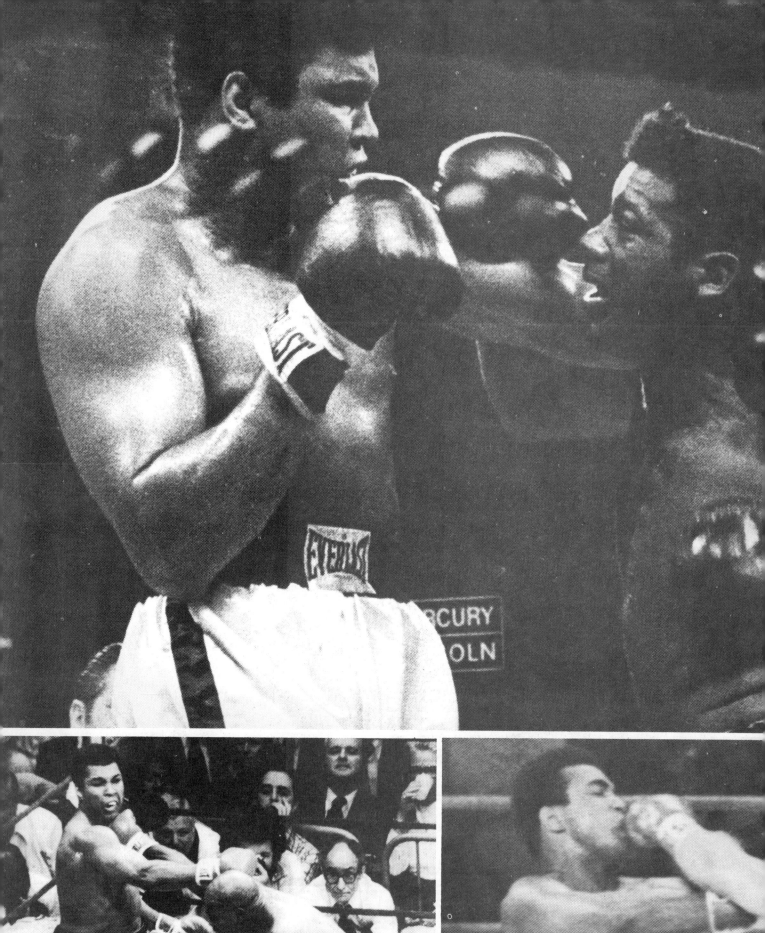

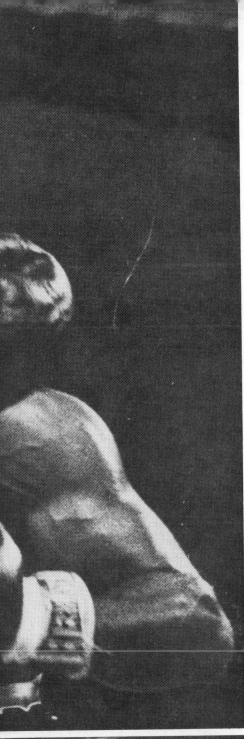

ADDING VERBAL FOOTWORK TO HIS amazing agility in the ring, Ali brought a touch of the theatrical to boxing, his jabberwocky making his opponents' heads spin as much as his fast hands.

Everything had a name or a meaning: His opponents were called "the Bear," "The Mummy," "The Washerwoman," and "The Rabbit"; his moves were "The Ali Shuffle," "The Rope-a-Dope," and "The Anchor Punch." And all became part of the language of fistiana. He even took to predicting the rounds when his opponents "must fall," and he rarely was an emotional welsher, delivering the results almost as reliably as the newspaper.

Ali made great copy with his wonderfully engaging remarks, calling Leon Spinks, "So ugly that when a tear runs down his face, it only gets halfway down and then runs back . . ." or, in answer to whether he was scared of Sonny Liston, "Listen, black guys scare white guys a lot more than black guys scare black guys." But it was one of these off-the-cuff remarks that came back to haunt him and short-changed "The Greatest" of almost three years of his career when he was still at the peak of his glory.

For when Ali, a.k.a. Selective Service Number 15–47–42–127, was reclassified 1–A and asked by the press what he thought of the action of his local Louisville board, he said, "I ain't got no quarrel with them Viet Congs." That and his decision not to serve his country during the Vietnam conflict in keeping with his Black Muslim beliefs gave the local Babbits who controlled the boxing commissions enough ammunition to defrock him of his title and bar him from the ring.

He survived as few others could have survived, bucking the system. But in the end he was victorious, the United States Supreme Court unanimously ruling in his favor, and he came back in 1970 to take up where he had left off as the undefeated heavyweight champion of the world.

Now Muhammad Ali was bigger than boxing, he was a symbol of the seventies, a man who had bucked the system and won. And despite his 15-round loss to Joe Frazier, he remained "The People's Champion," a championship he converted into the World Championship with a stunning 8-round knockout of George Foreman in "The Rumble in the Jungle" in 1974.

And although he was to fight for four more years—with two unfortunate attempts at a comeback—Muhammad Ali had acquitted himself on his claim as "The Greatest," if not in the ring, at least in history.

Born Cassius Marcellus Clay, Jr., 1/17/42, in Louisville, KY . . . National AAU champion, 1959–60 . . . Olympic light heavyweight champion, 1960 . . . Western Golden Gloves champion, 1959 . . . Intercity Golden Gloves champion, 1959 (defeated Australian Tony Madigan to win intercity title, also faced Madigan in semi-finals of Olympics) . . . First pro bout, 10/29/60 . . . Won world heavyweight title, 2/25/64, by seventh-round TKO of Sonny Liston . . . First champion to change name after winning title—after Liston bout became Muhammad Ali . . . Won rematch, 5/25/65, by first-round knockout . . . Made 5 title defenses in 4 countries, 1955—most heavyweight title defenses in a year since Joe Louis' "Bum of the Month" tour in 1941 . . . Forced inactivity, 3/23/67 to 19/25/70, due to draft status problems with U.S. Government . . . 3/8/71 bout with Joe Frazier—heavyweight championship bout between 2 undefeated heavyweight champions set new standards for closed-circuit ticket prices and paydays—$25 picket to watch closed circuit telecast and $2.5 million purse for each boxer . . . Classic 15-round battle won by Frazier . . . Ali won 12-round nontitle rematch, 1/28/74 . . . Broke jaw in 12-round loss to Ken Norton, 3/31/73; defeated Norton in rematch, 9/10/73 . . . Regained heavyweight championship from George Foreman by eighth-round knockout in Kinshasa, Zaire, first heavyweight title bout in Africa, nicknamed by Ali "Rumble in the Jungle" . . . Defended title 4 times in 1975: 10/1/75 bout with Frazier in Manila, one of boxing's greatest bouts, stopped Frazier in fourteenth round . . . 4 more title defenses in 1976, plus one exhibition against Japanese wrestler, Antonio Inoki, in Tokyo . . . Lost title to Leon Spinks, 2/15/78, by 15-round decision, huge upset . . . Only Spinks' eighth pro bout . . . Won title third time in 9/15/78, rematch with Spinks . . . Retired 1979, attempted comeback 1980, and was stopped by Larry Holmes in eleventh-round—first time in career did not go the distance in losing effort . . . Fought additional bout, 12/11/81, in Bahamas, against Trevor Berbick and lost 10-round decision . . . Truly a world champion—fought title bouts in North America, Europe, Africa, Asia, Canada, England, Germany, Zaire, Malaysia, Philippines, Puerto Rico . . . Fought nontitle bouts in Switzerland, Japan, Ireland, Indonesia, Bahamas . . . Fought exhibitions in Sweden, Scotland, Venezuela, Trinidad, Argentina . . . Fought in all parts of U.S. from Lewiston, Maine, to Miami Beach and from New York to Las Vegas . . . Won 22 of 25 heavyweight championship bouts, more than any other boxer except Joe Louis . . . Fought more heavyweight championship rounds (255) than any other man . . . Complete record: 61 bouts, 56 won, 5 lost, 37 knockouts.

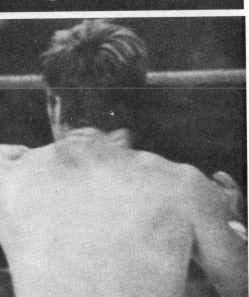

Top: Ali stops Floyd Patterson at Madison Square Garden in 1972. Far left: Ali outpoints "The Acorn" Earnie Shavers, in 1977. Left: The triumphant return of Ali after a 40-month enforced "retirement" October 26, 1970, vs. Jerry Quarry.

11 JOE GANS

JOE GANS

Depending upon which yellowing newsclip one reads, Joe Gans was either the cleverest man ever to grace the prize ring or one of the slickest. Sometimes both. Nick-named "The Old Master" for good reason, Gans used the ring as his own private laboratory. George Blake, the one-time manager of Fidel La Barba and former second of such men as Packey McFarland, thought Gans was the greatest lightweight in the world. Said Blake, in comparing Gans to Benny Leonard and others, "I was very impressed with the way his brain worked. One day he said to me, 'If you happen to hit a man in a certain place that hurts, that is the place to hit him again. You only have to hit him half as hard there as any other place to finish him.'

NOT LONG AFTERWARDS I REFEREED the match between Gans and Mike Sullivan. As the fight progressed one of Joe's hooks caught Mike beneath the ear, and Mike winced. It wasn't long after that when Mike was nailed under the ear again. The blow did not seem very hard, but it did the trick."

Having already lost to Frank Erne in his quest for the lightweight crown, Gans sought—and got—a second fight with the champion. While in training, Gans decided to put into effect something he had seen in their first fight: Erne would start his left and check it for just an instant to see his opponent's reaction; if his opponent moved to block his punch, he would turn it into a hook; if his opponent anticipated a hook, he would deliver a straight left. Gans determined to literally beat Erne to the punch and "shoot my right over the moment I saw the left start." When the two met again, Gans wasted precious little time putting the theory into practice and, as Erne started his first left, let fly with his right putting the soon-to-be ex-champion down for the full count just 100 seconds into the first round.

Gans, born Joseph Gaines, was the master of all he surveyed. The only quality he lacked was a sense of discrimination, associating himself on a scam with confidence men who would exploit their own mothers if the price

Clockwise from right: Young Peter Jackson (left) shakes with Gans; Gans squares off with Mike (Twin) Sullivan; Gans and Battling Nelson before famous 42-round battle for lightweight title.

Born Joseph Gaines, 11/25/74, in Baltimore, MD . . . Known as "The Old Master" . . . Began pro career 1891 . . . Early record incomplete . . . Boxed mostly in Baltimore area first 6 years . . . Lost to Frank Erne in twelfth-round in bid for lightweight title, 3/23/00 . . . Won lightweight title in rematch with first-round knockout, 5/12/02 . . . Second boxer in history to win world championship by first-round knockout . . . First black to win lightweight title . . . Fought 20-round draw with Joe Walcott for welterweight title, 9/30/94 . . . Defeated Battling Nelson in round 42, 9/3/06, when Nelson deliberately fouled to avoid losing by knockout—longest bout ever to end on a foul, third longest bout in twentieth century, and largest gate in history at the time, $69,715, earned only $11,000 to Nelson's $23,000 . . . Stopped by Nelson in seventeenth round of rematch, 7/4/08, and lost title . . . Challenged Nelson two months later, 9/9/08, and was again stopped—this time in round 21 . . . Fought one additional bout, ND 10 against Jabez White, 3/12/09 . . . Died of tuberculosis following year, 8/10/10, in Baltimore, MD . . . Fought 3 bouts in 1 night, 7/15/01 . . . Complete record: 156 bouts, 120 won, 8 lost, 10 draws, 18 no-decisions, 55 knockouts.

was right. The despoiling of Gans began at the tender age of 17, as his manager threw him to the wolves in long-distance fights against far more mature battlers. His very first bout went 12 rounds, his second 22. But still, his intuitive ring knowledge and hand speed carried the day. His manager, Al Hereford, tried to make money with Gans any way he could, once "arranging" a fight with bantamweight champion Terry McGovern in Chicago, a 2-round stoppage of Gans that rivaled the odor of the neighboring stockyards.

Wearing no man's collar, not even his own, Gans finally rid himself of those who exploited him, and fought, on the level, several of the turn-of-the-century greats, including Sam Langford, Jimmy Britt, and Joe Walcott, the latter for his welterweight title. But Gans's greatest fight was his 42-round classic against the human battering ram, Battling Nelson, in Goldfield, Nevada, in a fight where everything, including the weights, was loaded against him. Round after round, he blunted the attack of the Durable Dane by sidestepping his charges and frustrating Nelson's attacks with well-timed counterpunches. Finally, frustrated by his inability to get at Gans, Nelson took to fouling him, losing in the forty-second on a well-placed shot below the border. After the fight, Gans sent his mother a telegram which read, simply, "Bringing home the bacon," a phrase which has now become part of our language.

Within four years, Gans would be gone, the victim of consumption. But he is remembered today by the only boxing statue that stands in the Madison Square Garden Hall of Fame, a statue of a handsome, ebony-skinned boxer that bears mute testimony to the skills of "The Old Master," Joe Gans, one of the "greats."

WILLIE PEP

The man who scissored his given name "Papaleo" into the pallindronic "Pep" was boxing's version of the three-card monte player: Now you see him, now you don't. His movements, which took on the look of tap dancing with gloves on, left his opponents to speculate on their meaning and his fans to listen for accompanying music. Willie Pep fought as if he didn't like to get hit, which he didn't, having developed a great respect for his teeth at a very early age. He fought as a survivor, practicing a form of reverse polarity with the uncanny ability to anticipate an opponent's blows—and then parry them, pick them off, or just plain beat them with his own form of rat-a-tat punches. Throughout his long career, Pep substituted shiftiness and cunning for a lack of power, most of his knockouts coming not from a malicious blow but from his opponents falling to the ground in utter exhaustion, unable to keep up with the man labeled "Willie the Wisp," soon to be contracted, like his own name, to "Will o' the Wisp."

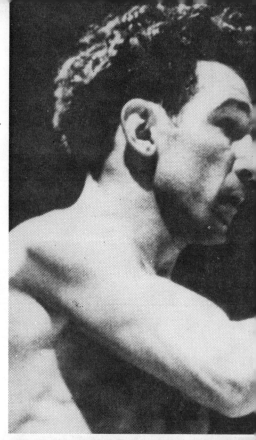

MANY OF HIS OPPONENTS LIKENED fighting the "Will o' the Wisp" to battling a man in the Hall of Mirrors, unable to cope with an opponent they couldn't find, let alone hit. Others compared the experience to catching moonbeams in a jar, or chasing a mirage or a shadow. And yet another, Kid Campeche, said after a fight in which Pep had pitched a no-hitter, "Fighting Willie Pep is like trying to stamp out a grass fire."

Pep's greatest virtuoso performance came the night he gave the fans a run for their money, literally, winning a round without throwing a punch. His opponent on this occasion was Jackie Graves, a TNT-southpaw puncher with more than his share of knockouts. Pep had already tipped off a few friendly sportswriters that he would not throw a punch in anger during the third round. Despite their incredulity, they found that what happened was incredible. For Pep moved; Pep switched to southpaw, mimicking Graves; Pep danced; Pep weaved; Pep spun Graves around and around again; Pep gave head feints, shoulder feints, foot feints,

and feint feints. But Pep never landed a punch. In the words of one sportswriter, Don Riley, "It was an amazing display of defensive boxing skill so adroit, so cunning, so subtle that the roaring crowd did not notice Pep's tactics were completely without offense. He made Jim Corbett's agility look like a broken-down locomotive. He made even Sugar Ray Robinson's fluidity look like cement hardening. Never has boxing seen such perfection!" Suffice it to say, all three judges gave Pep the round.

Willie Pep's long 22-year career was, in reality, two careers. During his first career, one that spanned seven years, Pep outclassed and outraced 109 of his 111 opponents—losing only to the hard-hitting ex-lightweight champ Sammy Angott—and won the featherweight crown at the tender age of 20 years and 2 months. Then, on January 8, 1947, Pep suffered near-fatal injuries in an airplane crash. His career, if not his ability to walk, were seemingly behind him. Miraculously, five months later, rather than sitting at home and watching his bones mend, Pep came back—not only to walk, but to fight,

Top: Willie Pep regains his featherweight crown from Sandy Saddler, Feb. 11, 1949. Bottom: The "Will O' The Wisp" connects on Charlie Riley.

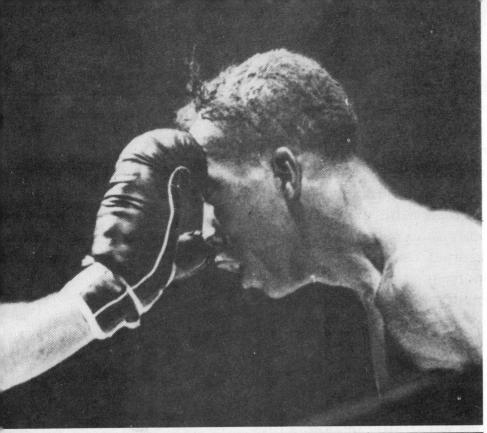

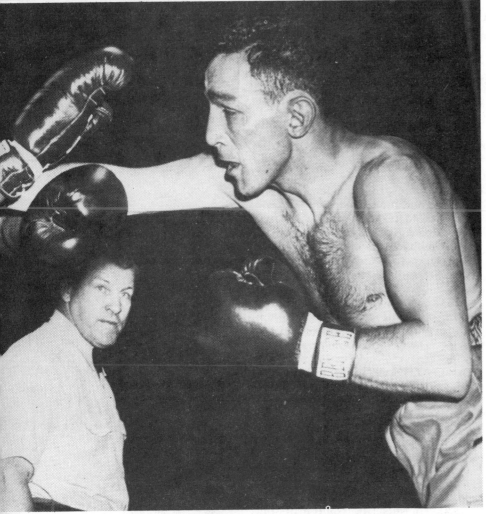

Born Buglielmo Papaleo, 9/19/22, in Middletown, CT ... Connecticut State amateur champion, 1938–39 ... First pro bout 7/3/40 ... Fought early years almost exclusively in New England ... Reputed to have won a round without throwing a single punch, called "The Will o' the Wisp" by sportswriters for his great defensive skills ... Held record of 54–0 when he defeated Chalky Wright for the world featherweight championship, 11/20/42, in 15-round decision ... Consecutive 63-win streak when defeated in 10-round decision by Sammy Angott in nontitle bout, 3/19/43 (Angott had retired as undefeated lightweight champion 4 months previously and was making a comeback) ... Defended title once annually, 1943–48, while fighting 10 to 12 nontitle bouts each year ... Successful defenses: 6/8/43, Sal Bartolo, W 15; 9/29/44, Chalky Wright, W 15; 8/19/45, Phil Terranova, W 15; 6/7/46, Sal Bartolo, KO 12; 8/22/47, Jock Leslie, KO 12; 2/24/48, Humberto Sierra, KO 10 ... Broke his back in crash of small airplane, 1/8/47, but back in action in less than 6 months ... Lost title to Sandy Saddler by fourth-round knockout, 10/29/48 ... Fought 73 consecutive bouts without a loss (only 1 draw) between losses to Angott and Saddler ... Won 135 of first 138 bouts ... Regained featherweight title, 2/11/49, by 15-round decision over Saddler ... Defended crown 3 times, 1949–50 ... Again lost title to Saddler by eighth-round knockout, 9/8/50 ... Lost title rematch, 9/26/51 ... Continued fighting until 1959 and won 60 of 66 bouts during that period ... Elected to Boxing Hall of Fame, 1963 ... Made comeback, 1965–66, at age of 44 and won 9 of 10 ... One of only 2 men to box after election to Hall of Fame ... Complete record: 242 bouts, 230 won, 11 lost, 1 draw, 65 knockouts.

and win again.

Pep continued to denude the featherweight division of contenders, winning 26 more times and defending his title twice. With the supply of challengers all but exhausted, Pep accepted the challenge of what he called "a thin, weak-looking guy who looks like you could go poof and knock him over." However, it wasn't Pep who was the knocker but the knockee as the "thin, weak-looking guy," who went by the name of Sandy Saddler, knocked Pep over with a vagrant left in the third and a right in the fourth that finished off the soon-to-be ex-champion.

The rematch was the highlight of Willie's career(s). For on the night of February 11, 1949, in that creaky, hallowed hall where dreams are made, Madison Square Garden, Pep made his dream come true by recapturing *his* featherweight title. Possessing all the nervous courage of a small pup and the speed, guile, and ability to recognize pain immediately, Pep stayed true to his instincts and gave Saddler nothing to hit. In return, Pep hit Saddler with his best shots, his combinations, and his target-bound left. Nothing. "But," said Willie, seeing a small straw, but a straw nevertheless, "when I stepped on his toes, he said 'Ouch!' so I stepped on his toes all night." It was more than enough. He had won the fight of his life and the last big fight he was ever to win, his long-running career at an end.

The name Willie Pep will forever be remembered as a name put to melody and symphony, a balletic will to grace that made him the "Will o' the Wisp."

JACK JOHNSON

Nobody knew just how good Jack Johnson really was, including Jack Johnson himself. Never bothering to combine delusions of grandeur with delusions of honesty, Johnson lived as he fought: unpredictably. A clever, scientific boxer the size of all Galveston, Johnson could move around the ring as gracefully as a cat, catching punches with his elbows, his hands, and the upper portions of his arms, or time his blocks and parries to set up his opponent for alternate right or left thrusts to the head, all done with the ease of a featherweight. Like a bullet, each one of his gloves had someone's name written on it. Unfortunately, he would rarely pull the trigger, fighting each fight as if he were merely cruising on his batteries, using little or no energy, all the while smiling his sweet smiles of inscrutability. To assess Jack Johnson's place in boxing history is as difficult as attempting to categorize Shakespeare's Othello merely as a Moor. And as misleading. The rise and fall of Jack Johnson was shaped as much by his being black as by America's reaction to it, and in many ways, his was as much a preordained tragedy as that of Othello.

DENIED HIS CHANCE TO FIND HIS ROOTS in big-time boxing, Johnson blossomed in bootleg fights, *Battle Royales*—a barbaric pastime in which between six and eight fighters, all blindfolded and almost all black, would fight until the last man left standing was adjudged the winner—and on the Chitlin' Circuit against other blacks. Relegated into their own isolated world, some black heavyweights had gained a measure of celebrity: Peter Jackson, Sam Langford, Sam McVey, and Joe Jeanette, to name a few. But few got further than that. Jack Johnson was to defy one of boxing's ineluctable verities—that no black man could ever become the heavyweight champion of the world.

Johnson menaced the heavyweight division like Tamerlane the Tartar and his yellow hordes had menaced the populace in the fourteenth century, beating the likes of Bob Fitzsimmons, Sam Langford, Joe Jeanette, and Jim Flynn. Finally, the man the papers called "the Playful Ethiopian" tracked the titleholder, Tommy Burns, down to

Australia, and there, more by dint of pleading and wheeling and dealing than by shrewd negotiations, Johnson got his long-awaited opportunity.

On the day after Christmas 1908, a large black cat played with a small white mouse in a combination boxing match-game, less for fistic nourishment than for sadistic pleasure. The fight was, in the words of columnist Jack London, "No fight," as Johnson fought with the armor of arrogance, expressing a contempt for opponent and fans alike as he played his audience like a band leader checking his sections, flashing his gold teeth and taunting Burns with verbal winks—"Come on, leedle Tahmmy, come right here where I want you."

Finally, with Burns tottering helplessly and unable to defend himself, the Sydney police took matters into their own hands and rushed into the ring, mercifully stopping the fight. The worst fears of white men everywhere were confirmed: the white man's burden had become his master.

The winner not only took the heavyweight championship of the world, he also unleashed a dammed-up wall of hatred. With sanctimonious smugness, white men everywhere demanded that other white men, called for lack of a better name, "White Hopes," rescue back *their* title, *their* heritage, *their* world. And every hardy, if not foolhardy, white fighter of more than 175 pounds came running to answer the call to arms.

But Johnson, whose natural ability was only rivaled by his contempt for white society, paid no heed to the seismic quake his win had wrought, instead flaunting everything society held sacred with his flamboyant ways. Johnson wanted it all. But it was too much. It always is. And, in the end, society would have the last laugh. But not before Johnson had taken the measure of two of society's appointed saviors—Stanley Ketchel and Jim Jeffries—in almost mirrored morality plays.

For the next few years, Johnson drove a jagged unpredictable path, practicing a total lack of self-control. A subtle spirit defiant, he lived the life of fast women, fast cars, and sloe gin, flaunting every excess to excess and living life to the fullest. But his high style of living, his marriages to three white women, and his opening of a free-wheeling Café de Champion in Chicago—which served all comers and none of society's mores—brought, like decaying fish, the redolent stench of scandal to the nostrils of moralists. And so, what man couldn't do, government now attempted to do: Get Jack Johnson. And get him they did, enacting legislation designed to forbid interracial fights and interracial marriages as well, and, for good measure, convicting him for violating the Mann Act.

But no one could legislate against Johnson's style of fighting, and Johnson fled the country to pursue his career abroad. Unfortunately, his less-than-

grand tour of Europe begot him few dollars and fewer fights and, when an offer came to fight yet another "White Hope"—this one, Jess Willard, called a "White Hope" for the same reason an aging lady of the streets applies rouge to her cheeks, to dress up her credentials—he succumbed to the financial fandangos the promoters offered.

The fight, held in Havana, Cuba, was not one of boxing's most memorable fights, even if it was one of its most memorable moments. For 19 rounds, the 37-year-old Johnson had his own way with the 6-foot, 6½-inch boxing Leviathan. Then, in the twentieth, Willard drove a hard right and a left to Johnson's body just at the bell, and from that point until the finish, in the twenty-sixth, Willard had far the better of it, finally ending the battle with a right-hand swing that landed on the point of Johnson's jaw. Johnson went down in a pose reminiscent of "The Dying Gladiator," his right arm covering

Born John Arthur Johnson, 3/31/78, in Galveston, TX . . . Early record incomplete, first recorded bout, 1897 . . . Boxed first 5 years mainly in Galveston then moved to West Coast . . . Known as "Li'l Artha" . . . Won so-called "Negro heavyweight title," 2/3/03, from Denver Ed Martin in 20-round decision . . . Mixed bouts unpopular at the time and many of his early bouts were with such top black boxers as Sam Langford, Sam McVey, and Joe Jeannette . . . Fought 8 bouts with Jeannette, 1905–06 . . . Defeated by Marvin Hart, 3/28/05, 20-round decision . . . Won world heavyweight championship from Tommy Burns in Sydney, Australia, 12/26/08, in bout stopped by police when Burns was unable to continue in fourteenth-round . . . Made first title defense against future Academy Award-winning actor Victor McLaglen, 3/10/09, in 6-round no-decision bout . . . Fought 3 more no-decision title defenses in 1909: Philadelphia Jack O'Brien, 5/19; Tony Ross, 6/30; Al Kaufman, 9/9 . . . Knocked out middleweight champion Stanley Ketchel in 12 rounds, 10/16/09 . . . First black heavyweight champion, but lifestyle made him highly unpopular and caused ex-champion Jim Jeffries to come out of 6-year retirement in attempt to reclaim title for white race . . . Knocked out Jeffries in fifteenth-round, 7/4/10 . . . Next defense 2 years later, 7/4/12, KO 9 of Fireman Jim Flynn . . . Moved to Europe to escape pursuit by U.S. Government . . . Boxed 10-round draw with Battling Jim Johnson in Paris, 12/19/13, and broke bone in left arm during third round of that fight and fought dull, defensive bout—one judge actually voted for Jim Johnson while referee and other judge scored it a draw—only draw in a heavyweight championship bout until 1983 . . . Competed in wrestling tournament in Paris, November 1910, and won 2 bouts before being eliminated by Jimmy Esson, a Scottish wrestler . . . Won 20-round decision from Frank Moran, 6/27/14, in Paris . . . Moved to Argentina same year . . . Fought Jess Willard, 4/5/15, in Havana, Cuba and lost by knockout in round twenty-six of scheduled 45-round bout—longest heavyweight championship bout in gloved era . . . Continued boxing until 1928 at age of 50 . . . Actually fought two 3-round exhibitions, 11/27/45, at age of 67 . . . Killed in auto accident, 6/10/46, in Raleigh, NC . . . Elected charter member of Boxing Hall of Fame, 1954 . . . Wrote autobiography (without ghost-writer), 1927, *Jack Johnson—In the Ring and Out* . . . Fictionalized account of his life by Howard Sackler, *The Great White Hope*, made into award-winning Broadway play and movie . . . Complete record: 112 bouts, 78 won, 8 lost, 12 draws, 14 no-decisions, 45 knockouts.

Left: Johnson and Joe Jeannette pose before one of their fights. Right: Jackson behind bars after his "illegal" fight against Joe Choynski.

his face. After the decision had been rendered and the frenzied crowd surged forward to collect around the ring as the faithful would around a shrine, he jumped up, and without catching an answer or a breath, raced for the dressing room. Years later, in a move reeking of prophetic hindsight, he would tell a so-called "confession"—that he had thrown the fight.

But, then again, Jack Johnson had played with boxing so long, when could we ever take him seriously? Or know when he was putting forth his best efforts?

BARNEY ROSS

Ring archaeologists can date the lowest point in boxing history as the year 1933. Attendance and gate receipts had hit an all-time low, and the heavyweight champion was Primo Carnera, a joke. Nat Fleischer, venerable publisher of *The Ring*, was moved to write, "I dare venture that 1933 is the worst on record." If boxing had been a wake, it would have been an insult to the deceased. But, if it had nowhere to go but up, that up would be in divisions other than the heavyweight division, which had quickly become the sandbox of boxing. There were "To Let" signs in five of the other seven traditional boxing classes as well. If there was to be a revival, it would have to be sparked by the only two divisions that had sustained interest in their continuity and their championships: the welterweight and light-weight divisions. And led by the one man who had, by now, given life to both of them: Barney Ross.

A GREAT FIGHTER IS ALWAYS BEFORE HIS time. Or after it. Barney Ross *was* his time. For not only was this graduate of the Chicago Golden Gloves and Maxwell Street ghetto, the vehicle used by Mike Jacobs to start his 20th Century Sporting Club—initiated informally with the annual Milk Fund fight in 1934, an over-the-weight match between Ross, then the lightweight champion, and the Fargo Express, Billy Petrolle—but in the thirties, when men fed their bellies with hope rather than food, he served his supporters a healthy portion of ethnic pride.

In an era when the descendants of Daniel Mendoza so dominated the sport—with four champions at the beginning of the thirties and identification with the sons of David so endemic that Max Baer took to wearing the Star of David on his trunks, even though he wasn't of the faith—boxing spokesman Joe Humphries was to write, "The United States today is the greatest fistic nation in the world and a close examination of its four thousand or more fighters of note shows that the cream of the talent is Jewish." But if they dominated the sport, one man, in turn, dominated their talent, personally decimating half the Jewish pugilistic popula-

tion. That one man was Jimmy McLarnin, a heavy-handed battler who, not incidentally, added insult to injuries by being Irish.

But over and above ethnic considerations, Ross was perceived by the boxing purist as a smart fighter, a thinking fighter, a "Fighter's Fighter." Remembered by Ray Arcel as "a great student of boxing," and by Jimmy McLarnin as "smart," Ross, with rare ring intelligence, could adapt to different styles, to any attack or defense, all the while setting up his opponent. And, although he had a good punch, his strong suit was his boxing ability. Stabbing repeatedly with his left jab, Ross could make any boxer look bad, giving him a good beating and, in the process, embarrassing him for good measure. He threw his punches in bunches, like grapes, especially in the last ten seconds of a round when he would always finish with a big flurry, all the better to catch the conscience of the judges. But Ross' one true permanent characteristic was his permanence. He was the perfect man to even the score with Jimmy McLarnin, the fellow with the Indian sign on Jewish fighters.

By 1934, Ross had won the lightweight and junior welterweight cham-

pionships of the world—both from Tony Canzoneri in the same fight—and had beaten such worthies as the aforementioned Mr. Canzoneri (twice), Billy Petrolle (twice), Battling Battalino, Ray Miller (the only man to knock out McLarnin), and others too numerous to mention. Driven by fistic upward mobility and an impulse to redirect his destiny, he challenged the welterweight titlist, Jimmy McLarnin. McLarnin's manager, figuring the seven-to-ten-pound pull in the weights to his fighter's advantage, took the challenge and the fight. But he hadn't figured on Ross.

Like two warring gods, one standing like Horatio on the bridge, the other like the Colossus of the welterweight roads, these two warriors fought each other three times, giving the welterweight division its finest hours and greatest fights ever. The tenor of the three fights was set in the opening

Opposite top to bottom: Ross outpoints Jimmy McLarnin; beats Tony Canzoneri; draws with Frankie Klick; relaxes with the Saxon sisters.

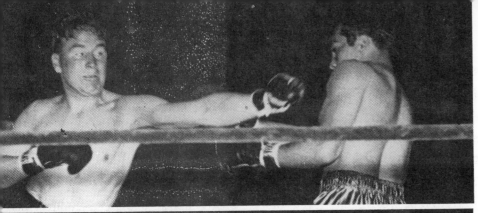

stanza of the first fight when McLarnin came out and landed a terrific left hook that staggered Ross and followed with a right cross that drove Ross into the ropes. But Ross, with his own spark of divine fire, decided that two could play the same game. Eschewing his traditional technique of deftly sliding punches and quickly moving out of the way, Ross instead, full of cannonade, fiber, and acid, came back with his own fusillade, and forced McLarnin to retreat. It was to go like that for 45 non-stop rounds, kindling and supercharging the face of boxing in the hour it needed it most.

Fighting with a resolution unknown since the days of Battling Nelson, Ross was rewarded with decisions in bouts one and three, losing the one sandwiched in between. But even then, Ross had lost in controversy, the split decision for McLarnin in fight two being decided by referee Arthur Donovan's 10-5 scorecard for McLarnin. This despite the hammering McLarnin had taken in the last five rounds when he could hardly see out of his left eye, closed by Ross's pinpoint jabs. One writer was moved to comment, "Obviously, Donovan's eyes were worse than McLarnin's. He couldn't see Ross at all."

Now Ross was more than just the pride of New York; he was the pride of boxing fans everywhere, idolized and lionized as the best fighter in the world. And for three years, with an occasional welterweight title bout thrown in to break the monotony, he would remain the king of the welterweight mountain. But by 1938, a new threat had emerged to challenge his supremacy, this from the most unlikely candidate, the current featherweight champion, Henry Armstrong. Ross, despite the fact that like last year's straw hat he had spent more time than not on the shelf since the previous September, took the fight. It was to be the end of his fistic journey, as a human hurricane, who went by the name of Armstrong, first battered him, then beat him, and then, with great compassion for a great champ, carried him. Ross, hopelessly beaten, his reflexes as dead as his chances, was begged by his cornermen to quit, to let them throw in the sponge. His reply was that of a champion: "I won my title in the ring and I'll lose it there . . . I won't quit."

That was Barney Ross. Courageous. Competitive. Champion.

15 JIMMY WILDE

JIMMY WILDE

The "flies" have normally commanded far less public attention than the international trade balance. But Jimmy Wilde lit up the flyweight division like fireflies in August, capturing the imagination of boxing fans on both sides of the Atlantic. Jimmy Wilde was a physical freak: a scrawny, almost anemic-looking schoolboy with pipestem arms and skinny legs who, at 5 feet 2 inches, stood no taller than a breadbox and weighed no more than 105 pounds, dripping wet. Suffice it to say that the great English cartoonist Tom Webster caricatured Wilde as a stickman, just a head with a few lines for the body and limbs. And yet, for the purposes of his trade, this frail matchstick boy was a demon, called by Gene Tunney the best fighter he ever saw.

ACCORDING TO ONE WRITER IN THE London *Evening Standard*, Wilde "could be compared to nobody who came before him for unique and dramatic background. He just happened." The happening started near the little Welsh coal mining community of Merthyr Tydfil, where Wilde was born into a family of colliers. Literally the runt of the litter, Wilde dropped out of school at the age of 14 to pursue his family's noble profession, becoming a coal miner at the going rate of two bob, or fifty cents, a day. It was there, while wedging his small frame into narrow seams and shafts too small for most men and hacking away that Wilde developed the back and shoulder muscles that were to become the source of his power in the ring.

Soon the little 56-pound mine boy had found a way to supplement his meager wages: sparring with his fellow coal miners in the narrow shafts for the vagrant pennies thrown by appreciative onlookers. Beating Wilde was like trying to mine coal with a nail file, and Wilde was able to beat much larger lads who by all rights should have been able to send him home crying.

From there it was a short hop, skip, and a right cross to England's classic laboratory for boxers, the boxing booths of the country fairs that fairly dotted the English summer landscape.

In one 3½-hour session, meeting all comers, he knocked out 19 men, rested for half an hour and then knocked out 4 more within 45 minutes. Dating from 1905, it is estimated that Wilde's career consisted of more than 1,000 fights, including his booth bouts.

It was in the boxing booths that Wilde developed the skills which would carry him to the top of the boxing world. And make him virtually unbeatable. Constantly driving in on his opponent with his head moving to and fro and his body swaying, his hands held at waist level, he would throw blows from all angles, driving his opponent across the ring under duress. His vigorous aggressiveness won him many battles. And many fans.

Turning pro, Wilde continued to drive his opponents to the floor, which, considering their size, wasn't too far away. But size still posed a problem for "The Mighty Atom," as he was now called. More often than not, he had to give away anywhere from 20 to 30 pounds, fighting featherweights and bantamweights—then the lightest class in boxing and, at 115 pounds, a full 10 pounds more than what Wilde could scale with his mining boots on. In fact, he even had difficulty locating sparring partners. As one story would have it, Wilde conscripted his wife, 'lizabeth, into action, outfitting her with a breast-

Right: Wilde beats Joe Symonds for the world flyweight championship, Feb. 14, 1916.

Left: Wilde covers up as Pete Herman presses the attack, Jan. 3, 1921.

Born 5/15/92, in Tylorstown, Glamorganshire, Wales . . . One of the lightest champions of all time, weighed between 98 and 108 pounds . . . Began boxing, 1910, in Wales, early record sketchy, probably had many more unrecorded bouts . . . Scored over 100 recorded knockouts, on all-time top-10 regardless of weight class . . . Lost only 2 bouts in 1911, did not lose any in next 3 years—in first 103 bouts, won 91, drew 2, 8 no-decisions, lost 2 . . . Scored 25 knockouts in 32 bouts in 1912 . . . Scored 19 knockouts in 33 bouts, 1913 . . . Challenged Tancy Lee, 1/25/15, for British and European flyweight titles, knocked out in seventeenth round . . . Won next 16 by knockout . . . Won world flyweight title froJoe Symonds, 2/14/16, with eleventh-round knockout . . . Defended title successfully against: Johnny Rosner, 4/24/16, KO 11; Tancy Lee, 6/26/16, KO 11, and Young Zulu Kid, 12/18/16, KO 11 . . . Scored 4 eleventh-round knockouts in title bouts in same year . . . Defended against George Clark, 3/12/17, with fourth-round kayo . . . Lost third-round decision in finals of Inter-Allied tournament to Memphis Pal Moore, 12/12/18 . . . Defeated Moore in 20-round rematch, 7/17/19 . . . Came to U.S. in late 1919 and fought there through May, 1920 . . . Knocked out by Pete Herman in seventeenth round, 1/13/21 . . . Inactive for next 2 1/2 years—final bout, 6/18/23, stopped by Pancho Villa in seventh round and lost world title . . . Had unusual distinction of scoring knockout in every round, from 1 to 15 in career . . . Elected to Boxing Hall of Fame, 1959 . . . Died, 3/10/69, Cardiff, Wales . . . Complete record: 153 bouts, 132 won, 6 lost, 2 draws, 13 no-decisions, 101 knockouts.

plate and making a few rounds of sparring a nightly ritual in their bedroom.

Wilde was not yet 21 when he won the British 98-pound title, and not yet 24 when he won the newly minted world flyweight title, gaining universal recognition when he knocked out the American champion, Young Zulu Kid, the next year. It was a title he would hold for six years and six months, the longest reign ever.

On January 13, 1921, Wilde met Pete Herman, the ex-bantamweight titlist, who came in at 121 pounds, 3 more than the bantam limit allowed by the contract, and some 15 pounds more than "The Mighty Atom." Told that the Prince of Wales was in a ringside seat, Wilde agreed to go with the bout. And although he put up a courageous fight, he was beaten badly. The fight was stopped in the seventeenth when the referee put his arm around Wilde and said, "It's the best thing, Jimmy. I can't let you take any more." After retiring for 2 years because his competition had evaporated, Wilde came back to defend his title against Pancho Villa in front of 23,000 fans at the Polo Grounds, the largest crowd in flyweight history. Jimmy was then 31, and the hundreds of fights he had fought plus his long layoff, had taken their toll. Villa ended Jimmy Wilde's amazing career by knocking him out in the seventh round.

Although this Lilliputian stood only 5 feet 2 inches, he was larger in the public eye than most. In a world of comparing stature and greatness pound for pound, Jimmy Wilde will never be outweighed.

GENE TUNNEY

It has been said that great fighters are born, not made. But you can't prove that by Gene Tunney. Nor his success. Gene Tunney was clearly an artist with predecessors—other fighters whose styles and genres he appropriated and adopted. Coming to the sport without the basic physical equipment of the greats before him, Tunney became a one-man laboratory for the analysis of strengths and weaknesses of fighters, his own and his opponents. He drew on the style of that prince of the middleweight division, Mike Gibbons; sparred for a moving picture short with the master boxer of all time, James J. Corbett; and listened to Benny Leonard's advice on how to beat Harry Greb. He then mixed and braided their input into an independent and eclectic talent that made him a winner, one who got there through sheer will power.

GENE TUNNEY'S CLAIM TO GREATNESS lay not in his two fights with Jack Dempsey, but instead, in his five fights with Harry Greb, "The Human Windmill."

Having returned from the great war with the light heavyweight championship pinned to his Marine Corps khakis, Tunney depended on the ring for his livelihood, making himself available to any promoter worthy of his salt who would ballyhoo him as "The Fighting Marine" and wrap him in the red-white-and-blue to artistically cover up his lack of a record. For the better part of a year, Tunney kept himself in a state of perpetual preparedness, campaigning against never-wases, has-beens, and fighters who weren't even household names in their own households.

After a cameo appearance on the undercard at the Dempsey-Carpentier fight, Tunney got his first big chance—challenging the swashbuckling Battling Levinsky for the American light heavyweight championship. Tunney won, going away, literally, in 12 rounds. His first defense some four months later, came against the aforementioned Mr. Greb and was hardly family viewing. Greb destroyed Tunney in a bout that Grantland Rice said looked like "a butcher hammering a Swiss steak." The fight, a classic in How to Foul, commenced with Greb rushing Tunney and butting him squarely in the face, fracturing Tunney's nose. While Tunney tried to stem the flow of blood down his face, Greb held Tunney's head with one hand and with the other used Tunney's unguarded face as a punching bag. By the end of the third, Tunney was literally wading in his own blood. And by the end of the fight, he looked like a second-place finisher in an abatoir. His body sore, his face a mess, Tunney was convinced that if Greb couldn't finish him off, he was a better man than Greb. And set out to prove it.

Nine months later, Tunney went back in against Greb to win back *his* title and avenge the one stain on his all-winning escutcheon. The nine months proved to be a proper gestation period for Tunney to give birth to a plan of attack, aided and abetted by the greatest ring scientist of all time, Benny Leonard, who taught Tunney how to come in under Greb's overextended elbows with body punches under the heart, all the better to take the steam out of Greb. The lesson took and Tunney gained his revenge. And his championship. But Tunney was possessed of an obsession, Jack Dempsey, and he made the man-tiger, then the heavyweight champion of the world, his own personal Everest.

Gene Tunney and Jack Dempsey meet twice, once before their second fight (top) and during their famous "Long Count" bout (bottom).

Born James Joseph Tunney, 5/25/97, in New York, NY . . . Started as a pro boxer in 1915 . . . Enlisted in U.S. Marines during World War . . . Won championship of American Expeditionary Forces while in service in France . . . Fought mostly in New Jersey and New York after return from war . . . Won so-called "American light heavyweight" title via 12-round decision over Battling Levinsky, 1/13/22 . . . Lost it to Harry Greb, 5/23/22, only true loss in career . . . Charged with "newspaper decision" loss in no-decision bout with Tommy Loughran, 8/24/22 . . . Regained "title" in rematch with Greb, 2/23/23, and defended against Greb, 12/10/23—both 15-round decisions . . . "American title" became irrelevant after American, Paul Berlenbach won world championship, 5/30/25 . . . Met Greb twice more in no-decision bouts, 1924 and 1925 . . . Won world heavyweight championship from Jack Dempsey by 10-round decision, 9/23/26 . . . Won rematch following year, 8/22/27, also via 10-round decision although down in seventh round for "long count" . . . Received $990,445 purse for that bout—the largest until Patterson-Liston 1963—acually received check for $1 million and wrote own check for difference . . . Made only one additional title defense, against Tom Heeney, 7/26/28, KO 11 . . . Retired as undefeated champion shortly afterwards . . . While definitely one of boxing's greatest, fact that he quit while on top helped to preseve his stature among boxing fans . . . Elected to Boxing Hall of Fame, 1955 . . . Died, 11/7/78, Greenwich, CT . . . Complete record: 77 bouts, 65 won, 2 lost, 1 draw, 1 no-contest, 8 no-decisions, 43 knockouts.

Many who were more jaundiced in their appraisal of his skills believed that Tunney's title wish was parent to a death wish. But not Tunney, who not only believed that he possessed the speed of hand and foot to beat Dempsey, but that if his right hand, the same right he had used to knock out some 40 opponents, could get in on Dempsey the same way he had seen Carpentier land his, he could control the fight. And win. Tunney did, and drove home his first right seconds into the fight as Dempsey cocked a wicked left-hand punch, destined never to land. The fight was Tunney's right then and there.

In their return match, a cool and efficient Tunney again controlled the tempo of the fight with the exception of one moment—perhaps the greatest moment in all of boxing—when Dempsey's triphammer left *did* connect, followed by a baker's dozen of equally murderous blows. And the fight and Tunney both turned over on their backs. But Tunney was able to get up—whether because of the "long count" or in spite of it—and ride his particular hobbyhorse out of trouble for the remainder of the fight. After one more fight, a valedictory against Tom Heeney, Gene Tunney retired, keeping his promise to his father-in-law that he would never fight again.

Shortly after their last meeting, the great Harry Greb said, "I'm through fighting Gene Tunney. There's one man that I never want to meet again," going on to explain why he believed that Tunney was a greater fighter than anyone at the time appreciated. Or has since. But Gene Tunney was a self-made champion, one who had his cards dealt to him and played them very well indeed.

Grossinger
ROBERTO DURAN

Just as at one time the universal way for a woman to proclaim ownership over a man was for her to pluck some invisible thread from that man's lapel, Roberto Duran also had a way of proclaiming ownership over his opponent: storming straight into the chest of his opponent and leaving a devastating punch to the liver as his calling card. Roberto Duran was the quintessential warrior, a predatory fighter who epitomized the Spanish word meaning "courage and aggressiveness"—"Machismo." Fighting with a conscious will to destroy, this street kid from the ugly barrios of Panama City fought every fight with the remembered resentment of his childhood: his cruel eyes burning brightly with contempt for anyone crossing his path; his teeth biting into his mouthpiece in a half-sneer, half-smile; his burning desire to own his opponent, body and soul. He had the look of an assassin and the assassin's conscious will to destroy.

THE ONE-TIME SHOESHINE BOY FOUGHT the first 24 fights of his career in the steamy, hot flyblown cauldrons that pass for fight clubs in his native Panama, rendering 21 of his 24 opponents into instant walking obituary columns. Some were also-rans who also ran; others were up-and-coming fighters who gave flight until no longer possible and then were destroyed by the man who was becoming known as "Manos de Piedra," or "Fists of Stone." But Duran viewed them only as stepping stones to the top, his sadistic street upbringing permitting him no remorse. Time and again his prefight oration would consist of "I will show him, I will *keel* him." (In a later life, after he had won the lightweight championship, he would glance at the mortal remains of a former challenger named Ray Lampkin being carted off to a hospital and announce on television in a deadly derringer tone, "The next time I send him to the morgue.")

Duran brought his street skills and inner fire to Madison Square Garden, where he took out Benny Huertas in the first round. Within one year he had a new trainer, Ray Arcel, and the lightweight championship of the world,

knocking out Ken Buchanan in brutal fashion. Over the next 6 years, he would defend his lightweight crown 12 times, knocking out all but one of his challengers and evening the score with the only man ever to beat him, Esteban DeJesus, by dealing with him twice in the traditional Duran fashion: taking him apart in sections with body punches and then making sure the head would follow by ripping it off, manually.

On the night of June 20, 1980, Montreal Olympic Stadium was too big for an insane asylum and too small for a nation. But that night it was both, as Roberto Duran stepped up in class—both in terms of weight and caliber of opponent—to challenge the darling of TV, Sugar Ray Leonard, for his welterweight title. Duran fought as if protected by diplomatic immunity, bullying his way inside and raking the body of the faster and taller Leonard with punch after punch, dominating the action. And the fight. It was vintage Duran, as he feinted with his head and his body, managing to stay away from Leonard's Gatling-gun flurries, and continually nosing his Satanically bearded head right up into Leonard's chest. And,

at the last bell, Duran gave final evidence that he still possessed the inner fury that had made him the proud carrier of the word "macho" by disdaining Leonard's extended handshake with a contemptuous "stick-it-in-your-oreja" gesture. The crowd let the word "Duran" sit on its tongue until the decision made it official: Roberto Duran was now the welterweight champion of the world.

But the man who had been called "The Ring Monster" would not have long to rest on his laurels. Five months later he went back into the ring to defend his newly won title. And the unthinkable happened: The man whom all had believed would have to be carried out on his shield before he would ever be defeated gave up, crying, "No Mas! No Mas!" It was the schoolyard bully syndrome, pure and simple: You can beat the schoolyard bully (as Esteban DeJesus had), but he will ultimately

Top: Duran and Sugar Ray Leonard trade shots in their Montreal fight. Bottom: Duran buries a "hand of stone" below the border of Ken Buchanan.

Born in Guarare, Panama, 6/16/51 ... Started boxing professionally at age of 15 in Panama ... First pro bout, 3/8/67, won 4-round decision ... Next 8 bouts won by first-round knockouts ... First came to U.S. in 1971 and defeated Benny Huertas in first round ... Ended career of junior lightweight champion Hiroyshi Kobayashi with seventh-round knockout in next bout ... Won world lightweight title from Ken Buchanan, 6/26/71, by thirteenth-round knockout although Buchanan claimed a foul ... After 31 straight victories, lost first bout to Esteban DeJesus, 11/17/72, 10-round decision ... First 10 title defenses, 1973–77, were knockout victories ... In eleventh defense, went 15-round limit with Edwin Viruet but won decision, 9/17/77 ... Knocked out DeJesus in twelfth round of 1/21/78 rematch ... Relinquished lightweight title, 2/1/79 ... Defeated Ray Leonard by 15-round decision, 6/20/80, to win world welterweight crown ... Lost title in rematch, 11/25/80, when he quit in eighth round, claiming stomach cramps—suffered great loss of prestige after the bout—especially since 2 Leonard bouts resulted in multi-million dollar purses ... Unimpressive comeback attempt, 1981–82 ... Lost 15-round decision in attempt to gain WBC junior middleweight title from Wilfred Benitez, 1/30/82 ... Considered washed-up after lacklustre loss to Kirkland Laing, 9/4/82 ... Regained lost prestige with decisive KO 8 victory over Davey Moore to win WBA junior middleweight title, on his thirty-second birthday, 6/16/83, Lost to Tommy Hearns in devastating second-round knockout, 6/15/84, to end career ... Seventh fighter to win 3 world championships ... Challenged Marvin Hagler for middleweight title, 11/10/83–lost decision but received public acclaim for strong performance ... Scored 18 first-round knockouts throughout career—fifth best among all champions ... Accomplished unusual feat of scoring a knockout in every round from 1 to 15 ... Still active—1984 ... Complete record: 82 bouts, 76 won, 6 lost, 57 knockouts.

come back and beat you (as Duran had, twice); you can run from the schoolyard bully (as many had), but he will ultimately catch you and beat you (as Duran had to almost all); but if you taunt the schoolyard bully, he will merely throw up his finger and tell you where to go. Unfortunately, when Duran threw up his finger—and his glove—millions of people witnessed it. And remembered.

Suddenly, Roberto Duran was no longer the symbol of "machismo." Where once he had been revered, he was now vilified. There was now no way out but to fight back, literally. And so, against all advice, after a decent interval to mourn the loss of his career, Roberto Duran assayed a ring comeback. And despite his loss to an unknown named Kirkland Laing (made even shabbier, if that were possible, by Laing's manager saying on national TV, "He's a fuckin' old man"), Duran continued, trying mightily to regain the glory that was once his. It came in back-to-back fights with Pipino Cuevas and junior middleweight champion Davey Moore. "The Monster" was back, one "Mas" time.

The assessment of Roberto Duran's career must take into account both his masterly comeback and his "No Mas!" comedown. But wherever that assessment lies, it must rate him as one of the most magnificent ring warriors of all time and the greatest of the modern warriors.

JOHNNY DUNDEE

Johnny Dundee was boxing's version of "Old Man River." He just kept rolling along. Already a seasoned veteran of some 75 fights by the time he fought featherweight champion Johnny Kilbane in an over-the-weight match at the ripe old age of 18, he won the crown in his fourteenth year as a prizefighter and campaigned for a grand total of 23 years and 330 fights. His endurance was to win enduring fame in the hearts and minds of thousands. And in the small print under his name in *The Ring Record Book*. But if endurance was all there was to Johnny Dundee, his name would grace only a yellowing clip of Ripley's *Believe It Or Not*. There was much more to the man known as "The Scotch Wop," a lasting greatness to go with his lasting perseverance. It would be nice to note that Dundee was earmarked for greatness right from the start. But, truth to tell, all that was marked was his ear, a cauliflower one worthy of the name that looked like a cabbage with a canvas education. Denied entrance into the amateur ranks because his ear connoted "professionalism" to those rank know-nothings running the program, Dundee turned to professional boxing. And to Scotty Monteith as his manager.

MONTEITH LIKED EVERYTHING ABOUT the young kid. Except his name, Guiseppe Carrora. "Carrora," said the voluble Monteith, "sounded like carrots. Which made sense because his father used to run a market. I told him, 'If you fight with that name, they'll start throwing vegetables at you. You should take the name of my hometown in Scotland, Dundee.' It stuck."

And so, Johnny Dundee he became, the beloved "Scotch Wop." The name tripped easily over the tongue and rebounded from the rafters of countless small clubs throughout the country—and big ones, too: "Dun-dee, Dun-dee . . ." They cheered the man who moved with the agility of a fistic Nijinsky—always up on his toes, pirouetting in mid-ring, ricocheting off the ropes, and bouncing up and down in jumping-jack tactics that looked like balletic *entrechats* complete with leaping left hooks.

Dundee was little more than a hint of a man, standing but 5 feet 4½ inches and weighing only 126 pounds to 130, at most. Still, with an elasticity that seemed almost as if he were growing on the spot, he took on the era's top lightweights. And handled them with ease. His eight no-decision fights with Benny Leonard, then the accepted master of the game, were some of the greatest scientific encounters of all time. Sportswriter Hype Igoe, commenting on Dundee's nimble method of boxing, wrote, "In the fifth, Dundee was moving so fast that Leonard, the master boxer, got his legs crossed. Dundee shot over a right and the champ went to his glove tips."

He took on the heaviest hitters of his day, men like Charley White, Pal Moore, Joe Shugrue, George "KO" Chaney, Leach Cross, Ever Hammer, Joe Rivers, Matt Wells, Frankie Callahan, Ritchie

Mitchell, Lew Tendler, and Benny Leonard. Only once during the course of his career was he floored and that time by accident, by Willie Jackson, an average New York fighter. Contrary to popular belief, Jackson did not catch Dundee coming off the ropes in his famous ricochets. Johnny Attell, a New York matchmaker, was in Philadelphia for the bout and remembered, "Speedy Oscar (Jackson's real name being Oscar Tobinsky) was scared of Dundee's fast-hitting power and he backed away from Dundee and into the ropes. Dundee started a left hook and, more in desperation than anything else, Jackson threw a right. He was not a puncher but he must have hit the right spot. Dundee went limp."

But Dundee was only biding his time campaigning amongst the lightweights. His real goal was Johnny Kilbane, that vanishing American titleholder. Kilbane, since winning the featherweight title in 1912, had defended it but nine times in nine years. One of those defenses had been against the same Johnny Dundee back in 1913, in a 20-round fight that saw Kilbane keep his title with a face-saving draw, although many thought Dundee had won the fight.

Dundee, who continually had to make the 126-pound weight by not drinking water unnecessarily, had dried out for the Kilbane fight, as he had for all his featherweight bouts, by sucking on marbles. And when none were available— he substituted gum. When he drew against Kilbane, Dundee blamed his draw on his drying-out agent, gum. Seems that he had stum-

Born Guiseppe Carrora, 11/22/93, in Sciacca, Sicily, Italy . . . First pro bout, 1910, New York . . . Won 13 of 14 bouts in 1910 . . . In 1911, fought incredible number of bouts, 45, won 24, lost only 1, 20 no-decisions . . . Total of 31 bouts in 1917 and lost only 1 . . . Fought 20-round draw with Johnny Kilbane for world featherweight title, 4/29/13 . . . Won vacant world junior lightweight title on fifth-round foul against George "KO" Chaney, 11/18/21 . . . Defended against Jack Sharkey (not the heavyweight) 7/6/22 . . . Won world featherweight crown, 8/15/22, one of few champions to win second title by moving down in weight class . . . Defended junior lightweight title twice before losing it to Jack Bernstein via 15-round decision, 5/20/23 . . . Won undisputed world featherweight title with 15-round decision over Eugene Criqui, 7/26/23 . . . Never defended featherweight title . . . Relinquished it, 8/10/24 . . . Regained junior lightweight title from Bernstein, 12/17/23, via 15-round decision . . . Lost it to Steve Kid Sullivan in first defense, 10-round decision, 6/20/24 . . . Challenged Tony Canzoneri for world featherweight championship, 10/24/27, but lost 15-round decision . . . Continued boxing until 1932 . . . Has most recorded bouts of any champion, 330 . . . Has one of all-time low knockout percentages, with less than 7 percent . . . Died, 4/22/65, in East Orange, NJ . . . Elected to Boxing Hall of Fame, 1957 . . . Complete record: 210 won, 56 lost, 31 draws, 32 no-decisions, 1 no-contest, 22 knockouts.

* includes newspaper decisions

Right: Dundee sends defending champion Eugene Criqui down on one knee in the first round on his way to winning the featherweight title on July 26, 1923.

bled getting up into a shoeshine boy's chair and accidentally swallowed the entire wad. "That load felt like a lump of lead in the pit of my stomach," lamented Dundee. "Within ten minutes I was sick and all during the fight the next night, I thought I'd throw up."

Kilbane, realizing that without the ingested gum he would never have kept his title on the wafer-thin basis of a draw, turned a deaf ear to Dundee's challenges, content to sit on his laurels. And his title. Dundee kept at it everlastingly, campaigning against anyone and everyone, and even petitioning the New York State Athletic Commission—or, as they were called at the time, the "Three Dumb Dukes." Finally, someone came to Dundee's rescue; Tex Rickard who created an ersatz title with Dundee in mind: the junior lightweight title. This time Dundee took no chances, training with a marble instead of gum and defeating "KO" Chaney for the obviously vacant title. But that wasn't the title he wanted; he coveted the featherweight title. And so, in one of those intriguing little bits of politics that every now and again goes down in boxing, the New York Athletic Commission "vacated" Kilbane's title—at least within their sovereign borders—and matched Dundee against someone named Danny Frush, fresh from a knockout at the hands of Kilbane. Dundee, accepting a proxy as the target of his wrath, dispatched Frush in nine rounds and awaited Kilbane.

Kilbane, unable to avoid defending his title but able to avoid Dundee, selected as his challenger a much-decorated and much-injured French war hero, Eugene Criqui, to defend against. In six rounds, Criqui knocked out the reluctant warrior. And then, true to his word, Criqui defended it against Dundee not six weeks later. For all of Criqui's martial glamour, he wasn't much of a fighter and Dundee scored an easy win, knocking down the Frenchman in each of the first two rounds and then bedazzling the six-week champion with an ad hoc display of fighting that looked like hundreds of little kids jumping up and down on Christmas morning.

By the end of his long career, Johnny Dundee had boxed more than 3,050 rounds, met 13 champions, and fought 330 fights. His was not only the honest bustle of a great, but the honesty of one, and his efforts were appreciated by the dues-paying fans and the praise-paying press.

19 ROCKY MARCIANO

ROCKY MARCIANO

Noah Webster defines the word "determination" as "a strong resolve; the quality of being resolute or firm in purpose." But then again, Mr. Webster never saw Rocky Marciano fight. It would have lent an entirely new dimension to the word. Christened Rocco Francis Marchegiano, the man known as "The Rock" hardly had an auspicious ring beginning, fighting—and knocking out—one Lee Epperson in three rounds in March 1947. Little could anyone then appreciate that Epperson would be the beginning of one of the most memorable streaks in the annals of sports, the first of 49 straight victims Rocky Marciano would notch on his belt before he hung up his gloves. Before Marciano would face his second opponent, some 16 months later, he would take his somewhat more than limited skills to New York to sculpt them into those of a fighter.

HE WAS FORTUNATE IN FINDING CHARlie Goldman, a miracle worker who performed the alchemy of turning the piece of rock into Rocky Marciano. As Goldman told it, "Marciano was so awkward we just stood there and laughed. He didn't stand right, he didn't throw a punch right. He didn't do anything right."

But under Goldman's competent eye and with his own sense of destiny, Marciano dedicated himself to becoming a fighter. And more. A champion. Fed a steady diet of stiffs, he stepped over their prone bodies on his way up the boxing ladder of success, continually honing his half-polished skills.

Determined now to become "great," Marciano worked diligently with Goldman on the bare-bones rudiments of jabbing, hooking, basic footwork, and other such techniques, spending untold hours in isolation. But one thing Goldman wouldn't touch was Marciano's power punch, his right hand, called the "Suzie-Q." It was one of the most devastating weapons ever brought into a ring, and Goldman wanted to preserve it in all its unadulterated purity and prowess.

The combined work of boxing's version of Pygmalion and Galatea wrought one of the most brilliant success stories in fistic history. Once nothing more

than a semblance of a fighter, by the sheer force of his will and the skills of his trainer, Marciano now stood astride the heavyweight division, ready to battle for the championship.

As indestructible as any fighter in history, Marciano walked into—and through—thousands of hard, clean, jolting shots in the manner of a human steamroller, wrecking his opponents with baseball-bat swings to the arms, the midsection, the head, and just about anything else within his reach. Always ready to take two or three punches to land one, the determined Marciano melted down the guards of his opponents, and with the shortest arms in the history of the heavyweight division, hewed them down to size.

When he left Jersey Joe Walcott for dead with one deep-dish beauty of a right that couldn't have traveled more than six inches, he became the first man to become heavyweight champion with an absolutely perfect record since John L. Sullivan, some 70 years before. It was the beginning of the Marciano legend.

He was to build on that legend with each and every fight thereafter, until he retired with a perfect 49 and 0 record, with 43 knockouts, the only champion in the history of boxing to retire with an unblemished record. His determina-

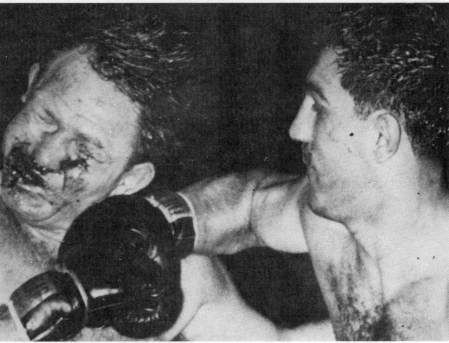

tion, his will, and his eminence had created a depth of affection and a hold on his fans that not only outlasted his career, but his life as well, making the name "Marciano" a shrine to determination and excellence.

Born Rocco Francis Marchegiano, 9/1/23, in Brockton, MA . . . Fought first pro bout as Rocky Marsh, 3/17/47, in Holyoke, MA . . . Returned to amateur ranks after that bout . . . Lost to Coley Wallace in preliminary round of Tournament of Champions Golden Gloves 3/1/48 . . . Billed as Rocco (Socko) Marchegiano for that bout . . . Reopened professional career, 7/12/48, in Providence, RI . . . Won first 16 pro bouts by knockout . . . Ended Joe Louis' career with eighth-round knockout, 10/26/51 . . . Won heavyweight title with thirteenth-round knockout of Jersey Joe Walcott in Philadelphia 9/23/52 . . . Ended Walcott's career with first-round knockout in rematch 5/15/53 . . . Made successful defenses against: Roland La Starza, KO 11, 9/24/53; Ezzard Charles, W 15, 6/17/54; and KO 8, 9/17/54; Don Cockell, KO 9, 5/16/55; Archie Moore, KO 9, 9/21/55 . . . Retired as undefeated champion, 4/27/56 . . . Shortest reach of all heavyweight champions—only 68 inches . . . Fought an average of fewer than 5 rounds per bout . . . Only 6 bouts were not won by knockout—2 of those opponents, LaStarza and Charles, were knocked out in rematches . . . Fought only 2 bouts outside the eastern seaboard . . . Returned to training for filming of computer fight with Muhammad Ali 1968 . . . Known as the Brockton Blockbuster . . . Killed in a crash of a private plane, 8/31/69, near Des Moines . . . Elected to Boxing Hall of Fame, 1959 . . . Complete record: 49 bouts, 49 won, 0 lost, 43 knockouts.

Top left: Marciano catches challenger Archie Moore in his last fight Sept. 21, 1955. Top right: Lee Savold's face shifts like pudding from the force of Marciano's rock-like right Feb. 14, 1952.

JOE WALCOTT

When Arnold Cream first embarked upon the ring career that would carry him to the heavyweight championship, he adopted the *nom de guerre* of Jersey Joe Walcott. The "Jersey" came easily, being his home state; the "Joe Walcott" was a little more difficult. Walcott-Cream, when asked why he chose the name, first said that the Original Joe Walcott was his father's favorite. Later he was "quoted" as saying, "I chose the name because Joe Walcott was the greatest fighter who ever lived. If I use his name maybe I can hope to be one-tenth as good as he was." Walcott-Cream was right on both scores, even when penalized one point for hyperbole. For the Original Joe Walcott was not just, as some fight experts are wont to say, "one of the greatest welterweights the ring has ever known," he was also one of the greatest fighters the ring has ever known as well.

SOME 30 YEARS AGO ONE OF THE BOX-ing-hyphen-wrestling magazines that dotted the newsstands called Joe Walcott the second greatest fighter of all time, stating that he was "welter champion but whipped top middleweight, light heavies, and heavyweights when only weighing 138 pounds." It then went on to describe him as a "Physical freak with reach and punch of a heavyweight."

Boxing observers at the turn of the century referred to Walcott as a sawed-off Hercules. Standing just one-half inch above five feet, Walcott had long, muscular, heavyweight-length arms, a pair of shoulders that would be the envy of any heavyweight, a pair of biceps that were muscled like those of a wrestler—which Walcott had been once—with a chubby face that sat close to his shoulders without any discernible connecting neck.

Walcott's style was, in reality, no style at all. He fought every fight with but one thought in his mind, to destroy the man in front of him. And he went about his purpose by swarming all over his opponent—jumping up at him if necessary, which more times than not, was—throwing punches from every angle imaginable. And some not. Several ancients with hardened arteries who saw both Henry Armstrong and Walcott lik-

Born 3/13/73, Barbados, British West Indies . . . Came to Boston, 1887 . . . First pro bout, 1890 (date listed as 2/29/90, but incorrect since 1890 was not a leap year, reported as 2/29/90, in 1895 record book and erroneous date perpetuated thru several generations of record books) . . . Early bouts primarily in Boston, 1890–93 . . . Fought 15-round draw with Mysterious Billy Smith, 3/1/95 . . . Lost 15-round decision to George Lavigne, 12/2/95 . . . Fought 19-round draw with Tommy West, 12/9/96, bout scheduled for 20 rounds but timekeeper's error ended bout 1 round early . . . Challenged Lavigne for lightweight crown but lost decision, 10/29/97 . . . One of a handful of boxers who lost title challenge at lighter weight but later won world title at heavier weight . . . Fought 25-round draw with Mysterious Billy Smith for welterweight title, 4/4/98 . . . Lost to Smith in 20-round rematch later that year, (12/6/98) . . . Defeated Smith on a tenth-round foul after Smith had lost the title to Jim Ferns 9/24/00 . . . Knocked out Ferns in fifteenth round, 12/18/01, to finally win world welterweight title . . . Defended title successfully against Tommy West, 6/23/02, 15-round win ; and Billy Woods, 4/2/03, 20-round draw . . . Lost title on foul in the twentieth round to the Dixie Kid, 4/30/04 . . . Rematch with Kid 2 weeks later ended in 20-round draw . . . Fought 20-round draw with Joe Gans, 9/30/04, and claimed world welterweight title as a result, since Dixie Kid had abandoned claim . . . Lost title in 15-round decision to Billy "Honey" Mellody, 10/16/06 . . . Lost rematch with Mellody, 12-round decision, 10/16/06 . . . Continued boxing until 1911 but lost more than he won in last few years . . . Killed in auto accident, 10/35, Massilon, OH . . . Elected to Boxing Hall of Fame, 1955 . . . Complete record: 150 bouts, 81 won, 24 lost, 30 draws, 15 no-decisions, 34 knockouts.

ened Armstrong's swarming windmill style to Walcott's, a trait made all the more comparable by Armstrong's similar disregard for personal safety.

Walcott was in fear of no man, no matter how big or how strong. The only trouble was, as George Underwood, of the New York *Telegram*, wrote, "They were all running away from Walcott—the big ones, the middle-sized ones. The only fights Tom

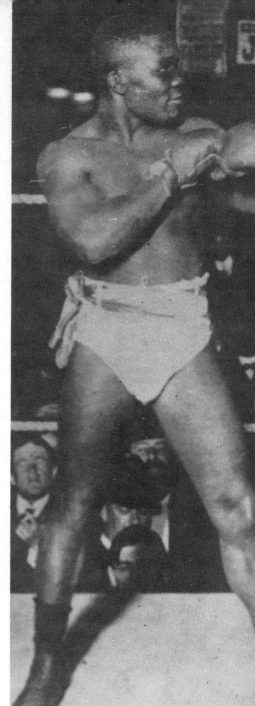

O'Rourke, his manager, could make were outlandish affairs in which Walcott was at a striking disadvantage." Still, this man who looked more like a featherweight than a welterweight fought the aristocracy in four turn-of-the-century divisions including such opponents as: Joe Gans, George Gardner, Dan Creedon, Mysterious Billy Smith, Philadelphia Jack O'Brien, Sam Langford, Young Peter Jackson, and Joe Choynski.

The man they called the "Barbados Demon" was at his peak during 1899 and 1900 when he stopped Joe Choynski—the man who had fought a draw with Jim Jeffries and would beat Jack Johnson—and knocked down Tom

Sharkey during a sparring session prior to the Sailor's bout with Jeffries for the heavyweight title. Other heavyweights began to look away when Walcott began hurling challenges at them, including Jim Corbett, Bob Fitzsimmons, and Jeffries himself, all hiding behind the pretext that he was too small.

O'Rourke's problems in making matches for Walcott reached a point where the only times he could find fights for his Demon came when Walcott, in the quaint vernacular of the day, "did business." In one such odiferous affair, Walcott was leading Tommy West by a big margin in a bout held in New York in 1900 when he simply held up his arm in the eleventh round and in-

sisting, "I broke my arm," and quit. O'Rourke later admitted, "If Walcott hadn't pulled up that night, both he and his manager would have wound up on slabs in the morgue."

In yet another fight, he had to make the lightweight limit of 133 to fight Kid Lavigne and "knock him out in fifteen rounds—or lose." Weakened by a sub-sistence-level diet that had him do without water, a drastically weakened Walcott entered the ring on legs strangely not his own. And yet, by the end of the fight he had rallied back to sever Lavigne's ear, leaving it hanging barely attached, had closed both of his eyes, and battered him thoroughly. But it still wasn't enough. The weight loss

and the conditions that prevailed proved his undoing, and, unable to knock out his foe, he lost the decision.

As if those in-the-ring conditions weren't enough of a handicap, Walcott inflicted an additional one on himself. In 1903, the then-welterweight champ was at a dance hall in Boston where he was exhibiting the workings of a newly store-bought pistol to a friend. While his right hand was over the muzzle, the gun went off, killing his friend and disfiguring his right hand so badly that he could never again close it properly.

The lasting legacy of the Original Joe Walcott is the name he left to Arnold Cream—and the reference amongst the *cognoscenti*, to the *other* Walcott.

Above left: Joe Walcott (left) and Joe Gans square off before their 20-round draw for the title, Sept. 30, 1904. Above right: At his janitorial job later in life.

STANLEY KETCHEL

The first thing you must understand about Stanley Ketchel is: He wasn't human. Any of the greybeards still alive who saw him fight remember him as a man-made tornado, rushing head-down, almost bull-like, into his opponent, his briar patch of cowlicks flying, his nose aimed sideways and his eyebrows a dishonest match. What would have been a straight smile had it but been on a face that was human was instead an off-center sneer on the face of Stanley Ketchel, which, when accompanied by a gutteral sound, gave him a Renfieldesque quality. With hate in his heart and murder in his eyes, the man known as "The Michigan Assassin" would try everything, up to and including stepping on his opponent's thorax, to win.

LIKE DEMPSEY, KETCHEL'S DEFENSE WAS his offense. A murderous puncher with death at the end of each arm, Ketchel kept exploding six-inch shells in five-ounce gloves until something happened—and that something rarely happened to him. In one fight, against Farmer Jim Smith, Ketchel had been frustrated for five of the scheduled six rounds, only to come roaring out of his corner with the bell for the final round and catch the Farmer with a thunderous right which seemed to emanate from somewhere behind the shoulder. Without looking back to see the effects of the blow, Ketchel merely vaulted the ropes and ran down the aisle to his dressing room, so sure was he of the

knockout power in his punch.

Another time, against Philadelphia Jack O'Brien, the then light heavyweight champion of the world, Ketchel spent eight of the ten rounds on the receiving end, having "his puss jabbed off." But in the tenth, and final, round, he doubled up O'Brien with a murderous left to the pit of the stomach—an adaptation of Fitzsimmons's famous shift, but far more deadly—and then crunched over a right to the jaw. O'Brien fell back, out cold, with his head in the resin box in Ketchel's corner where he lay, the count at six when the final bell sounded. He was

one of the lucky ones, "earning" a draw with "The Michigan Assassin."

Turning pro after 250 or so "unofficial" barroom fights, "Steve" Ketchel raced through the middleweight division, knocking out 47 of his 60 opponents and effectively denuding it of competition. Only once had he been knocked out, that once by Billy Papke when, in defense of his title, he had extended his hand to Papke at the commencement of hostilities. All he got for his troubles was a murderous right in the windpipe. Down 4 times in the first round and literally beaten to a bloody pulp, Ketchel hung on for 11 rounds, the blood on his trunks testament to his bravery. Finally, even raw courage was not enough and Papke prevailed. With the words, "Shake hands and come out fighting," a permanent part of boxing as a result of Papke's unsporting gesture, Ketchel came back just 80 days later to settle his debt of violence, dispatching Papke in one less round.

But Stanley Ketchel is best remembered for one fight: his fight with Jack Johnson for the heavyweight championship of the world. Supposedly prearranged, the bout was to have been a half-hour fight for the benefit of motion picture cameras with the champion emerging victorious at the end of the movie. But Ketchel, in the same reckless manner as a condemned man forsaking the traditional blindfold in favor of a cigarette, disdained the "X" and leapt in with one of his famous right-hand wallops to the head of the champion in the twelfth, driving him to the floor. As Johnson arose, Ketchel raced in to put the finishing touches on his partially completed work. It was a work that would remain forever incomplete as Johnson met his ferocious charge with an outstretched right, stretching out the challenger for the count and shearing off four of his teeth in the bargain.

One year—less one day—later, Stanley Ketchel was dead. John Lardner said it best when he wrote, "Stanley Ketchel was 24 years old when he was fatally shot in the back by the common-law husband of the lady who was cooking his breakfast." But the legend of Stanley Ketchel will never die and many of his believers identified with the words of Wilson Mizner who, when informed of the death of "The Michigan Assassin" merely said, "Boys, start counting ten over him. He'll get up at nine."

orn Stanislaus Kiecal, 9/14/86, in Grand Rapids, MI ... Known as the "Michigan Assassin" (although he never fought in Michigan) ... First pro bouts, 1903 ... Fought first 4 years in Montana ... Knocked out 41 of first 49 opponents ... Knocked out Mike (Twin) Sullivan in first round, 2/22/08, and knocked out Sullivan's twin brother, Jack, in next outing, in twentieth round, 5/9/08 ... Only man to knock out twin brothers in consecutive bouts ... Won world middleweight title in latter bout ... 3 defenses in next 3 bouts: 6/4/08, Billy Papke, W 10; 7/31/08, Hugo Kelly, KO 3; 8/18/08, Joe Thomas, KO 2 ... Lost title to Papke, 9/7/08, when stopped in twelfth round ... Regained title, 11/26/08, by eleventh-round kayo of Papke ... Made 4 defenses in 1909: 3/26/09, Philadelphia Jack O'Brien, ND 10; 6/2/09, Tony Caponi, KO 4; 6/9/09, O'Brien, KO 3; 7/5/09, Papke, W 20 ... Challenged Jack Johnson for world heavyweight title, 10/16/09, outweighted by 35 pounds (170 to 205), knocked out twelfth round ... Last middleweight champion to challenge for the heavyweight title ... Defended middleweight title, 3/23/10, Frank Klaus, ND 6 ... Faced Sam Langford in nontitle bout, 4/27/10, ND 6 ... 2 more title defenses: 5/27/10, Willie Lewis, KO 2 and 3/10/10, Jim Smith, KO 5 ... Shot and killed, 10/15/10, in Conway, MO ... Placed title on line in 9 of 12 bouts, 1908–10, unusual for era in which nontitle bouts were the norm ... Although champion only 3 years, won more middleweight championship bouts (12) than anyone except Carlos Monzon ... Charter member of Boxing Hall of Fame, 1954 ... Complete record: 66 bouts, 53 won, 4 lost, 5 draws, 4 no-decisions, 50 knockouts.

Left: Ketchel (left) and Joe Thomas in the fight that made Ketchel famous, a 32-round knockout, Sept. 2, 1907. Above: Ketchel and Billy Papke pose for their rematch, Nov. 26, 1908, won by Ketchel.

22 JIMMY McLARNIN

JIMMY McLARNIN

As sure as Uncle Wiggley's rheumatism served as an omen for the coming of a storm, the coming of economic hard times meant that the "little men" became the dominant focus of boxing fans. And as the feverish twenties exploded into an economic panic that soon became known as the Great Depression, and bread lines and bonus armies took the place of the boom-and-bust atmosphere of the early twenties, there seemed to be added impetus to identify with the "little men." One of those so-called "little men" was 5-foot, 6-inch Jimmy McLarnin, whose face was a cross between that of a choirboy and an angel—with a little bit of the map of Ireland thrown in for good measure—and whose hands were those of an assassin. "The Boy Wonder" had started out as an even smaller man, if that were possible, beginning his career as a wee 4-foot, 11-inch flyweight. But with growth—and the addition of a manager-mentor named Pop Foster—McLarnin soon began ascending in class, both up the weight ladder and up the ladder of success as well. He had begun as a speedster, believing, "If they can't hit you, they can't beat you, and can't hurt you, which is the great science of boxing."

AND SO THE INFERNALLY FAST McLarnin sped through his early fights without a glove being laid on him. Soon Foster had him switch to power, adding a right hand to his arsenal—the left hook would be perfected later. The transformation took effect as McLarnin used his clever ducking, pulling away, and sidestepping to add greater force to his blows. He became known as the greatest lightweight hitter in the world.

And it was as a lightweight that McLarnin was first introduced to the City of Brotherly Shove in a fight against Sid Terris, then heralded as the uncrowned lightweight champion and pride of the ghetto. As New Yorkers watched in awe, McLarnin feinted at Terris in such an unusual move that he pulled Terris toward him almost as if he had charmed him with a four-leaf clover. Terris, baffled by McLarnin's feint, led with his right. Terris's right hand traveled about a foot when BANG!, McLarnin threw a whiplike

right to the chin. No sooner had the punch connected than Terris did a neat one-and-a-half gainer, spun right on top of his head, and settled into the resin. Time: 1 minute, 36 seconds.

McLarnin's right-hand wizardry, together with his new-found left hook, were so impressive that New York sportswriters—in those days before there was a Sugar Ray Robinson—called him "The greatest pound-for-pound fighter in the ring today." He followed up his victory over Terris by personally wiping out the best Jewish fighters in New York: Joe Glick, Joey Sangor, Ruby Goldstein, Al Singer, and the greatest of them all, Benny Leonard, who was now merely the ghost of the splendid fighter he had once been. And after each victory, this one-man wrecking crew would further add leprechaunic insult to Hebraic injury by performing a handspring in the ring to celebrate his victory.

But McLarnin wasn't discriminatory,

Top left: McLarnin ends the career of Benny Leonard, Oct. 7, 1932

orn James Archibald McLarnin, 12/19/06, in Inchacore, Ireland ... Began boxing career on West Coast in 1923 as a flyweight ... Scored victories in 1925 over Fidel La Barba, Pancho Villa, Jackie Fields, and Bud Taylor ... In bid for lightweight title, lost to Sammy Mandell, 5/21/28, by 15-round decision ... Subsequently defeated Mandel twice in nontitle rematches in 1929 and 1930 ... Ended Benny Leonard's comeback attempt with a 6th-round winning knockout, 10/7/32 ... Won world welterweight title by first-round knockout of Young Corbett III ... Only man to win world welterweight crown via first-round knockout ... Alternated 15-round decisions with Barney Ross in next 3 bouts—losing, winning, and losing title—both losses on May 28 (1934 and 1935) ... Reitred after 11/20/36 victory over Lou Ambers ... Last 16 bouts were against champions or Hall of Famers and won 11, lost of them: 1930—defeated Sammy Mandell, Young Jack Thompson, Al Singer, lost to Billy Petrolle; 1931—defeated Petrolle twice; 1932—lost to Lou Brouillard, defeated Benny Leonard and Sammy Fuller; 1933—defeated Young Corbett ; 1934—lost and won with Barney Ross; 1935—lost to Ross; 1936—lost and won with Tony Canzoneri, defeated Lou Ambers ... Fought 27 of 77 career bouts against champions or Hall of Famers and won two thirds of them ... Elected to Boxing Hall of Fame, 1956 ... Complete record: 77 bouts, 63 won, 11 lost, 3 draws, 20 knockouts.

just good, taking them all on and out, regardless of race, creed, national origin, or credentials. The iron-chinned Phil McGraw of Detroit was a good fighter, as good fighters go, and as good fighters go, he went, in the first round, Stanislaus Loayza of Chile got as far in the fourth. Joe Glick took the count in the second and Sammy Baker in the first. Finally, McLarnin—having strained himself to make the lightweight limit in a losing effort against Sammy Mandell, finding his natural fighting weight to be 140—took on Young Corbett III for the welterweight title. With about 30 seconds left in the first round, both McLarnin and Corbett threw punches at the same time. McLarnin's lightning-like right landed first, and he had added another pelt to the ever-growing list of champions he had conquered—enough to start his own Hall of Fame.

Then came the three Little Big Horns with Barney Ross for the welterweight title, three fights in 365 days that lit up the New York skyline like no other fireworks display since the centennial celebration almost half a century before.

McLarnin's manager, Pop Foster, who guarded McLarnin like a mother lion protecting her young, had always sought an edge in weight for McLarnin and figured that at 145 pounds his warrior would have a decided edge over the 135-pound Ross, who was moving up from his lightweight championship to challenge McLarnin's title. The odds were with McLarnin: McLarnin had no fewer than eight wins over champions, almost permanent possession of any and all Jewish fighters, and the welterweight advantage.

For 45 rounds neither man stepped down. Nor back. First it was the air shattered by the force of McLarnin's blow, then Ross', as the two locked horns like two bull moose in heat. The first fight went to Ross on a split decision, the second to McLarnin, likewise, and the third went to Ross on a verdict that didn't meet with the approval of ringsiders, several, like Gene Tunney, calling it a disgrace, scoring it 13 to 2 for McLarnin.

After two more wins over ex-champions, Tony Canzoneri and Lou Ambers, Jimmy McLarnin called it a day. But what a day it had been! Wins over 13 men who at one time or another held world championships, and a reputation as one of the greatest hitters in the history of boxing. Not bad for one of its "little men."

McLarnin "carries" his manager, "Pop" Foster.
Top right: McLarnin, in his last fight, staggers lightweight champ Lou Ambers.

ARCHIE MOORE

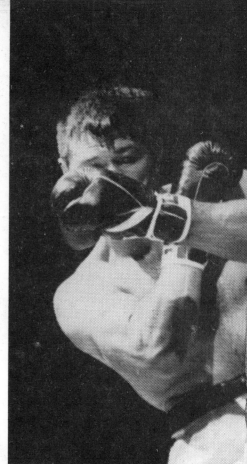

Archie Moore is proof positive that boxing builds character as well as characters. At an age when most men are already planning what to do with their Social Security checks, Archie Moore finally got what had been a long time in coming: the light heavyweight championship. But the road to that championship had been paved with detours and plenty of hard knocks. Born in either Collinsville, Illinois, or Benoit, Mississippi, on either December 13, 1913, or December 13, 1916—depending on who was keeping score, Moore or his mother—Moore was either 36 or 39 when he won the light heavyweight crown. Asked about the discrepancy in his birth date, the quick-witted champion sidestepped and countered, "I have given this a lot of thought and have decided that I must have been three when I was born." Moore's first bout came in 1935 against the picturesque-sounding Piano Man Jones. His pay for the night was the small coins collected in a hat that was circulated amongst his fellow CCC camp members. The result was a knockout, the first of many more than any man in history would record.

FOR THE NEXT 17 YEARS, WITH TIME out for a severed tendon in his wrist, acute appendicitis here, a perforated ulcer or an organic heart disorder there, Moore treaded the highways and byways of America in search of recognition and an elusive title shot—always lining up first to be second. Just another of the many talented "colored" fighters trying to break into the big time, Archie had to go through a lot of back doors so that the black fighters of today could go through front doors, fighting in bootleg battles, tanktowns, and small clubs on the Chitlin' Circuit. Hardly one to suffer in silence, he responded to his second-class treatment with the only means available to him, his fists. And with hopes blowing on those fists to keep them warm, he scored knockout after knockout.

Moore survived where few could have survived, and 17 years and 110 knockouts after Piano Man Jones, he stood on the threshold of his greatest dream: the light heavyweight champi-

onship of the world. On December 17, 1953, he finally achieved that dream, decisively beating Joey Maxim for the title. But even then Moore got the fuzzy end of the lollipop, earning only $800 for climbing into the ring and to the pinnacle of his profession, as well. However, in the strange and wondrous way of boxing, Moore got something more than merely the championship belt and $800; he also got Maxim's manager, wiley old Doc Kearns, the man who had guided Maxim—and before him, Jack Dempsey and Mickey Walker—to the title.

Over the next 6 years, Moore would go to the post 43 times, taking on all comers regardless of weight and class, dispatching 25 of them in fewer than the scheduled number of rounds. Looking less like a fight figure than a father figure, Moore rowed with muffled oars, peering out from behind his crossed-arm "Armadillo" curtain, making a slight insouciant move and then, Bam!, scoring with his devastating right. He

Top: Moore comes back to meet Yvonne Durelle in one of the greatest fights of all time. Bottom: "The Old Mongoose" destroys Carl "Bobo" Olson.

orn Archibald Lee Wright, 12/13/13, in Benoit, Mississippi . . . Birth year questionable . . . Began boxing professionally in mid-1930s—early record sketchy . . . Earliest recorded bout, 1935 . . . Started as middleweight in St. Louis area and moved to San Diego in 1938 . . . Spent most of 1940 in Australia and won 7 bouts there . . . Fought on West Coast during early 1940s and East Coast during late 1940s—won most of his bouts by knockout but did not receive title shot . . . Fought in South America in 1951 . . . Finally got first world championship bout, 12/17/52, at age of 39—won light heavyweight championship from Joey Maxim by 15-round decision . . . Defended against Maxim in 1953 and again in 1954 winning both by 15-round decisions . . . Won defenses over Harold Johnson and Bobo Olson by knockout in 1954 and 1955 . . . Challenged Rocky Marciano for world heavyweight title, 9/21/55, but was knocked out in ninth-round—Marciano retired after bout—Moore, 10 years younger, remained active boxer for 10 more years . . . Won 8 nontitle bouts in 10 weeks in 1956 in tune-up for light heavyweight title defense . . . Matched with Floyd Patterson, 11/30/56, for vacant heavyweight title—Patterson, age 21 to Moore's 42, stopped Moore in fifth . . . Defended successfully against Tony Anthony, 9/20/57 . . . Title defense against Yvon Durelle, 12/10/58, one of most exciting in history—both men down 4 times—Durelle knocked out in eleventh round . . . Rematch, 8/12/59, knocked out Durelle in 3 . . . NBA (forerunner of WBA) withdrew recognition as light heavyweight champion, 10/25/60, for failure to defend within a year . . . Still recognized by NY and European boxing commissions and won 15-round decision, 6/10/61, in defense against Italian, Giulio Rinaldi . . . Championship recognition withdrawn by NY and Europe, 2/10/62 . . . Scored one-round knockout over Howard King, 5/7/62, at age 48 . . . Stopped by Cassius Clay in fourth round, 11/15/62 . . . Last bout, 3/15/63, won third-round knockout over wrestler, Mike DiBiase . . . Fought exhibition, 8/27/65, at age of 51 and won by knockout . . . Scored more knockouts than any other man—145 . . . Oldest man to hold world championship—48 years, 59 days old . . . Probably oldest man to score first-round knockout . . . Starred in the motion picture "The Adventures of Huckleberry Finn," 1960 . . . Elected to Boxing Hall of Fame, 1966 . . . Complete record: 234 bouts, 199 won, 26 lost, 8 draws, 1 no-contest, 145 knockouts.

would half-talk and half-punch his opponents into oblivion, scoring psychological as well as physical knockouts over members of the beaten-upon in good standing, which included such recognizable names as Bob Baker, Harold Johnson, Bobo Olson, Nino Valdes, James J. Parker, Eddie Cotton, Willie Besmanoff, Charlie Norkus, and Howard King.

But perhaps Moore's most spectacular moment came when he got up from the canvas four times—saying to himself as he lay prostrate on the canvas, "This is no place to be resting; I'd better get up and get with it"—and came back to outpunch and outpsyche Durelle in one of the greatest comebacks of all time. (Moore remembers that after being floored for the fourth time, he went to his corner and "waved" to his wife just past Durelle's corner, when all the while she was seated behind him. The effect of this outrageous bravado on Durelle was even more devastating than one of Moore's right hands which came six rounds later.)

Nobody who ever saw this man, who wore trunks that looked like they were made by Omar and not Everlast, will ever forget him. For Archie Moore was a good wine that traveled far. Very far.

TOMMY RYAN

By the eighth decade of the twentieth century, what the boxing community knew about Tommy Ryan could be written on a postcard crowded with a description of the obscenely awful view on the obverse side, with more than enough room left over for a long address and an oversized postage stamp. This is patently unfair to the memory of Ryan, one of the ring's greatest strategists and students. Spanning both the bareknuckle and gloved worlds of boxing, Ryan was master of all he surveyed. Called by Nat Fleischer, "one of the cleverest boxers and ring generals of the Queensberry era," Ryan could beat more men with his head than most could beat with their fists. He was to boxing what A.D. was to everything else, the finesse school of boxing dating from his entry onto the scene. In a day and age when most fighters got all the schooling they needed to be able to sign a contract, Ryan made the ring his university. And, adopting Jem Mace's scientific philosophy that the "left hand is the brains and the right the muscle," he embroidered it until his left and right were his Yale and his Princeton.

THE STATE OF BOXING BACK IN ITS primitive days was not unlike that of Nathan Detroit's famed "Floating Crap Game," with runners, always one step ahead of the local constabulary, telling anyone with a fiver in their pockets where the "action was." During a "Meeting-All-Comers" tour in the summer of 1889, Ryan chanced to find himself in Detroit, where the "action" could be found not in Nathan Detroit's sewer, but in two even more unlikely locales: Detroit's ice house and a beach on the shores of Lake St. Clair. In the first fight, against one Martin Dunn, Ryan, with enough coolness of his own to chop it up and sell it on the spot, underlined his opponent's eyes with straight lefts and rights and left him out cold in the ninth. In the second, under glowing bonfires, Ryan took 46 rounds to do away with another local worthy named Martin Shaunghnessy, ending the bout the following morning just when the fires were finally ebbing, along with the tide.

As the tour continued wherever box-

ing was tolerated, the sight of the milk-white Ryan with bobbed nose, dark black hair parted down the middle, in the fashion of the day, sinewy arms, and sloping shoulders all swathed in knee-high britches bound by a stars-and-stripes sash became a familiar one. So, too, did his style, a classic boxing style with punches as calculable as his fight plan. Constantly adding and subtracting as he approached perfection, Ryan had added something new to his arsenal: a deadly kidney punch, one which stoked the fires within. Ryan could use what had become known as the "Tommy Ryan Kidney Punch" with telling effect, timing its delivery from either long-range or from inside in a clinch. Many a wild-charging opponent was felled by one of Ryan's deftly administered chops over the kidneys—such was the fate to befall one of his early opponents, Dick Guthrie, who lay paralyzed on the ropes just as the Naugatuck police interfered to save the helpless boxer from further punishment at the hands of Ryan in the third.

By now the man promoter Jack Curley referred to as a "rare combination of English, Irish, Indian, French, and Jew" had made enough fans among all of the above, plus thousands of others, to be considered as one of the two best "little men" in the boxing world. The party of the second part was Mysterious Billy Smith, a fighter so unrelenting he gave the impression that after he had been called by that Great Referee in the Sky, he would have had his ashes thrown in his opponent's face.

They had first met at the Coney Island Athletic Club on August 29, 1893, and the result was a face-saving, but disappointing, draw. Rematched in Boston, the two again fought six rounds to another draw. Both claiming victory, they met again, in Minneapolis, with Smith's welterweight title thrown in for good measure. This time Ryan took a 20-round decision after 20 hard-fought rounds.

While training for his Minneapolis title fight with Smith, Ryan had taken a liking to the shifty McCoy, one of boxing's early snake oil salesmen, and taken him under his wing, hiring him as a sparring partner. However, even though Ryan had taught McCoy some of the finer points of the game, he had also taught him some of the more sadistic as well, trying out his kidney punch and other maneuvers on McCoy in preparation for his bout with Smith. Leaving Ryan's nest after the fight, McCoy determined to come back to befoul it, swearing revenge on his former instructor and tormentor.

That revenge would take place in the spring of 1896 when McCoy, laying down a path to his trap as enticingly as the witch baiting Hansel and Gretel, sent a note to Ryan imploring him to give McCoy a fight. The disarming note read: "I can't go four rounds with you. . . . I'm sick. . . . I need the money. . . . " Ryan, who had a poor opinion of McCoy as a fighter anyway, followed the handwritten breadcrumbs and fell into the trap, giving McCoy the fight, a fight he didn't even bother to train for, believing the note. It was a gross mistake, 144 times worse than a normal one. And one Ryan, woefully out of shape, knew upon entering the ring. For there, on the other side, stood Kid McCoy, with a knowing smile on his lips like that of a Cheshire cat. And in anything but the condition he had described in the mendacious note. Springing the trap, McCoy toyed with the unprepared Ryan, cutting his face to ribbons and

Born Joseph Youngs, 3/31/70, Redwood, N.Y. . . . First pro bout, 1887, Midwest . . . Early record incomplete . . . Fought in transitional era, from bareknuckles to skin-tight gloves . . . Early bouts included ones of 33, 46, 57, and 76 rounds . . . Defeated Mysterious Billy Smith in 20-round decision to win world welterweight championship, 7/26/94 . . . Successfully defended title 6 times, including 3-round KO of Jack Dempsey, the Nonpariel, 1/18/95 . . . Won vacant world middleweight championship with 20-round decision over Jack Bonner, 10-24/98 . . . Abandoned world welterweight crown . . . Defended middleweight title successfully 4 times, 1889–1902 . . . Recognized as champion despite lack of title defenses 1903–1907 . . . Inactive 1905–06 . . . Final bout, 3/4/07 . . . Fought exhibition, 8/4/07 . . . Only lost 2 of 109 bouts . . . Never lost a world championship bout—only man to win 2 world titles and not lose either in the ring . . . Died 8/3/48, in Van Nuys, CA . . . Elected to Boxing Hall of Fame, 1958 . . . Complete record: 109 bouts, 86 won, 2 lost, 6 draws, 9 no-decisions, 6 no-contests, 68 knockouts.

knocking him down 12 times before the fight was mercifully stopped in the fifteenth round.

Recognized now as both welterweight and middleweight champion, the lusty Ryan took them all on: the long, the short and the tall. But the one he wanted was Kid McCoy. He got his wish on September 8, 1897, in his home bailiwick of Syracuse. Ryan went into the fight vowing revenge, his hard visage looking like a book of rules bearing out his determination. And, for two rounds, he had it. But, in the third, McCoy rushed Ryan to the ropes, and they both went down. Ryan was the first to hit the canvas, and before referee George Siler had tolled off the first second, McCoy toppled over. Authorities finally jumped into the blood-spattered ring in the fifth, stopping the contest. Ryan still did not have his pound of flesh.

The following year, 1898, Ryan finally perfected his claim to the middleweight crown with a 20-round decision over Jack Bonner and proceeded to meet all comers in its defense, much

as he had at the start of his career. But it was still Kid McCoy he wanted. Badly.

And then, on May 29, 1900, at the Tattersall Club in Chicago, the two locked horns again. This time Ryan trained faithfully for McCoy, resolute in his desire to hand the Kid a thorough beating. But while Ryan fought like a bull moose in heat, McCoy's ring skills enabled him to withstand Ryan's continual assaults. At the close of the sixth, and final, round, honors were about even, even slightly in favor of Ryan. Nevertheless, referee Malachy Hogan calmly stepped forward and declared McCoy the winner. Ryan stood stock still for a second, and then, inexplicably made a tiger-like spring at Hogan, staggering the surprised referee with a lusty right to the jaw. Hogan, one of the most dangerous rough-and-tumble street fighters in the history of Chicago, was not the sort of man who would take a punch without replying in kind and tore into Ryan like a pit-dog freed from his leash. The hall was in an uproar, and several partisans of both men jumped into the ring while peace-

makers struggled desparately to separate Ryan and Hogan. Finally, Chicago's "Finest" jumped into the ring, and after an interval that included billy clubs, the ring riot was brought under control, and Ryan was escorted out of the ring by the blue coats—still vowing vengeance not only on McCoy, but also on Hogan. But there was a reason for Ryan's outburst: when Ryan had signed the contract, it had mandated that should the battle last the scheduled limit of six rounds, a draw would be announced. Hogan argued that he knew of no such conditions or pre-arrangement. Meanwhile, the news wires carried the "result," and bets were paid accordingly on Hogan's announcement. The Tattersall Club, anxious to clean up the nasty mess, met hastily, announced that the referee's decision had been reversed and that the fight was officially a "draw," regardless of what the record books showed.

Tommy Ryan was to continue fighting for another seven years, giving boxing lessons to anyone who applied. But never again to Kid McCoy. The Kid was now too busy trying his scams in other areas and arenas.

Still, Tommy Ryan will be remembered as one of the greatest students of the game of boxing, and one of its greatest ring artists as well, who threw himself, whole timbre and pallette, into each and every one of his fights.

Above: For Auld Lang Syne: old-timers Ryan (left) and Billy Papke try to recapture some of their past glories while Kid McCoy looks on.

GEORGE DIXON

Fate has a fickle habit of bestowing its fame upon those it later takes by the scruff of the neck and hurls overboard. George Dixon, the famed "Little Chocolate," was one of those, reduced from a graven image to the grave in but a few short years. In any lineup of greats, George Dixon's name must rank right up there with the immortals. Like so many others, however, his greatness has been distorted in the telling and retelling, bent out of its honest shape by tiresome old gentlemen born at the age of 80 who recount the story of the willowy silhouette who fought with unbelievable dexterity and poise only to come apart at the seams in his later life. It is a tale with a moral, but a tale worth telling nonetheless.

BORN IN HALIFAX, NOVA SCOTIA, IN 1870, Dixon next turned up in Boston around 1886—nobody can be very precise about dates in that early era—where, as a messenger boy, he is reputed to have gotten into his first fight, a street fight with a white messenger over some slur, giving his tormentor a "hiding," to use the quaint catchall phrase of the day. Boxing in those days was something less than an honorable calling, held in cellars and back rooms of saloons. But billing himself as "George Dixon, Little Chocolate," the 87-pounder, who, in the words of one ancient observer, "looked no bigger than a cigar holder," tried it "for the fun of it."

It was in a so-called arena in nearby Cambridge, in 1889, where, as chance would have it, one of his efforts was witnessed by Tom O'Rourke, a pretty good-looking welterweight himself and an expert in boxing flesh. O'Rourke saw in the waiflike fighter a natural boxer and a natural resource as well. After seeing him score a knockout over a white boy named "Kelly"—no more, just "Kelly"—O'Rourke said to his companion, "It's a pity he hasn't got someone to teach him the finer points of boxing," noting that the ebony sliver's "left hand shot out like a rattlesnake's poisoned tongue . . . but he hardly ever used his right."

O'Rourke was to take this raw, talented prospect with the rapid-fire left, agile feet, nonstop endurance, and fearless mien and graft new skills onto his already substantial ones. Taking what was left, O'Rourke went to work on his right, teaching him all the conventional uses of the right hand: how to sneak the short right behind his stinging left, the full-armed straight right alone, and the solar plexus punch riding in directly behind the lifting left hook. Now a complete fighter, Dixon was ready to venture into the world of little men.

By 1890, the reputation of the fighting gamecock had grown, along with his maturing skills. With a wistful smile playing on his lips and as devoid of fear and nervousness as any man who ever entered the ring, Dixon conceded weight to all, but the fight to none, snapping off his left like an electric light switch and using his right like a gun to drop his opponents in their tracks. O'Rourke used to tell his charge, "Remember that old Irish drinking toast, 'May the wind always be at your back'? Well, that's the way I feel when I saddle you up, laddie boy." And saddle him up, O'Rourke did. With the lighter weights overloaded with talent, so much so that their talent was at a discount, O'Rourke threw him in against every manner of small man: bantamweight, featherweight, and lightweight. And always Dixon acquitted himself, winning most by knockout. When he couldn't finish them off, he had to be satisfied with a draw, although it was evident to all who had won.

One day in the spring of 1890, O'Rourke dropped by the Anthenium, where Dixon was making routine money, $100 for a fight. "I've got news," the excitable O'Rourke screamed, "real big news. England wants us to box Nunc Wallace at the Pelican Club in London with the four-ounce gloves. The winner will get $2,000 to $500. . . . And what's more, the winner will be accepted as world's bantamweight champion." Dixon knocked out Wallace and returned home the conquering hero. Two years later, although still actually a bantamweight—and capable of making the present flyweight limit if necessary—Dixon added the featherweight belt to his almost nonexistent waist. He now stood taller, much taller, in the eyes of the boxing world than his mere 5-foot 3-inch frame. He was peerless.

After beating the amateur titleholder, Jack Skelly, in the New Orleans Olympic Club's three-day fight carnival, Dixon returned to New York where, with no towering buildings then to obscure his greatness, he promenaded down the streets, a champion with every stride, fairly gliding over the sidewalks much as he did the ring. Atop his head was a brown derby, always tilted to one side to expose his bronze-colored head. And always in his wake twenty to thirty kids, none of whom seemed to ever get in his way. Or so Dixon made it appear. He had become a *boulevardier,* a *salonierre,* a *bon vivant.* And he lived like one, sparring more with John Barleycorn than with others, his great ring skills beginning to suffer permanent deterioration.

Over the next eight years, Dixon hit the bottle more than he hit opponents, defending his championship whenever O'Rourke got him a bout, and then, indifferently. Sometimes his opponents were able to penetrate his greatness, and beat him. But always O'Rourke would reclaim the featherweight championship, holding that one opponent or another had come in over the featherweight limit of the time—118 pounds.

Finally in 1900, unable to reach his charge in any other way, O'Rourke tried appealing to his pride, signing Dixon to fight "Terrible" Terry McGovern in a 25-round championship bout. Pride was all Dixon had, as McGovern abused the ghost of Dixon past for eight rounds. Finally, O'Rourke had had enough, even if Dixon hadn't and threw

Top: Caspar Leon and "Little Chocolate" (right) prepare to fight an exhibition for the new innovation, moving pictures. Bottom: At Coney Island.

in the sponge, ending the fight. And effectively ending the career of the great "Little Chocolate."

The defeat cast a spell over Dixon. He returned to New York—with a side trip to England to display his quickly eroding wares—where he contrived a feud with O'Rourke and took refuge in the bad booze served him by bartenders with white aprons, patent-leather haircombs, and memories of his greatness. Finally, the bad booze, aided and abetted by hunger, neglect, and exposure, took its toll and "George Dixon, Little Chocolate" died without two coppers in his pockets with which to cover his dead eyes.

Tom O'Rourke, who was in England at the time of Dixon's death, remembered the once-great Dixon, his spic-and-span ring togs, his light-as-air movements around the ring on his toes, the crowd lifting his light body above their heads in their acclaim. And he returned to take what had been the matchless "Little Chocolate" to Boston where he laid him to rest under a tombstone reading: "Here rests the gamest pugilist that ever lived."

Born 7/29/70, in Halifax, Nova Scotia, Canada . . . Known as "Little Chocolate" . . . First recorded pro bout, Halifax, 1887 . . . Came to Boston, 1887 . . . Fought Tommy Kelly, the Harlem Spider, 5/10/88, in bout stopped after 9 rounds—claimed bantamweight title afterwards although Kelly was not a clear titleholder . . . Matched with Cal McCarthy for the "American" bantamweight title, 2/7/90, in bout called draw after 70 rounds using 2-oz. gloves . . . Traveled to England to fight Nunc Wallace, 6/27/90—knocked out Wallace in 18 rounds to claim world bantamweight championship . . . Kayoed Cal McCarthy, 5/31/91, in 22 rounds in American bantamweight title bout . . . Won world featherweight title with fourteenth-round knockout of Fred Johnson, 6/27/92 . . . Fought Jack Skelly, 9/6/92, in original "Carnival of Champions"—defended featherweight crown with eighth-round knockout . . . Fought in an era in which distinction between championship and non-championship bouts was not always clearly made or reported—may have had as many as 27 defenses of featherweight title . . . Lost title to Solly Smith on 20-round decision, 10/4/97 . . . Regained title with 10-round victory over Dave Sullivan, via disqualification, 11/11/98 . . . Had 10 bouts in 1899, most of them with the title at stake, undefeated in all . . . Lost featherweight title to Terry McGovern on eighth-round knockout, 1/9/00 . . . Fought at a time when a draw decision was common—had 42 draws in career, 10 in 1903 . . . Fought in England, 1902–4 . . . Continued boxing until 1906, but with limited success—from 1900–06 had 59 bouts, won 11, lost 21, drew 24, 3 no-decisions . . . Died 1/6/09, in New York City . . . Elected to Boxing Hall of Fame, 1956 . . . Complete record: 130 bouts, 50 won, 26 lost, 42 draws, 7 no-decisions, 5 no-contests, 27 knockouts.

EDER JOFRE

Just when it seemed that ring technicians had disappeared entirely, save for a few preserved as classroom fossils, a little necromancer by the name of Eder Jofre lifted himself to the plane of other men called "The Greatest Pound-for-Pound" something-or-other with his prodigious skills. Coming on the scene in 1960, when the gyms were an isolation ward of protesting ghosts, the talent in boxing threadbare, undistinguished and uninspiring, and the bantamweight division hardly a going concern, Jofre pumped life back into the sport with his fistic derring-do. But the splendor of his achievements would obscure his talents, which were many. Possessing all the tools and *materia* of the craft, the perfectly symmetrical Jofre used his lightning left jab like a paintbrush to coat his opponents with layers of lefts, his left hook like a megaphone to capture their attention by assaulting their ears, and his right like a battle-axe to decapitate them. The sum total of his actions was a work of art, one seen infrequently down the dreadful chute of time.

Born 3/26/36, in Sao Paulo, Brazil . . . Competed in 1956 Olympic Games, bantamweight class and won first bout against Burman, Thein Myint but lost in quarter-final round to Chilean, Claudio Barrientos (later knocked out Barrientos in pro bout) . . . Began professional boxing career in Sao Paulo, 1957 . . . Fought primarily in Brazil, 1957–60 . . . Won South American bantamweight title, 2/19/60, with 15-round decision over Ernesto Miranda . . . Came to U.S. with record of 34 won, 3 lost, 2 draws, and won vacant NBA world bantamweight title with sixth-round knockout of Mexican, Eloy Sanchez . . . Won undisputed title recognition with 10-round knockout of Piero Rollo, 3/25/61 . . . Defended title successfully 7 times, 1961–64, all by knockout . . . Held record for most consecutive bantamweight title defenses won by knockout (since broken by Carlos Zarate) . . . Included in string were 5 bouts won in opponents' homelands . . . Title defenses were: Caracas, 8/19/61, Ramon Arias, KO 7; Sao Paulo, 1/18/62, Johnny Caldwell, KO 10; San Francisco, 5/4/62, Herman Marquez, KO 10; Sao Paulo, 9/11/62, Jose Medel, KO 6; Tokyo, 4/4/63, Katsutoshi Aoki, KO 3; Quezon City, 5/18/63, Johnny Jamito, KO 12; Bogota, 11/27/64, Bernardo Caraballo, KO 7 . . . Lost decision and title to Japanese, Fighting Harada, Nagoya, Japan, 5/17/65 . . . Lost rematch with Harada in Tokyo, 6/1/66—only 2 losses in career . . . Retired 1/2/67 . . . Made most successful comeback in boxing history—8/27/69–10/8/76 won 25 of 25 bouts and regained world title . . . Defeated Jose Legra, 5/5/73, to capture world featherweight title . . . Defended successfully, 10/21/73, Vicente Saldivar, KO 4 . . . Recognition as champion withdrawn, 1974 . . . Continued boxing until 1976 . . . Complete record: 78 bouts, 72 won, 2 lost, 4 draws, 50 knockouts.

EDER JOFRE CARRIED THE BLOODLINES of a champion, almost as if he had been bred to fight. On both his mother's and father's sides, Jofre's family tree was fully leafed-out with boxers and wrestlers: one uncle had been European middleweight boxing champion; another had been lightweight champion of Brazil; an aunt had been one of Brazil's leading women wrestlers; and his father had been a lightweight who had fought under the name Kid Jofre.

It was in his father's gym, or "Academy," that young Eder first started his climb to greatness, his father handing down his talents like an heirloom. At nine, he had his first bout, a family affair against a cousin. At 12, he won his first amateur tournament and continued in the amateurs for the next eight years. In 1956, he qualified for the Brazilian Olympic team, but lost in the quarter-finals to Claudio Barrientos of Chile. With a 148–2 amateur record, it seemed that Eder had been fighting forever. Maybe he had, his father once answering a question as to when the younger Eder had started by saying, "when he was so small you could sit

him in a glove."

But, truth to tell, Eder Jofre *always* looked like he could sit in a glove. Turning pro in 1957, Jofre became a 5-foot, 4-inch fighting machine as he ran under, around, and over his opponents, leaving them foundering like beached craft on the shores of his native Sao Paulo. After 32 bouts, he was undefeated, with 20 KOs.

When bantamweight champion Joe Becerra announced his retirement in August of 1960, the bantamweight division took on the look of a supermarket line, with everyone crowding to the front. One of those was Eder Jofre, who was matched with Eloy Sanchez for the vacant NBA championship. For four rounds, Sanchez came at Jofre, who guilefully evaded most of his punches, countering and biding his time. Jofre dropped Sanchez with a triphammer right in the fifth, but Sanchez roared back and bloodied Eder's nose in the sixth. Jofre, who "was just looking for a spot to throw a straight right," landed with a right to the jaw midway in the sixth. Sanchez dropped on his face, there to be counted out. Jofre was now

the NBA bantamweight champ.

But the NBA crown was only the first olive out of the jar. It was a title that Jofre would have to win three times, like the Lonsdale Belt, to actually own.

Right: Jofre with his father, Aristides, at father's "Academy."

He added the second leg with a ten-round knockout over European claimant Piero Rollo four months later. And then, in 1962, beat the previously unbeaten Johnny Caldwell, the European Boxing Union's designated champion, when Caldwell, suffering from temporary loss of intellect, one made permanent by Jofre's fists, also folded in the tenth and silently stole away. Now Jofre was the universally-recognized bantamweight champion.

Jofre would go on to defend *his* bantamweight title five more times, Herman Marquez falling in ten, Jose Medel ditto in six, Katsutoshi Aoki ditto in three, Johnny Jamito ditto in twelve and Bernardo Caraballo ditto in seven. By the end of 1964, Jofre had successfully defended his title eight times, winning all by knockout, and had gone undefeated in 50 fights with 37 knockouts—the last 17 coming in his last 17 outings. Now people were beginning to view him as not only the greatest all-time bantamweight champion, but the greatest pound-for-pound boxer.

But a funny thing happened to Eder Jofre on his way to lasting immortality: Fighting Harada. Harada, the former flyweight champion, kept the fluid Jofre at bay with a nonstop assault and beat him in 15 rounds to take his title in May of 1965 and then repeated his performance an unlucky 13 months later—proving only that the great Eder Jofre was mortal.

Suddenly, it seemed that the great Eder Jofre was finished, his fights fewer and fewer, his incentive gone, and his weight no longer that of a bantamweight. Seven months later he confirmed the rumors; he was retiring from the ring to attend to his outside business interests. But, just as incredibly, in August of 1969, after a hiatus of 26 months, the sound instinct that prompts the most enlightened man to come in out of a rainstorm seemed to be sadly missing from Jofre's mental makeup as he essayed a comeback. In the long history of boxing, efforts at comebacks often fail and sometimes succeed rather absurdly. It seemed that Jofre's comeback, especially as a featherweight, was destined to fall into one of these two categories.

But Eder Jofre was no ordinary fighter. Nor was his comeback an ordinary comeback. Moving more like an institution than a fighter, Jofre would go on to win 25 consecutive fights—and the world featherweight championship—to close his remarkable career.

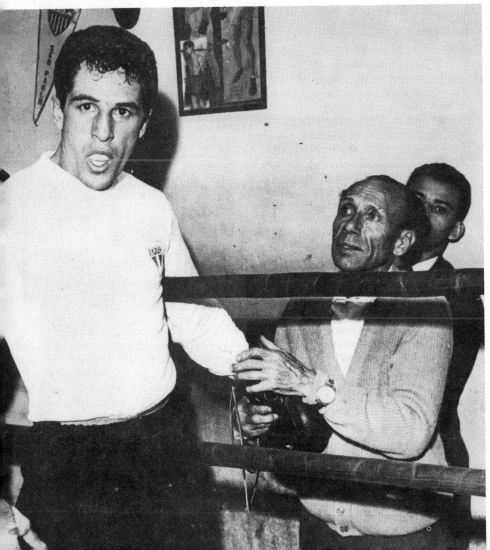

75

ABE ATTELL

Abraham Washington Attell, born February 22, shared the same birth date as another man named Washington, known better as the "Father of Our Country." And that's about all he shared with the man who said, "I cannot tell a lie." For no man in the history of boxing ever combined the feeble union of brutality and rascality better than Attell. As slick in the ring as the brilliantine which coated his hair, Attell was equally slick outside, where he continually waited for a scam like an old taxi cab waiting in line for whatever designation came up. Attell was fond of cards, horses, fights, whatever, and they were reciprocally affectionate. But this man who craved action—any action—could usually find it in the ring, where he was called by Charley Harvey, the manager of Jim Driscoll and Owen Moran, two fighters who faced Attell six times, "The best fighter in ring history, pound for pound. . . ." And for close to 14 years, he was one of the all-time greats.

IT WAS IN THE ARENA OF BOXING THAT Abe Attell was larger than life-sized, which in his case was not stupendous, his size being only 5 feet, 4 inches, and 122 pounds. But what those 64 inches and 122 pounds could do inside the ring! With all the ease and grace of an early-day sand dancer, Attell could block, slip, duck, and sidestep, darting in and out and around his opponent, all the while feinting him into knots, and then, with the greatest arm-to-body coordination in ring history, land his own devastating punches on his by-now frustrated and beaten opponent. It's little wonder that this spidery ring magician was accorded the same honorary title that had been given to Young Griffo before him—and would be given to Willie Pep after him—"The Will o' the Wisp."

Coming from the same south of the market section of San Francisco that had spawned the great James J. Corbett, Attell copied many of the moves that had made Corbett the first great scientific fighter. Watching Corbett, and, after him, the "Old Master," Joe Gans, Attell learned that, "a fighter could be a fighter and not get hurt—if he were clever enough."

Attell borrowed liberally from others, his ring plagiarism also including the adoption of the style of George Dixon, the great "Little Chocolate." When the featherweight crown—which had blown around like a feather in a windstorm, from claimant to claimant—came up vacant with Terry McGovern was unable to make the 122-pound weight limit, Attell and Dixon were paired to fight for the title. Everyone, Dixon included, was surprised to find that Attell had been an apt student and had mimicked the ring tactics of Dixon to perfection. The result of the two mirror images was just as it should have been: a draw. Rematched 8 days later, Attell won the "title" in 15 rounds, a title that was later solemnized by *The Police Gazette*, which put its official stamp on his ascension by giving him a championship belt, complete with the picture of its publisher, Richard K. Fox.

From 1901 through 1912, "The Little Champ" risked his belt some 75 to 80 times, according to his estimate, and several times, having exhausted the division of worthy challengers—even recycling a few—ventured into the lightweight division to do battle with some

of the all-time greats: Al Wolgast, Freddie Welsh, George Chaney, Charlie White, Battling Nelson, Jim Driscoll, Memphis Pat Moorel, and Harlem Tommy Murphy. Finally, on his birthday in 1912, he risked his belt one time too many, and Johnny Kilbane walked off with a 20-round decision. And the belt.

Sixteen days later Attell was back to do battle with Harlem Tommy Murphy, one of the toughest of the old timers. Having spent his entire training period—including the night before the fight—playing high-stakes stud poker, Attell came to the realization that his condition and the 11 pounds Murphy had on him would be too much, even for Attell, to handle, so he turned his magic to a darker side, and, with contemptible mischief in his heart, approached Murphy to do a "hippodrome." The referee caught wind of it and warned Attell that he would not stand for any such shenanigans, and At-

tell was forced to fight Murphy on the "up-and-up," losing a 20-round blood-spattered battle. That same year Attell fought Knockout Brown in New York. After the fight the New York State Athletic Commission, taking offense at the fact that Attell showed no offense, claimed Attell had "faked" the fight and barred him from fighting in New York for six months.

After losing his title to Kilbane and

Top: Abe Attell (left) and Harlem Tommy Murphy in one of their 20-round bloodbaths, 1912. Bottom: "The Little Champ" with Joe Gans, 1907.

fighting Murphy twice, Attell's career began to wind down, the once laudatory fighter showing only glimpses of his one-time greatness. Drifting away from boxing, the next time his name was in the papers occurred in 1920 when he was headlined as the go-between in the World Series fix of 1919.

Toward the end of his life, an industrious fight reporter uncovered a loss on his record, going back half a century. "Shh," whispered Attell, "keep it quiet. It can hurt my standing . . . I never told anybody I lost that one." That was Abraham Washington Attell, the idol of American boyhood and American hoodhood as well, a man whose crooked nose covered a crooked mind, but whose greatness stands for all time in spite of it, debased but never defiled.

Born Abraham Lincoln Attell, 2/22/84, in San Francisco (Albert Knoehr, according to book entitled *Eight Man Out*) . . . Only man to win and lose world championship on his birthday . . . First year as a pro, 1900, fought mostly kids: Kid Lennett, Kid Dodson, Kid O'Neill, Kid Jones, Kid Dulley, Kid Powers . . . Scored 15 kayos in 16 bouts in first year . . . Won 11 more in a row before fighting 20-round draw with George Dixon, 8/24/01 . . . Fought second draw with Dixon, 20 rounds, 10/20/01, and then won 15-round decision from him 8 days later . . . First loss, 11/4/01, to Harry Forbes, bantamweight champion, in non-title bout . . . Claimed world featherweight title after kayoing Forbes in fifth round, 2/1/04, although Forbes never held featherweight title and Young Corbett was still recognized as champion . . . Lost to Tommy Sullivan, 10/13/04, by fifth-round kayo in bout billed for vacant world featherweight title . . . Sullivan abandoned title in 1906, Attell then defeated Jimmy Walsh, 2/22/06, and established valid claim to title . . . Successfully defended title 22 times, 1906–12, including 6 in 1906 and 5 in 1908 . . . Had 4 draws in title defenses— 2 with Owen Moran in 1908—1/1/08, 25 rounds and 9/7/08, 23 rounds . . . Fought 15-round draw with Battling Nelson, 5/31/08, just prior to Nelson's winning the lightweight title . . . Made 2 title defenses in 2 weeks in Calgary, Alberta, Canada, 1910 . . . Defended successfully against Johnny Kilbane, 10/24/10, 10-round decision . . . Lost title to Kilbane, 2/22/12, via 20-round decision . . . Last pro bout, 1917 . . . Involved in baseball Black Sox scandal, 1919 . . . Elected to Boxing Hall of Fame, 1955 . . . Died 2/7/70, New Paltz, NY . . . Complete record: 165 bouts, 92 won, 10 lost, 18 draws, 45 no-decisions, 51 knockouts.

JACK BRITTON

Jack Britton rewrote *The Guiness Book* for boxing. At least, in terms of active ring service. For although *The Ring Record Book* lists "just" 327 times this great lightweight and welterweight climbed through the ring ropes to do battle, 1930s ring historian George Pardy insists that Britton had been fighting for over seven years before his name appeared in any of the tabulated chronicles of fights. And Britton himself insisted he had fought over 400 times, a fact you could almost attest to personally by looking at his cauliflower ears, so outsized you could have covered them with a liberal serving of Hollandaise sauce. But it wasn't merely his remarkable record of more than 400 fights over a span of 30 years that entitles Jack Britton to join the pantheon of greats: It was his marvelous ring generalship. And a left hand that speculated like a doctor in search of a vein.

BORN WILLIAM J. BRESLIN IN CLINTON, New York, and raised in New Britain, Connecticut—from whence he stole his *nom de guerre* which was later mangled badly by a tongue-tied ring announcer—Britton made his name in the small boxing clubs around Chicago. And against one of Chicago's greatest fighters ever, Packey McFarland. McFarland, resenting Britton's popularity in his native burg, accepted the challenge of the new kid on the Loop, all the better to teach him a lesson for invading his home turf. However, it wasn't Britton who was taught a lesson, but McFarland, as he had to extend himself to the limit for eight rounds, fending off Britton's whirlwind charges and rapid-fire flurries. After eight fast-paced rounds, the fight was ruled a "Draw," although most of the local newspaper reporters insisted that Britton had won the fight. No matter what the outcome, it was the beginning of Jack Britton's ring career, catapulting him into the boxing spotlight, one he would dominate for the remainder of his long, illustrious career.

Britton combined his legendary left with an uncanny ring artistry that made everyone he fought look bad, dancing out of trouble with little more than a

Born William J. Breslin, 10/14/85, in Clinton, NY . . . Began pro boxing, 1905, early record incomplete . . . Averaged more than one bout per month for 26 years—For 327 total bouts, most of any champion . . . Fought first 10 years in U.S., mostly no-decision bouts . . . Won welterweight title from Mike Glover, 6/22/15, on 12-round decision . . . Lost title to Ted Kid Lewis in next bout, 8/31/15, 12-round decision . . . Fought Lewis 20 times in career—won 4, lost 3, 1 draw, 12 no-decisions . . . Welterweight crown alternated between the 2, 1915–22 . . . Regained title, 4/24/16, lost it, 6/25/17, rewon it, 3/17/19, on ninth-round kayo—only knockout in series . . . Had total of 37 welterweight title bouts—9 wins, 4 losses, 6 draws, 18 no-decisions—most title bouts of any boxer in history . . . Included among title opponents, Pinky Mitchell, Dave Shade, Benny Leonard, and Johnny Griffiths . . . Fought Griffiths 10 times throughout career without a decision (1 draw, 9 no-decisions) . . . Lost title to Mickey Walker, 11/1/22, 15-round decision . . . continued boxing until 1930 . . . More than 300 of his bouts went the distance . . . Consecutive 26 years of boxing surpassed, among champions, only by Archie Moore's 28 years . . . Boxing instructor at Downtown A.C., N.Y.C. after retirement . . . Elected to Boxing Hall of Fame, 1960 . . . Died, 3/27/62, Miami, FL . . . Complete record: 327 bouts, 100 won, 29 lost, 20 draws, 177 no-decisions, 1 no-contest, 21 knockouts.

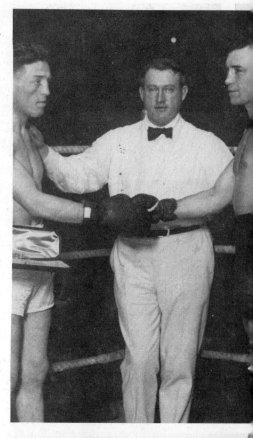

Top left: Jack Britton (right) and Mickey Walker, Nov. 1, 1922, the night Britton lost his welterweight title to the "Toy Bulldog".

glide and a slide, or moving his head in time with his opponent's swings. One time, according to his manager, Dumb Dan Morgan, Britton was fighting "a nonentity in Wilkes-Barre who managed to slap a gold tooth out of his mouth while he was counting the house." Jack saw the tooth fall into the sawdust in his corner and wanting it back, directed Morgan to find it. Standing flat-footed in the corner, all the time watching his opponent out of the corner of his eye and bobbing and weaving to avoid the oncoming punches, Britton called out to his manager, "To your left, Dan. . . . Now a little more to your right. . . . That's it! . . . Now dig for it. . . . " Morgan found the tooth and Britton went back to defang his opponent, now arm-weary from his efforts.

But perhaps the anchor of Britton's fame was his traveling road show with Ted "Kid" Lewis, a series that featured 20 bouts in almost as many cities. Fighting on any day ending in "Y," these two greats fought in four different cities in just 37 calendar days in 1917. However, their six-year series occurred during the height of boxing's infamous "No-Decision Days," and the "winner" was usually the fighter whose manager got to the telephone first to call in the result. However, Britton took care of such shenanigans by knocking out his British rival to regain custody of the welterweight crown fittingly on St. Patty's Day, 1919.

Britton would defend his title against the same Lewis, Dave Shade, and the great Benny Leonard before risking it, at the advanced age of 37, against the 21-year-old Mickey Walker. And although the gallant old champion made excellent use of his fabulous left and dazzled Walker and the crowd with his breathtaking footwork, he could not hold off the younger pit terrier, whose body attack wore down the tiring champion. After the inevitable decision, ring announcer Joe Humphries commandeered the center of the ring, and through his ever-present megaphone hollered, "Wait a minute! Here's to one of the all-time greats . . . three rousing cheers!" The Garden echoed in tribute to one of boxing's most beloved champions ever. And one of its greatest.

BOB FITZSIMMONS

The word, or demi-word, "Fitz" in auld Irish lore stands for, literally, "the left hand of God." And nobody in fistic lore stood taller when it came to the left hand than "Ruby" Robert Fitzsimmons. In any shape-up of fighters, "Fitz" would have been rejected. His prematurely bald terra-cotta coiffure and silver dollar-sized freckles which flecked his body made him look like a curious piece of goods. Add to that his muscular shoulders which resembled those of a village smithy—which he had been in his previous career—atop a tapering 28-inch waist set on spindly, pipestem legs and it was obvious why some called him a "sandhill crane," while others, like John L. Sullivan, labeled him "a fighting machine on stilts."

BUT IT WASN'T HIS LOOKS THAT MADE Bob Fitzsimmons a great fighter; it was his left. For it was that left, complete with a curious shifting of the feet, that won him the heavyweight championship from James J. Corbett.

And almost immediately after the fight, boxing writers, never having seen anyone use his left as Fitz had to knock the air out of Corbett and the crown off his head, called it "the solar plexus punch," describing the area to which the blow had landed rather than the blow itself: the first pure left hook ever thrown.

Throughout his storied 25-plus-year career, "Fitz" threw his patented left hook into the gullets of the large, the tall, and the small, often fighting elephantine opponents twice his size, which rarely exceeded 170 pounds. But Fitzsimmons fought them all, merely proclaiming, "The bigger they are, the harder they fall." And fall they did, all 32 of them.

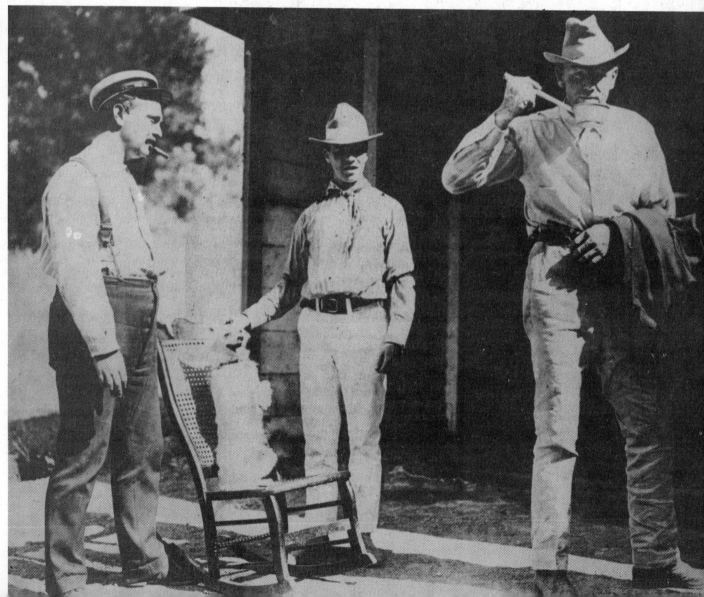

His style was one that almost defied normal nomenclature. He threw lefts and rights to both body and jaw with equal devastation. And then seducing his opponent into a momentary torpor, turning southpaw, he would shift his feet to loosen a tide of bafflement in his opponent's mind and implant his left almost up to the wrist in his opponent's waist—or, as his contemporary Bob Armstrong said, "He tore de gizzards out of his opponents."

Fitzsimmons was to ride his left hook to three separate titles, the middleweight, heavyweight, and light heavyweight titles, the first man ever to win three boxing titles, winning the last at the advanced age of 40, a tribute to the man who believed "a good head is better than good legs."

And a good left hook is better than most heads, especially when it was thrown by a man named "Fitz," who lived up to his name.

Born Robert James Fitzsimmons, 5/26/63, in Cornwall, England . . . Started boxing professionally in the early 1880s in Sydney, Australia . . . Known as "Ruby Robert" for red hair . . . Came to United States, 1890 . . . Won world middleweight championship from Jack Dempsey, "The Nonpareil" by thirteenth-round knockout, 1/14/91 . . . Made only one defense of title, 9/26/94, second-round knockout of Dan Creedon . . . Scored first-round knockout against Peter Maher, 2/21/96 . . . Defeated James J. Corbett by fourteenth-round knockout to win world heavyweight championship, 3/17/97 . . . Only champion to successfully move up in class and win world heavyweight title . . . Lost title to James J. Jeffries in first defense, 6/9/99, by eleventh-round knockout . . . Only weighed 167 pounds for both heavyweight title bouts—lightest man to win heavyweight crown . . . Lost rematch with Jeffries, 7/25/02, for heavyweight title by eighth-round knockout . . . At the age of 40, defeated George Gardner, 11/25/93, to win third title—world light heavyweight championship . . . Defended title in 6-round no-decision bout with Philadelphia Jack O'Brien, 7/23/04 . . . Lost title to O'Brien, 12/20/05, by thirteenth-round knockout . . . Had 5 additional bouts from 1907–14—last bout, 2/20/14, 6-round no-decision bout at age of 50 . . . First man to win 3 world championships . . . Died, 10/22/17, Chicago . . . Charter member of Boxing Hall of Fame, 1954 . . . Complete record: 62 bouts, 40 won, 11 lost, 10 no-decisions, 1 no-contest, 32 knockouts.

Below right: Fitzsimmons (right) and George Gardner before "Fitz" wins light heavyweight title, 1903.

TERRY McGOVERN

30 TERRY McGOVERN

Turn-of-the-century Brooklyn was a wondrous place to behold. Only recently absorbed by New York City, it was a borough filled with every conceivable classical incubus of architecture: Victorian mansions decorated with cupolas; fanciful gingerbread designs with curlicues; and houses festooned with Gothic lacework. All of these wedding-cake structures decorated tree-lined neighborhoods with august names, tenanted by working-class families, many of whom were second-generation Americans. Brooklyn also was the proud home of the Brooklyn Bridge—that crowning masterpiece of Victorianism—Coney Island, the Brooklyn Trolley Dodgers of the National League, and "Terrible" Terry McGovern. "Terrible" Terry McGovern was one of Brooklyn's most important monuments. And a work of art unto himself. Born in Johnstown, Pennsylvania, Terry was brought to Brooklyn at the tender age of six months, thereby qualifying him as a homegrown native. Raised in one of Brooklyn's many Irish-American "nabes"—the borough having supplanted Boston as the Irish-American capital of America—Terry not only came from Brooklyn, but was Brooklyn through and through.

HIS FIRST BOXING BOUT, HELD AT Brooklyn's Jackson Club, against one Jack Shea one month after his seventeenth birthday, resulted in a first-round kayo and a $25 victor's purse for Terry. His blood-letting doubled as group therapy for his Irish followers, and soon his fame began to spread beyond the Williamsburg section to the entire borough as his ruthless and savage style caught the imagination of the sporting crowd.

Truth to tell, McGovern's style was no style at all, but was his own version of mass mayhem. With sloping shoulders, thick forearms and heavy fists, small waist, deep chest, and the legs of an acrobat, a bobbed nose and bushy beetle eyebrows framing a pair of embers that doubled for eyes, McGovern had the look of a fighter (one he played to the hilt outside the ring, wearing the turtleneck sweater and Gallic cap, called a *caipin,* of a pugilist) and the

fighting technique of a human volcano. Fighting like a bearcat—albeit a 5-foot, 4-inch one—the Little Harp waded into his opponent without nuances or subtleties, throwing a frenzied orgy of punches with lightning speed, tireless aggressiveness, and a punching power qualitatively different from anything ever thrown by a bantamweight before. His object: to destroy his opponents, forcing them to look for a clean, well-lit place in which to collapse. "No bantamweight or featherweight," wrote Nat Fleischer, keeper of boxing's flame, "ever packed a more dangerous punch than did 'Terrible' Terry. No fighter of his weight piled up such a consistent record for tearing pell-mell into his adversaries and smothering them with wicked jolts, hooks, uppercuts and vicious swings. In every sense of the phrase, he was a pugilistic marvel."

McGovern clawed his way hand-over-glove up the ladder of success, breaking into the front ranks of the pugilistic

world late in 1898 by knocking out George Munroe, Harry Forbes, and Austin Rice. A twelfth-round KO over the Italian idol, Caspar Leon, an eighteenth-round stoppage of Patsy Haley, and a twenty-fifth-round decision over tough Joe Bernstein led the little warrior to a bout with England's undefeated Pedlar Palmer for the vacant world bantamweight title.

Palmer, the British champion, was known as the "Box o' Tricks" for his cleverness. But it hardly mattered to McGovern, as he let the Englishman throw two puerile left "feelers" before battering him into a helpless heap in 1:15 of the first round.

Four months later, McGovern, unable to make the bantam weight, moved up to the featherweight division, fighting the immortal "Little Chocolate," George Dixon, for his crown. For seven rounds Terrible Terry slashed and ripped at Little Chocolate with a murderous assault that the champion withstood only with superlative courage. In the eighth, his legs giving way under the relentless attack, the little black fighter went down seven times. Again and again, according to the rules of the day, McGovern pulled the bruised and groggy Dixon to his feet only to belt him into the resin dust one more time. Finally, the savage McGovern dragged the game soon-to-be ex-champion to the center of the ring and hit him under the heart with a fearful blow. Dixon fell to the canvas with a sickening thud. A second later there was a plop in the center of the ring as Dixon's corner threw in the sponge in surrender.

Terry the Terrible One next ventured into the lightweight ranks, starting, as one would expect, with the lightweight champion, Frank Erne. Erne agreed to take the short end of the purse if he couldn't knock out McGovern within the allotted ten rounds. Further, Erne held that since, due to weight, he couldn't claim McGovern's title if he won, McGovern would have to agree not to claim the lightweight title if he won. But all Erne was to win were his demands, as McGovern, firmly planting his head in Erne's chest, took but three rounds to beat Erne into a plowshare with body punches, using his crude, young strength to wear down the lightweight titlist and then, as Erne's actions became more hesitant, accelerating his own. McGovern was to finish out the year 1900 by beating the supposedly invincible Joe Gans in a fight that had a

rancid odor about it.

It was beginning to look like Terrible Terry couldn't be beaten down by mortal fists. But all that was to change when McGovern faced an unknown from the West named Young Corbett. Corbett had bet his entire purse on himself and then went out to make it "happen," baiting the fiery, flint-hearted demon of the feathers with words rather than punches. Before their fight, Corbett dressed in his ring toga hurriedly, then went over to McGovern's dressing room and knocked on the door, hollering, "Hurry up, McGovern, you big bum . . . . Come on up in the ring for your licking!" McGovern, his perilously short fuse made all the shorter, wanted to get it on right then and there. But his managers held him back as Corbett taunted, "Oh, no! I want your friends to see what a lousy fighter you are." In the second round, as each of the battlers

fought savagely, wishing that he had had the foresight to have fitted a dagger or rattlesnake into his gloves, Corbett caught McGovern with a terrible swat to the head. McGovern went down. Hard. And out.

They carried McGovern from the

canvas to his cot. Refusing to move he lay there and wailed, "I'm just a bum now . . . just a bum. I can lick that guy . . . "

That was Terrible Terry McGovern,, whose fearlessness was matched only by his carelessness. An original American tintype.

Born John Terrence McGovern, 3/9/80, in Johnstown, PA . . . First pro bout, 1897, Brooklyn, NY . . . Fought 10-round draw with future champ, Brooklyn Tommy Sullivan, in sixth pro bout . . . Kayoed future world bantamweight champion, Harry Forbes, in 15 rounds, 10/1/98 . . . Won world bantamweight title, 9/12/99, with first-round KO of Pedlar Palmer . . . Scored 18 straight knockouts, 1899–1900, including 11 consecutively within 3 rounds . . . Never defended bantamweight championship . . . Won world featherweight title with eighth-round KO of George Dixon, 1/9/00 . . . Defended title successfully 6 times, all knockouts . . . Lost title to Young Corbett, 11/28/01, stopped in second round . . . Lost rematch with Corbett, 3/31/03, on eleventh-round knockout . . . Continued fighting until 1908 . . . Died, 2/26/18, in Brooklyn, NY . . . Elected to Boxing Hall of Fame, 1955 . . . Complete record: 78 bouts, 60 won, 4 lost, 4 draws, 10 no-decisions, 42 knockouts.

"Terrible Terry" McGovern (left) and Young Corbett before Corbett knocked out McGovern for the first time in a match Nov. 28, 1901.

EZZARD CHARLES

For that rare boxing fan with an eye for fistic delicacies, the name Ezzard Charles suggests one of the greatest boxers in the history of the sport. But for the general boxing public, especially those weaned on the exploits of Joe Louis, the name of Ezzard Charles initiates a banquet of the malicious. To traditionalists, of whom there are many, daring to succeed to the mantle of the great Joe Louis was irreverent. But, even worse, to actually beat the great Joe Louis in combat bordered on blasphemy. It was almost as if the boxing crowd suddenly realized that what they had in front of them was not the dish they had ordered. And so, Charles, instead of being hailed as the heavyweight champion of the world, became known merely as the man who beat Joe Louis, destined forever to become an antihero to one of the most popular names in all of sports.

THIS WAS PATENTLY UNFAIR TO CHARLES, one of the great boxers of all time, heavyweight or otherwise—and one of its most underrated as well. Not because, following in Louis' rather large footsteps, it was inevitable that he had to suffer in comparison to the man who had served as an idol to all for the previous twelve years. But because boxing fans, confused by the entrance of a new player—as they always are—failed to recognize the genius in this warm, sensitive man.

For even before Ezzard Charles entered the heavyweight ranks, he had carried a flame of achievement, first as a middleweight and then as a light heavyweight. Some, including that venerable boxing voice, Ray Arcel, hold that Charles was one of the greatest light heavyweights of all time.

Charles started boxing at the age of 14, fighting in amateur contests in and around his adopted city of Cincinnati. During his illustrious 4-year amateur career, he won not only all 42 of his bouts but also the Diamond Belt, the Ohio AAU Welterweight title, and the National AAU Middleweight title (twice). Turning pro in March of 1940, he ran off 20 straight wins, including 14 knockouts, before being matched against ex-middleweight champion Ken Overlin. The cagey Overlin proved too ringwise for the 20-year-old youngster and outcutied him over 10 rounds.

But Charles came back, scoring three victories before the end of 1941, including one over Teddy Yarosz, the ex-middleweight king. Soon he was being hailed as "The Cincinnati Cobra," testimony to his lightning speed and deadly aim, not to mention his growing number of knockouts. In 1942, "Ez" fought 12 times, beating such worthies as Charley Burley, the man rated by many as one of the all-time middleweight greats; Joey Maxim, the future light heavy champ; and Anton Christoforidis, the former light heavyweight king.

The winds of war were beginning to gust over the country and everybody, athletes included, was caught up in the ensuing draft, Charles included. Barely 21, Ezzard enlisted in the Army, and for the next three years, while "open" vacancies pocked the boxing world like bomb craters, he had only two fights, both taken while on leave with little time for training. He was to lose both, a ten-round decision to the "Duration" champion in both the heavyweight and light heavyweight divisions, Jimmy Bivins, and a knockout at the hands of one of the great "hitters" of all time, Lloyd Marshall.

Born Ezzard Mack Charles, 7/7/21, in Lawrenceville, GA ... Won U.S. national amateur middleweight championship, 1939 ... First pro bouts, 1940 ... Won first 20 bouts, 1940–41 ... Lost 10-round decision to Ken Overlin, 6/9/41 ... Drew with Overlin in rematch, 3/2/42 ... Defeated Joey Maxim twice, 1942 ... In service, 1943–45 ... Defeated Archie Moore 3 times in 3 years and won 28 of 29, 1946–48 ... Won vacant NBA heavyweight championship with 15-round decision over Jersey Joe Walcott, 6/22/49 ... Extemely active champion—9 defenses in 2 years ... Knocked out Gus Lesnevich, 8/10/49, in seventh round ... Stopped Pat Valentino in eighth, 10/14/49; kayoed Freddie Beshore in fourteenth, 8/15/50 ... Won universal championship recognition with unanimous decision over Joe Louis, 9/27/50 ... Stopped Nick Barone in eleventh round, 12/5/50; kayoed Lee Oma in tenth, 1/12/51 ... Won 15-round decision over Jersey Joe Walcott, 3/7/51; decisioned Joey Maxim, 5/30/51 ... Lost title when kayoed by Jersey Joe Walcott in seventh round, 7/18/51 ... Lost decision in rematch with Walcott, 6/5/52 ... Had 2 other attempts at regaining title against Rocky Marciano—6/17/54, L 15, and 9/17/54, KO 8 ... Continued fighting until 1959 but definitely past prime, lost 13 of 23 bouts, 1955–59 ... Had more heavyweight title fights than all but 3 champions, (Louis, Ali, Holmes) ... 4 bouts with Walcott for title—most heavyweight title bouts between 2 men ... Lost more heavyweight title fights than all but 2 others (Walcott, Patterson) ... Outweighed in 10 of 13 title bouts ... Fought more bouts than any other heavyweight champion ... Elected to Boxing Hall of Fame, 1970 ... Complete record: 122 bouts, 96 won, 25 lost, 1 draw, 58 knockouts.

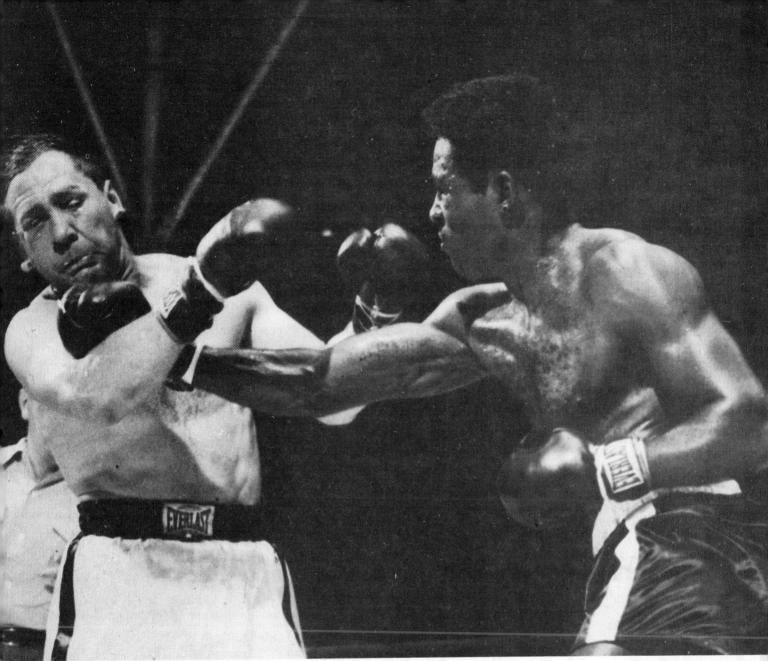

Four years later, Charles picked up where he left off. Twice he avenged his loss to Bivins and knocked out Marshall to even their score, while also taking the measure thrice of an oldster named Archie Moore. Still a light heavy, Ez seemed on the verge of a championship bout with the then-champion, Gus Lesnevich, but Lesnevich wanted nothing to do with him. Charles marked time, taking bouts with men 10 to 50 pounds heavier—and beating them.

Boxing is more wrapped up in the human, the person, the incalculable element than any other sport in the world. And, on the night of February 20, 1948, all of those came into play, as Ezzard Charles's world was to be redefined, radically. On that night, Charles mercilessly beat a top light heavyweight named Sam Baroudi, literally destroying him. Baroudi died a day

later, and with him a piece of Charles died too.

Suddenly Charles was no longer "The Cobra," no longer possessed of a killer's instinct, no longer relentlessly pursuing his hurt foe with TNT-laden gloves. Instead, driven by an impulse to redirect his destiny, he became a technician, a fighter whose assault was more leisurely: not a rash judgment, but slow and measured. And the boxing crowd answered this new player with an enveloping silence.

Despite his eventual climb to the top of the heavyweight heap, the fact that he sidestepped the challenge of no aspirant for top honors but met each of them and took each apart like a workman administering a scientific beating, and hung in, as gallantry itself, against Rocky Marciano, losing the fight but not his composure, Ezzard Charles has

always been dismissed by the public and press alike as a pugilist lacking in color—boxing's versions of Mt. Rushmore.

Time does not relinquish its rights either over human beings or monuments. And Ezzard Charles was both: a rare human being and a monument to greatness, one who should be judged higher in boxing's pantheon than merely as the titular successor to Joe Louis.

Above: "The Cincinnati Cobra" knocks out Gus Lesnevich in the seventh round to keep his title, Aug. 10, 1949.

PACKEY McFARLAND

Someone once said the only time that an opponent ever put a glove on Packey McFarland was when they shook hands before a bout. For although Packey McFarland never won a championship, he was one of the most skillful boxers who ever drew on gloves. Born in the tough stock yard district of Chicago where fighting was considered a natural pastime and where a lad's lot was measured by his ability to use his fists, Packey passed his baptism of fire by showing he was made of pretty good stuff, possessing the requisite courage to survive. (In fact, the only scars he ever suffered came "from the battles of my youth".) Having passed his boyhood survival course, Packey turned pro at the age of 15, taking on Pete West in his first "real" fight at Chicago's Park Manor Athletic Club. Packey started West heading east in the fifth round, running him out of the club-cum-barn in which they were fighting and ten blocks down the street. For his pains, Packey received a purse of $3, half of which he gave to his mother.

LIKE EVERY OTHER NOVICE BEFORE him, in the beginning McFarland felt there was only one way to prove himself—and that was by knocking out his opponents. His knockout punch earned him a reputation throughout the Southside as a "banger," as he rolled up knockout win after knockout win.

After two years of matching Mrs. O'Leary's cow for laying waste to the Chicago landscape, McFarland tried to export his somewhat limited skills to nearby Milwaukee and Davenport. That's when he learned that there was more to boxing than merely imposing his own strong will on an opponent. Faced with the prospect of matching wits and mitts with such experienced and capable performers as Benny Yanger, Kid Goodman, and Maurice Sayers, Packey made some adjustments, sacrificing punching power for movement. It was to be the beginning of his career as a scientific fighter, his speed and ring intelligence keeping him one step ahead of his opponent at all times. Packey disposed of all three and very likely would have scored knockouts over all of them had he been more experienced. These victories, followed by a 15-round no-decision bout with Kid Herman—back in those dark ages of boxing when state boxing regulations

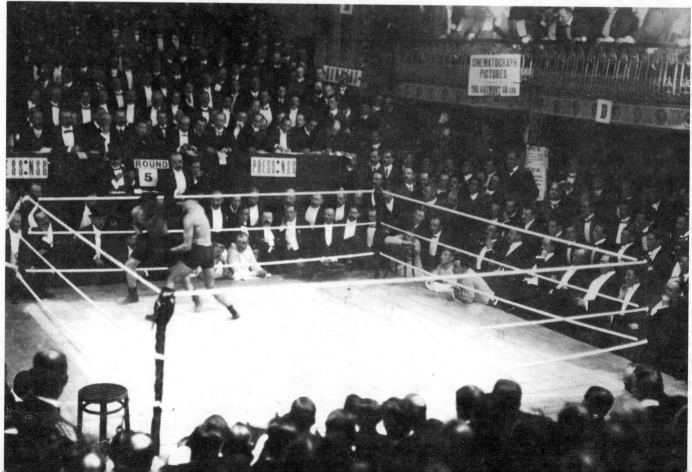

made no-decision bouts the norm—suddenly catapulted McFarland to the top of the lightweight division, and created a wide demand for his services, as well.

By 1907, McFarland was established in the Midwest, having knocked out Benny Yanger in four for his thirty-fourth consecutive victory. Now he set his sights on the two coasts—the right coast and the left coast. Coming East, first he fought the dangerous Bert Keyes in Boston in January of 1908. And although Keyes was in line for a title shot, McFarland, in the words of writer George T. Pardy, "handled Keyes with the cold indifference of a professor giving a pupil a lesson."

In that same year, Packey scored what were probably his two most notable victories: in back-to-back fights he outscored future lightweight champion Freddie Welsh, one of the most masterful boxers the division has ever seen, and knocked out Jimmy Britt, the same Jimmy Britt who twice beat Battling Nelson.

Then, on July 4, 1908, the same day Joe Gans lost his lightweight crown to Battling Nelson, Packey fought a rematch with Welsh in Los Angeles. In what ring historians call the fastest lightweight battle ever seen, McFarland blunted Welsh's inside attacks and proved superior at long range. The result: a 25-round draw.

Now the curly-headed son of the Chicago stockyards tried to get a title fight with Nelson. But the Durable Dane, knowing full well he didn't stand a chance against the clever McFarland in a 20- or 25-round fight, imposed his usual laundry list of conditions he knew McFarland could not comply with, consenting only to a 45-round, or "finish," fight. McFarland, who stood at 5 feet, 8 inches, tall for a lightweight, normally fought at a weight anywhere from 137 to 140 pounds. He could make 135 without too much effort, but like Gans, had trouble with the 133 pounds Nelson demanded he make for a title fight. And so he remained a lightweight in name only, in the same way raisins are fruits, technically and only in a manner of speaking. In effect, he was a junior welterweight in a day and age when there were no such halfway houses. So he continued to ply his trade as a heavy lightweight, disposing of Phil Brock and fighting no-decision fights with Harlem Tommy Murphy, Dick Hyland, and Leach Cross, all top

performers of his day.

For three more years McFarland fought all the greats in both the welterweight and lightweight divisions, finally retiring in 1913. From 1905 through the end of his career—with the exception of two early "street" fights held on Southside handball courts in 1904, one in which he was knocked out when his head struck the hard wooden floor—Packey McFarland didn't lose a single fight. And he fought some of the best, some of the toughest, retiring from the ring undefeated.

Packey McFarland was a fistic genius, and the few yellowing newspapers still remaining bear tribute to his skills. Cool and calculating, he performed wizardry when moving at top speed or when on the defensive, never missing an opening and timing his punches to perfection. But his forte was his accuracy when on the retreat, cutting and slashing an opponent to ribbons.

Perhaps Matt Wells, the hairy-chested British lightweight champ and world welterweight claimant, paid Packey the greatest compliment on the occasion of their fight at Madison Square Garden, April 1912. After being outpointed soundly by the boxing master, Wells was asked by his cockney trainer, Dai Dollings, "Why didn't you 'it 'im, Matt?"

"Aw, shut up!" Wells shouted back through puffed and bleeding lips. "Ah couldn't 'it that bloke with a 'orsewhip!"

Born Patrick McFarland, 11/1/88, Chicago, IL . . . Began boxing professionally, 1904 . . . Knocked out by Dusty Miller in fifth round of bout in first year, never lost another bout in next 10 years . . . Never fought for a championship although faced many top contenders in U.S. and England, 1904–15 . . . Knocked out 14 of 15 opponents, 1906 . . . Defeated 42 of first 43 opponents, 33 by knockout, 1904–07 . . . Most bouts 1908–15 were no-decision . . . Met Freddie Welsh (future lightweight champion) 3 times—2/21/08, W 10; 7/4/08, D 25; 5/30/10, D 20 . . . Knocked out Jimmy Britt (ex-lightweight champion) in 6 rounds, 4/11/08 . . . Defeated Cyclone Johnny Thompson, (middleweight title claimant) in 10 rounds, 11/8/09 . . . Fought Jack Britton (future welterweight champion) 3 times: 1/30/11, 8-round draw; 3/7/13 and 12/8/13, 10-round no-decisions . . . Met Matt Wells, British lightweight champion in 10-round no-decision bout, 4/26/12 . . . Final bout, 9/11/15, 10-round no-decision with Mike Gibbons . . . Died 9/23/36, Joliet, IL . . . Elected to Boxing Hall of Fame, 1955 . . . Complete record: 104 bouts, 64 won, 1 lost, 5 draws, 34 no-decisions, 47 knockouts.

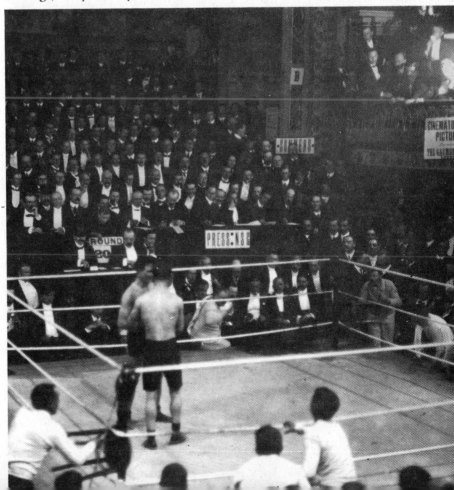

Opposite and below: Two of the most talented defensive boxers of all time, Packey McFarland and Freddie Welsh, fight to a 20-round draw at the National Sporting Club in London.

TED "KID" LEWIS

At dawn on a June day in 1837, a very young lady was called from her virtuous davenport with the news that she had become queen of England. She was to give her name to an age as no other person had before. During the 65 years she reigned, the world was complex in its simplicity. The effort it made was worthy of a better cause. The Victorian Era began by making women angels and ended by making everything else that could pass for entertainment devilish. One such amusement frowned upon by Victorian England was the pastime of prizefighting, as police became less tolerant, clergymen more adamant, and attacks on the sport more frequent. It wasn't until the death of Queen Victoria and the ascension of King Edward VII that the sport of prizefighting came back into favour (spelled with a "U.") And that several clubs started "programmes" dedicated to "The Sport of Manly Self-Defense," including The King's Hall, The Albert School of Arms, the Brockley B. C., Premiereland, and the Judean A. C. It was at the Judean A. C., also spelled with a U, that a little ashen-faced boy named Gershon Mendeloff, born in a gas-lit tenement in the nearby Aldgate Pump section of London's teeming East End, first took up the sport. He was to go on to become Britain's greatest pound-for-pound fighter, Ted "Kid" Lewis.

THE KID CALLED LEWIS MADE HIS TENtative start in one of the Judean A. C.'s weekly Sunday shows, fighting at the tender age of 14 for sixpence and a cup of tea—actually, the net was fivepence; he had to pay back a penny for the tea. Later, he was to win the club's flyweight competition and come home with a "silver" cup as a token of his growing proficiency. Unfortunately, the cup, not all what it was held out to be, melted on the mantelpiece overnight. That was to be the start of the man who would go on to win nine official championships, become a claimant to three others, and earn over 200,000 pounds in the ring. And become known as "The Smashing, Bashing, Crashing, Dashing Kid."

The young Kid won the British featherweight crown 18 days before his eighteenth birthday and went on to win the European title a year later. Taking his newly-won Lonsdale Belt with him, he first toured Australia, where the local burghers found him to be "the goods," as Lewis fought as many as five 20-round bouts in 63 days. Now campaigning as a lightweight-cum-welterweight, a concession to his maturing body, Lewis next invaded the States, rather than return home to his country, which was embroiled in a minor skirmish that would ultimately become known as "The War to End all Wars." Humorist Rube Goldberg, at ringside for Lewis' American debut, wrote, "Kid Lewis, the English lightweight, came to this country with a few hundred yards of red, white, and blue bunting and a reputation for being one of the fastest things raised on British soil for many moons. Lewis fought ten fast rounds with Phil Bloom, a Brooklyn gentleman with many friends, and gained the decision by a good margin. Lewis is blonde, fast, and bony, and can rest assured that he will have plenty of American money in his pockets while his own country is straining its neck looking for zeppelins."

Lewis now reached out with more than just his long left and "claimed," in the custom of the day, the long dormant and virtually moribund welterweight title. There was only one problem: another fighter named Jack Britton was also claiming the 147-pound title. And so was born boxing's most famous rivalry, the Britton-Lewis series, a series of 20 bouts in 12 different cities over a span of five years, reviving interest in a division which had failed to attract public attention for almost a decade.

Britton-Lewis was a rivalry in fact as well as in name. Britton, a proud Irishman, hated Lewis, and for far more than merely being an Englishman. Britton felt that Lewis was "a dirty fighter," and refused to shake hands before any of their 20 fights. The rivalry was also fueled by the managers of the two greats, Dumb Dan Morgan and Jimmy Johnston, both born hustlers. With 12 of their 20 fights of the no-decision variety, the "victory" belonged to the spoilsport who got to the telegraph office first to flash his version of the match to the out-of-town papers. On one occasion, both men left their charges in the middle of the fight and raced to the Western Union office to make the wires hum. One New York editor, who got two different versions of a bout which had gone to a no-decision, printed both telegrams, commenting, "Johnston's wire reporting Lewis had won was 'sent' in the fifth round and Morgan's with Britton the winner in the ninth. But Morgan had a head-start and beat Johnston by half an hour." Another time, Lewis climbed into a Boston ring with his "gumshield," the first time a mouthpiece had been seen in America. Morgan, viewing the mouthpiece as trickery of the first order, first asked to see it, then threw the offending rubber piece out into the audience, from whence it was never to be retrieved.

But there was still business during altercations, and Lewis managed to perfect his "claim" to the title by beating Britton in their second fight in Boston—the first time a Brit had ever won a title on American soil—and successfully defended it the next month,

Ted "Kid" Lewis "smashes and bashes" Johnny Basham in a fight June 9, 1920.

slashed with reckless abandon in his "smashing, bashing" style.

Lewis returned to England in 1919 allegedly "washed up." And yet it was to be the beginning of a second career, as he savaged the leading British welterweights, middleweights, and even heavyweights, winning the British and European welterweight and middleweight titles and beating the reigning light heavyweight champion.

After almost permanently retiring the entire middleweight population of Great Britain two-handedly, Lewis went after bigger fish, the heavyweights. He knocked out Tom Gummer, a full-fledged dreadnought, in one round, and then faced another heavyweight who, when he came out for the eighth round, was astonished to find Lewis offering his gloves for the traditional last-round "touch." "This isn't the last round," complained the somewhat flustered heavy. "It *is* for you," replied the carefree Lewis as he proceeded to fulfill his prophecy.

But the one big fish Lewis wanted was the biggest *poisson* of them all: Georges Carpentier, the world light heavyweight titlist and European heavyweight champion. Many in the crowd at London's Olympia the night of May 11, 1922, not only thought that the 150-pound Lewis stood a good chance of beating his 25-pound heavier rival and of redeeming Britain's flagging international prestige, but that the Kid could actually better Jack Dempsey's time of four rounds in disposing of the "Orchid Man." And for almost two minutes it looked like Lewis would accomplish everything he set out to do, hammering Carpentier to the body with his right while draping his left around the Frenchman's extended right arm. But then the referee intervened, lecturing Lewis on his tactics and touching the Kid's right wrist while Lewis merely stood there dumfounded, his arms stretched out an imploringly, his head turned to the referee arguing his case. It was at that pregnant moment that Carpentier landed a full-blooded right which floored Lewis and ended the fight. And his career.

When the British Boxing Writers honored their "Smashing, Bashing, etc. etc. Kid" in 1964, they presented him with a trophy inscribed, "The Best Old Boxer of the Year—or any Other Year." And he was one of Britain's, and boxing's, greatest, "The Smashing, Bashing etc. Kid."

again in Boston. But, after two no-decision bouts, complete with differing versions of the fights sent out by the two madcap managers, Britton turned the tables on Lewis and won the crown in New Orleans the next year. By 1917, in one of three fights with Britton in June, Lewis would win back the crown, which had become a shuttlecock between these two excellent gamesmen, only to lose it a second time to Britton on March 17, 1919. This time Morgan had a legitimate reason to send out a wire, celebrating his fighter's St. Patrick's Day victory with a telegram addressed to Buckingham Palace announcing Lewis' defeat at the hands of an Irishman. The final score of their road show was Britton 4, Lewis 3, 1 draw, and 12 no-decisions.

Normally, familiarity with the dangers of the ring makes a brave man brave, but less daring. Lewis, once famous for boxing "along safe lines," now became more daring. Starting out his career as an evasive boxer with a long left that he could snap on and off like an electric light switch from afar, the Kid underwent a metamorphosis during his six years in America, changing his style to that of a swarming combination boxer-fighter. He became more tigerish, his punches more deadly, his moves more economical. He traded in his puerile right-hand slap to the body for a straight right cross, one he would land time and again in the infighting while tenderly holding onto his opponent with his left. Swiftly, he threw a bewildering array of punches, coming onetwothreefourfive that fast, as he

Born Gershon Mendeloff, 10/24/94, London, England . . . Lost first recorded pro bout to Johnny Sharpe, 9/13/09 . . . Fought primarily in London through 1914 . . . Won British featherweight title with seventeenth-round knockout of Alec Lambert, 10/6/13 . . . Won European featherweight championship on twelfth-round foul by Paul Til, 2/2/14 . . . Fought in Australia part of 1914 . . . Traveled to U.S. in 1915 and won world welterweight title from Jack Britton, 8/31/15, on 12-round decision . . . Faced Britton 20 times, 1915–1921 . . . Lost title to Britton, 4/24/16 . . . Regained title from Britton, 6/25/17 . . . Lost title again to Britton on ninth-round KO, 3/17/19 . . . Returned to England, 1920, and won British welterweight title from Johnny Bee, 3/11/20, KO 4 . . . Won European welterweight title 6/9/20, with nineteenth-round KO of Johnny Basham . . . Lost final bout with Britton in unsuccessful attempt to regain welterweight crown . . . Won British middleweight and European middleweight titles in subsequent bout with Basham, 10/14/21, KO 12 . . . Challenged Georges Carpentier for world light heavyweight title, 5/11/22, was knocked out in first round . . . Continued boxing until 1929 . . . Kayoed Basham in final bout, 12/13/29 . . . Elected to Boxing Hall of Fame, 1964 . . . Died 10/20/70, in London, England . . . Complete record: 279 bouts, 170 won, 30 lost, 13 draws, 66 no-decisions, 70 knockouts.

MARCEL CERDAN

The two greatest names to come out of Casablanca during World War II were Rick Blaine and Marcel Cerdan. Rick Blaine was, of course, the fictional owner of Rick's Café Americain, made famous by Humphrey Bogart in the film "Casablanca." Marcel Cerdan was a real-life figure who could whip any fighter worth his mouthpiece. He was also a man who carried the tragic dignity of heroism. And greatness. Born in Sidi-Bel-Abbes, Algeria, the sentinel city of the storied French Foreign Legion, Cerdan soon became as much a legend as the Legion throughout the French colonies, especially in the nearby city of Casablanca, where he fought 18 of his first 28 fights, winning all. The *pied noirs* loved the handsome, rugged fighter with the determined chin, beetle brow, and delicate nose looking for a final resting place on his face, a man who bore a Gallic resemblance to Jimmy Cagney. He fought the same way, too, almost as if he said, "Here I am and here I stay." (*"J'y suis, j'y reste"*) standing resolutely in the face of his opponents and contemptuously walking through their punches to land his *crochet du droit* (right hook) or his famed left hook.

BY THE OUTBREAK OF THE WAR, THIS gutsy little performer with the swarming style, limitless stamina, and pinpoint accuracy had fought 53 times with only one loss to show for his efforts, and that a dubious "foul" claim in London. He had won the French and European welterweight titles and had had six epic encounters with Omar Kouidri, the great Algerian welterweight who extended Cerdan the distance on five of those occasions.

With hobnailed jackboots goose stepping their way across the Continent, boxing and Cerdan both went into limbo, Cerdan joining the French Navy. After the temporary fall of La Belle France, he was persuaded to come back and fight in occupied France, and did so, running off a string of 9 straight KOs—the last in 21 seconds against someone by the name of Gustave Humery. He made one more pitstop in Paris, the briefest possible, fighting for the advertised "Middleweight Championship of Europe" against José Ferrer. Guaranteeing that French sports fans and German occupation troops would reach their appointed shelters by blackout time, Marcel ended the fight in just 83 seconds. Without waiting for the scheduled victory dinner or his paycheck, Cerdan cleared out by using a forged exit visa. The Nazis, obviously unamused, gave the "championship" to the fallen Ferrer.

Six weeks after Cerdan's unceremonious retreat from Paris—the only time he had ever taken a backward step—the Allied Armies invaded North Africa. Prizefighter Cerdan was only too happy to join the Free French Navy and accept an assignment to box exhibitions in the former French colonies in order to raise funds for the Resistance. And, not incidentally, to provide a therapeutic diversion to war-weary fighters of a different sort. The fame of Cerdan was soon to spread as he whipped his weight in GIs, adding an international dimension to his growing legend.

Brought to the States, Cerdan was matched against Georgie Abrams, the perennial middleweight contender. Unaffected by what the wisenheimers call "Gardenitis," Cerdan fairly rushed Abrams off his feet, pounded away with both hands, and walked away with a unanimous decision. Here was no wartime accident, here was an accidental warrior, an out-of-the-ring gentleman who charmed the press with his laugh, his gleeful display of gold-capped teeth, displayed at just the right time, and his emotional expressions—even taking his time to properly enunciate in English, punctuated with a grin, "I also admire your beautiful women here in America. . . ." When he knocked out Harold Green and Laverne Roach and beat Anton Raddik, his abilities were, like his charm, no longer suspect. He was the real thing, a fighter better than his reputation—and that was substantial.

His next fight in America was against Tony Zale, famous for his thunderous body shots and the two knockout wins over Rocky Graziano, the "Dead-End Kid." Cerdan's superior speed, quicker reflexes, and more accurate punches wore down the "Man of Steel" until, in the eleventh, Zale seemed to be walking on legs no longer his own, his knees

Born 7/22/16, in Sidi Bel-Abbes, Algeria . . . First pro bout, 1934 . . . First 3 years boxed exclusively in North Africa, won 28 straight bouts . . . Went to Paris, October 1937, and continued winning streak with 6 more victories . . . Won French welterweight title, 2/21/38, with 12-round decision over Omar Kouidri . . . Lost first bout in career, 1/9/39, on foul to Englishman, Harry Craster in London . . . Won European welterweight title, 6/3/39, from Saverio Turiello, on 15-round decision in Milan, Italy . . . Successfully defended European title with first-round knockout of Jose Ferrer, 9/30/42 . . . Won Inter-Allied welterweight tournament in Algiers, 2/15–2/20, 1944, won second tournament with 3 knockouts in Rome, 12/12–12/16, 1944 . . . Won French middleweight title, 11/30/45, with third-round knockout of Assane Diouf . . . Successfully defended French title twice in 1946 . . . Defeated Holman Williams in Paris, 7/7/46 . . . Came to U.S. for bout with Georgie Abrams, 12/6/46, won 10-round decision . . . Won vacant European middleweight title, 2/2/47, with first-round knockout of Leon Foquet . . . Defended European title twice in 1948 before losing only decision of career and title to Belgian, Cyrille Delannoit in Brussels, 5/23/48 . . . Regained title in Brussels rematch, 7/10/48, via 15-round decision . . . Knocked out Tony Zale in twelfth round to win world middleweight title, 9/21/48 . . . Lost world middleweight title to Jake LaMotta, 6/16/49, on tenth-round knockout . . . Return bout with LaMotta scheduled for 9/28/49, but postponed to 12/2/49, due to training injury suffered by LaMotta . . . Rematch never took place as Cerdan killed in plane crash en route to the U.S., 10/27/49 . . . Elected to Boxing Hall of Fame, 1962 . . . Complete record: 115 bouts, 111 won, 4 lost, 66 knockouts.

Marcel Cerdan knocks out the "Man of Steel," Tony Zale, Sept. 21, 1948, to win the crown (top) and rejoices with his brother.

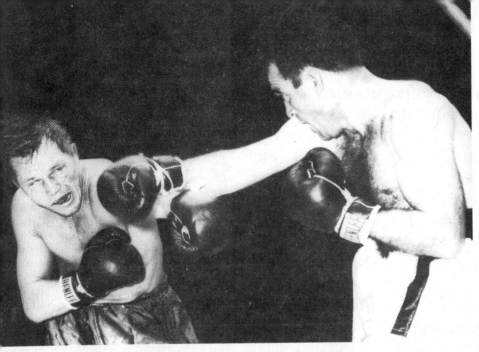

pointed every which way. Finally, at the bell, Cerdan caught the faltering Zale with one unambiguous left hook. Zale hung in the air for a brief second and then started to pitch forward, his crown perceptibly tumbling from his head. Marcel Cerdan was the new middleweight champion of the world, the first non-American to own the crown since Bob Fitzsimmons half a century before.

One of the things that goes down in the sport of boxing is its sub-rosa deals. And the IBC, then the landlords of boxing, had made a deal for a shot at the middleweight championship with a contender named Jake LaMotta, who was coming off a dishonorable showing against Billy Fox. He was part and parcel of the baggage the sport carried and Cerdan, whose dream had been realized but who knew that the realization carried with it a certain bonus and a certain burden, accepted the burden in LaMotta, an overstuffed light heavyweight in middleweight's clothing. There was absolutely no way LaMotta could beat Cerdan. But it was possible that Cerdan could lose to LaMotta. And that's exactly what happened when, in the first round, LaMotta wrestled Cerdan to the ground and Cerdan fell heavily on the back of his neck, tearing a muscle in his left shoulder. At the end of the round, his cornermen asked him politely, "Marcel, do you want to 'retire'?" to which the fiercely proud Cerdan barked, "I'm a fighter, not a dressmaker. . . . If I must fight him with one hand, I will!" For nine more rounds the courageous Cerdan fought with one hand, trying to keep away "The Bronx Bull" with a chopping right hand, his left useless. Finally, his shoulder smashed, his hopes dashed, even Cerdan saw that raw courage was not enough and, for the first time in his career, "retired."

After the fight, Cerdan, groggy with sentimentality, would utter, "I win back my title—or die." He was to proudly proclaim those exact words, a mixture of Gallic emotion tinged with tragic dignity, as he enplaned for his return bout with LaMotta four months later. It was a bout that fate in the form of the eternal referee would see never happened, as one of the most underrated fighters in a long history of underrated fighters met his death in an airplane on his way back to redeem *his* title, becoming one of boxing's most heroic—and tragic figures.

35 KID CHOCOLATE

KID CHOCOLATE

Suffice it to say, there are more great pictures of fighters than there are pictures of great fighters. But there was one great fighter called a "picture fighter" by everyone who ever saw him. And for good reason. For that "picture fighter" was Kid Chocolate, accent on the last syllable, a fighter with ring movements as smooth and supple as the cured calf-skin in the brown wing-tips he wore as "el campeon." And one of the first smooth stones to hit the boxing waters and break, in never-ending circles, until half a century later virtually every challenger and champion would be of Hispanic forebears. But we're getting ahead of our story. A story with an accent as well.

THE STORYLINE FOR THE "PICTURE" OF this picture-book fighter starts back in the proud old days of 19-aught-25 near The Prado, Havana's elegant walk-along street. One block away, in a restaurant fronting a flower-drenched square, stood one of those quiet yet comfortable-looking outdoor cafes which beckon to the well-to-do and those who looked well-to-do. On the afternoon in question, nobody looked more well-to-do than the man seated at one of the shaded outdoor tables, a well-appointed gentleman with a well-manicured mustache named Luis "Pincho" Guiterrez, a man about town and about Cuba who, not incidentally, just happened to be the sports editor of *La Noche*, one of the island's leading newspapers. Guiterrez, like many of the other patrons, was idling away his time throwing small coins to some of the urchins of the street who stood, appropriately, in the gutter, away from a part of Havana that was destined never to become part of their lives.

One of those who picked up the coins, as fate and the story would have it, was an ebony 15-year-old newsboy too timid to come close to the railing that separated the two worlds of Havana in 1925. But the coin-tossing became a regular afternoon ritual, an occasion for the two to continue their meetings. And soon Guiterrez got to know the shy youth, finding out that he was an aspiring boxer, one with a streak of lightning in his hands and an ambition in his head to become "el

campeon."

Guiterrez and the boy—then known to Guiterrez as "The Keed" and to his street friends as Eligio Sardinias—formed an alliance, one destined to make "The Keed" "el campeon." But not before the two in concert had determined that collectively they didn't know much about boxing. They decided that the best thing to do was to study the methods of the so-called "masters." And where better to do this than at the local cinema where pictures of boxers were being shown that very afternoon?

As Guiterrez would tell Wilbur Wood of the old-old New York *Sun,* "I had read that Joe Gans had a marvelous left hand. It happened that moving pictures of the Gans-Nelson fight were being shown in Havana. So 'The Keed' and I went to see those pictures every day as long as they were in town. We studied how Gans used his left hand. When the show was over we would go to my house and there 'The Keed' would try to throw his left hand just as Gans did. Study pictures of both Gans and 'The Keed' and you will know that Chocolate's left hand is just like Gans'."

And so, just as the making of the best *Cuba libre* lies in correctly mixing rum, cola, and lemon or lime juice in the right proportions, Guiterrez and "The Keed" began mixing the right proportions of great fighters, seeking the proper balance in their equation of greatness.

"Next, we saw movies of the

Leonard-Tendler fight," Guiterrez went on. "And in that we studied how the great Leonard used his right hand and blocked and feinted and moved around. And 'The Keed' practiced until he could do them as well as Leonard.

"Then we saw the pictures of the Jeffries-Johnson fight and studied how Johnson tied up the mighty Jeffries so easily in the clinches so that he could not make a move. We studied that and practiced it until 'The Keed' had the trick perfect."

And then Guiterrez and "The Keed" mixed them all together, threw in a liberal garnishing of Chocolate, and came up with an amalgam that became known as "The Picture Boxer."

After "practicing these things" both in and out of the ring—becoming world-famous, all over Havana, where he won all 100 of his amateur fights,

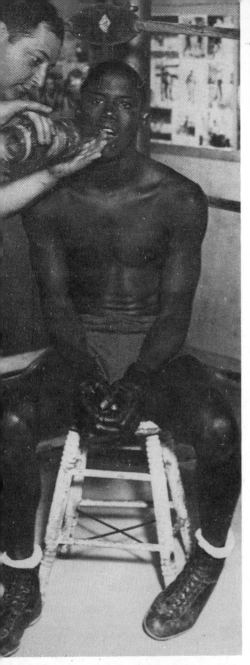

Guiterrez and the Havana Bon Bon sailed for New York. The arrival of this "Picture Boxer" was a sight for sore eyes for wearied New Yorkers, just then beginning to feel the end of the Golden Age of Boxing. All of a sudden, "The Keed" became a crowd favorite in that hallowed mecca of hopes, Madison Square Garden. His classic upright stance, his boxing skill, his defensive agility, and his all-around boxing ability, combined with his windmill style of boxing—his hands ablur as he threw a baker's dozen punches in the time it took to say "Eligio Sardinias"—and his little touches, like tying his laces behind his shoes, made the tall, graceful Cuban one of the most exciting fighters of the day. And a double titleholder in no time, winning the featherweight and junior lightweight titles and challenging for the lightweight and junior

Born Eligio Sardinias, 1/6/10, in Cerro, Cuba . . . First pro bouts, Havana, 1928 . . . Came to New York later that year . . . Undefeated in first 53 bouts (1 draw), 1928–30 . . . Included among 23 victories in 1929 were wins over Bushy Graham, 4/12/29, Fidel LaBarba, 5/22/29, and Al Singer, 8/29/29—all ex-champions or future champions . . . First loss, 10-round decision to Jack Kid Berg, 8/7/30, junior welterweight champion in nontitle bout . . . Lost to Chris "Battling" Battalino in bid for world featherweight title, 12/12/30 . . . Won junior lightweight title from Benny Bass with seventh-round knockout, 7/15/31 . . . Failed in bid for additional titles in 15-round loss to Tony Canzoneri, world lightweight and junior welterweight title holder, 11/20/31 . . . Only man in boxing history to fight for 4 different world titles in less than 12 months—one of very few to fight for 4 world titles in lifetime . . . Defended junior lightweight crown, 4/10/32, via 15-round decision over Davey Abad in Havana, and 8/4/32, over Eddie Shea in 10-round decision . . . Won double-or-nothing bout on 10/13/32—placed junior lightweight title on line while fighting Lew Feldman for vacant N.Y. State world featherweight title, stopped Feldman in twelth round to win title . . . Defended both titles against Fidel LaBarba, 12/9/32, and won 15-round decision . . . 3 more defenses, 1953-5/1/33, Johnny Farr, W 10; 5/19/33, Seaman Tony Watson, W 15; 12/4/33, Frankie Wallace, W 10 . . . Lost junior lightweight title to Frankie Klick on seventh-round TKO, 12/26/33 . . . Relinquished featherweight crown, 2/17/34 . . . Continued boxing until 1938, closed career with streak of 25 wins and 3 draws in last 28 bouts (including 24 bouts in 1937) . . . Unusual record in that he lost most of his bouts during the peak of his career . . . Elected to the Boxing Hall of Fame, 1959 . . . Complete record: 148 bouts, 132 won, 10 lost, 6 draws, 50 knockouts

welterweight crowns.

Soon the Roman candles he had sparked were being held aloft by acolytes to light his deeds. But the candle, burned at both ends by the fun-loving Chocolate, soon began to flicker,

his efforts lumbered by the social disease that ravaged his body. He returned to Havana, there to wind up the career he had started, as boxing's greatest "Picture Fighter."

"The Keed" lands a picture-perfect left on Seaman Tom Watson in defense of his featherweight and junior lightweight titles, May 19, 1933.

PASCUAL PEREZ

36 PASCUAL PEREZ

Greats come in all sizes, but none smaller than Pascual Perez, who looked like any heavyweight who had been caught in a trash compactor. And fought the same way, reducing most of his opponents to candidates for litter bags. Nicknamed "El Terrier," this 4-foot, 10½-inch Lilliputian with the Brobdingnagian punch gave special meaning to the time-honored saying, "It's not the size of the dog in the fight but the size of the fight in the dog," as he personally decimated the entire fifties flyweight population. Pascual Perez desired only what he could accomplish. And he could accomplish almost anything he wanted to inside the four ring posts. But first he had to get past his parents, those two sturdies who offered young Pascual stiffer opposition than most of his opponents, denying him his wish to leave the family vineyards for the greener pastures of the ring.

AGAINST HIS PARENTS' WISHES, PEREZ fought, winning the Argentine amateur flyweight championship four years fighting, and capping his string of successes with a gold medal in the 1948 London Olympics. Still, his parents compelled him to give up his heart's desire, preferring that he toil in the fields at home. But Perez, determined to pursue boxing, merely changed his name to "Pablo Perez" and continued his amateur career. After again winning the Argentine amateur flyweight title in 1950, losing the Pan American Games finals in 1951, and winning three more amateur bouts, Perez decided to try his glove at professional boxing. It was a decision based not so much on going against his parents' wishes as it was on countering his own dire economic predicament: "I was a janitor in the civil service of my government in Mendoza," Perez would remember years later, "and didn't have enough money . . . So I decided to take a chance as a professional. As such, I made the grade," he added with characteristic understatement.

Saying hello to professional boxing at the ancient age of 26 when most others are already saying goodbye, Perez not only made the grade, he set the curve, winning his first 18 pro bouts by

knockout and winning 21 of his first 22 fights by KO. The swarthy, bull-necked little battler with the square shoulder muscles and bushy brows had become a national hero, given superhuman powers by his countrymen.

But then, in his twenty-third fight, in front of thousands of his cheering countrymen at Buenos Aires' Lunar Park Stadium, Perez was held to a draw in a nontitle fight by reigning flyweight champion Yoshio Shirai. Even the most optimistic Argentine didn't expect Perez to fare any better on Shirai's home turf than he had the first time they met. However, they hadn't figured on the dogged desire of "El Terrier," who had gone to Japan with the paramount objective of toppling the flyweight crown from the head of Shirai, even though he couldn't possibly reach the head of his seven-inch-taller opponent.

For 15 rounds, Perez swarmed into Shirai, coming in underneath his gloves and planting his head on either the champion's chest or his navel—whichever came first—all the while working both hands to the body and head and hammering his taller opponent all around the ring. As the short wave commentary carried the unbelievable news back to Buenos Aires, crowds be-

gan to gather in the Plaza de Mayo, hoping against hope that Perez would bring home Argentina's first professional boxing championship. By the time the inevitable decision was announced, the Plaza was packed with a frenzied crowd of some 100,000 worshippers shouting, as they had many times before at political rallies, "Viva Peron! Viva Perez!" commingling, in their excitement, Argentina's two most famous names.

Pascual Perez and Yoshio Shirai were to fight yet again, in that inevitable rematch which always followed the losing of a crown in the fifties. This time, however, the powers-that-be ruled that the title rematch was to be held not in Argentina, which had yet to see its new champion in action, but instead back in

Above: Perez knocks out Yoshio Shirai to retain his flyweight championship, 1955.

Japan. Perez was indignant over the slight to his country, and arrived in Japan filled with resentment over having to make his first title defense back on Shirai's turf.

Shirai didn't help Perez's disposition when, seconds into the fight, Perez turned back to his corner having just discovered that he was without benefit of mouthpiece. The opportunistic Shirai took that occasion to nail the champion on the jaw with a vicious right. There were strings in Perez's heart that were better off not vibrated. Unfortunately, Shirai had found them. Shaking off the effects of the right that would have floored a less hardy warrior, the sturdy Perez came back hellbent on devastation and on bending his opponent in two like a bedsheet. His

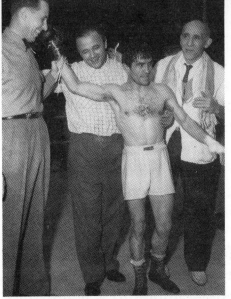

eyes firing and then his gloves, he gave his opponent a fearful battering, leaving the beaten Shirai on his knees as the bell ended the fifth round. There

would never be a sixth round. Nor another in Shirai's future, Perez having literally retired him on the spot. And on the floor.

Having proved that a gamecock can crow just as loudly out of its own backyard as in, Perez returned to Argentina in triumph, a legend of substantial size. Over the next four years, Perez was to bring pride and pleasure to millions of his fellow countrymen as he continued his march through the by-now depleted flyweight ranks, running off 25 more victories and bringing his streak to 51 fights without defeat.

Born 3/4/26, in Tupungate, Mendoza, Argentina . . . Won 1948 Olympic gold medal in flyweight class with 5 victories in 5 bouts . . . Started as professional, 1952 . . . Won first 18 bouts by knockout . . . Won Argentine flyweight title, 11/11/53 . . . Held world champion Yoshio Shirai to 10-round draw in nontitle bout, 7/24/54, was rewarded with title shot . . . Won world flyweight title in his first bout outside of Argentina, 11/26/52, with 15-round decision to Japanese, Yoshio Shirai in Tokyo . . . Won rematch with fifth-round knockout of Shirai, 5/30/55 . . . Made 8 subsequent successful defenses including first-round kayo of Dai Dower, 3/30/57 . . . Also fought 7 nontitle bouts in which title theoretically was at stake, since both boxers were under the weight limit . . . Lost first bout of career in fifty-second bout (1/16/59, Sadao Yaoiata, 10-round decision in Tokyo, nontitle bout) . . . Stopped Yaoita in 13 rounds in title bout, 11/5/59 . . . Lost title to Thai, Pone Kingpetch by decision, 4/16/60, in Bangkok . . . Kayoed by Kingpetch in rematch, 9/22/60 . . . Continued boxing until 1964, including 10 straight knockouts in 1961 . . . Had more career knockouts than all but 2 heavyweight champions . . . Died 1/22/77, in Argentina . . . Elected to Boxing Hall of Fame, 1977 . . . Complete record: 91 bouts, 83 won, 7 lost, 1 draw, 56 knockouts.

But his ring skills, once those of a fighter whose blistering and sustained attack took no survivors, were now beginning to show the gentle and relentless erosion of age, his opponents now ending the fight on their feet where once Perez had been able to look down on their mortal remains from his 4-foot, 10½-inch mountain. Finally, the sand in his fistic hourglass began to sift through rapidly. He lost a ten-rounder to one Sadao Yaoita in Tokyo in 1959 and a 15-rounder, and his title, to Pone Kingpetch in 1960. In the obligatory rematch with Kingpetch, Perez was stopped for the first time in his long career, rescued by the referee in the eighth round.

Incredibly, that did not end the career of Pascual Perez, who would go on to win 28 consecutive fights, 19 by knockout, before the gilt of his ring greatness began peeling off at the very end of his fistic journey.

Small wonder the small wonder known as Pascual Perez is considered one of the all-time greats. The smallest champion of them all, he proved that size alone does not make grandeur any more than territory makes a nation.

TOMMY LOUGHRAN

Tommy Loughran possessed boxing's most talented left, a left that was almost independent of conscious effort. Using his left with all the guile of a pickpocket to pick his opponents clean, Loughran came by his nickname, "The Phantom of Philly," quite naturally. It was that left, in challenger Jim Braddock's face all night, that caused a beaten Braddock to ask after the fight, "Loughran? Has anybody here seen Loughran? I was supposed to fight the guy tonight." He was *that* good. The Loughran left came of necessity. His right hand had betrayed him, become his enemy, the ill-healed bones broken on other men's jaws, the veins so bloated they threatened to rupture, and the gnarled cast of it so unsuited to the "Manly Art of Self-Defense" rendered all but useless. In his first 24 fights, he posted 11 knockouts; in his next 148 fights, he only had 7, so ineffective had his right become.

IT WAS THAT UNCANNY LEFT, COMBINED with skillful displays in the art of boxing and an almost wraithlike presence in the ring that made Loughran next to unbeatable. Loughran not only single-handedly reduced the light heavyweight division into a vast wasteland at the end of this century's third decade, but relinquished his title to campaign among the big boys and to administer boxing lessons to the likes of Max Baer, Paolino Uzcudun, Johnny Risko, Ernie Schaaf, Tuffy Griffiths, King Levinsky, and Steve Hamas amongst many. (In fact, Loughran made such a fool of Baer with his educated left that after several rounds of trying to locate the elusive Loughran with his bombs, the disoriented Californian merely stopped trying and turned to the crowd with his arms extended with a, "What-the-hell-can-you-do?" expression on his befuddled face.)

After years of apprenticing as a middleweight in and around Philadelphia, Loughran got his first big break by answering Jack Dempsey's call-to-arms for fast, clever sparring partners to help him train for the first Tunney fight. The workout made Loughran famous and Dempsey mad, as Loughran handled the heavyweight champion with ease,

avoiding his rushes and his punches with some of the famous finesse he would show in later years. With a win over Jack Delaney in the semifinal event to the "Fight of the Century," Loughran gained more of a following, one he followed up with a win over Mike McTigue the next year for the light heavyweight championship of the world. After defending his newly-minted championship 6 times in the next 21 months (and beating, among others, Mickey Walker, Jimmy Braddock, and Jimmy Slattery), Tommy decided that he would enter the heavyweight tournament being held on the occasion of Gene Tunney's abdication of the crown.

Even though Loughran weighed just 175 pounds, tops, and looked like a choirboy in heavyweight clothing, he was the sentimental—if not the betting—favorite of the boxing crowd to win the tournament. Long viewed by fight afficionados as the lineal descendant of Jim Corbett's scientific boxing, which even extended to his winding up in his own corner at the end of each round, Loughran was, in the words of Jack Johnson, "The only modern boxer I know who can really pick off punches." Floored only 4 times in 117

Opposite top: Loughran easily handles Max Baer. Opposite bottom: He outpoints Braddock in last successful defense before turning heavyweight.

Born 11/29/02, in Philadelphia, PA . . . First bout 1919 . . . Undefeated in first 49 bouts through 1922, although 33 were no-decisions . . . Lost 15-round decision to Harry Greb for "American light heavyweight" title, 1/30/23 . . . Fought 6 bouts with Greb, 1922–24—1 won, 2 lost, 1 draw, 2 no-decisions . . . Won world light heavyweight championship from Mike McTigue in 15-round decision, 10/7/27 . . . Made 6 successful defenses, all by decision, 1927–29: 12/12/27, Jimmy Slattery; 1/6/28, Leo Lomski; 6/1/28, Pete Latzo; 7/16/28, Pete Latzo; 3/8/29, Mickey Walker; 7/18/29, Jim Braddock; (Walker and second Latzo bouts went 10 rounds, others 15) . . . Abandoned title to move to heavyweight class, 1929 . . . Stopped by Jack Sharkey in 3, 9/26/29 . . . Decisioned Max Baer, 2/6/31 . . . Defeated Sharkey in rematch, 9/27/33 . . . Challenged Primo Carnera for world heavyweight title, 3/1/34—outweighed by 86 pounds, 270 to 184—greatest weight difference in a world championship bout, and lost 15-round decision . . . Boxed in South America and Europe, 1934–36 . . . Last bout, 1/18/37 . . . Only 18 knockouts in 172 bouts—one of the lowest KO percentages of all champions . . . Defeated 10 champions in all classes from welterweight to heavyweight . . . Refereed Paterson-Rademacher heavyweight championship bout, 8/22/57 . . . Elected to Boxing Hall of Fame, 1956 . . . Died, 7/7/82, Altoona, PA . . . Complete record: 172 bouts, 96 won, 23 lost, 8 draws, 45 no-decisions, 18 knockouts.

fights and never knocked out, Loughran was a firm believer in the precept that, "They have to hit me to hurt me," adding, "and they can't hit me!"

Unfortunately, Loughran's first opponent in the heavyweight box-off was Jack Sharkey, boxing's version of the little girl with the curl. And on the night he met Loughran, he was very, very good, hitting Loughran in the third with a huge right that exploded in his face and drummed him to the canvas. Up at the count of nine, Loughran wandered over to the referee and asked, "Where's the chair? I want to sit down." Loughran sat down, temporarily, only to stand up again almost five years later to challenge "The Tower of Gorgonzola," Primo Carnera, for the heavyweight crown. Outweighing Loughran by some 89 pounds, Carnera used his weight and his feet—starting with his first foray, a left foot delivered to Loughran's right instep—to win a 15-round decision. Carnera was even to prove himself invulnerable to garlic, Loughran having eaten much of it and rubbed his body with it before the fight to repel the "Ambling Alp." But in the words of Loughran, "He liked it."

Although Tommy Loughran could not vault the moat that forever seems destined to separate the light heavyweight and heavyweight worlds, he will go down in history as one of the past masters of the Sweet Science. No left-handed compliment when applied to one of the greatest left hands of all time.

JIM DRISCOLL

Since the Brits invented the bloody sport of boxing, it was only fair that they would also invent their own standards of fame and octaves heralding their contributions to the game. One of those eight-line chauvinistic verses proclaiming their fistic supremacy went thusly: "Since boxing is a manly game/And Britons recreation/By boxing we will raise our fame/'Bove any other nation./Throw pistols, poniards, swords aside/And let all such deadly tools/Let boxing be the Britons pride/The science of their schools."/By the turn of the century, when fighters were considered animals, and not necessarily of the highest order, the British featherweight known as "Peerless Jim" Driscoll had come to create his own standard. And his own school of boxing as well.

9685

THE DRISCOLL SCHOOL OF BOXING WAS a throwback to the old Belcherian, or Bristol, School of a century earlier. Named after Jim Belcher, the bare-knuckle champion who reigned from 1800 to 1803, the Belcherian School incorporated the hard, quick, and straight-hitting moves of the champion, a style that begot the following comment from a periodical of the time: "You heard his blows, but did not see them. He threw his hits with such adroitness that you could not discern how the damage was done. His style was perfectly original and extremely difficult to avoid or to withstand."

Jim Driscoll was considered by many to be the perfect boxer, his ring artistry and punching perfection held by no less a ring authority than Nat Fleischer to be a "relevation." With a rigid stand-up style and heavy ears belying his elegant movements, Driscoll had a befuddling admixture of punches and an array of moves that often had his opponents looking like contortionists who had finally come into their own, off-balance and at his mercy. And then, Driscoll would "bang them real good," according to one of his great admirers, matchmaker Jimmy Johnston, who added, "He really was smart!"

A product of Cardiff, Driscoll began his career in the boxing booths that abounded in turn-of-the-century South Wales, expanding his sphere of activity to include a few gloved fights in his native town. Still, he was known only to those few in and around Bristol Bay who had seen him or heard of his exploits, his fame extending no farther. It was not until he beat Joe Bowker, then substituting for Johnny Summers, that he began to attract national attention. A second and far more decisive win over Bowker for the vacant British featherweight title and a win over Charlie Griffin for the British Empire featherweight title firmly established Driscoll. And placed him on a pinnacle as one of Great Britain's greats.

With his reputation secured on a national basis, Driscoll sought to enhance his international standing. It was at this point in his career that Charley Harvey, the personification of John Bull, right down to his mutton chops, and his partner, Jimmy Johnston, nicknamed the "Boy Bandit" for reasons other than his youth, brought him over to the Colonies. Going down to the dock to meet their incoming import, they scanned the crowd, without finding anything vaguely resembling their world-beater in sight. One step away from hopping back in their cab, they were approached by a snaggle-tooth "has-been" who looked like he never was, with a terminal case of cauliflower ears. He introduced himself as "Jim Driscoll," his name coming out sounding like "Jem." Johnston, knowing of

Driscoll's reputation as a defensive master, merely stared at this obvious imposter. Without so much as a "How do you do," Johnston, who had done some boxing in his day, threw a punch at "Driscoll," who merely moved his head a sixteenth of an inch one way; then he threw another, and "Driscoll" moved his head imperceptibly the other. Finally, after two or three more shots had hit nothing but wind, the winded Johnston accepted the man's introduction. Later, recounting the story, Johnston would embroider it a little, and then add, "It turned out he had such wonderful reflexes he could dodge a punch by a sixteenth of an inch, and that's how he got his ears so torn up."

Although Driscoll, known in America as "Jem," never weighed more than 9

Above: "Peerless Jim" Driscoll (right) schools Spike Robson in some of boxing's finer points, in successful defense of British featherweight title, 1911.

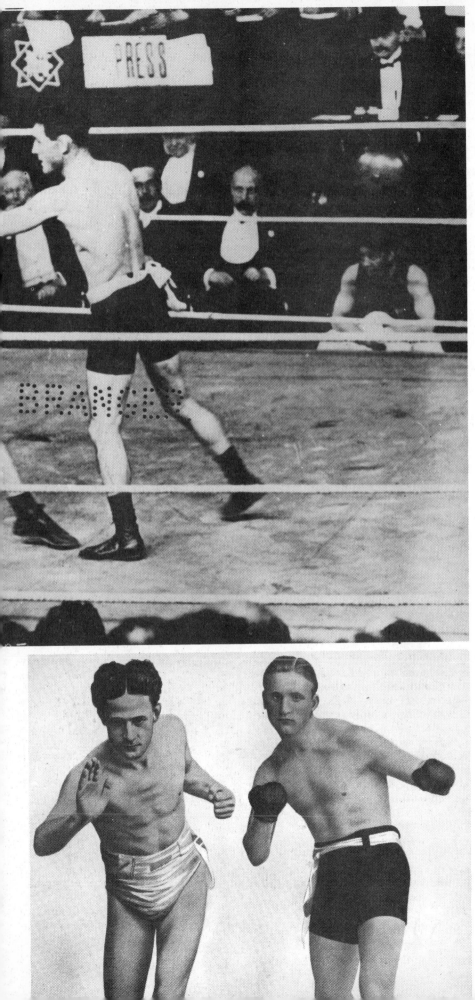

Born 12/15/80, in Cardiff, Wales . . . First pro bout, 1901, Cardiff, Wales . . . Won Welsh featherweight title, 12/24/01, on 10-round decision over Joe Ross . . . Defeated George Dixon in 6-round bout, 1/24/03 Won British featherweight title, 6/3/07, with seventeenth-round knockout of Joe Bowker . . . Won British Empire featherweight title by defeating Charlie Griffin, 2/24/08, on a foul in the fifteenth round . . . Came to U.S. in 1908, fought Matty Baldwin twice, 11/13/08, ND 6 and 12/29/08, W 12 . . . Fought 10-round no-decision with Abe Attell, 12/19/09 . . . Returned to England, 1910 . . . Twelfth-round knockout victory over Jean Poesy, 6/3/12, to win vacant European featherweight title; the bout was recognized in Britain as world title bout . . . Defended against Owen Moran in 20-round draw, 1/27/13 . . . Relinquished titles, 1913 . . . Inactive during war years, 1914—18 . . . Fought 3 bouts in 1919, then retired . . . Died, 1/31/25, in Cardiff, Wales . . . Elected to Boxing Hall of Fame 1956 . . . Complete record: 69 bouts, 52 won, 3 lost, 6 draws, 8 no-decisions, 35 knockouts.

stones—or 126 pounds—he fought several of the hardest-hitting lightweights of the day, including Leach Cross, Matty Baldwin, John Marto, Tommy Langdon, and Grover Hayes.

But it was to be his fight with Abe Attell that would forever cement his greatness. In a fight called by Nat Fleischer, "one of the best exhibitions of ring science ever seen in New York," Driscoll moved around the man thought to be the greatest ring scientist ever seen with an elegance and ease, feinting him into openings, which, like a vacuum, he filled with lefts, ducking and sidestepping Attell's every move, countering continually, all the while keeping his straight left in Attell's *punim*. In a day and age when no-decision fights were boxing's speakeasy answer to total prohibition of the sport, all Driscoll had to show for his magnificent efforts after ten one-sided rounds was a no-decision. But it begot him fame and recognition, the boxing public now accepting him as the undisputed, if uncrowned, champion. And a nickname, "Peerless Jim," coined by former gunslinger-turned-word-slinger, Bat Basterson.

Asked to remain in America by one of his sponsors, Jimmy Johnston, Driscoll responded, "Jimmy, my friend, this isn't a bad place. But it isn't home, now is it? I miss Cardiff and I miss London. And you don't want me to forget my wife and kiddies, now do you?" And with that, he left to return to his wife and kiddies and his Lonsdale Belt.

But even though "Peerless Jim" would leave America and four years afterward leave boxing—forever, except for an ill-fated comeback—he also would leave his legacy: a school named in his honor to rank with the Mendoza and Belcher Schools that would stand for the English School of boxing. And excellence.

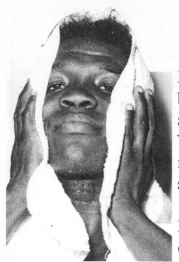

39 EMILE GRIFFITH

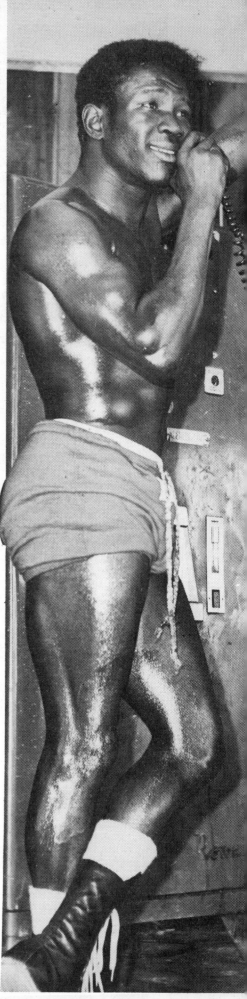

Madison Square Garden is at once a building and a symbol. But it has not always been thus. Originally a New York, New Haven & Hartford Railroad freight yard and depot, the structure had been converted in 1874 by none other than P.T. Barnum into a magnificent hall called the Great Roman Hippodrome. That first night 15,000 curiosity seekers who crammed into the Hippodrome were treated to a veritable Circus Maximus: Arabian horses, waltzing elephants, cowboys and Indians, tattooed men, chariots driven by women, fire-eaters, and just about everything else imaginable. Three incarnations and 94 years later the fourth Madison Square Garden opened its doors to the public for the first time with a boxing double feature—Emile Griffith defending his world middleweight crown against Nino Benvenuti in front of some 20,000-plus fans. This was only fitting, Emile Griffith having fought more main events in the Garden—Gardens III and IV—than any other headliner in history.

BUT TO CALL EMILE GRIFFITH MERELY A "house" fighter is to do an injustice to one of the foremost scrappers of all time. For not only had Griffith settled permanently in boxing's mecca, but he had also settled in the hearts of its fans as well, where they never recognize a trend until it has become a tradition.

In his prime, when he won the world welterweight title for the first time—the first of his five championships; six, if one counts European recognition of his junior middleweight title—he was a "Y"-shaped youngster with a pinch waist and shoulders big enough to support water buckets, with a sparkling style of fighting to match the sparkle that danced and played in his dark eyes. Moving around the ring with all the grace of a ballet dancer, he would employ his formidable right and snaky left, which snapped out like a towel popping—pop! pop!—to maneuver his opponent into a position where he could corner him.

One horrible night he surrounded his opponent, Benny "Kid" Paret, in a corner and, made berserk by "mean sayings by Paret," avenged an unen-

durable insult with a homicidal assault. Afterward, the normally happy-go-lucky Griffith, still smoldering like a volcano at Paret's words which had hit like bullets, could only say, "A man who wants to fight for the title must gamble." Paret did, and lost, both his title and his life in a miscalculated gamble that cost him everything.

Normally, however, never was heard a discouraging word from the voluble Mr. Griffith. After he had been knocked out in one round by Ruben "Hurricane" Carter—only one of two times in his 112-fight career that he failed to finish or be in at the finish—Emile, seated on a rubbing table in his dressing room, looked out to see boxing's version of the Inquisition, the press, gathered around and palpably ill at ease as to how to begin their professional probing. It being just five days shy of Christmas, Emile broke the ice by chanting, in his sing-song Virgin Island accent, "Merry Christmas to you," and followed with an ear-to-ear smile that split his face. And the silence.

That was the Emile Griffith the press and the public knew and loved. For the

100

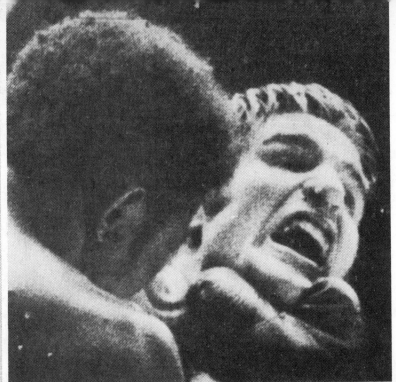

man who always fought just well enough to win and had renewed flagging interest in the welterweight division by winning the title for the first time—one of two titles he held and reheld almost as if they were on a rubber-band umbilicus—lit up boxing and Madison Square Garden as much, if not more, than any boxer in history.

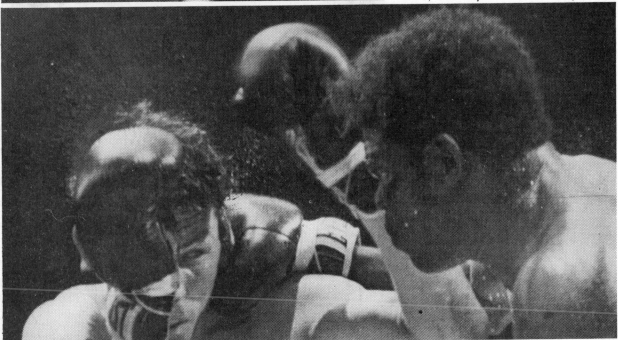

Top: Griffith regains middleweight title from Nino Benvenuti, 1967. Bottom: Griffith vs. Joey Archer, 1966.

Born Emile Alphonse Griffith, 2/3/38, in St. Thomas, U.S. Virgin Islands . . . Won New York Golden Gloves titles, 1957–58, also Eastern Regional and Intercity Golden Gloves, 1958 . . . Only 1 knockout in 14 Golden Gloves bouts . . . Began professional boxing career in 1958 in New York, won 22 of 24 in first 3 years . . . Defeated Benny Kid Paret, 4/1/61, with thirteenth-round knockout to win world welterweight title . . . Defended successfully, 6/3/61, against Gaspar Ortega, twelfth-round kayo . . . Lost title to Paret, 9/30/61, via 15-round decision . . . Rubber match with Paret, 3/24/62, ended in tragedy as Paret never regained consciousness after twelfth-round knockout—ironic in that Griffith was never known for knockout punch, either as amateur or pro . . . Decisioned Ted Wright in Vienna, 10/17/62, for world junior middleweight title . . . Defended welterweight title twice (Ralph Dupas, 7/13/62, W 15; Jorge Fernandez, 12/8/62, KO 9) before losing title by decision to Luis Manuel Rodriguez, 3/21/63 . . . Won title for third time in rematch with Rodriguez, 6/8/63 . . . Became world traveler in 1964 with nontitle bouts in Australia, Italy, and Hawaii and title defenses in U.S. and England . . . Won world middleweight title from Dick Tiger, 4/25/66, via 15-round decision . . . Relinquished welterweight title in mid-1966 . . . Defended middleweight crown twice against Joey Archer, 7/13/66 and 1/23/67 . . . Lost title to Nino Benvenuti, 4/17/67 . . . Rewon crown from Benvenuti, 9/29/67, first man to regain both welter and middleweight titles . . . Lost title again to Benvenuti in first bout in new Madison Square Garden, 3/4/68 . . . Continued boxing for 10 more years with 4 unsuccessful bids to recapture titles: 10/18/69, Jose Napoles, welterweight title, L 15; 9/25/71, Carlos Monzon, middleweight title, KO 14; 6/2/73, Carlos Monzon, middleweight title, L 15; 9/18/76, Eckhard Dagge, WBC junior middleweight title, L 15 . . . Retired from active competition after 7/30/77, loss to Alan Minter . . . Fought 22 recognized world championship bouts (won 14, lost 8) and also had 4 other bouts of limited title recognition . . . Fought in 5 continents, 12 foreign countries, as well as Hawaii, Puerto Rico, and U.S. Virgin Islands . . . Became trainer after retirement from active boxing . . . Elected to Boxing Hall of Fame, 1981 . . . Complete record: 112 bouts, 85 won, 24 lost, 2 draws, 1 no-contest, 23 knockouts.

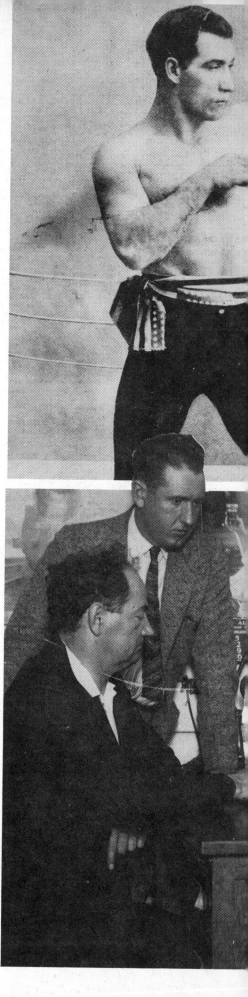

40 "KID" McCOY

"KID" McCOY

Charles "Kid" McCoy jumped out of the womb a born hustler. He played his scams across the early face of boxing with all the breeze, bluff, and buncombe of a claim jumper, becoming the middleweight champ and the shrewdest boxer the ring has ever known. His calling card was the famous "corkscrew" punch, a punch which gave him the curious ability to cut up an opponent and which was the forerunner of the twisting, slashing left made famous by Sandy Saddler a half century later. A perpetual student of the game, McCoy had developed the corkscrew punch after watching his kitten toying with a cloth ball. He noticed that the kitty's paw came toward the ball at an angle instead of in a straight line, punctuated by a twist at the end, similar to the spin given a bullet by the riffling in a barrel.

PRACTICING HIS NEW-FOUND PUNCH on a bag of cement, he found that he could reduce the dry cement into powder. McCoy's opponents felt the same way, one describing his corkscrew as feeling like "a telephone pole had been driven into my stomach sideways."

Although never more than a natural middleweight, McCoy fought elephantine men who dwarfed him in size, taking on men like Joe Choynski, Tom Sharkey, Peter Maher, Jack Root, Philadelphia Jack O'Brien, Jack "Twin" Sullivan, Gus Ruhlin, and James J. Corbett, all leading heavyweights of the time—and more than made up for his lack of size with a ring ingenuity, grace, and generalship never equaled.

The Kid stopped at little. One of his favorite tricks was wrapping his knuckles up in mounds of friction tape, all the better to stab his opponents' faces apart, giving them the look of second-place finishers in knife fights. He practiced his ring witchcraft on many, dropping tacks on the floor to beat a barefoot South African who had stopped to investigate the strange tingling on the bottoms of his soles, and once beat a Gallic lady's man by asking him during combat, "Who is that mademoiselle in the stands?" and then delivering the famed McCoy right to *le*

Opposite top and bottom: Losers to McCoy, Joe Choynski and Jack Sullivan. Left: McCoy with heavyweight Tom Sharkey. Bottom left: McCoy questioned by LA detectives after he shot his ninth wife.

Born Norman Selby, 10/13/72, in Rush County, IN . . . Began as a pro, 1891 . . . Fought early years in Midwest . . . Knocked out welterweight champion Tommy Ryan, 3/2/96, credited by some sources as being world welterweight champion as a result of this bout, but never claimed title . . . Defeated Mysterious Billy Smith on sixth-round foul, 5/18/96 . . . Knocked out George LaBlanche and Beach Ruble in first round, each on same night, 11/12/97 . . . Won vacant world middleweight title with 15-round kayo of Dan Creedon, 12/17/97 . . . Never defended title . . . Scored 13 consecutive knockouts, 1897–98 . . . Knocked out Peter Maher in fifth round, 1/1/00 . . . Knocked out by Jim Corbett in 5 rounds, 8/30/00 . . . Knocked out 3 men in 1 night, 12/2/01, in London, England . . . Fought Jack Root in first world light heavyweight championship bout—lost 10-round decision . . . Continued boxing on and off until 1916 . . . Died by own hand, 4/18/40, Detroit, MI . . . Elected to Boxing Hall of Fame, 1957 . . . Complete record: 105 bouts, 81 won, 6 lost, 6 draws, 9 no-decisions, 3 no-contests.

whiskers when his French opponent made a mistake, turning his head for a *voir-see* a moment too long. But perhaps his most famous ring scam was one he practiced on Jack Wilkes, a man billed as the champion middleweight of the Southwest. On the night of the fight, the normally pale and delicate-looking McCoy employed a gambit that would have made Sarah Bernhardt proud: He had powdered his face with a liberal dose of talcum and feigned illness in his corner. Wilkes, believing that his opponent was "too weak and ill to fight anyone," spent the entire first round trying to inflict little or no damage to the damaged merchandise masquerading as his opponent. But in the second McCoy tore out of his corner like a tornado and finished off his supposed benefactor with a left to the solar plexus. It was vintage McCoy.

Kid McCoy left yet another legacy to boxing. And to the English language. As one of the many stories goes, it was in one of the Kid's favorite watering holes that he was once approached by someone who had eyes for the blonde the Kid was squiring. "Beat it, bum," he said. "My name's Kid McCoy." "Yeah?" supposedly replied the interloper. "Well, my name's Gesundheit," (or something to that effect) "and you don't look like no fighter to me." The Kid's right hand came over to emphasize his point, and one hour later when his quasi-antagonist recovered, he rubbed his chin and was reputed to have said, "That was the *real* McCoy!"

Today there is still only one *real* McCoy, one of boxing's legends—the man who invented "the corkscrew" and thought the same way.

JAMES J. CORBETT

James J. Corbett straddled the two worlds of boxing at the turn of the century like the Colossus of Rhodes, uniting the rough-and-tumble world of the bareknuckle days with the futuristic world of the Marquis of Queensberry. His technical virtuosity, underwritten with speed, would forever be recognized as beginning the "scientific school" of boxing—and would date everything from before his advent as B.C., Before Corbett. The history of prizefighting would turn forever on the substantial skills of "Gentleman" Jim Corbett, a slight, 6-foot 1-inch fashion plate who came out of San Francisco to challenge the invincible John L. Sullivan for the heavyweight championship of the world—and to challenge the inviolate standards that had dominated boxing for more than a century. Corbett would upset both.

THE YOUNG BANK CLERK WITH HAIR SO black it made his face seem bleached had made a career out of beating the best amateurs on the northern and Barbary coasts. He had also made a reputation for himself extending the entire length and breadth of the Olympic Club. Corbett would add to his notoriety with a 27-round knockout of his crosstown rival, Joe Choynski, in what was called by Billy Delaney, who handled both Corbett and Jeffries, "the hardest heavyweight battle I have ever seen. . . . For cleverness, gameness and endurance displayed, I've never seen it's equal."

Corbett further bolstered his fame by besting Jake Kilrain, the one-time claimant to the bareknuckle championship, only to then challenge the great Australian black heavyweight, Peter Jackson, a man even John L. Sullivan had sidestepped drawing something he called the "color line." In a 61-round fight, using gloves and the Marquis of Queensberry rules, these two greats tried everything at their disposal. Fighting like tigers, each took everything the other could throw and came back with his own. Finally, after 61 rounds of blood-letting, the referee stepped into the middle of the ring and declared the bout "No Contest . . . as neither Corbett or Jackson is able to continue. . . .

" After the exhausting marathon, Jackson was overheard saying, "Corbett, Corbett, James J. Corbett. A truly great fighter."

The draw was a disappointment to Corbett but a revelation to his followers who had just seen their hero hold at bay the man the great John L. had refused to fight. Now the name Corbett was linked to Sullivan. And when Sullivan issued a challenge to "any and all bluffers to fight me," citing specifically "James J. Corbett, who has uttered his share of bombast. . . ," the fight was arranged to be held in New Orleans on September 7, 1892. It was a fight that would change the course of boxing history.

In fact, the fight was no fight at all. It was Corbett three furlongs in front of John L. the entire time, fighting in balletic arcs around his prey, much like a moth tempting a flame, while never coming close enough to damage its wings. For 20 rounds, Corbett, using footwork of a sort previously unknown, had turned the huge suffocating bear once known as John L. into a dancing bear. Then, in the twenty-first, the most important round in boxing history, Corbett lowered the boom, raining blows on the helpless heap before him. Wobbling under the cumulative effect of the nonstop assault, Sullivan took a

right to the ear and a left to the jaw, and then pitched forward, the soon-to-be ex-champion of the world.

A portcullis had fallen, a new age in boxing had dawned: James J. Corbett was the new heavyweight champion. And even though he would lose his prized possession to Bob Fitzsimmons—to then, in one of the greatest comeback fights in ring history outpoint Jim Jeffries for 23 of the 25 rounds only to lose when his aging vitality deserted him—he would always wear his crown with grace and aplomb,

suggesting proud ring virtues, For James J. Corbett had served as the mid-wife of modern-day boxing, replacing strength with skill and immobility with finesse. Boxing will be forever indebted to him.

Below right: Corbett, right, fends off Bob Fitz-simmons' probing left in early rounds of "Solar Plexus" fight, March 17, 1897.

Born James John Corbett, 9/1/66, in San Francisco, CA . . . Known as "Gentleman Jim" . . . Early record sketchy, fought both amateurs and professionals, 1884 . . . Fought in transition era, bareknuckles, skin-tight gloves, and padded (5 oz.) gloves . . . 3 bouts with Joe Choynski, 1889—5/30/89, 2 oz. gloves, stopped by police in fourth; 6/5/89, (held on a barge), kayoed Choynski in twenty-seventh; 7/15/89, won 4-round bout . . . Bout with Dave Campbell, 7/29/89, called draw after 10 rounds when Corbett failed to score knockout as agreed . . . Defeated Jake Kilrain via 6-round decision, 2/18/90, 5 oz. gloves . . . Boxed Peter Jackson for 61 rounds, 5/2/91, bout declared no-contest by referee, Hiram Cook, after neither fighter threw a single punch in the sixty-first round; elapsed time, 4 hours and 5 minutes; battling actually ended after twenty-fifth round when Jackson's shoulder and Corbett's right arm were severely damaged . . . Won world heavyweight championship, 9/7/92, in first world heavyweight title bout under Marquis of Queensberry rules—huge underdog, outweighed by 34 pounds (178 to 212), knocked out John L. Sullivan in twenty-first round . . . Seconded by Jack Demp-sey, the Nonpareil, for defense against Charley Mitchell, 1/25/94—won by third-round kayo . . . Appeared on London and Broadway stages, 1895 . . . Scheduled bout with Bob Fitzsimmons, 11/3/95, Dallas, called off due to adverse legislation, Fitzsimmons arrested . . . Announced retirement, 11/11/95, presented championship belt to Peter Maher . . . Finally matched with Fitzsimmons, 3/17/97, lost title when stopped in fourteenth round. . . . Lost on foul to Tom Sharkey, 11/22/98 . . . Challenged Jim Jeffries for heavyweight title, 5/11/00, knocked out in twenty-third round . . . Defeated Kid McCoy, 8/30/00, with ninth-round kayo . . . Final bout, 8/14/03, again challenged Jeffries for heavyweight title, again knocked out, tenth round . . . Had 19 recorded bouts, fewest of any heavyweight champion . . . Autobiography, The Roar of the Crowd, 1925 . . . Auto-biographical movie, "Gentleman Jim", starred Errol Flynn, 1942 . . . Died, 2/18/33, in Bayside, NY . . . Street in Bayside (Corbett Street) named for him . . . Charter member of Boxing Hall of Fame, 1954 . . . Complete record: 19 bouts, 11 won, 4 lost, 2 draws, 2 no-contests, 7 knockouts.

42 BILLY CONN

BILLY CONN

Whenever shall we see the likes of a Billy Conn again? A feisty, brash little leprechaun who fought every fight with all the bravado of somebody going down aboard an ocean liner humming "Nearer My God to Thee . . . " Billy Conn was the prototypical Irish sprite, a charmingly raffish character with an elfin grin and a puckish stance; so elfin, in fact, that if ever a fighter could tug at a forelock with his gloves on, Conn would have been the one to do so. Bringing to the ring all the blarney and headstrong qualities of the "ould sold," this more spectacular version of Tommy Loughran was able to weave castles in the air with his fists and leave trails of gold with his fistic triumphs, spun over the greats and near-greats of the late thirties with his skills as a clever fighter, rather than as a boxer. What very few remember about this little kid with the honest bustle who started as a skinny elbowy welterweight and worked his way to the cusp of the heavyweight championship is that along the way he worked his way through the boxing alphabet, too, taking the measure of no less than ten men who held titles at one time or another—from A to Z: Fred Apostoli, Melio Bettina, Young Corbett III, Vince Dundee, Solly Kreiger, Gus Lesnevich, Babe Risko, Teddy Yarosz, Tony Zale, and Fritzie Zivic.

NEVER FED A SCHEDULE OF STIFFS, Conn took them all on, beating them with his speed of foot, his agility of hand and the balls of a cat burglar. In one fight, local rival Oscar Rankins floored Conn early in the fight with a straight right. Conn arose and, through the fogbanks of his memory, proceeded to bang out a ten-round decision. Afterward, he apologized to his manager, John Ray, for "getting knocked out," still not knowing he had won. That was Billy Conn, an artistic practitioner who always got his job done.

After having won the light heavyweight championship and defending it three times, Conn crossed the divisional Rubicon and tried his hand in the heavyweight division. Very successfully, thank you!, as he beat Bob Pastor, Al McCoy, Lee Savold, Gunnar Barlund, and Buddy Knox—three of them by

knockout. Suddenly, Conn began to harbor a desire to try for the heavyweight championship of the world, then held by the immortal Joe Louis. It sounded like whistling in the dark, even from the brash "Pittsburgh Kid."

Both Joe Louis and promoter Mike Jacobs were tiring of that group of life's losing stuntmen labeled by Falstaffian writer Jack Miley "The Bum-of-the-Month Club," who had been half-led, half-carried into the ring in the past six months. They were looking for something new, something fresh. And there was nothing newer or fresher than Conn.

In a scenario that has been repeated time and again since David and Goliath, a great little man went out to battle a great big man on June 18, 1941, at the old Polo Grounds. The great little man was Billy Conn, who weighed in at

Right: Conn, left, moves away from Joe Louis, 1941. Far right: Conn, left, smothers attack of Tony Zale, 1942.

174½ pounds against the great big man, Louis, who scaled 199½. It was to be boxer versus puncher. Machine gun versus howitzer.

Conn's consummate boxing skill, with his flashy left hand the centerpiece, made him a lineal descendant of Gentleman Jim Corbett, the first of the great scientific boxers. Conn could block punches with his arms, elbows, and gloves, and further nullify his opponent's punches by "rolling" with them. Even when hit, Conn had remarkable recuperative powers, having been knocked down only twice in his career and having gotten up both times. If there was any rap against Conn, it was that he was headstrong. But bumptious Billy was determined not to let that happen. "I know that I have lost my temper in some fights," the strong-willed challenger said before the fight, "but you can bet I won't this time." And bet his followers did, bringing the last-minute odds down to 11-5, making him the shortest-priced underdog in a heavyweight title fight against Louis since Max Schmeling.

Forgetting that while being wrong is an occupational hazard in most of life, in boxing it's endemic, many of those in the crowd of 60,071 believed Conn could do it. Members of the press, such as Hype Igoe and Willard Mullin, picked the "Pittsburgh Kid." So too, did several members of the busted-beak fraternity, including champions like Jim Braddock, Fred Apostoli, Gus Lesnevich, Lew Jenkins, and Fritzie Zivic. And they were almost right!

Starting out like Leon Errol on a casting call, Conn stumbled around the ring in the first round, almost falling from fright. Finally getting his ring legs. But by the third, he was swatting Louis with his quick left, and when he turned the other cheek, swatting him there too. His in-and-out, hit-and-run tactics, punctuated by quick combinations, first flustered Louis, then caused him to hold on. Whenever Louis got through his defense, mostly to the body with wrist-deep punches, Conn dashed out of difficulty or tied up Louis before he could follow up his momentary advantage. And then, in the twelfth, the hunted became the hunter as Conn, his eyes razor-sharp taking in all the deliciousness of the moment and of his opponent's exposed chin, caught Louis in a savage exchange, staggering the champion with a left hook to the jaw. Louis's mouth flew open as much with

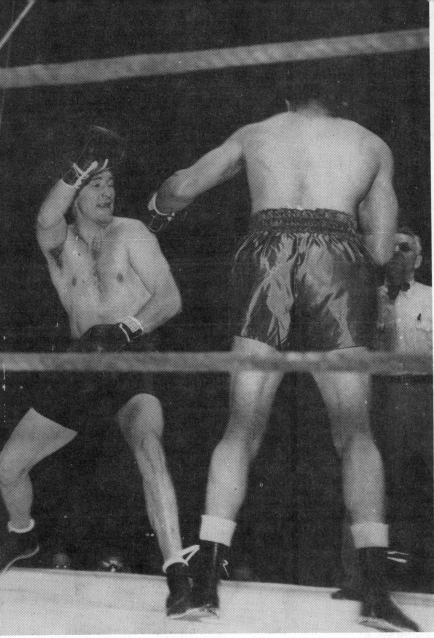

surprise at the audacity of the blow as with the blow itself. At the bell the crowd was on its feet.

But Conn, who only had to stay in command for the final three rounds, had determined on a course of slugging it out with the seemingly faltering champ. Unknowingly, he had chosen a course of dancing at his own wake. For Louis, revived by the smell of ammonia burning in his nostrils and the ringing words of his trainer Jack Blackburn—"You've got to knock him out to win"—stinging his ears, went out for the past 12 rounds hell-bent on destroying his tormentor. And, as Conn tried to pick up where he left off, Louis landed a hard right of his own, jerking Conn's head back. Louis followed up with three more hard rights to Conn's jaw. But, unfaithful to his prefight prediction that he would run away to stay another day, Conn fought back. Turning as slowly as a leaden door, the cham-

pion now set his sights on Conn, who stood his ground, much like a prisoner lighting a cigarette without a blindfold, unmindful of what fate had in store for him. Louis followed with a volley of rights and lefts to Conn's head. Yet another right to the head spun Conn partway around and he fell, as if he were filmed in slow motion, there to take the ten count looking like a carney doll waiting to be claimed.

Afterward, Caswell Adams of *The Herald Tribune* best summed up Billy Conn: "It was nationality that cost Conn the title. If he hadn't been Irish, he would have won. But being Irish, he wanted to finish it the way all Irishmen want to finish a fight. He wound up on the floor, hoping Irish legs would save what Irish spirit had thrown away, the heavyweight championship." And in his dressing room, Conn himself acknowledged that he had shown the stubbornness born of Irishness by saying,

"What's the use in being Irish if you can't be thick?"

That was Billy Conn, professional Irishman and professional boxer. And great at being both.

Born William David Conn, Jr., 10/8/17, in East Liberty, PA . . . Began pro career, 1935, Pittsburgh, PA . . . Lost 6 of 18 in first year . . . Undefeated in 19 bouts in second year, including decision over Fritzie Zivic, 12/28/36 . . . Defeated 4 ex-champions in 1937, scored decisions over Babe Risko, Vince Dundee, Teddy Yarosz, and Young Corbett, III . . . Defeated middleweight champion Fred Apostoli twice in nontitle bouts, 1938 . . . Won vacant world light heavyweight title with 15-round decision over Melio Bettina, 7/13/39 . . . Defended title successfully twice against Gus Lesnevich, 11/17/39 and 6/5/40, both 15-round decisions . . . Relinquished light heavyweight crown to campaign as a heavyweight, May 1941 . . . Challenged Joe Louis for heavyweight title, 6/18/41, nearly won but was knocked out with 2 seconds left in the thirteenth round . . . In military service, 1943—45 . . . Rematch with Louis for heavyweight title ended in eighth-round knockout victory for Louis . . . Won 2 final bouts in 1948 with ninth-round knockouts, surprising ending to career since only 12 kayos in 73 prior bouts . . . Boxed 6-round exhibition with Louis in final ring appearance, 12/10/48 . . . Elected to Boxing Hall of Fame, 1965 . . . Complete record: 75 bouts, 63 won, 11 lost, 1 draw, 14 knockouts.

43 JAKE LaMOTTA

JAKE LaMOTTA

Jake LaMotta. His name evokes memories of a fighter who had no passing familiarity with the canvas; "The Bronx Bull," who brought the strategy of "Playing Possum" to life, charading as a beaten fighter one second and then, the trap sprung, coming back to life to catch a surprised opponent with a devastating fusillade the next; the only fighter to beat Sugar Ray Robinson in the Sugarman's first 132 fights; and the man who incensed some of the more sensitive boxing fans by admitting to a Senate subcommittee that he had "thrown" a fight to Billy Fox. Jake LaMotta was all these things—and more. He was a throwback to the barge fighter, one to whom every fight was a war with no survivors taken; a rough-and-tumble fighter who gave every fan his money's worth; and a fighter whose name was never taken in vain when the words "art" or "science" were employed. He was, indeed, "The Raging Bull," and that was the basis of his fame.

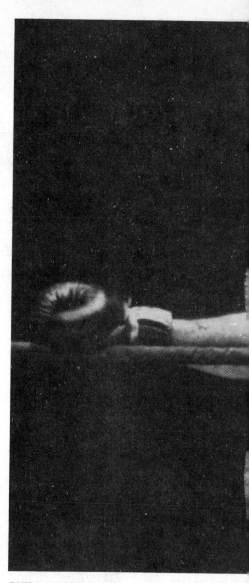

BUT LaMOTTA WAS A CURIOUS PIECE OF goods as well. His fists—messengers of some outlaw corner of his psyche—were as delicate as those of a concert pianist, forcing him to eschew the head and direct his attack almost exclusively to the body. His heart was that of a thoroughbred trapped inside the body of a mule. His body was that of a short, squat fireplug, physically full enough to qualify as a heavyweight or light heavyweight—both of which he had been in his earlier movies—and yet housing a full-fledged middleweight. And his style was that of a street kid, no subtlety, no finesse, just straightforward, unabashed balls-out mauling.

To LaMotta, fighting was a personal statement. He fought with an anger that seemed as if it would spring forth from the top of his head like a volcanic eruption. And yet it was just this crowd-pleasing, bull-like style that made being a street kid a negotiable commodity. And made LaMotta popular.

Together with Jake's "knock-the-stick-off-my-shoulder" approach to boxing was his style. Or lack of it. In a fighter, a stance is as expressive as a punch. With his legs fully planted—as if they had been glued to the floor—and spread akimbo to support his massive frame, LaMotta challenged anyone to knock him off his pins. Even in the face of Sugar Ray Robinson's onslaught in their sixth fight, forever known as "The St. Valentine's Day Massacre," there was no unconditional surrender by LaMotta to undeniable facts. He withstood the assault and stood upright on legs that were strangers to him, absorbing Robinson's barrage like a sponge. One could almost hear the sound of metal fatigue as the ironman sagged, crumbled, but never fell.

But if in the ring he was his opponent's worst enemy, outside of it he was his own. As a bona fide street kid, LaMotta never trusted the establishment; in fact, he never trusted anyone.

To some, he was the kind of guy even a Dale Carnegie would have hit in the mouth. Denied a title shot, which he thought was his divine right after he had savaged the middleweight division, LaMotta, no stranger to the cliquey clubhouses of boxing, sold his soul to boxing's landlords. He indulged in several odiferous bouts, including the Billy Fox bout—which paid the last installment of his dues—and finally got his title shot against Marcel Cerdan, winning it after Cerdan retired with a torn shoulder, compliments of being wrestled to the canvas by "The Bronx Bull."

Other times, LaMotta, believing he was indeed "The Raging Bull," would take hormone shots while reducing on a diet of water and water to make the weight. His hands and his body were up for retirement long before he even began to think of retiring, so sure was he that he could "play possum" with fate much as he had with his opponents.

But even if Jake LaMotta's greatness is the hypocritical homage virtue must pay to vice, he was great nevertheless. And that's no "Bull."

Born Giacobe LaMotta, 7/10/22, in the Bronx, NY . . . First pro bout, 1941, New York City . . . Lost 10-round decision to Ray Robinson, 10/2/42 . . . Avenged loss by defeating Robinson, 2/5/43, first professional loss for Robinson after 40 victories . . . Lost rubber match 3 weeks later . . . Beat Fritzie Zivic in 3 of 4 bouts, 1943–44 . . . Won 10 of 12 with 7 knockouts in 1945 (only 2 losses to Robinson) . . . Only 10 knockouts in previous 4 years . . . Stopped in fourth round by Billy Fox, 11/14/47, in tainted bout . . . Knocked out Marcel Cerdan in 10 rounds to win world middleweight title, 6/16/49, only fourth loss for Cerdan and first by knockout . . . Cerdan killed en route to rematch . . . Successfully defended twice: 7/12/50, Tiberio Mitri, W 15 and 9/13/50, Laurent Dauthuille, KO 15 . . . Lost title to Ray Robinson, 2/14/51, via thirteenth-round knockout . . . Continued in the ring until 1954 but did not receive another title shot . . . Won more bouts by decision than by knockout, unusual for middleweight class . . . Nicknamed "The Bronx Bull" . . . Biography, *Raging Bull*, made into motion picture starring Robert DeNiro as LaMotta . . . Complete record: 106 bouts, 83 won, 19 lost, 4 draws, 30 knockouts.

Left: LaMotta, wife Vikki and their three little champs. Above: After being gored by Sugar Ray Leonard, 1951.

MAXIE ROSENBLOOM

"You couldn't hit him in the backside with a handful of buckshot," said trainer Cus D'Amato of this original American tintype, Maxie Rosenbloom, arguably the best defensive boxer in the history of the sport. A member of the jab-and-grab club, Rosenbloom was a bona fide "cutie" who gave his opponents very little to hit, throwing his "tush" up at them, crouching low to the floor, and, in his eccentric style, doing everything he could to keep from getting hit. He was so good at not getting hit that he was the only fighter Joe Louis ever ducked, not because he couldn't beat Rosenbloom, but because he wouldn't look good and couldn't knock him out. But, then again, very few could; Rosenbloom suffering only two knockouts in 289 fights.

ON THE OTHER GLOVE, ROSENBLOOM'S offensive arsenal was comparable to the 1906 Chicago White Sox, "The Hitless Wonders" of baseball; he had no knockout punch, KO-ing just 18 of his 289 opponents.

His best punches were of no special consequence, delivered in a slapping, open-handed manner; hence his nickname, "Slapsie" Maxie. But they made up cumulatively for their deficiency in power, coming 13 to the dozen, the last merely to attract the attention of the judges. His left was akin to an umbrella thrust by a lady weighing approximately 80 pounds; his right he called a "potch." It was his ringmanship that won him his bouts and the light heavyweight title.

Rosenbloom was a globetrotter who took his act on the road to more places than Hope and Crosby ever imagined, fighting along the highways and byways of America, all the better to shake the money from the rubes. In one month, December 1932, he fought—and

won—in Stockton, San Jose, San Francisco, Albuquerque, and Chicago. It got so that his manager, Frankie Bachman, only asked, "If we win can we at least get a draw?", which may account for the 23 draws on Rosenbloom's record.

However, another reason Rosenbloom had to take his title on the road was because he was about as exciting as watching a tree form its annual ring. His style was the kind that would cure insomnia and it was hinted that vendors would package hot dogs to go during his fights. Dan Parker once wrote of Slapsie, "Is it the cheese that fills the breeze/ with rare and deadly perfume?/ Oh, no, it isn't the cheese, It's Rosenbloom" to the tune of "Love in Bloom" to explain Rosenbloom's somewhat boring style.

But Rosenbloom made up in excitement outside the ring what he failed to supply inside the ropes, viewing training with about the same affection as welcoming towns viewed the invading Huns. More often than not, he would remain out all night prior to a fight and have a good time on the day of the battle itself, then romp off with the victory. Add to this his working *un*familiarity with the English language—he once turned to his manager who was pleading with him to "open up" and said, "This guy might nail me. You want me to get 'conclusion' of the brain?"— and the time he found himself out of cash to pay his chauffeur and paid him off by driving him around—and you have a boxing original, as well as its greatest defensive fighter.

Left to right: Rosenbloom, left, pushes and punches Ad Heuser in defense of light heavyweight title, 1933. Rosenbloom, left, slaps Abie Bain on way to one of his rare knockouts, 1930. Rosenbloom, right, gives Jimmy Slattery a left and a "potch" in defense of title, 1931.

Born 9/6/04, in New York City . . . Started professional boxing career, 1923 . . . Known as "Slapsie Maxie" for knockout-punchless technique, won only 6 percent of bouts by knockout, averaged only 1 knockout per year, one of lowest knockout percentages of all time . . . Engaged in more bouts that resulted in 10-round decisions than any other champion—boxed nearly 3000 rounds . . . Averaged 17 bouts per year in 17-year career . . . Defeated champions in welterweight through heavyweight divisions . . . Boxed 10-round nontitle no-decision bout with middleweight champion Harry Greb, 7/16/25 . . . Defeated middleweight champion Tiger Flowers on ninth-round foul, 10/15/26 . . . Challenged Jimmy Slattery for world light heavyweight title, 8/30/27, but lost 10-round decision . . . Won New York State recognition as world light heavyweight champion by defeating Jimmy Slattery, 6/25/30 . . . Matched with future heavyweight champion, Jim Braddock, 11/10/31, but both men disqualified for stalling in the second round . . . Fought 107 bouts while champion, 1930–34, but only 9 of them were for title, all 30 bouts in 1932 went the distance . . . Defended title successfully against: Abie Bain, 10/22/30; Jimmy Slattery, 8/5/31; Lou Scozza, 7/14/32; Adolf Heuser, 3/10/33; Bod Godwin, 3/24/33; Mickey Walker, 11/3/33; Joe Knight, 2/5/34 . . . Stopped Bain and Godwin in 4 rounds each, drew with Knight, won others by 15-round decision . . . Gained universal championship recognition after Scozza bout . . . Lost title to Bob Olin, 11/16/34 . . . Lost bout, 6/26/39, resulted in ironic third-round knockout victory over Al Ettore (less than 7 percent of all world champions scored knockouts in their final bout) . . . Became comic movie and television actor after retirement from ring . . . Elected to Boxing Hall of Fame, 1972 . . . Died 3/6/76, in Los Angeles . . . Complete record: 289 bouts, 210 won, 35 lost, 23 draws, 19 no-decisions, 2 no-contests, 18 knockouts.

PANCHO VILLA

Philippine folklore would have it that Malakas and Maganda, their Adam and Eve, were born full-grown from bamboo shoots. And like the mythological twosome, Pancho Villa looked like he, too, was born from the same source, hard and springy, growing straight and slender and only a few feet high. And almost as godlike. Born in the town of Iloilo on the Philippine island of Panay as Francisco Guilledo, Villa came by his name naturally—years before a Mexican bandito with the same handle began to dominate headlines—taking his surname from his foster father and his first name from the nickname for Francisco, "Pancho." Migrating to Manila to pursue his dream of becoming a fighter, Villa competed in the *novatos* (for beginners) and took to hanging around the streets of Manila shining shoes for *pesetas* and sleeping on newspapers on the stone floors of office buildings, all the better to fulfill his dreams. Soon the vicious rip-snorting boxer who could go 15 rounds at blinding speed and finish as fresh as when he started had decimated the Philippine flyweight and bantamweight divisions, winning both Oriental titles. Seeking more worlds to conquer, his manager, Frank Churchill, brought him to the United States, where he was to gain fame as the most colorful small man in boxing. But not immediately.

VILLA FIRST LABORED IN OBSCURITY OF New Jersey rings, fighting future bantamweight champion Abe Goldstein and future flyweight champion Frankie Genaro in two no-decision bouts. With the mentality that gave voice to the phrase "Anything West of the Hudson is Hicksville," the New York press made scant mention of his exploits. But when he came to New York's old, old Madison Square Garden to fight a semiwindup against someone known only as Johnny Hepburn, the New York papers "discovered" the colorful Villa, making him the smaller version of Jack Dempsey. "After that," explained his manager, "Villa was a big star."

But "big" was an adjective that would never be pinned on Villa, his height a bare 5 feet and change in bare feet. But the shadow he cast was longer, made so by his increasing fame in the ring, as he won the American Flyweight title with an eleventh-round KO of Johnny Buff and defended it twice before losing it to the abovementioned Frankie Genaro in 1923.

But even though Genaro was to beat Villa, he never deceived himself. "What's the use?" he lamented. "You can beat Villa all you want, but he's the guy the fans go for. He's a living doll." And a living doll at that, one of the Dresden china variety without the accompanying Dresden china chin.

Ironically, it was his loss to Genaro that paved the way for Villa's immortality. Apparently eliminated from a shot at Jimmy Wilde's title on the basis of his loss to Genaro, the popular little battler was offered up to Wilde when Genaro proved difficult to deal with. Villa's manager buttonholed the powers-that-be and sold them on the premise that "More people would come out to see Villa after he lost than Genaro after he won. Make the match!"

And so, on the night of June 18, 1923, a crowd of 40,000 fans flocked to New York's Polo Grounds—the largest crowd ever to see a flyweight fight, title or no—to see Wilde and Villa stand center-stage and give the flyweight division its greatest show ever. The very first punch Villa landed, a left hook to the body, won the fight for him. "As soon as I hit the Wilde with that punch he clinched and I could feel his fingers pressing hard against my arm, as if he was afraid to let go," said Villa after the fight. "I say to myself, Pancho, you win 'em the fight, and you win 'em easy, begorra." And he did, with a vicious right after the bell ending the second round, although Wilde managed to last five more rounds. As the referee helped the helpless Wilde back to his corner, Villa was greeted by burst after burst of cheering, rushing together like a roaring surf at the edge of Manila Bay. He had finally arrived as a legend in his own right. Or left.

The lead commander of boxing's so-called "Mosquito Fleet" was now the toast of New York. And of sports fans everywhere. His every word, his every move, was newsworthy. The papers were filled with the man they now called "Puncho Pancho." Quoting Villa on his best punch, they reported him as saying, "My best punch is my double left. First I hook the body and then, with the same movement, I hook the jaw. It was how I surprised 'The (Johnny) Buff.' When I hooked him to the stomach he expected me to step back. But I no step back. Instead I hook him to the chin with the same hand and 'The Buff,' him drop to the mat." And his out-of-the-ring exploits were faithfully followed by the press. For Pancho Villa's fighting style and lifestyle both matched the gaudy spirit of the times, nonstop. Possessed of an "eat, drink, and be merry for tomorrow we may die" spirit, he provided his own musical accompaniment, playing both the drums and the ukulele—appropriately translatable in Hawaiian as "the little flea."

It was to be this dual consumption by contrary desires, to fight and to enjoy life, that would tragically cost the seemingly indestructible Villa his own fight for life. For, while negotiations were equivocally renewed for yet another Villa-Genaro fight, Villa took a fight on the coast, signing to joust at

Top: Villa, left, with Jimmy Wilde, before winning flyweight championship. Bottom: Fight night at Manila Stadium where Villa took first steps to greatness.

catchweights with a young flyweight-cum-bantamweight named Jimmy McLarnin. But then again, to Villa, the whole world was catchweights. And the fact that McLarnin weighed 120 pounds and he only weighed 108, didn't bother him at all. What bothered him, instead, was a painful wisdom tooth which had been extracted just a few days before the fight, leaving a painful jaw as a constant, and nagging, reminder. Villa would rather fight than eat, and so, against his manager's orders and his doctor's wishes, he went into battle with McLarnin, all his senses affected by his teeth. Once in the ring, Pancho gave the best he had, even blackening both of McLarnin's ears with his constant punches to the head in the in-fighting. But it was far from the form he had shown on previous occasions, and lost a decision.

The morning after, Villa would tell the noted boxing writer, Tom Andrews, "Me too weak to give away so much weight and do my best. Two nights I had no sleep and soon I found myself weak in the ring." The next day Villa went to see a dentist, who told him he had three more infected teeth. The dentist took them out on the spot and admonished Villa to stay in bed for three days and return to his office. It was a directive that was destined to go unheeded as Villa went on a one-week binge, playing on his ukelele and living out the words to the hit song of 1925, "Running Wild." Ten days after the fight, Pancho Villa succumbed to Ludwig's Angina, a dangerous infection of the soft glands of the neck caused by neglected and decaying teeth.

By the time of his death, at the age of 23, Pancho Villa had managed to occupy his own sparsely populated island of greatness—one which made him the greatest Asian boxer in history.

Born Francisco Guilledo, 8/1/01, in Iloilo, Phillipines . . . First pro bout, 1919, Manila . . . Early career incomplete . . . Fought exclusively in Manila until 1922 . . . Came to New york, 1922 . . . Fought future junior lightweight champion, Mike Ballerino 10 times, 1920–21, won 6, others no-decisions, or draws . . . Lost 10-round decision to Frankie Genero, 8/22/22 . . . Knocked out Johnny Buff in eleventh round to win American flyweight title, 9/14/22 . . . Successfully defended against Abe Goldstein, 11/17/22, and Terry Martin, 12/29/22, both on 15-round decisions . . . Lost title to Frankie Genaro, 3/1/23, 15-round decision . . . Won world flyweight championship by stopping Jimmy Wilde in 7 rounds, 6/18/23, First world flyweight championship bout held in U.S. . . . Retained title in 4 successful defenses . . . Lost non-title bout to Jimmy McLarnin, 7/4/25, 10-round decision . . . Died 10 days later, 7/14/25, in San Francisco, CA, of blood poisoning caused by infected tooth . . . Elected to Boxing Hall of Fame, 1961 . . . Complete record: 105 bouts, 73 won, 5 lost, 4 draws, 23 no-decisions, 22 knockouts.

JOSE NAPOLES

46 JOSE NAPOLES

Technology usually doesn't reverse itself, but in the case of Jose Napoles it did. Napoles was a throwback to the classic fighters of yesteryear, a methodical boxer whose sleek, slick style won him the admiration of millions of fans throughout Mexico. And won him everlasting fame everywhere as "Mantequilla" for his smooth-as-butter moves. Using his left jab to set up an Aladdin's lamp of punches, "Mantequilla" delivered his butter in a stylish dish, throwing lefts, double lefts, triple lefts, a hook off his jab, and a punctuating right uppercut with bewildering speed, every punch synchronized, every movement fluid. It was almost as if each punch determined new rules for how punches were to be thrown. If Napoles had an Achilles heel, it wasn't in his style, it was in his Achilles eyebrows, eyebrows which came apart in the final days of his career like *Mantiquilla* cut by a hot knife, his skin finally betraying him after more than 20 years in the ring, dating back to his early childhood.

BROUGHT UP IN THE DIRTIEST SLUM IN Santiago de Cuba, young Napoles fought for his three *tios*, three uncles who served as matchmakers, lining up suitable opponents for their nephew, sometimes for as little as five cents a bout—proving that fighters are born, not paid. And when the youngster failed to acquit himself in an adequate fashion, his uncles took turns taking the strap to him. But, according to Napoles, "They weren't as tough as my mother. When she found out about my getting in all those fights, she'd grab hold of me, assume a fighter's stance and yell, 'Come on, you're such a great fighter, let's see you fight me.' Those were the only fights I had no chance to win."

Growing up, the young Napoles would hitch rides over to Havana and sneak into gyms to watch fighters train. There, serving as a general "Go-fer"— as in go-for coffee, go-for wraps and go-for anything else that might be needed—Napoles began imitating the fighters, aping their moves, especially the moves of the great ones, like Kid Gavilan. Soon he was boxing in the amateur ranks, and from 1954 to 1957, he had 114 amateur bouts, winning all but one.

On August 2, 1958, Napoles made his pro debut as a bantamweight in Havana's Arena Trejo, knocking out his opponent with his first punch. During the next two and a half years, he fought 17 more times, losing twice in ten-round bouts to more experienced fighters. But even then, Napoles' days in Cuba were numbered as the guerrillas of Fidel Castro, then massed in the mountains in Napoles' home province of Oriente were on the threshhold of taking over the government. Soon the new regime would deny him his chance to fight by skewering him through and through with the pushpins of politics and binding him hand and foot with declarations against the sport of boxing. Denied his chance to fight by politics, a word he had no passing interest in, Jose "went to Mexico City in 1961 and resumed my boxing career there."

From the moment he arrived in Mexico City—there to be greeted at the airport by Sugar Ramos, Chico Veliz, Baby Luis, and other well-wishers—he became a national hero, adopted by fight-loving Mexicans as one of their own. Fighting first as a featherweight and then as a lightweight, he outclassed the best boxing had to offer. One of his friends also noticed that, "All of a sudden, he was knocking out everybody. In Cuba, he had been a boxer. In Mexico, he was a killer. And they love killers in Mexico."

Napoles' first fight in front of the fans he was to call "*marveloso*" took place on July 21, 1962, a second-round knockout before a packed house at Arena Mexico. His second fight, also a sell-out, came one month later, this time a knockout in nine rounds. As knockout followed knockout, the fame and legend of Napoles flourished. He

Above: Napoles butters up Jean Josselin with an overhead right en route to a 5th-round knockout, Aug. 23, 1971.

could climb into any Mexican ring and make any madding crowd of dues-paying boxing fans feel tense and giddy with anticipation. And their mustachioed hero rarely disappointed them, using his left like a *banderilla* and his right like a machete to swat his opponents into enforced obsolesence.

By the end of 1962, the boxing world also began noticing him as he edged into *Ring* magazine's junior welterweight ratings. In 1963, he had risen to the fourth-rated junior welterweight contender. And by 1964, the top-rated contender, a position he also held in 1965. But the landlords of boxing, the WBA and the WBC, didn't seem to care about Napoles. By 1967, he had grown into a full-fledged welterweight, and gained a national ranking there as well. And still, no one was interested.

Sometime during 1968, a Los Angeles promoter named George Parnassus came out of retirement to correct the oversight. Aggravated at what seemed to him to be a catch-22 situation, that no fighters would go to Mexico to meet the leading contenders nor would any of the promoters then doing business in southern California bring the ranking Mexicans north, Parnassus set up shop on his own. And, in so doing, became Napoles' patron.

Finally, on April 18, 1969, Parnassus, his voice tinged with the tinkling sound of money, offered the reigning welterweight champion, Curtis Cokes, the unheard-of sum of $80,000 to risk his title against Napoles. Napoles was

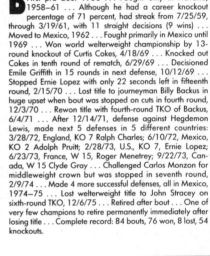

Born 4/13/40, in Santiago de Cuba, Oriente, Cuba . . . First pro bout 1958 . . . Fought only in Havana, 1958–61 . . . Although he had a career knockout percentage of 71 percent, had streak from 7/25/59, through 3/19/61, with 11 straight decisions (9 wins) . . . Moved to Mexico, 1962 . . . Fought primarily in Mexico until 1969 . . . Won world welterweight championship by 13-round knockout of Curtis Cokes, 4/18/69 . . . Knocked out Cokes in tenth round of rematch, 6/29/69 . . . Decisioned Emile Griffith in 15 rounds in next defense, 10/12/69 . . . Stopped Ernie Lopez with only 22 seconds left in fifteenth round, 2/15/70 . . . Lost title to journeyman Billy Backus in huge upset when bout was stopped on cuts in fourth round, 12/3/70 . . . Rewon title with fourth-round TKO of Backus, 6/4/71 . . . After 12/14/71, defense against Hegdemon Lewis, made next 5 defenses in 5 different countries: 3/28/72, England, KO 7 Ralph Charles; 6/10/72, Mexico, KO 2 Adolph Pruitt; 2/28/73, U.S., KO 7, Ernie Lopez; 6/23/73, France, W 15, Roger Menetrey; 9/22/73, Canada, W 15 Clyde Gray . . . Challenged Carlos Monzon for middleweight crown but was stopped in seventh round, 2/9/74 . . . Made 4 more successful defenses, all in Mexico, 1974–75 . . . Lost welterweight title to John Stracey on sixth-round TKO, 12/6/75 . . . Retired after bout . . . One of very few champions to retire permanently immediately after losing title . . . Complete record: 84 bouts, 76 won, 8 lost, 54 knockouts.

later to confess, "I would have fought Cokes for nothing," so sure was he that he could win. It was a big chance for Napoles and a huge mistake for Cokes as Napoles dominated the fight. And Cokes as well. Ripping and slashing away at the veteran champion with his talented left and then throwing a befuddling admixture of punches behind it to cut up the champion, "Mantequilla" forced Cokes to surrender in his corner at the end of the thirteenth. Jose Napoles was awarded with a sombrero and a belt in mid-ring, the welterweight champion of the world and hero of all Mexico.

Napoles was to hold the welterweight belt twice for six years, less a short period of six months when Billy Backus parted his eye. The china eyebrows of Napoles were now showing the tensile strength of wet tissue paper, his face starting to come apart like that of Dorian Gray, testimony to his long career in the ring. And when, finally, after 13 successful title defenses, he lost to John Stracey, he retired and took his lumpy eyebrows back to Mexico, where the word "mantequilla" translates into "one of the greatest."

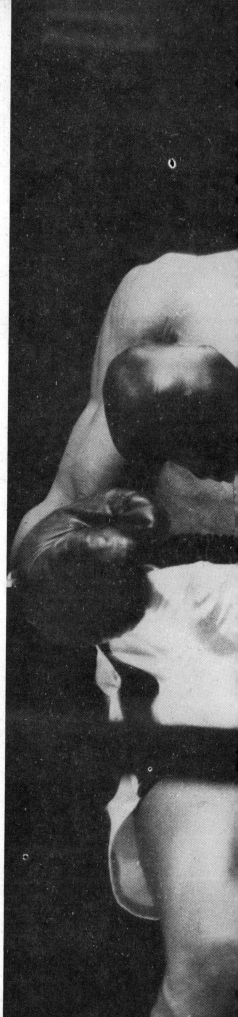

47 SANDY SADDLER

SANDY SADDLER

James Figg may have founded modern-day boxing, but Sandy Saddler dumfounded it. To the boxing traditionalist, the sight of this physical freak was astounding: a featherweight who measured 3½ inches short of 6 feet laid end-to-end, possessing the same construction as a baseball bat with a deficient thyroid. It was almost as if this walking case of malnutrition could be cut in half and two featherweights made of the equal parts. But it wasn't just his physical equipment that stunned the fans, it was what Saddler could do with the different parts of his anatomy. For this hyperpituitary specter was a jangling medley of arms, elbows, fists, and all manner of rough edges, harmonized beautifully into one fighting machine. It was a style designed to make his opponents feel as if they had been caught in a fistic Waring blender, each limb a weapon. If that's all there was to Sandy Saddler, he might have been acceptable, even if not accepted. But it wasn't.

SADDLER WAS A THROWBACK TO THE rough-and-tumble style of fighting fashionable under the old London Prize Ring Rules which allowed everything up to, and including, keel-hauling. Hardly a graduate of Mrs. Denton's finishing school, Saddler was a cross between one of nature's irregularities and the darker side of human nature, using all the fine arts of collaring, heeling, holding, thumbing, and wrestling—with an elbow thrown in as an exclamation point. One got the impression that Saddler could hurt his opponent even if he was in a tin can and the lid had been closed. The critics, without really knowing whether his actions were a code of morality, a code of convenience, or merely a reflex action, viewed his style a little like belching in church.

And the teary-eyed sentimentalists, who had come to view Willie Pep as a patron saint, treated Saddler as if he had just pointed out a terminal case of hoof and mouth disease in their personal favorite in the herd. Ignoring his greatness but concerned only with his tactics, they dismissed him as a mere purveyor of the black arts of boxing. Nothing more. All of which was pa-

tently unfair to Saddler, forever destined to stand in the dock charged with dirty tactics. And to stand in the smaller shadow of Pep.

Forgotten to many were Saddler's greatness and his graceful movements, his ability to stick and move or with one swat of his praying-mantis arm remove a man from his sensibilities. Forgotten too are his precise ring movements: the snapping of his left so that it came back to, but never beyond, the top of his outstretched left foot, or his twisting and hurtful left jab, delivered in the fashion of Kid McCoy's famed "Corkscrew Punch." Gone, too, are memories of his other 158 fights and 103 knockouts, and the fact that he fought them all, featherweights and lightweights alike, retiring as the undefeated champion.

Instead, his name will forever more be linked irrevocably to that of Pep as two magnificent fighters whose greatness intersected for four years back in the late forties and early fifties when they held annual affairs that could have doubled as get-togethers of two warring Irish clans.

Four times the human eraser known as Saddler and the "Will o' the Wisp"

116

Born Joseph Saddler, 6/23/26, in Boston, MA . . . Started pro career, 1944 . . . Knocked out in second professional bout by Jock Leslie (future top-10 contender) . . . Won 19 of 22 in 1944; won 24 of 24 in 1945 (including 14 straight knockouts) . . . Defeated Willie Pep for featherweight title, 10/29/48, by fourth-round knockout . . . Lost title in rematch, 2/11/49, on 15-round decision . . . Junior lightweight title resurrected for match with Orlando Zulueta, 12/6/49, won 10-round decision and became first junior lightweight champion since 1934 . . . Defended title against Lauro Salas, 4/18/50, KO 9, and against Diego Sosa, 2/28/51, KO 2, before abandoning claim—title dormant for next 8 years . . . Rewon world featherweight championship from Willie Pep by eighth-round knockout in rubber match, 9/8/50 . . . Fourth and final Pep-Saddler battle, 9/26/51, ended in ninth-round knockout victory for Saddler . . . Lost next 3 nontitle bouts, 1951–52 . . . After fifth-round knockout of Tommy Collins in nontitle bout, 3/17/52, inactive for nearly 2 years while in U.S. Army . . . Resumed boxing career, 1/15/54, but did not defend title until 1955 . . . Decisioned Teddy "Red-top" Davis in 15-round title defense, 2/25/55 . . . Final title defense, KO 13 over Gabriel "Flash" Elorde, 1/18/56 . . . Final bout, 4/14/56, 10-round loss to Larry Boardman . . . Injured in auto accident, 1956, and retired 1/21/57, due to failing vision . . . Occasionally boxed exhibitions with Willie Pep into mid-1960s . . . On top-10 all-time knockout list with 103—most of any featherweight . . . Elected to Boxing Hall of Fame, 1971 . . . Complete record: 162 bouts, 144 won, 16 lost, 2 draws, 103 knockouts.

Left: Saddler stops Willie Pep, regaining the featherweight title, Sept. 8, 1950.

known as Pep engaged in epic feats of arms, legs, and virtually every other anatomical appurtenance known to boxingkind. And three times Saddler came out the victor. Their dislike purely platonic, they answered each other's indiscretion one for one, boxing being a mere window decoration to their other skills, as they used each other as 126-pound throw rugs. In the first fight Saddler put Pep down twice in the third and out with a right in the fourth, Pep deciding that the 10-count was something that could be better listened to sitting down. In their second fight, Pep came back to out-distance Sandy, who spent the entire 15 rounds regarding the punches of the "Will o' the Wisp" with the mild dismay of a man annoyed by an errant fly, looking to land one of his own, but never quite getting close enough to do so. In their final two fights, Saddler outmugged Pep, who, although ahead in both at the time of his quitting, quit nevertheless, as if drugged by some scent of his reconstituted past—being stopped in the eighth and ninth rounds respectively, but not respectfully.

But while Willie Pep's one win was to be the cornerstone of his fame, Sandy Saddler was to gain no such immortality for his three. For it was his plight to have dumfounded boxing's critics and historians who couldn't bring themselves to understand his greatness—or classify him, rightfully, as one of the great "Little Champs."

FREDDIE WELSH

Welshmen have always been famed for their fighting ability, from the chieftains of old, who, in the rocky fastnesses of their native land, defied all the might of England, down through the centuries to the Welsh fusiliers who were permitted to fly a piece of black ribbon at the back of the neck of the tunic as a special mark of esteem for their bravery. It would be nice to note that one Frederick Thomas out of Pontypridd, by way of Philadelphia, adopted the surname Welsh as his *nom de guerre* in testimony to the ferocity of his ancestors. However, there is no need to embroider the truth, which makes all things plain. Thomas acquired the name quite unceremoniously, taking it to prevent his mother from knowing he was making his living as a boxer. Of such stuff are legends made.

BUT FREDDIE WELSH WAS A LEGEND, name and all. He took that inexact science called "The Sweet Science" and developed it through experimental investigation and application of disciplines of his own making. Having learned the basic fundamentals of prizefighting back in Wales, he was to do his graduate work while serving as a porter, general handyman, occasional sparring partner, and all-around factotum in a New York gymnasium. He explained the difference: "The English boxer is too orthodox, he sticks to his style, despite all else. The American fighter conforms to the situation. If he misses a left hook, he swings right back with a right. The English boxer swings back to his position and starts again."

Adopting the American methods, he was to superimpose his own science onto the sport. His daily regimen included sprinting, instead of the normal long-distance runs fighters had traditionally taken, and precision punching with his left jab, hitting a white dot he had painted on the punching bag with accuracy and impact. It was his left jab and his footwork—footwork that would have Irene and Vernon Castle envious and which numbered among its many variations sidestepping, feinting, wheeling, and ducking in and out after coming to a complete stop—that were to make Freddie Welsh a complete boxer.

Welsh took to leap-frogging the Great Pond as if it were a small pond, commuting regularly between the States and England on several of the new ocean steamers then studding the seas. And always in quest of something. In 1909, he returned to London in pursuit of something new, the Lonsdale Belt, put up by the National Sporting Club. Unable to generate enough money to attract the top names in boxing, the National Sporting Club had hit upon a promotional gimmick worthy of P.T. Barnum: A Belt emblematic of the British championship and only available to the "accepted" champions who won it at the National Sporting Club. Welsh was to win the first Belt offered, beating Johnny Summers in a 20-round boxing lesson, thus establishing both his credentials and his reputation.

But still Welsh didn't have what he coveted most: the world's lightweight title. And so, once again, he boarded a New York-bound steamer in Southampton for yet another round of Trans-Atlantic champion-chasing. He had challenged Battling Nelson when he held the world's title, but Nelson hadn't even cupped an ear to his challenge. He had gotten his successor, Ad Wolgast, to within hours of a title fight, but Wolgast had been stricken by appendicitis and a substitute, Willie Ritchie, took his place. Now Willie Ritchie was champion, having beaten Wolgast, and al-

though Welsh had come within four days of answering the call of the bell against Ritchie in Vancouver in the summer of 1913, Ritchie, too, had pulled out. Welsh continued his quest for the Golden Fleece nevertheless and continued to meet, and beat, the best around including Leach Cross, Joe Rivers, and Johnny Dundee. But it still wasn't the championship.

A championship was damnably serious business, especially in England, which hadn't owned a piece of the lightweight championship since Dick Burge lost to Kid Lavigne some 18 years earlier. Welsh was finally to get his chance when theatrical impresario C. B. Cochran tempted Ritchie with a guarantee that translated into approximately $20,000 for putting his title on the line at London's Olympia. To get his shot, Welsh pawned more than a few promises; he pawned the crown jewels, settling for a percentage of the profits. But he didn't care a fig about money; he had what he wanted, a shot at the title.

For 20 rounds, Welsh was, in the words of one reporter, to "bounce three or four thousand light jabs off the

anatomy of Willie Ritchie and dance away. Satisfied to clinch, flop a right to the kidneys, grin, and do it all over again, his punches were as harmless as the drop of a butterfly . . . ." But Welsh wasn't interested in challenging the harder-hitting Ritchie, only in winning, which he did handily, beating Ritchie to the punch, throwing successions of lefts with intoxicating headiness, and even resorting to what Pierce Egan called "Milling on the Retreat," landing punches as he went backward. At the end, the title was his, even though he didn't have a ha'penny to show for his efforts, profits being as invisible as the phantomlike Welsh.

Tucking his freshly won 135-pound championship belt under his arm, the man they now called "The Pride of Pontypridd" sailed for the land of dollars for the express purpose of exploiting it "for the money being offered." Fighting in every town that had an armory—and a state law calling for no-decision bouts—Welsh took them all on: Charley White, Ad Wolgast, Joe Shugrue, Willie Ritchie, Ever Hammer, and a youngster out of New York named Benny Leonard.

Born Frederick Hall Thomas, 3/5/86, in Pontypridd, South Wales . . . First pro bout, 1905 . . . Fought during "no-decision" era . . . Fought 23 bouts in 1906 in area of Philadelphia, PA . . . Scored 3 knockouts, remainder draws or no decisions . . . Returned to Wales, 1907 . . . Returned to U.S. in 1908 and defeated Abe Attell in 15 rounds, 11/25/08 . . . Won British lightweight championship, 11/8/09, with 20-round decision over Johnny Summers . . . Successfully defended against Jim Driscol, 12/20/10, winning on tenth-round foul . . . Fought throughout Canada in 1913 . . . Won world lightweight championship from Willie Ritchie on 20-round decision, 7/7/14 . . . Defended title successfully only twice, both in 1916: against Ad Wolgast, 7/4/16, W 11; and Charley White, 9/4/16, D 20 . . . Lost title to Benny Leonard on ninth-round knockout, 5/28/17 . . . Joined U. S. Army during WWI . . . Inactive until 1920 . . . Fought only 6 more bouts before retiring in 1922 . . . Only fighter whose last name was also his nationality . . . Died, 7/29/27, in New York, N.Y. . . . Elected to Boxing Hall of Fame, 1960 . . . Complete record: 167 bouts, 77 won, 4 lost, 7 draws, 79 no-decisions, 24 knockouts.

Welsh was outclassed from the start, the ten-year-younger Leonard not only keeping up with his sprinter's pace, but incredibly outsprinting him and occasionally looking back to see if Welsh was still in the race. In the ninth, Leonard caught the tiring Welsh with a powerful right that put the champion down for one of the few times in his career. Under Leonard's merciless assault, he went down two more times and then, arising, fell over the top rope, unable to defend himself. As the referee tried to ease him off, he fell over the middle strand, out cold, the only time he was ever knocked out in his long career.

A purist's delight, Welsh was an artful dodger who gave his opponents a come-hither look, but when they came a-knocking, they would never find anyone at home. Abe Attell, when asked how Welsh could be beaten, had the final word on the skills of Welsh when he said, "How do you beat Freddie Welsh? If you can lay a glove on that guy five times in twenty rounds, let alone beat him, you'll get the verdict, sure! If you don't want to be made to look like a sucker, take my advice: go away and train. Train good and hard. Then sprain yer ankle the night before the fight."

That was Freddie Welsh, ring magician extraordinaire.

Above left: Welse extends hand in sporting gesture to former stablemate Jim Driscoll, after Driscoll slipped in bout won by Welsh, Dec. 20, 1960.

JOE FRAZIER

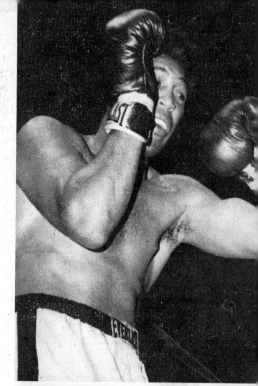

The roots of Joe Frazier, like those of almost every other successful boxer, were literally planted in economic deprivation. Born in a one-room shack on a small farm, Joe grew up in dirt-poor poverty, picking radishes for 15 cents a crate to help his father, who had lost his left arm in an automobile accident before Joe was born. "I was his left hand," Joe said. "If he had the hammer, I held the nail." And for the majority of his adult life, Joe Frazier would use that same left hand to hammer his way to fistic greatness. But if chance hadn't twice lit up like a small electric lightbulb in a small room the size of the farmer's shack of his youth, it is doubtful if Joe Frazier would ever have risen to the heights of greatness he achieved.

THE FIRST BIG CHANCE CAME WHEN Buster Mathis, the only man ever to beat Joe as an amateur, hurt his hand before the 1964 Olympics and Frazier, an alternate, stepped in to represent the United States, doing Uncle Sam proud by bringing home a Gold Medal from Tokyo. Returning to his adopted city of Philadelphia as a hero, Frazier repaired home to nurse a broken thumb and a bruised bank account. Once again, on the borderline of poverty, he took a job in a slaughterhouse waiting for the chance to turn pro and for his thumb to heal. Finally, a group of Philadelphia businessmen put together an athletic corporation called "Cloverlay" to underwrite Frazier's career, and in August of 1965, he turned pro with a one-round knockout over Woody Goss.

Frazier won his next 14 fights as well, his straightforward, businesslike style—punctuated by his deadly left hand—taking out 13 of his opponents within the allotted number of rounds. And then chance again lit up, this time in the form of Muhammad Ali who refused to step forward for induction on April 18, 1967. Within scant hours, boxing's Babbits and political chest-thumpers had withdrawn Ali's title, scattering the heavyweight title like crumbs to the wind. Almost immediately every Tom, Dick, and WBA rushed in to fill the vacuum in an "Ali, Ali, All in Free" fashion, advertising for anyone and everyone to campaign for the right to ascend to Ali's throne as heavyweight champion. Joe Frazier was one of those who threw his left into the ring.

Less than one year later Joe Frazier was matched against the man New York Boxing Commissioner Ed Dooley called "Buddy" Mathis for their split

Born Joseph Frazier, 1/12/44, in Beaufort, SC . . . Made 1964 U.S. Olympic team as an alternate after losing to Buster Mathis in Olympic trials—Mathis unable to compete and Frazier selected as replacement . . . Won 1964 Olympic gold medal in heavyweight class . . . Started pro career in Philadelphia, 1965 . . . Won first 11 by knockout and 21 of first 23, 1965–68 . . . Defeated Buster Mathis, 3/4/68, in inaugural card at new Madison Square Garden in bout recognized by New York State as world heavyweight championship bout . . . Defended N.Y. title against Manuel Ramos, 6/24/68, with second-round knockout . . . Decisioned Oscar Bonavena, 12/10/68; knocked out Dave Zyglewicz in first round, 4/22/69, and stopped Jerry Quarry in 7, 6/23/69, in title defenses . . . Bout with WBA heavyweight champion, Jimmy Ellis, billed for undisputed world heavyweight title, although many still recognized the inactive Ali as titleholder—defeated Ellis with fifth-round knockout, 2/16/70 . . . Defended against light heavyweight champion, Bob Foster, 11/18/70, with second-round kayo . . . 3/8/71 bout with Muhammad Ali billed as "The Fight,"—first bout between 2 undefeated world heavyweight champions, $2.5 million purse for each (highest in history by far to that date), closed circuit prices of $25 also highest in history . . . Bout lived up to billing with Frazier winning 15-round unanimous decision but hospitalized after bout . . . Made 2 soft defenses in 1972—knocked out Terry Daniels in 4, 1/15/72; knocked out Ron Stander in 5, 5/25/72; neither Daniels nor Stander ever rated in top 10 . . . Lost title to George Foreman, 1/22/73, on second-round knockout in Kingston, Jamaica—first time title changed hands outside U.S. since Willard-Johnson bout in 1915 . . . First title bout between 2 Olympic heavyweight champions . . . Lost to Muhammad Ali, 1/28/74, in nontitle bout . . . Faced Ali in third bout, 10/1/75, for championship in Manila, considered among greatest bouts of all time; Frazier's corner would not let him come out for final round . . . Retired after fifth-round knockout by George Foreman, 6/15/76 . . . Made ill-advised comeback, 12/3/81, after 5 years of inactivity—bout with Floyd Jumbo Cummings was called a draw but Frazier's talents were obviously missing . . . Elected to Boxing Hall of Fame, 1980 . . . Complete record: 37 bouts, 32 won, 4 lost, 1 draw, 27 knockouts.

version of the heavyweight championship of the world. Frazier won with an eleventh-round KO against Mathis, the first of three times he would have to perfect his claim to the title. The second time he perfected his claim by knocking out Jimmy Ellis, whom the WBA called champion, and the third time by knocking Muhammad Ali down, but not out.

The man who had by now come to be known as "Smokin' Joe" fought Muhammad Ali for the undisputed world heavyweight title on March 8, 1971, in a bout so big it was merely called, with uncharacteristic understatement, "The Fight." Both men entered Madison Square Garden that

Top: Frazier knocks out WBA champion Jimmy Ellis, Feb. 16, 1970. Bottom: "Smokin' Joe" and Muhammad Ali put their best fists forward at prefight press conference for "The Fight," while NY State Athletic Commissioner Ed Dooley intercedes.

night undefeated. Only one would leave it undefeated. That man was "Smokin' Joe," who came at Ali as one writer put it, "like a wild beast caught in a thicket." His head bobbing up and down to the metronomic movement of his body, his mouth pursed, sucking air much like a fish out of water, Frazier moved in relentlessly—no qualms, no hesitations, no questions, just straight in like a hurricane—his right a mere throat clearing for his devastating left. Time and again he rocked Ali, until at last Ali, hit so hard he couldn't even limp, joined the ranks of the walking wounded. But even though he was floored in the last round, Ali was able to finish the fight—even though he was

never able to wash away the improbability of the calendar.

Joe Frazier had, at last, emerged from the shadow of Ali. He was no longer the "pretender" to Ali's throne, but instead became *the* heavyweight champ.

However, Frazier's savage style of boxing, and the small pieces of himself he had left behind, had already started taking their toll. He would fight only ten more times, losing almost as many as he would win. His plain vanilla strategy of coming straight into the blazing guns of his opponents cost him dearly in Jamaica, where George Foreman used him for fungo practice, knocking him down six times in two rounds. And then, in a bout billed as "The Thrilla in

Manilla," he took Muhammad Ali to what Ali called "the closest thing to death" only to be retired at the end of the fourteenth by his compassionate trainer. The following year he made a last-scene appearance as a character actor instead of a star against the same George Foreman, who repeated his earlier insult. And then, as a coda, he made an embarrassing comeback against someone named "Jumbo" Cummings. That was enough for anyone, even Joe.

But Joe Frazier's greatness—like the greatness of all—is not based on what he did when fighting from memory. It was when he was at his peak. And when he was at his peak, Joe Frazier was a gladiator, one of boxing's greatest.

Above: Frazier knocks Jerry Quarry down and out in the fifth round, June 17, 1974.

JOHN L. SULLIVAN

Back in the days when men were men and women were damn glad of it, the man most men wanted to be was a boxer with swaggering virility named John L. Sullivan—simply stated, the strongest man in the world. In a day and age when America was cocksure and confident of its future but in need of a national hero to tie its patriotic kite tail to, John L. Sullivan provided just such a hero. And more. Much more. He was an institution, a deity, a national obsession. The preoccupation with Sullivan took on the form of myth-making and nicknaming, as he became known as "The Boston Strongboy," "The Hercules of the Ring," "The Prizefighting Caesar," "His Fistic Highness," and just plain ol' familiar "Sully."

HIS PRIDE WAS THE PRIDE OF A NEWLY emerging nation, and his "I-can-beat-any sonuvabitch-in-the-house" defi was the rallying cry of a young nation intent upon making itself heard in the world back in those early days of Manifest Destiny. It was a pride that inspired anyone who had ever met him, with thousands of men holding out their hands to others and proclaiming, "Shake the hand that shook the hand of John L."

Sullivan was part real man, part folk legend. But he continued to rewrite the legend with his fists, devouring his opponents as easily as he devoured the free food and drink at his neighborhood saloon. One opponent was to remember nothing of his battle with John L. other than that his awesome right "felt· like a telephone pole had been shoved against me endways." Another said his right "felt like the kick of a mule."

He drank as he fought, prodigiously, never meeting a saloon he didn't like. And, again, the nation loved him for it. He lived for the din of the brass bands, the raucous cheers of the crowd, and the acceptance of the fans, especially the Irish fans to whom he became a special symbol.

For almost twelve years he led the parade himself, usually fighting in secluded spots one step ahead of the local constabulary and always winning. It

was said that if the government had toppled and our most precious assets were stolen during a Sullivan fight, nobody would much notice, such was the excitement he engendered. Finally, his living and lack of training caught up with him and a John L. with a tumorous belly, sagging skin and eyes hanging low in the sockets to match, was beaten by James J. Corbett. But even then he became a martyr, less to failure than to booze, and as such, retained his place in the hearts of fight fans everywhere.

The figure of John L. Sullivan cast a hulking shadow upon the American boxing landscape in that curious era characterized by bare knuckles and white gloves. And yet, ironically, it was Sullivan who would bring together the two worlds of boxing by demanding the use of gloves. That may be his biggest contribution. And one which becomes a legend most.

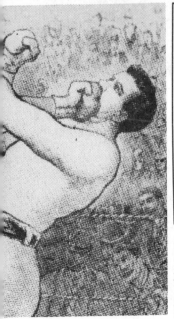

Born John Lawrence Sullivan, 10/15/58, in Roxbury, MA . . . Fought mostly bareknuckles . . . First pro bout, 1878 . . . Won the world heavyweight title from Paddy Ryan in 10 minutes, 30 seconds in bareknuckle bout that ended in ninth round . . . Fought in era when not all bouts engaged in by heavyweight champion were for title—won 16 bouts by knockout, 1882–84, but no title bouts . . . Fought 39-round draw with Charley Mitchell, Chantilly, France, 3/10/88, in title bout lasting 3 hours, 10 minutes under London Prize Ring rules (bareknuckles) . . . Defended title against Jake Kilrain, 7/8/89, in Richburg, MI in last bareknuckle heavyweight championship bout—bout lasted 2 hours, 16 minutes, 23 seconds and ended in a knockout victory for Sullivan in the seventy-fifth round . . . Spent 1890 in theatre as an actor . . . Defeated by James J. Corbett, 9/7/92, in the first heavyweight title bout under Marquis of Queensberry rules—Sullivan knocked out in twenty-first round, winner-take-all bout that was the last competitive bout . . . Fought exhibitions until 1905 . . . Died 2/2/18, in Abingdon, MA . . . Charter member of Boxing Hall of Fame, 1954 . . . Complete record: 42 bouts, 38 won, 1 lost, 3 draws, 33 knockouts.

Left: Adhering to Marquis of Queensberry rules in 1st championship fight, Sullivan takes one of James J. Corbett's rights, 1892. Above and right: The fight that marked the end of Bareknuckle Era, Sullivan's 75-round knockout of Jake Kilrain, 1889.

123

CARLOS MONZON

Picture, if you will, a swashbuckling Errol Flynn in the part of James J. Corbett, assuming the classic stand-up fencing pose of the time, his confidence and contemptuousness oozing from every glistening pore of his matinee-idol body and his body swaying like a reed in the soft summer breeze. Now, add muscular shoulders large enough to serve a sit-down table of six a full five-course meal, rotate the wrists ever so slightly in the modern boxing pose, and abbreviate the trunks into a modern cut, complete with the words "Fernet-Branca" inscribed on the waistband. And you have Carlos Monzon.

CARLOS MONZON WAS HARDLY THE stock-model pug with a nose you could hang your hat on. Instead, he had the reserved looks of a matinee idol, one with delicately marked brows, an unmarked face, and a remarkable body that could serve as a model for Hollywood beefcake pictures. And he fought the same way, with a coolness that could no more be melted than ice welded, his style a cross between aggressive caution and cautionary aggression. With a long right hand thrown in for good measure.

For seven years, this tall, willowy Argentine with the punch of a giant oak labored in the stadia of his native land, leaving more stretched-out opponents than breadcrumbs as a trail to his growing greatness. Fighting shrewdly and intelligently, albeit more in a flawless technical sense than one marked by finesse, he used his long propeller-like left, which came from somewhere across his country's borders, to set up his axe-like right, as he hewed down opponent after opponent.

Losing only three fights—and all of those in the first 20 fights of his youth—Monzon turned the tables on all three who had beaten him, having done with losing much as a youth who once had measles had gotten it out of his system, never again to suffer blemishes. He then went undefeated in his next 62 fights, with a few draws thrown in to make him look like a mere mortal. But aside from the thousands of art lovers who packed Buenos Aires' Luna Park to pay tribute to his growing fistic genius, few outside the reaches of Argentina knew anything about this towering inferno.

He was so well-unknown, in fact, that when he arrived in Rome as the South American middleweight champion to fight Nino Benevenuti for the world middleweight title, he was unranked, unappreciated and unheard of, the newspaper, *Corriere dello Sport*, asking "Monzon, Ma Chi Sei?," or "Monzon, Who Are You?"

There were those who tried to explain the unknowable Monzon in terms not worth knowing. And others who called him a "calm and tranquil" warrior who "lacked finesse and boxing skills." But his finesse was of a foreign language, mispronounced by all who had not seen him in action, too busy trying to study the package without considering its contents.

The 3-to-1 underdog, fighting outside the friendly confines of his homeland for the first time in 83 fights, answered all of his critics the only way he could: with his fists. Brimming with so much confidence he could have franchised it, Monzon took command of the action at the opening bell, throwing a sharp left to the features of Benvenuti. Monzon would never lose control as he raked Benvenuti's head from the outside, roughed up his body on the inside, and dominated the champion thoroughly for the first 11 rounds. Then, in the twelfth, as Benevenuti peered out from behind anguished eyes, unable to stave off the inevitable, Monzon caught him flush on the chin with an overhand right. A religious silence fell over the partisan Italian crowd as their favorite whipping boy sank to a prayerful position on his knees, there to surrender to the obvious. Carlos Monzon had answered all of his critics.

Monzon would continue to answer them over the next seven years, defending his middleweight title 14 times. Fighting more for prosperity than posterity, he took his title on tour, beating the likes of Nino Benvenuti, again, Emile Griffith, twice, Jose Napoles, and Rodrigo Valdez. And always with that

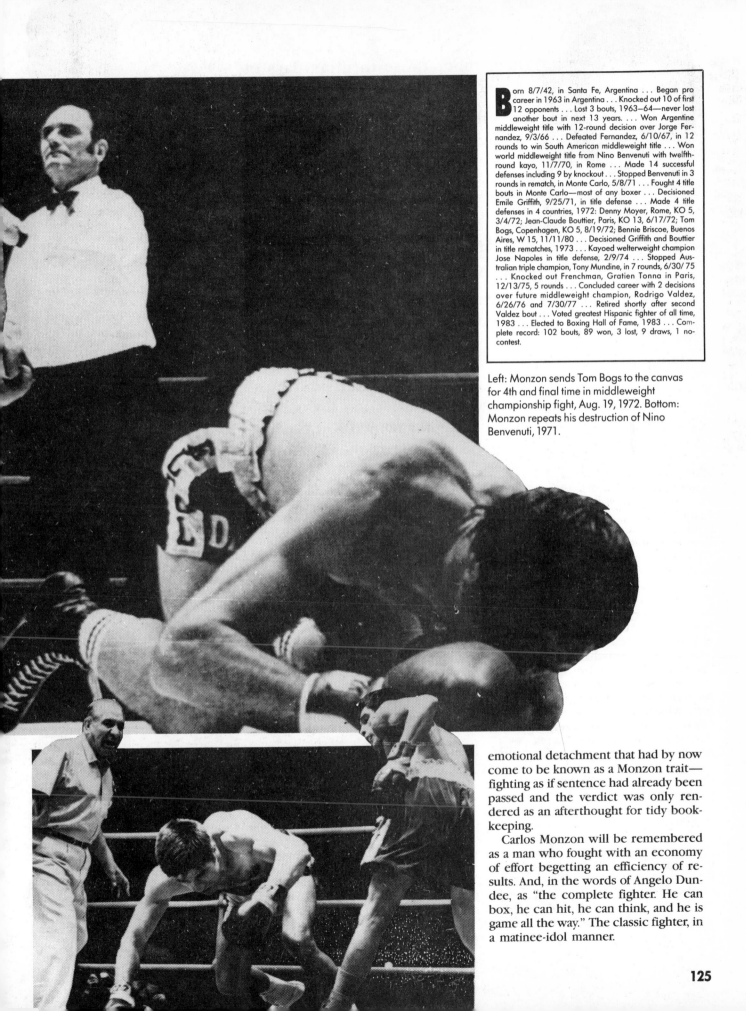

Born 8/7/42, in Santa Fe, Argentina . . . Began pro career in 1963 in Argentina . . . Knocked out 10 of first 12 opponents . . . Lost 3 bouts, 1963–64—never lost another bout in next 13 years. . . . Won Argentine middleweight title with 12-round decision over Jorge Fernandez, 9/3/66 . . . Defeated Fernandez, 6/10/67, in 12 rounds to win South American middleweight title . . . Won world middleweight title from Nino Benvenuti with twelfth-round kayo, 11/7/70, in Rome . . . Made 14 successful defenses including 9 by knockout . . . Stopped Benvenuti in 3 rounds in rematch, in Monte Carlo, 5/8/71 . . . Fought 4 title bouts in Monte Carlo—most of any boxer . . . Decisioned Emile Griffith, 9/25/71, in title defense . . . Made 4 title defenses in 4 countries, 1972: Denny Moyer, Rome, KO 5, 3/4/72; Jean-Claude Bouttier, Paris, KO 13, 6/17/72; Tom Bogs, Copenhagen, KO 5, 8/19/72; Bennie Briscoe, Buenos Aires, W 15, 11/11/80 . . . Decisioned Griffith and Bouttier in title rematches, 1973 . . . Kayoed welterweight champion Jose Napoles in title defense, 2/9/74 . . . Stopped Australian triple champion, Tony Mundine, in 7 rounds, 6/30/ 75 . . . Knocked out Frenchman, Gratien Tonna in Paris, 12/13/75, 5 rounds . . . Concluded career with 2 decisions over future middleweight champion, Rodrigo Valdez, 6/26/76 and 7/30/77 . . . Retired shortly after second Valdez bout . . . Voted greatest Hispanic fighter of all time, 1983 . . . Elected to Boxing Hall of Fame, 1983 . . . Complete record: 102 bouts, 89 won, 3 lost, 9 draws, 1 no-contest.

Left: Monzon sends Tom Bogs to the canvas for 4th and final time in middleweight championship fight, Aug. 19, 1972. Bottom: Monzon repeats his destruction of Nino Benvenuti, 1971.

emotional detachment that had by now come to be known as a Monzon trait—fighting as if sentence had already been passed and the verdict was only rendered as an afterthought for tidy book-keeping.

Carlos Monzon will be remembered as a man who fought with an economy of effort begetting an efficiency of results. And, in the words of Angelo Dundee, as "the complete fighter. He can box, he can hit, he can think, and he is game all the way." The classic fighter, in a matinee-idol manner.

KID GAVILAN

Remember those thrilling days of yesteryear when every Friday night we were entertained by a little bird named Sharpie, an animated parrot who sounded like Donald Duck with a herniated vocal chord, who, accompanied by the familiar three-chime slogan—"Look Sharp, Feel Sharp, Be Sharp," in F#, A#, and C#—announced proudly to the fistic faithful: "The Gillette Cavalcade of Sports Is On the Air"? And remember the fighters who were served up to us more times than fish on Friday? Or Monday, or Tuesday, or Wednesday, or Thursday, or Saturday, all of them fight nights, when prime-time was a veritable gymnasium? The 23-inch, black-and-white miniaturized boxer who most readily comes to mind to those of us to whom TV was the babysitter of our youth was a fighter named Kid Gavilan, "The Cuban Hawk," who appeared on national TV no less than 34 times.

THE CUBAN "KID"—PRONOUNCED "Keed" by Gavilan, as in "I ween this fight"—was a show and a showboat unto himself, the equal of another early Cuban television favorite, Desi Arnez, as he rhumbaed and danced his way through his fights in sort of an early-day form of fistic break dancing. And then, for good measure, he would throw in his beau gest-ure, the bolo punch, developed in the sugar cane fields of his youth, sort of a cross between an uppercut and a softball pitcher's underhanded delivery.

Those viewers of what was then network TV—the coaxial cable stretching from Schenectady, New York, to Richmond, Virginia then back—got their first look at the elegant style of "The Keed" on Friday, December 13, 1946, when he slicked his way to a 10-round decision over Johnny Williams. For 12 months Gavilan took his dancing-cum-fighting act back to Havana and then toured the small clubs that dotted the Eastern United States, winning 11 of 12 fights. He came back to New York for two draws, sans TV, and then, appearing on the January 23, 1948, Gillette Cavalcade for the second time, registered his second win, this one by a two-round knockout of Joe Curcio, one of

his infrequent knockouts, but frequent enough for him to merit another look-see by the giant maw called television which was so shy of programming that boxing had become its main staple.

Now the Gavilan bandwagon began to roll, all to the staccato beat of an ever-present rhumba band, whether in or out of the ring. He lost to Ike Williams on TV, knocked out someone named Rocco Rossano in front of the kleig lights and, in his spare time, even fought away from the cameras, beating Buster Tyler and Tommy Bell—the same Tommy Bell who had given Ray Robinson a life-or-death struggle for the welterweight crown. Gavilan's reward was an over-the-weight match with the Sugarman himself. In a fight that saw a distinguished cast in an undistinguished fight (read: boring), Robinson won a close decision over "The Keed." Now Gavilan picked up the pace, beating Ike Williams twice (both times on TV), Al Priest, Cliff Hart, Ben Buker, and Tony Pellone. (Three of these bouts were again on the 23-inch magic lantern.) The by-now popular Gavilan was given a title shot at Robinson for his efforts. In a close 15-round fight in which Gavilan cut Sugar Ray's eye and staggered him, Robinson held on to

outpoint "The Cuban Hawk." But Gavilan's reputation had been made; he was a force to be reckoned with in the welterweight division.

For the next two years Gavilan bided his time, fighting, and beating, welterweights and middleweights. Possessed of an energy born of a rhumba dancer, he fought 15 times in 1950, against such noteworthies as Robert Villemain, Billy Graham, Georgie Small, Sugar Costner, Eugene Hairston, Sonny Horne, Tony Janiro, Joe Miceli, and Paddy Young, beating almost all the welters and a majority of the middles. Finally, on the night of Friday, May 18, 1951, he got his chance, fighting Johnny Bratton for the by-now vacated welterweight title (Robinson having gone "upstairs" to the middleweight division). It was a fight made for Gavilan,

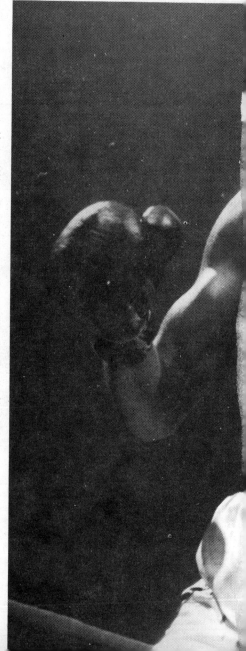

Right: Gavilan prepares to uncork his patented "Bolo Punch" to head of Bobo Olson, 1954.

his shop-worn opponent being a fighter who depended on the other fighter to make the fight. Gavilan accommodated him, swooping down like a hawk on his unsuspecting prey. He won easily.

In the homeopathic discipline of medicine, minute quantities of a substance are administered, which if given in massive amounts will produce effects similar to the disease being treated. Boxing's equivalent was Chuck Davey. For by 1953, televised boxing was suffering from overexposure, and its excesses were no more apparent than in the case of Davey. A college-educated white southpaw out of Detroit, he had become TV boxing's "glamour boy," his record built on over-the-hill fighters who looked like TV had emptied out the mission. In 1952 alone, he had appeared on the regularly

Born Gerardo Gonzalez, 1/6/26, in Camaguey, Cuba . . . Assumed name "Gavilan," meaning "hawk" in Spanish . . . Began professional career in 1943 . . . Fought primarily in Cuba, 1943–46 . . . Came to New York, 1946 . . . Lost 10-round non-title bout to Ray Robinson, 9/23/48 . . . Challenged Robinson for world welterweight title, 7/11/49—lost 15-round decision . . . Won welterweight crown, 5/18/51, in bout with Johnny Bratton for Robinson's vacated title . . . Successfully defended against: Billy Graham, 8/29/51, W 15; Bobby Dykes, 2/4/52, W 15; Gil Turner, 7/7/52, KO 11; Billy Graham, 10/5/52, W 15; Chuck Davey 2/11/53, KO 10; Carmen Basilio, 9/18/53, W 15; Johnny Bratton, 11/13/53, W 15 . . . 3 title defenses won by split decisions—Graham (first bout), Dykes, and Basilio . . . Second bout with Graham held in Havana, Cuba—first world championship bout in Havana since Johnson-Willard bout in 1915 . . . Unsuccessfully challenged Bobo Olson for middleweight title, 4/2/54, lost 15-round decision . . . Lost welterweight title in next bout to Johnny Saxton, 10/20/54, 15-round decision . . . Not known as knockout puncher—only 27 knockouts in 143 bouts . . . Scored only 3 knockouts in 35 bouts during prime of career, 1948–51 . . . Fought in South America and Europe, 1955–56 . . . Last 5 years (1954–58) definitely downhill—17 losses in last 30 bouts . . . Retired 9/11/58 . . . One of most televised boxers during television's "Golden Age" . . . Famed for "bolo" punch . . . Never knocked out—gave fans their money's worth—went the distance in 80% of his bouts . . . Elected to Boxing Hall of Fame, 1966 . . . Complete record: 143 bouts, 106 won, 30 lost, 6 draws, 1 no-contest, 27 knockouts.

scheduled Pabst Wednesday night fights seven times. In a fight that was as revelatory of Gavilan's skills as it was embarrassing in its exposure of Davey's, Gavilan jabbed Davey, flailed away with his bolo, and even took to mimicking Davey by turning around and facing his foe from a southpaw stance. He finally knocked him down twice and stopped him in the tenth. It was a *tour de force* for the flashy Gavilan, one which would serve as the centerpiece of his career.

Soon Gavilan was to run down, his out-of-the-ring rhumbaing and his troubles with a manager with flypaper fingers catching up with him. But he will always be remembered as one of the greats of the television era of boxing.

PETE HERMAN

The last time anybody in New Orleans moved as fast as Pete Herman came when they raided one of the Storyville pleasure houses. A human dynamo with two cyclonic hands working nonstop, Herman fought like a gristmill imbued with animality. His infighting and triphammer body blows were not as deadly as a massacre, but in the long run more devastating, forcing his opponents to look for refuge in clinches. And even there the respite was at a high price. Little wonder that he became a municipal monument in his hometown of New Orleans, which absorbed him much as he absorbed it. Starting out as a shoeshine boy in a New Orleans tonsorial parlor, the-then 12-year-old Herman chanced to come across a copy of the national 10¢ weekly, *The Police Gazette.* There, sandwiched among features on barbers who could clip hair the fastest, bartenders who could make a *pousée-café* with the most layers, strongmen who allowed their craniums to be sledgehammered through blocks of concrete, and other such sundry acts of the unusual, Herman came across the boxing news. And, like thousands of others in turn-of-the-century barbershops, pool halls, saloons, police stations, and fire halls, was fascinated by the sport. Only Herman, unlike most of the others, decided to do something about his fascination.

CONSUMED BY HIS DESIRE TO BE A prizefighter, Herman spent his spare moments shadow-boxing in front of the floor-length mirrors that surrounded the barbershop, practicing those moves that would become famous in years to come. However, the owner of the barbershop was underwhelmed with his bootblack's adopted avocation, yelling at him to "Sit down! You'll never be a fighter as long as you got a hole in your ass." Discreetly relocating his extracurricular activities to the nearby athletic club, Herman worked out every lunch hour with a friend of his who was then posing as a preliminary fighter and making the princely sum of 15 Taft dollars a week. The little kid with the build of a racetrack hotwalker not only beat his friend, but beat him easily and began to think to himself, "Hell, I'm going to start making some of that big money myself."

The local promoters put him in the saddle, but he already knew how to ride and began to win. And win regularly. Soon the little human dynamo who fought through a threshing swirl of activity was winning bouts and fans up and down the Delta. He had to be fast, he was moving in fast company, by 1913 fighting Eddie Coulon, Jimmy Walsh, Johnny Fisse, and Nat Jackson, all bantams of promise in a tough league. But he continued to win, almost as if his performance chart read: "Start good, won handily."

Within another year, Herman had advanced himself still higher, to the likes of Eddie Campi, Kid Williams, Young Zulu Kid, and Jimmy Pappas, all of

whom were experienced at the testing distance of 15—and even 20—rounds. And, as becomes any burgeoning talent, he had also acquired a board of strategy, led by Sammy Goldman, who had brought several fighters from New Orleans up to Madison Square Garden. Now he began beating the drums for his young fighter. "He's good," said Goldman, "but I'd like to see him at the weight and at the championship distance of twenty rounds. Then I'd really be able to sell my fresh young merchandise."

And so, on February 7, 1916, Goldman arranged a match for Herman with the bantamweight champion, Kid Williams, in New Orleans. The concessions to Williams included a record guarantee of $5,000 expenses and the privilege of naming the referee. Williams named his friend, the nationally known referee from Philadelphia, Billy Rocap. It was a duel of punchers, both running in billy-goat style with their heads down and locking horns, all the better to get close enough to throw their triphammer body punches. The New Orleans *Item* reported: "Pete grew up last night, he gave Williams a boxing lesson." Unfortunately, the referee didn't agree, his vote constituting a majority of one, all it took—and he voted for a draw.

For five years Herman slashed and stung his way through the lighter weights, dealing out his own special brand of terror. Finally, he got his rematch with Kid Williams. His manager, ever a shrewd student of psychology, came to him with a plan that would have brought tears of joy to the eyes of Freud: "I know that Rocap did a job for Williams last time. He won't dare do it again. So I'll *demand* him as the referee this time." And so, on the night of January 9, 1917, in front of Herman's hometown rooters, Rocap, knowing that his reputation was on the line and that he was appearing before several thousand New Orleans critics, gave the decision to Herman in another slugging battle; a decision which put him back in good odor with the local burghers.

Three months later America entered the "War to End All Wars," and Herman entered the Navy. Stationed in Philadelphia, he was asked by one of the commanding officers to box on a charity card to benefit the sailors and soldiers. As Fred Digby, the sports editor of the New Orleans *Item* remembered: "Pete knew he was out of shape and

really didn't want to, but he couldn't very well refuse. He boxed a boy named Gussie Lewis, who palpably took advantage of Pete's condition. Well, he got mad and soon it was a vicious affair. When Pete hurt him, he lost his temper. . . . He could dish it

Born Peter Gulotta, 2/12/96, in New Orleans, LA . . . First pro bout, 1912, New Orleans . . . Early record sketchy—fought primarily in New Orleans, 1912–16 . . . Fought 10-round nontitle no-decision bout with bantamweight champion Kid Williams, 6/30/14 . . . Challenged Williams in title bout, 2/7/16, but 20-round bout was called a draw . . . Won title from Williams in third bout, 1/9/17 . . . Successfully defended against Frankie Burns, 11/5/17, in 20-round decision . . . Lost title to Joe Lynch, 12/22/20, via 15-round decision . . . Re-won title in 15-round rematch with Lynch, 7/25/21 . . . Lost title in first defense to Johnny Buff, 9/23/21 . . . Fought 2 bouts in 1922 and then retired . . . Died 4/13/73, in New Orleans, LA . . . Elected to Boxing Hall of Fame, 1960 . . . Complete record: 149 bouts, 69 won, 11 lost, 8 draws, 61 no-decisions, 19 knockouts.

out but he couldn't take it. And he stuck his thumb in Pete's right eye."

Soon after the charity match, Herman, unbeknownst to all, became a charity case, losing the sight in his right eye. But while he had one good eye, he was able to continue fighting out of the fogbanks of his memory. But sometimes even that fog was too much for him, like the night he defended his title against Joe Lynch in the old, old Madison Square Garden. Herman, bothered by the manmade smoke haze and the haze in his eye, recalled many years later, "The smoke was like fog in the arena. It was so bad, Lynch would be in his corner and I would be in mine and I couldn't see him." Popular prejudice running in favor of two eyes, the decision went in favor of Lynch.

His next fight came less than one month later against the legendary Jimmy Wilde, "The Mighty Atom." Herman, one eye or no, dropped the flyweight champion twice and stopped him in 17 rounds. But Wilde had been reluctant to enter the ring, not only because of the weight differential, but more importantly because the promoters had promised him a shot at the bantamweight title and missed a small point: Herman had left it with Lynch for safekeeping, having lost that small bauble between signing to fight Wilde. Promoters being what they are, they evened the score by skipping out of town with Herman's share of the purse, thus managing to skewer everybody involved.

Returning home, Herman redeemed his bantamweight crown in a rematch with Lynch outdoors in Ebbets Field where "the smoke didn't bother" him. And then, two months later, he rerouted it to Johnny Buff, who beat him in 15.

By this time, the demands his almost totally sightless right eye were making on his left had begun to strain that orb, too. And Herman was fighting almost totally in the dark, his endurance and infighting carrying him into his opponents and through fights, his punches depending on a divining rod instinct.

Within the year, Herman finally gave up the ghost, retiring at the age of 26. He had had his day. Some may have had longer ones, but none ever had a brighter one than Pete Herman, whose memories were as good as hindsight. Except that most hindsight is 20-20. But not in the case of Pete Herman, who was to leave the ring legally blind.

Far left: Herman (left) and Johnny Buff shake hands mid-ring before Herman loses bantamweight title, 1921. Left: Herman (left) and Jimmy Wilde in fight won by Herman, 1921.

129

TIGER FLOWERS

"Blessed be the Lord, my strength, who teacheth my hands in war and my fingers to fight." Before the start of each of his fights, the quiet, unassuming man known to the boxing world as Tiger Flowers would quietly intone the above passage from Psalm 144 as a prayer before he went into battle. And go into battle he did. Radiating a hard glow of high purpose and swinging his arms with a sort of prancing nervousness, he would wheel into action with a tigerish fury, throwing caution and punches to the wind. Some compared his unorthodox southpaw windmill style to that of Harry Greb, calling him "a left-handed Harry Greb"; others described it as a "clownish way of fighting." But whatever it was, his inartistic style worked, as he ripped and slashed at his opponent, throwing rights and lefts with blinding speed in an attempt to make his opponent yield to the force of his convictions. And his punches.

THE PUNCHES OF THE MAN THEY called "The Georgia Deacon" were less punches than slaps, cuffs, smacks, and slashes, most of his blows landing with the side of the fist almost as if he were incapable of landing a straight jab or swing. Flowers's best quasi-combination was a clubbed right to the rib or the heart, followed by a slapping, cuffing left, resembling neither a swing nor a hook, but a version of someone playing "Pease Porridge Hot." And yet, untidy as it was, it somehow got the job done, especially when combined with his own strange interpretation of the Golden Rule—which was, in fact, no Golden Rule at all—that mixed in more than a small garnishment of tugging, pulling, wrestling, holding and hitting, low punching, and general all-around mauling.

In contrast to his open-handed slapping in the ring, outside the ring Flowers held his emotions in a tight fist. After beating former light heavyweight champion Mike McTigue decisively and being victimized by a poor decision in favor of the white man, Flowers accepted the verdict gracefully and congratulated McTigue without any semblance of a complaint. After the bout, as one reporter walked back to Tiger's dressing room to "look for my sweater,"

Tiger started searching for something, too. When asked what he was looking for, Flowers, from whom rarely was heard a discouraging word, only responded, "Ah'm lookin' for that decision what they say Ah done lost."

But Tiger Flowers didn't lose many decisions. Starting at the advanced age of 23, Flowers fought other "colored" fighters throughout the South—it being somewhat less than good sport to a black "whuppin'" a white boy down in his home area in those quaint, compartmentalized days of yesteryear. Finally, seeing the cities between New York and Chicago as one vast arena, his manager, Walk Miller, moved him into the midwest. And into the big time. In 1924, he fought 36 times without a loss, fighting the likes of Johnny Wilson and Harry Greb.

Nineteen twenty-six was the year of Gertrude Ederle, Aimee Semple McPherson, Admiral Richard Byrd, the Hall-Mills murder trial, and Tiger Flowers. For, on February 26, Flowers would win the middleweight title from Harry Greb, beating "The Pittsburgh Windmill" the only way anyone could: by outroughing him.

The first black to hold the middleweight title and the first since Jack Johnson to hold any championship,

Flowers hardly shared Johnson's bold approach to race relations, instead subscribing to Ralph Ellison's theory that blacks were invisible, and to an overly deferential attitude that he was, in his own words, "a Negro man who knows his own place." But even when he knew his own place, he was reluctant to assume it. Shortly after he had become champion, Flowers was invited by the New York Boxing Writers to take his place at their "Table of Champions" at their annual dinner. "I know I'm a champion," he explained, "but I am a Negro and maybe some of the white folks might think it out of place for me to sit down with them. So you'll please have to excuse me if I stay away." In the overly condescending style of the day, ring announcer Joe Humphries called Flowers "the whitest Negro I have ever known since Joe Gans," the traditional way of complimenting the modest champion.

The freshly baptized champion, true

Right: Flowers comes into Harry Greb with hands ablur, beating "The Pittsburgh Windmill" at his own game. He wins middleweight title, Feb. 26, 1926.

Born Theodore Flowers, 8/5/95, in Camille, GA . . . Known as "The Georgia Deacon" . . . First pro bout, 1918, early record sketchy . . . Knocked out 4 times in 1923 . . . Fought 36 bouts in 1924, won 30, lost none, others were draws or no-decision bouts . . . Won 3 consecutive bouts on fouls . . . Knocked out 2 opponents in same night, 11/10/24 . . . First black middleweight champion . . . Won world middleweight title with 15-round decision over Harry Greb, 2/26/26 . . . Defeated Greb in title bout rematch, 8/19/26 . . . Greb died shortly later from complications following facial surgery—ironically Flowers died in the same way less than 1 year later . . . Lost middleweight title to Mickey Walker, 12/3/26, in 10-round bout . . . Final year in ring, 1927, lost only 1 of 18 bouts, and had 3 draws with Maxie Rosenbloom . . . Died, 11/16/27, in New York, following an operation . . . Elected to Boxing Hall of Fame, 1971 . . . Complete record: 149 bouts, 115 won, 13 lost, 6 draws, 14 no-decisions, 1 no-contest, 49 knockouts.

to his word, gave Greb a rematch and again beat Greb at his own game. He next put his title on the line against the former welterweight champion, Mickey Walker, thought by all to be washed up. Despite being knocked down twice—which he always came back from with one of his famous back-springs before tearing into action— Flowers ruthlessly slashed, cuffed, and ripped into Walker for eight of the ten rounds, inflicting by far the greater damage. Still, in one of those mysterious and wholly undeserved decisions that happen every so often in the sweet-scented game, referee Benny Yanger mugged Flowers and gave the verdict, and the crown, to Walker— proving that nothing fails like success, especially if you were a black. Afterward, a discouraged but not disgruntled Flowers pored through his Bible for guidance: "I haven't lost faith," Flowers said. "But I'm puzzled and hurt as to how the Lord could have let me down."

Walker had promised Flowers a return bout. It was a return bout that would never take place. Eagerly awaiting the return go, Flowers continued to campaign—fighting light heavies and heavies and winning almost all of his 18 fights in 1927—while Walker continued to look the other way. After knocking out Leo Gates, a full-fledged heavyweight, Flowers entered a private hospital in New York for the removal of scar tissue. It was a routine operation, so routine, in fact, that the doctor told Flowers's manager, "You can go home, he's fine, he's just resting." But during the night a nurse made a routine bed check. She found no pulse beat. The doctor was summoned and confirmed Flowers's death, a "one-in-a-million shot."

But that was Tiger Flowers, a one-in-a-million fighter who was described by Gene Tunney as "A great champion and a true man. . . . A credit to the boxing game and to his race." And if anyone was keeping score upstairs, they could have written his epitaph with the words from the Second Epistle of Paul the Apostle to Timothy: "I have fought a good fight, I have finished my course, I have kept the faith. . . ." Tiger Flowers did all three.

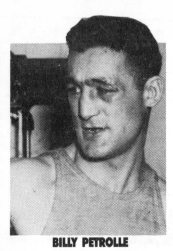

BILLY PETROLLE

You could connect the scars on Billy Petrolle's face. They had the look of an elaborate criss-crossing, like lines on a road map. And, although the map led to many memories, it never led to a championship. But it is not the scars that one remembers most about Billy Petrolle. Nor is it his style, a modified form of a one-man riot. It is something else that Billy Petrolle brought with him every time he fought—his Navajo blanket. No one who saw Petrolle fight will ever forget the sight of him hurrying down the aisle wrapped in his bright red and green Navajo blanket. It became, along with his wicked left hook, his trademark. From the first time he wore it into the ring, in Los Angeles, the crowd loved it, cheering wildly. The blanket sort of symbolized the gallery gods' reverse snobbism. And for the next 11 years, Billy Petrolle would never enter the ring without what he called his "good luck piece."

TO THE TRADITIONAL SIGHTS AND sounds of boxing, Petrolle was to add another—smell: He refused to wash the blanket because he was "afraid of washing the good luck out of it." And so, the blanket, stained with the sweat and blood of 11 years, became his red badge of achievement in the ring— smelly though it was—just as the blood on the aprons of doctors becomes their red badge of achievement in operating rooms.

But there was more to Petrolle. Much more. Petrolle was someone the average person on the street could identify with, a fighter who gave his all every second of every round, fighting as he looked, with hair on his chest. His nonstop aggression and streaking left hook combined to give him his nickname, "The Fargo Express"—after one contemporary New York cartoonist pictured the kid from Fargo, North Dakota, as a runaway locomotive. And, as "The Fargo Express," Petrolle became one of the ring's greatest crowd pleasers. Little wonder that, as Damon Runyon noted, "When 'The Fargo Express' climbs into the ring, the people climb in right behind him."

Petrolle first burst onto the boxing scene with a fifth-round knockout of

Jackie "Kid" Berg, the first of five world champions he was to beat—unfortunately, at a time when none of them possessed a championship to which he could lay claim. He followed that up with wins over Ray Miller, Tony Canzoneri, and former lightweight champion Jimmy Goodrich. And then, at what Mrs. Malaprop called "the pineapple of his career," he took apart Jimmy

McLarnin in a fight when 6–1 money went begging on Petrolle, sending McLarnin to the hospital for his efforts. Now, under a full head of steam, "The Fargo Express" roared through the lightweight division denuding it of contenders as first he ruined Eddie Ran, then Billy Townsend, and then Justo Suarez, the tough Chilean challenger.

By now, the Petrolle style was be-

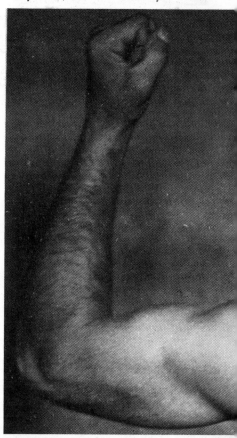

coming as familiar as the Navajo blanket. Coming in low in his patented crouch and bobbing his head to and fro, Petrolle would use his hands like Indian clubs to the body, feint a right to the head, and then try to bury his streaking left hook in his opponent's stomach, right up to the wrist.

Just one fight away from his big chance—a shot at the lightweight championship and Tony Canzoneri, the man he had already beaten—Petrolle took on Battling Battalino, the former featherweight champion who had relinquished his crown to do battle amongst the bigger men. In as two-sided and gory a fight as any ever seen, "The Fargo Express" knocked out Bat in the twelfth round, the only time Battalino was ever stopped. But in doing so, he injured his money arm, the left, and

after a lengthy layoff to recuperate, Petrolle came back to lose a 15-round decision to a Canzoneri at his best.

It was no disgrace, but it was also no brass ring for as great a warrior as the ring has ever known. And because he never held a title, no amount of fistic bookkeeping will ever be able to properly assess the greatness of the man they called "The Fargo Express."

Opposite bottom: Petrolle with manager Jack Hurley. Below and left: "The Fargo Express" roars in on classy Eddie Ran and leaves his wreckage on the canvas in the 6th round, 1932.

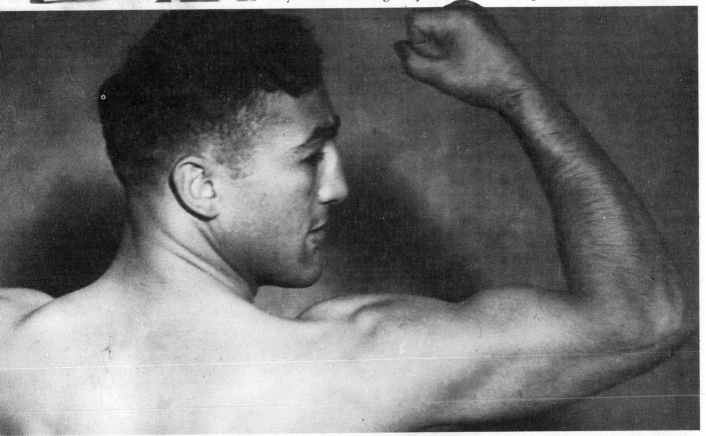

Born 1/10/05, in Berwick, PA . . . Began boxing professionally, 1924 . . . Never won a championship but faced 10 world champions and defeated 6 of them . . . Known as "The Fargo Express" after hometown of Fargo, ND . . . Undefeated in 24 bouts in first year as a professional . . . Fought Sammy Mandell, world lightweight champion in nontitle no-decision 10-round bout, 1/13/28 . . . Drew with Jack Kid Berg, 7/26/28, knocked out Berg in rematch, 8/24/28, first knockout loss for Berg . . . Defeated Jimmy Goodrich in 10 rounds, 7/26/29 . . . Defeated Tony Canzoneri, 9/11/30, 10-round decision . . . Met Jimmy McLarnin in 3 bouts, won the first, 11/21/30; lost the next 2, 5/27/31 and 8/20/31 . . . Defeated Battling Battalino twice, twelfth-round kayo, 3/24/32; 5/20/32, 10-round decision . . . Only one title bout, lost 15-round decision for world lightweight championship to Tony Canzoneri, 11/4/32 . . . Knocked out Dutch Olympic champion Bep Van Klaveren in 4 rounds, 7/12/33 . . . Defeated Sammy Fuller, 10/21/33, in 10 rounds after 10-round draw with Fuller, 9/8/33 . . . Lost twice to Barney Ross, 3/22/33, and 1/24/34, both 10 round decisions . . . Retired from ring after last loss to Ross . . . Elected to Boxing Hall of Fame, 1962 . . . Complete record: 157 bouts, 89 won, 20 lost, 10 draws, 37 no-decisions, 1 no-contest.

SUGAR RAY LEONARD

Many old-timers, for whom boxing goes in one era and out the other, believe that there was only one "Sugar" and that the accolade was reserved for one man and one man alone—Sugar Ray Robinson. In fact, Robinson had once tried to preserve his title in the face of a fistic avalanche of "Sugars." One time, so the story goes, when Robinson faced another of the so-called pretenders to the Sugar crown, George Costner, he reputedly told Costner before the fight, "Now I'll show you who's the real 'Sugar,'" and proceeded to prove his point by laying out Costner endwise in one round. Afterward, Robinson chided the artificial Sugar with, "Now go out and earn yourself the name!" But another "Sugar" Ray Charles Leonard was to earn himself the name. And with it a place in history.

welterweight division—if not all of boxing—was merely a rumor, devalued as much as the rest of society, sort of boxing's form of Gresham's Law with the bad fighters forcing out the good ones.

However, before he could make himself into a smooth coin negotiable in any market, he had to serve his apprenticeship in the ring. Already a celebrity, he quickly became a hero, as he flashed across the canvas to his own beat, with lightning fists and well-defined moves. But it was not grace without power nor beauty without substance, as Leonard won his first 25 fights, 16 by knockout.

In his twenty-sixth fight, he met another all-time great, Wilfred Benitez, for the welterweight championship. In a battle of greats where talent was the punch and determination the clever footwork, Leonard showed he had more of both—plus a schoolbook jab and his by-now patented flurries—and won by a knockout in the closing seconds.

Then, after defending his newly-

STARTING BACK WITH THE 1920 SUMmer games in Antwerp, when Frankie Genaro traded in his Olympic gold medal for the championship gold of professional boxing, the Olympics have been a shortcut to fistic gold and glory. Throughout the intervening years several gold medalists have translated their victories into successful professional careers and even championships, including: Fidel La Barba, Jackie Fields, Otto Von Porat, Pascual Perez, Floyd Patterson, Pete Rademacher, Nino Benvenuti, Cassius Clay, Joe Frazier, Chris Finnegan, and George Foreman. But no one summer Olympics gave us more champions who turned in their amateur trinkets for professional treasures than the 1976 games in Montreal. And no one fighter ever capitalized on his Olympic gold more than the darling of the 1976 Olympics: Sugar Ray Leonard.

In a day and age when the new buzzword among Madison Avenue executives was "charisma," Sugar Ray Leonard, with his infectious personality was someone who possessed what Clara Bow had a half-century before, that indefinable trait called "It," for lack of a better word. Highly marketable and properly packaged, Leonard became a commercial property before he ever stepped into a professional ring.

But Sugar Ray Leonard was to acquit the build-up and raise it some. For when he came upon the scene, the

Born Ray Charles Leonard, 5/17/56, Wilmington, SC . . . Named for jazz musician . . . Excellent amateur record: won U.S. National Amateur title, 1974–75; won Pan-American Games, 1975; won Olympic Games, 1976—all in light welterweight (139 lbs.) class . . . Only man to win Pan-American Games title and world professional championship . . . Much publicized career: first pro bout on national TV, 2/5/77, W 6 over Luis Vega, earned $40,000 for bout . . . Won first 25 bouts, 1977–79 . . . Matched with Wilfred Benitez for WBC world welterweight title in only third year as pro (11/30/79) stopped Benitez in fifteenth to win title—first loss for Benitez . . . Defended against Dave (Boy) Green, 3/31/80, KO 4 . . . Multi-million dollar defense against Roberto Duran, 6/20/80, lost title via 15-round decision . . . Regained title in rematch, 11/25/80, when Duran unable to continue in eighth round . . . Defended against Larry Bonds, 3/28/81, KO 10 . . . Won WBA world junior middleweight title from Ayub Kalule, 6/25/81, by ninth-round knockout, first pro loss for Kalule . . . Held 2 titles simultaneously before relinquishing junior middleweight title without a defense . . . Stopped WBA welterweight champion Thomas Hearns in fourteenth round, in unification bout, 9/16/81, first pro loss for Hearns . . . Defended against Bruce Finch, 2/15/82, KO 3 . . . Scheduled defense against Roger Stafford, May 1982, cancelled after Leonard underwent surgery, 5/9/82, to repair a detached retina . . . Announced retirement at special ceremony, 11/9/82 . . . Attempted comeback, 5/11/84, stopped Kevin Howard in ninth but lacklustre performance caused him to retire immediately following bout . . . Complete record: 34 bouts, 33 won, 1 lost, 24 knockouts.

the accomplishment by winning back the title he had "leased" to Duran five months earlier.

With just one more mountain to scale, that of solidifying his claim to the undisputed welterweight championship of the world—which had been halved by those two clowns of boxing, the WBA and the WBC—Leonard next faced the owner of the other "half" of the championship, Thomas Hearns, WBA titlist. In a fight called "The Showdown," but which could have easily become one of the hundreds of lesser battles known as the "Fight of the Century," Leonard beat the supposedly invincible Hearns in a fight with more twists and turns than could be found in an early O. Henry potboiler. Entering the ring with a robe emblazoned with the solitary word, "Deliverance," Leonard went to work to rid himself of the dybbuks and devils who had belittled his right to be called great by playing mongoose to the man introduced as "The Motor City Cobra." Finally, in the fourteenth, Leonard overcame Hearns, three judges who had him behind, and a by-now threatening mouse on his left eye with a nonstop effort to attain a fourteenth-round TKO and his thirty-first win.

There would be only two more wins left in the career of Sugar Ray Leonard, his illustrious career foreshortened by a detached retina, his celebrity still such that there arose a universal hymn of concern for his health. Still, in five-plus years, he had accomplished all he had set out to do when he took his Olympic gold medal and turned it into pure gold. And greatness. And the right to be called "Sugar."

minted title once, he faced the legendary Roberto Duran in the same Montreal ring where he had started his meteoric rise to fame just four years before. However, this time Leonard, eschewing the tactics that had brought him there, went right into the lion's den and tried to out-macho the "Hands of Stone," slugging it out with the barrio brawler from the streets of Panama City. As betrayed by his plumage as any bird, Leonard could never quite make restitution for his impetuosity, and lost the decision. And the title.

Five months later Leonard *would* fight "his" fight. And in so doing, reduce Duran to a frustrated battler, his punches re-routed, his bull-like charges thwarted, his manhood taunted. Finally, after following Leonard around the ring for seven rounds in much the same manner as trying to find a snail that left a faint recognizable thread out of itself but never quite finding it, Duran inexplicably threw up his "Hands of Stone" and capitulated with the infamous words, "No Mas . . . No Mas." Leonard immediately jumped up on the ring post, less in celebration of the attainment of greatness than a celebration of

Left: Leonard, complete with a picture of Ray, Jr. tucked in his sock, socks it to Augustin Estrada, Nov. 5, 1977. Above: Leonard shows winning form against Jose Bernardo Prada, Nov. 3, 1978.

JACK DEMPSEY, THE NONPAREIL

In one of those little tricks history continually plays on us to see if we are really paying attention—similar to the one that has become enshrined in our memories and books holding that Lindbergh was the first to cross the Atlantic when, in reality, he was the nineteenth, albeit the first to fly solo—we tend to forget that there were two Jack Dempseys. Without the second one, the original might well have enjoyed timeless fame as one of the greatest fighters of all time; instead he is known only as the second greatest fighter named Jack Dempsey, if he is known at all. And yet, this boxer whom very few know, over and above boxing's hard-core cognoscenti, was acclaimed as "the greatest fighter" of his time—which was back in boxing's antediluvian days, the 1880s—and by many of those who saw him and are no longer around to defend their opinions, "the greatest fighter in modern times." At his peak, he was without peer and accorded the nickname "The Nonpareil," meaning matchless or unrivaled, a name which theretofore had been the special unpoachable reserve of the great English bareknuckle champ Jack Randall.

THE CAREER OF THE FIRST JACK Dempsey, "The Nonpareil," was rooted in the boyhood camaraderie of four boxing-minded friends in a barrel-making plant in Brooklyn. Lunchtime was boxing time for the four. After wolfing down bowls of soup, they would wrap their cooperage aprons around their hands as makeshift gloves and have a Go at it, all four emulating the moves of Jem Mace, the current bareknuckle champion. The four, all of whom would go on to play leading roles in the world of boxing, were Jim Browne, who would become a prominent promoter; Jack Skelly, who would later box for the featherweight championship against the great George Dixon in his first professional fight; Jack McAuliffe, the undefeated American lightweight champion; and the aforementioned Jack Dempsey.

Actually, Jack Dempsey was not Jack Dempsey's real name any more than it was the real name of "The Manassa Mauler." "The Nonpareil's" christened name being John Kelly. But for purposes of wrestling, he had adopted his stepfather's surname, first using it to form a wrestling team with his brother, appropriately known as "The Dempsey Brothers."

His first fight was against Eddie McDonald, an experienced fighter, but one who was notorious for not going into the ring until he knew the probable planned result. Nothing happened for five rounds and then McDonald whispered in the clinch to Dempsey, "Time for you to lay down, boy." Dempsey laughed in his face. McDonald suddenly realized that no arrangements had been made with the handsome Irish lad with the rare roast beef complexion standing in front of him. On his own for once, McDonald held on until the twenty-first round when Dempsey knocked him out.

Within 15 months the peerless one had become the American lightweight champion—and the world's middleweight titleholder, as well.

Having fought 63 consecutive fights without a loss, he took on George LaBlanche, "The Marine," in a title defense in August of 1889. Warned by "those in the know" that LaBlanche might resort to some sort of a surprise maneuver, the haughty Dempsey ignored their warnings and went ahead with business as usual during altercations, using his lightning-like hands to war upon the features of "The Marine" for 31 rounds. But then, in the thirty-second, LaBlanche spun completely around. Gaining momentum, his right arm straight out, catching Dempsey with a perfectly executed pivot punch; or more correctly stated, he gave him the back of his hand, literally. Dempsey went down like a barrel filled with cement, out cold. Some excused LaBlanche's action on the grounds that, like Jack the Ripper's, it was human nature. But the referee disqualified LaBlanche for an illegal blow and Dempsey continued to be recognized as

the legitimate champion.

That recognition would continue for another 17 months, until he fought Bob Fitzsimmons at the famed Olympic Club in New Orleans for a purse of $12,000—$11,000 to the winner, $1,000 to the loser—the largest purse offered for a fight up to that time. The fight, however, was no fight, as Fitz established his mastery right from the start and began beating Dempsey to the punch and to the floor with equal frequency, knocking him down seven times in the eleventh. After the seventh knockdown, Fitzsimmons begged The Peerless One to resign. "If you want me to," Dempsey snarled, "you'll have to knock me out." Two rounds later Fitzsimmons accommodated Dempsey's demand.

Dempsey was to fight but three more times in the next four years. In his last fight, an exhibition against the up-and-coming Tommy Ryan, his weight had dropped to a startling 135 pounds. Something was wrong with the man who had once possessed the finest physical equipment in boxing. Drastically wrong. That June, the sporting life of New York, now aware of Dempsey's declining condition and his losing battle with consumption, gave him a benefit. The Nonpareil cried with unashamed tears. Shortly thereafter he left the East Coast to settle in Portland, Oregon, but within five months he was dead from the ravages of the dread disease. Inexplicably, the great Jack Dempsey was to lay in an unmarked grave for a long period of time, prompting a friend to write the poem that ended:

" 'Tis strange New York should thus forget
Its 'bravest of the brave'

And in the fields of Oregon
Unmarked leave Dempsey's grave."

Born John Kelly, 12/15/62, County Kildare, Ireland . . . Came to U.S. as youth . . . Fought during transition era from bareknuckles to gloves . . . First pro bouts, 1883 . . . Accepted challenge of Canadian, George Fulljames and claimed vacant middleweight title after twenty-second-round knockout—bout fought with heavy driving gloves . . . Defended title, 2/3/86, with twenty-seventh-round kayo of Jack Forgarty . . . Knocked out George LaBlanche in 3 rounds, 3/4/86, in second title defense . . . Defeated Johnny Reagan, 12/13/87, in 2 rings, first ring became submerged with water in fourth round, bout moved 20 miles away and finished in snow and cold after 1 hour and 13 minutes for a forty-fifth-round knockout . . . Knocked out by George LaBlanche, 8/27/89, in title bout but LaBlanche used illegal "pivot punch" to score kayo and was also over the weight limit, LaBlanche's title claim not recognized . . . Defended, 2/18/90, with twenty-eighth-round kayo of Billy McCarthy . . . Lost title to Bob Fitzsimmons when kayoed in thirteenth, 1/14/91 . . . Last bout, 1/18/95, challenged Tommy Ryan for world welterweight title, kayoed in third round . . . Died later that year, 11/2/95, in Portland, ORE . . . Charter member of Boxing Hall of Fame, 1954 . . . Complete record: 48 won, 3 lost, 7 draws, 7 no-decisions, 3 no-contests.

Above: Dempsey (insert left) knocks out George Fulljames (right insert) in the 22nd round to win world middleweight title, July 30, 1884.

DICK TIGER

Dick Tiger was the type of fighter who rolled up his sleeves, spat on his hands, and went to work, giving an honest laboring-man's effort. Each time. Every time. And therein lay the popularity of this simple, sincere, and solid warrior. The man who would be known forever to the boxing world as Dick Tiger was born Richard Ihetu—a family name with tribal origins, attested to by the tattoos scratched into his back and chest with blue dye, affirming his blood ties, like the hieroglyphics of a long-lost society—in the British trust territory of Nigeria. Moving to the nearby major city of Aba in 1947, Ihetu pursued an occupation as handyman and a preoccupation with boxing, joining the local boxing club and the regularly scheduled boxing shows held at the local British army base. As Ihetu-Tiger would later recall, "I don't remember exactly when it happened, but I do remember one day I had been jumping in at my opponent . . . fast, real fast. One of the Englishmen shouted, 'A tiger, that's what he is.' And that's how I got my fighting name." And so, Dick Tiger was born.

TURNING PROFESSIONAL ALMOST IMMEdiately, the fine print at the beginning of his pro record shows him fighting local strawmen, local lions, and local sacred cows with names almost as picturesque as their fabled tribal exploits: Easy Dynamite, Lion Ring, Black Power, and Super Human Power. After winning the Nigerian middleweight title from someone with the pallid handle of Tommy West, Tiger decided to further his career far from the big town of Lagos where he considered himself "lucky to get by," there being "too many fighters and not enough shows."

However, Tiger never asked much till fate, in the form of Jack Farnsworth, offered more. Farnsworth, a Brit who was chairman of the Nigerian Boxing Board of Control, was responsible for having started Hogan "Kid" Bassey on his way to becoming featherweight champion of the world. Anxious to help the crowd-pleasing battler with the catlike springiness, Farnsworth offered Tiger a hammock of hope, sending a telegram to Bassey, who was at the time fighting in England: "Dick Tiger could be a top middleweight fighting in England. Advise." Bassey, in turn, handed the telegram over to his manager, Bobby Diamond, who replied that he would be interested in seeing Tiger.

And yet, even at a time when there was a growing shortage of boxers in England, and West African fighters like Bassey could be sure of getting plenty of work, Tiger got none. Diamond instead consigned him to a job in a paint factory in Liverpool, telling Tiger to get to the gym and find his own instructor. Losing his first four fights and having to pull double duty as a working manfighter, Tiger was on the verge of packing it in when one of the Liverpudlians who had seen him fight advised him to "try again" like Robert of Bruce. Taking a new manager, Tiger set about correcting a few of the errors in his style. And began winning. By 1958 he had won 17 of 19 fights and the British Empire middleweight title as well.

Next he set sail for the States, like hundreds of British boxers before him. But unlike almost all of them, this import was not of the typical horizontal

variety. Instead, Tiger merely tested his opponent's will, the strongest will winning. He believed that in a man-to-man contest both risks and ring tricks were a denial of the old axiom: "May the *better* man win." It was a style as glamorous as an unmade bed, but popular among the fight fans who ap-

Born Richard Ihetu, 8/14/29, in Amaigbo, Orlu, Nigeria . . . Began professional career in Nigeria, 1952, early record sketchy . . . Early opponents include: Easy Dynamite, Mighty Joe, Lion Ring, and Super Human Power . . . Moved to England, 1955, lost 4 consecutive bouts, 12/55–3/56 . . . Won British Empire middleweight title, 3/27/58, with KO 9 win over Pat McAteer . . . Came to U.S., 1959 . . . Lost British Empire title to Wilf Greaves, 6/22/60, regained title from Greaves 11/30/60 . . . Won NBA world middleweight title from Gene Fullmer by 15-round decidion, 10/23/62; received more widespread title recognition, 11/9/62, when Paul Pender was stripped of his version of the title . . . Defended against Fullmer, 2/23/63, held to 15-round draw but retained title . . . Knocked out Fullmer in seventh round of third match, 8/10/63 . . . Lost title to Joey Giardello, 12/7/63; regained title via decision, 10/21/65, in rematch win Giardello . . . Lost title by decision in first defense, 4/25/66, to Emile Griffith . . . Won world light heavyweight title in next outing, 12/16/66, by decisioning Jose Torres . . . Defended successfully twice: 5/16/67, Torres, W 15; 11/17/67, Rouse, KO 12 . . . Lost title to Bob Foster on a fourth-round knockout, 5/24/68 . . . Continued boxing until 1970 . . . Announced retirement, 7/19/71 . . . Died, 12/14/71, in Nigeria . . . Elected to Boxing Hall of Fame, 1974 . . . Complete record: 81 bouts, 61 won, 17 lost, 3 draws, 26 knockouts.

Right: Tiger Outpoints Nino Benvenuti in a 10-round nontitle fight, May 26, 1969.

preciated his sincerity of effort.

However, Tiger's sincerity was not reciprocated and he was soon to learn the American way of insincerity, practiced by the American grandees of boxing. First of all, his American handler, Jersey Jones, attempting to go it alone, avoided dealing with Madison Square Garden and became embroiled in deals of his own making. Getting tangled up in an independent promotion in Edmonton, Canada, Jones put Tiger's Empire title on the line against a local, Wilf Greaves. Tiger hammered Greaves like a one-man strong-arm squad for 15 rounds. And yet at the end of the fight, the voting was a draw. Jones protested and on a recount, he was repaid for his impetuousness by having the decision overturned into a win for Greaves. Then, after winning the title from Gene Fullmer—and defending it two more times against him—Jones had Tiger defend it against Joey Giardello in another "off-Broadway" production in Atlantic City. The gatekeepers stole the gate by letting everyone in free and the referee, Paul Cavalier, who, according to Tiger, "didn't see the fight . . . He only saw Giardello"—"stole" the title from Tiger.

Promised a return "before anybody else," Tiger waited and waited while Giardello delayed and dickered. By now 33 years old and conscious that the sand in his hourglass slowly was ebbing away, Tiger became embittered. "I have met a lot of people in the United States," he was to say, "and they are good people. But it is lucky that I did not meet Giardello first. If I did," he went on, "I would never have any respect for Americans."

Tiger finally got his chance and made the most of it, winning back the title. Six months later he was to lose it in his first defense to Emile Griffith. But Tiger was not through, and in his next fight, he won the light heavyweight championship from Jose Torres in 15 close, exciting rounds, imposing his will on Torres and his style on the judges who gave him a narrow victory.

Nearing the end of his long, intercontinental fistic journey, Tiger put his light heavyweight title on the line three more times, the last time against Bob Foster. It was one risk too many as Foster caught Tiger with a right uppercut and left hook in the fourth round, knocking out the ebony block of granite for the first—and only—time in his career. Tiger tried a comeback at the tender age of 40, beating Nino Benvenuti. But time had run out on him and, after one more fight, old in body and equally old in spirit, he announced his retirement.

Then, like an old tiger, Richard Ihetu returned to the place of his last remembered beauty, Aba, now in Biafra, to die—whether from cancer, as reported, or just another unfortunate statistic of war, a warrior to the end, as had been rumored. But whatever it was, it was one more of the risks a great champion had to take. And Richard Ihetu, aka "Tiger," was a champion. And a great.

59 BEAU JACK

BEAU JACK

A large part of boxing's power structure is its internecine warfare, with struggles unseen since the early wars between the Italian feudal states. Back when boxing and the country were both on the relief rolls, courtesy of the Depression, which lay on the land like the pharaoh's plague, a desperate struggle took place for possession of Madison Square Garden between the forces of Garden matchmaker Jimmy Johnston and those of "Uncle" Mike Jacobs, head of something known as the 20th Century Sporting Club. Following that old boxing bromide that holds whoever controls the heavyweight champion controls boxing, Jacobs first gained control of the coming heavyweight champion, Joe Louis. Then, having gotten his nose under the Garden tent, he gained control of the Garden as well, his two major attractions Louis and Henry Armstrong. But if Louis and Armstrong were the building blocks that built the 20th Century Sporting Club, it would be battler Beau Jack who would retire the mortgage.

BEAU JACK CAME UPON THE NEW YORK boxing scene in late August of 1941, and became a main eventer in the Garden in November of 1942, just when the clouds of war were their blackest. But from his very first fight, the radiance of Beau pierced the wartime blackout, his handiwork less that of the occasional heroics sportswriters feed upon than that appreciated by dues-paying fans who flocked to see him.

From the very first moment Garden fans laid their eyes on the dynamic, nonstop punching machine known as Beau Jack, they welcomed him—and his brand of fighting—with open arms. Appearing in 21 main-event fights, more than anyone in the long history of Madison Square Garden, he would never wear out that welcome.

The Beau's broad, flat face gave him the look of someone who had stopped a runaway train at full speed in complete disregard of personal safety. He fought the same way. Barreling into his opponents like a pinwheel out of control, Beau would provide enough smoke behind the fire to suffocate his foes, causing them to suffer gentle and gradual erosion. Looking like a mar-

ionette with one string broken, Beau flailed away from every conceivable angle, his low-held hands throwing a smorgasbord of punches, bolos, hooks, crosses, and just about everything else imaginable, with either hand, always following his trainer's shouted command to "rip 'em all the time . . . " On defense he was a human backboard, totally indestructible and impervious to punishment. And after every fight, win or lose, he would unfailingly ask, "Was it a good fight? Did the people like it?" Small wonder that the New York sporting crowd loved their Beau idol. And flocked to see him fight.

But even though he had become the idol of a civilization that was measured by late-night newsstands, neon lights, and Broadway babes, Beau Jack had come a long way to get there. Raised in Georgia—pronounced "Jojah" by Beau—Beau Jack had started as a shoeshine boy at the same prestigious Augusta National Golf Club which annually hosts the Masters. A consistent winner in that southern pastime that rivals bear-baiting, "Battle Royals," the Beau had taken a shine to boxing rather than shoes, and asked the members if

anyone could grubstake him to his sought-after career. Finally, Beau asked golfing great, Bobby Jones, who asked some of the members and, as Beau remembers it, "He called me downstairs and said, 'Beau, I finally spoke to the members and fifty of them will give you fifty dollars apiece to begin your boxing life.' " Beau went north with one of the members and took up residence at the Long Meadow Country Club in Springfield, Massachusetts, which accounts for his early fights in nearby Holyoke.

Left: Jack beats Frizie Zivic for the second time in 28 days, March 5, 1943.

After 28 fights against the wheat and chaff of New England, Beau made his way south to New York and the emerald palace of every boxer's dreams, Madison Square Garden. In the five years before he made his first appearance at the Garden, the Garden had averaged 11,677 paying fans per show and a gate of $36,295. (And, if Joe Louis' five title appearances were expurged, the average would be reduced to 11,400 and $33,433.) Beau's first fight, a seventh-round KO of Allie Stoltz, brought out 14,249 fans paying $34,786. His second, a three-round KO of Tippy Larkin for the New York version of the lightweight title, turned out 18,817 and a gate of $58,468. Jack became the biggest little draw in boxing.

Over the next seven years, the man who mainlined excitement headlined the Garden card 21 times—including the incredible feat of appearing three times in the main event in one month, March of 1944—drawing more than 336,000 fans and $1,579,000. His "proudest" moment came August 4, 1944, when he faced Bob Montgomery

in a fight to benefit the War Bond drive and netted $35,864,900!

It would be nice to be able to write that some of the monies Beau Jack earned for the Garden stuck to his ribs. Unfortunately, such was not the case. For he was to run into the ineluctible lies and eloquent greed of boxing as his money hit a sea called "expenses" and was swallowed up without a trace. His manager, in name if not in fact, Chick Wergales—who, in the time-honored tradition of Jacobs Beach, had a cheerful contempt for the English language—once said, "Beau loves to fight. If he didn't get no pay for it, he'd still wanta fight just to relieve the monopoly." And unfortunately, although he did earn the Garden $1,579,000—and the War Bond drive almost 24 times that amount—Beau Jack "didn't get no pay for it," winding up penniless after almost single-handedly rekindling the dormant torch called boxing.

Still, he had no regrets, looking back and remembering how it was: "The people came week after week, month after month, carrying me along to win because they knowed I was doing my best at all times." That was Beau Jack, a crowd-pleaser without peer in the annals of boxing.

IKE WILLIAMS

60 IKE WILLIAMS

Writer Barney Nagler was once overheard asking of no one in particular, "Why won't sharks eat managers?" And then, without pausing for an answer—lest it be funnier—hurried to give the punchline: "Professional courtesy." Around boxing since Cain rendered Abel *hors de combat,* Nagler remembers all too well those days back in the late forties and early fifties when the shadow landlords of boxing all had numbers under their pictures. These boxing noblemen combined their efforts to form something called the "Managers Guild," a confederation whose stated purpose was to control the fighters and, through them, to control the sport of boxing and keep "uncooperative" fighters, matchmakers, and promoters in line. Led by two sharks of the first water—Paul John "Frankie" Carbo, a.k.a. "Mr. Gray," and his trusty sidekick, Francis "Blinky" Palermo, so nicknamed for his fluttering eyelids—the Managers Guild, rowing with muffled oars, laid anchor to some of the biggest names in boxing, including Ike Williams, the talented lightweight of approximately the same era.

IKE WILLIAMS WAS A GIFTED FIGHTER, on the one hand a ring general who combined speed and finesse and, in the words of one ringside reporter, "could have played piano with boxing gloves on." On the other hand, he was a murderous puncher who was relentless in his pursuit of his prey. With well defined moves worthy of some of the ancient greats, Williams used his lightning left to run interference for one of the heaviest rights in lightweight history, leaving most of his opponents with the same difficulty in their search for defensible borders as ancient Rome had.

Starting his career in 1940, Williams had 47 fights in four years, losing only four times. But in each of those losses, Williams was to "learn something," storing it away for future use. Finally, he was matched against former lightweight champion Bob Montgomery, who had been playing musical chairs with his championship, alternately winning it from, and losing it back to, Beau Jack. In 12 brutal rounds, Montgomery used all the tricks of the trade, head included, to knock out Williams with but 11 seconds left in the twelfth and final round.

But Williams, with the resiliency of a champion, picked himself up, brushed himself off, and started all over again. Over the next 15 months, he ran through and over 20 opponents, rendering the lightweight division a boxing wasteland. Finally, the National Boxing Association recognized his fistic achievements and made him their number-one challenger for their belt, then held by Juan Zurita. And even though Williams was to knock out Zurita in his own backyard, Mexico City—landing a beautiful right to the body and a picture-perfect left to the chin—he was never to own the belt, as the brick-throwing crowd stormed the ring, and one of the ungrateful banditos brandished a gun in mid-ring and took the belt back.

But the belt soon became the least of his problems. For Williams had determined to leave his manager, one Connie McCarthy, and strike out on his own. In the eyes of the Managers Guild, that was to be strike one against Williams, and they blackballed the newly crowned—if not belted—cham-

pion. Jimmy White, the president in name if not in fact, stated publicly, "We're going to show everyone just how powerful we are. We're going to stop Ike Williams from fighting. And, if anybody fights him, we're going to blackball them, too."

Ike Williams was suddenly an untouchable. None of the fistic caste would book him, none would promote him, and damned few would fight him. And what few there were existed in the Union Cities, Norwalks, and Oranges of the boxing world.

But there *was* one person who would touch Williams, Blinky Palermo. After one training session, Palermo sidled up to Williams and whispered something that sounded like, "Listen, Ike, you sign a contract with me, I'll straighten out the Guild." The economic realities being, in the words of Jimmy Durante, "them that is," it was an offer Williams could ill afford to refuse. The only condition Williams put on his signing the contract was that Blinky get him a return fight with Montgomery. And property. Soon he not only overflowed with Blinky's associations, he stood in their slop. In the Kefauver Committee investigations, Williams retold countless tales of Palermo approaching him with some offer or other, always offered as a suggestion, never an order, as in, "Ike, they want to give you fifty thousand dollars . . . " to do something or other. And then closing out the masked demand by couching it with an "If I were you I wouldn't take it, but it's not for me to say. . . . " It was an unholy alliance between Ike Williams, who always had his opponent's number, and Blinky Palermo, who would rarely let him dial it.

Magically, doors and dates opened up to Williams, courtesy of the Managers Guild. And Blinky Palermo. And, after six fights in 1947—including a main event at Madison Square Garden against Tippy Larkin—what to his wondering eyes should appear but a rematch with Bob Montgomery. This wasn't just to be a resumption of their bitter rivalry—one which had simmered since their first fight three years before when Montgomery had knocked out Williams to repay him for having knocked out a friend of his, and thrown in a gratuitous butt or two—but a title unification bout between two half-champions, Williams, the standard bearer for the NBA, and Montgomery, the New York State champion.

Williams fought like a man pos-

sessed, for five rounds holding off the onrushing Montgomery with his talented left and then, almost as if to prove he was no shrinking violet, swapping punches with the heavy-handed "Bobcat." Then, in the sixth, Williams saw the moment he had been waiting 43 months for: Montgomery had gone into a crouch. Williams knew he couldn't punch from a crouch and would have to come up to get leverage. And as he did, Williams, making a conscious move with unconscious ease, caught him with a perfectly timed right to the temple, dropping him to the ground heavily. Struggling to his feet at nine, Montgomery turned his veiled eyes to see Wiliams coming in atop him, flailing away with rights and lefts. Draped over the middle rope, Montgomery hung in the air and started to pitch forward. There would be no getting up this time, Ike Williams was now *the* lightweight champion of the world. And this time had a belt to prove it!

Above: Williams unites lightweight championship with knockout of Bob Montgomery, 1947.

Born 8/2/23, in Brunswick, GA . . . First pro bouts, 1940, New Jersey . . . Won 41 of first 47 bouts (2 draws) in first 4 years, total of 31 consecutive victories, 1942–43 . . . Stopped by Bob Montgomery, 1/25/44, in 12 rounds . . . Twice decisioned former champion Sammy Angott, 6/7/44, and 9/6/44 . . . Won NBA world lightweight title, 4/18/45, via second-round kayo of Juan Zurita . . . Defended successfully, 9/4/46, ninth-round knockout of Ronnie James in Cardiff, Wales . . . Won undisputed recognition with sixth-round knockout of Bob Montgomery, 8/4/47 . . . Defeated Kid Gavilan in nontitle bout, 2/27/48 . . . 3 title defenses, 1948: 5/25/48, Enrique Bolanos, W 15; 7/12/48, Beau Jack, KO 6; 9/23/48, Jesse Flores, KO 10 . . . Defended title twice in 1949: Enrique Bolanos, KO 4, 7/21/49, and Freddie Dawson, W 15, 12/5/49 . . . Fought 11 bouts in 1950 but did not defend title . . . Lost championship to Jimmy Carter via TKO in fourteenth round, 5/25/51 . . . Continued boxing for 4 more years . . . Last bout, 8/12/55, stopped Beau Jack in ninth round, final bout for both ex-champions . . . Elected to Boxing Hall of Fame, 1978 . . . Complete record: 153 bouts, 124 won, 24 lost, 5 draws, 60 knockouts.

Ike Williams may well have been the lightweight champion of the world, but he was also Blinky Palermo's champion.

Williams would admit to the Committee, that he had, in fact, carried one title contender, Enrique Bolanos. And, parrying the questions of the investigators much as he had his opponents' blows in the right, he also intimated that at times he had been at less than

his best dealing with others as he had Bolanos.

The biggest loser in all of this, though, was not boxing, but Ike Williams. For not only had he mortgaged his greatness to Carbo and Palermo, he had also seen his bank account foreclosed, his money, as with all good things, vanishing, courtesy of Blinky Palermo. Williams was to tell author Peter Heller in *In This Corner:* "Blinky just robbed the hell out of me from my money. Two fights I had I received thirty-three thousand four hundred fighting Beau Jack in Philadelphia. I never saw a penny of that. And thirty-three thousand five hundred, Jesse Flores, in New York. I never saw a penny of that. . . . "

No fighter ever came freighted with the baggage Ike Williams had to carry with him to greatness. He was a great wine, one diluted by water until only Williams, himself, and Palermo knew which part was the wine and which part the water—water in which only sharks could swim.

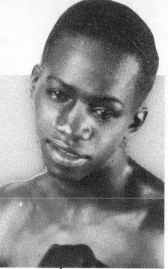

PANAMA AL BROWN

There was only one Panama Al Brown, even though he looked like two. An elongated bantamweight who stood a fraction under six feet and whose reach exceeded his height by five inches, Brown was a parcel of limbs tied together by a chance bond. Gaunt, almost to the point of being invisible from the side, this freakish physical specimen spread-eagled the bantamweight class for six years. But if the physical equipment of this ebony coat hanger made him an oddity, his fighting equipment made him an even bet to be the greatest bantamweight of all time. With a 76-inch reach, longer than most heavyweight champions except the super dreadnaughts, Brown could almost hit an opponent half the width of the ring away. Using his boardinghouse reach less like a spear than a rapier, Brown would stab his opponents from the front—Bat Battalino, who fought Brown back in 19-aught-29, remembered it almost as a sound, "Bing . . . bing . . . keeping me away . . . " all the while gesticulating unspeakable acts of destruction with his wing-like right. Bobbing and weaving like a bird of prey preparing for a takeoff, Brown was a difficult, if not impossible, target for his opponents, most of whom looked like the other half of the '39 World's Fair logotype when measured against this walking case of malnutrition. All in all, the whole was greater than the sum of his gangly parts, making Panama Al Brown a fighter who floated like a praying mantis and stung like a bee.

INCREDIBLY, BROWN STARTED HIS CAreer in the canal zone of his home country as a flyweight. And like the canal, took the shortest route to greatness by migrating to New York in 1922. Unknown to the trade and unable to get fights because of his freakish build, Brown took a job as a busboy in a Harlem beanery, spending his spare time in the Commonwealth Club at 135th Street and Madison Avenue. Finally, Jess McMahon, then matchmaker at the club, gave the youngster, now known as "Panama" Al Brown, a chance to show his wares. He became an instant sensation, using his long left as an hors d'oeuvre to set up his right and flattening his first opponent with the first solid punch he landed.

Brown ran off a brilliant record during his first two years of campaigning in and around New York, taking them all in his long stride. He knocked out the likes of Tommy Milton, Willie LaMorte, Al Kaufman, Willie Farley, Bobby Hines, and the clever Englishman, Frankie Ash, and added victories over Joe Coletti, Sparkplug Russell, Tommy Hughes, Willie Darcy, Eddie Flank, and Jimmy Breslin. His only defeat, at the gloves of Jimmy Russo, was avenged in a return match.

By 1925, as becomes a growing boy, Brown had become a bantamweight. And, although he still used New York as his base of operations, he began to

Born Alphonse Theo Brown, 7/5/02, in Panama . . . Began pro career, 1919, early bouts not recorded, first recorded bout, 1922 . . . Won Panamanian flyweight title, 12/6/22 . . . Came to New York, 1923 . . . Kayoed Willie La Morte, in second round, 6/7/24 . . . Shuttled between Paris and New York, 1927–29 . . . Defeated Eugene Criqui in 10 rounds in Paris, 4/2/27 . . . Lost 10-round decision to Andre Routis there, 12/10/27 . . . Returned to New York for 5 bouts, 1928, back to Paris . . . Returned to New York and won vacant world bantamweight title with 15-round decision over Vidal Gregorio, 6/18/29 . . . Defended title 11 times, 1929–35, all outside the U.S. even though he fought many nontitle bouts within the U.S. during that time . . . Defended title in Denmark, France, Canada, Italy, England, and Spain . . . Title defenses: 8/28/29, Knud Larsen, Copenhagen, W 10; 10/4/30, Eugene Huat, Paris, W 15; 2/11/31, Nick Bensa, Paris, W 10; 8/25/31, Pete Sanstol, Montreal, W 15; 10/27/31, Eugene Huat, Montreal, W 15; 7/10/32, Kid Francis, Marseilles, (split decision, 15, riot following decision); 9/19/32, Emile Pladner, Toronto, KO 1; 3/18/33, Domenico Bernasconi, Milan, W 12; 7/3/33, Johnny King, London, W 15; 2/19/34, Young Perez, Paris, W 15 . . . Lost title to Baltazar Sangchilli, Valencia, Spain, 6/1/35, 15-round decision . . . Continued boxing until 1942 . . . Truly one of boxing's world travelers, fought throughout Europe in 9 different countries, North Africa, Canada, Panama and U.S. . . . Died 4/11/51, in New York City . . . Complete record: 152 bouts, 120 won, 19 lost, 11 draws, 2 no-decisions.

Right: Panama Al Brown keeps hold of his bantamweight title against Eugene Huat, Oct. 27, 1931.

travel. Soon the same wanderlust that had brought him to the States sent him to Paris to fulfill a contract for three bouts. But, like the man who came to dinner and stayed, Brown became such an instantaneous hit with the Parisiennes that he remained for ten bouts—and a year and a half—beating the likes of former featherweight champion Eugene Criqui. It was to be the beginning of a regular commuter route for Brown, who liked the Parisians almost as much as they liked him. And liked the high life on Paris' Left Bank as well.

With Bud Taylor, Bushy Graham, and Charley Phil Rosenberg all moving up or out of the bantamweight class, those three worthies on the New York State Athletic Commission—called the "Three Dumb Dukes" by writer W. O. McGeehan—decided to do something novel in doling out a championship. They announced that the winner of an Al Brown-Vidal Gregorio 15-round bantamweight fight would be recognized as the "defending" champion. Staged at the Queensboro Stadium in the middle of June 1929, Brown became the "defending" champion by defending the title successfully against Gregorio, jab-

bing the smaller "challenger" back on his heels time and again and outscoring him in 15 rounds.

During the next six years, Brown fought more than 70 bouts in Europe and the States, no fewer than a dozen of those title defenses. But none was more bizarre than his title defense against Kid Francis in Marseilles in July of 1932. After the decision was rendered in favor of Brown, on a split decision, a riot broke out. During the melee, Lidro Spiripo, the head of France's underworld, and a leading "capo," pulled out his gun and aimed it at the judge who had voted against his "goombah," Francis. Despite the judge's bowing to reason and reversing himself, the International Boxing Union awarded the bout to Brown.

Now a globetrotter, Brown defended his title in Toronto, Milan, London, Paris, and all points north, east, and south. One of those title defenses was against Baltazar Sanchilli in Spain. (Another way of putting it is that Brown lost the fight, the first standing for the second, as Brown left his belt with Sanchilli for safekeeping.) Unfortunately, by the time he had caught up with Sanchilli on his adopted turf of Paris, Sanchilli had already misplaced the belt, losing it to Tony Marino in his first defense.

His landing gear no longer what it once was, Brown considered retirement. But the man who had money to burn and met his match in Paris was swiftly moving from affluence to poverty and was forced back into the ring to support his habit. Attempting more comebacks than Sarah Bernhardt, he stayed in Paris fighting until the sounds of Hitler's advancing hobnail boots were almost audible. Then returned first to the States and then to Panama, leaving behind him property worth over a quarter-million dollars, cold quid.

It all finally caught up with Panama Al Brown, who died penniless in a Staten Island hospital after a lingering bout with tuberculosis. Saved from Potter's Field by his countrymen, who remembered the tall, classy fighter who had brought pride and pleasure to his country, he was brought "home" to be buried at Amador Guerrero Cemetery as a national hero. Not as a broken old body that had been worn out by numerous ring battles and the battle of life, but as the graceful ghost of a sharpshooter who had been the class of the bantamweight class back in the thirties.

LARRY HOLMES

62 LARRY HOLMES

It was almost as if the biography of Larry Holmes began with Chapter Two. For here was a 28-year-old boxer laboring in the virtual anonymity of boxing's vineyards and backyards, undefeated, untied, and unwanted, when chance—in the form of the WBC and Don King—singled him out to fight for the so-called heavyweight championship. And therein lies a tale with all the elements found in a best-selling novel of the intrigue genre. The two alphabet-soup organizations known as the WBA and the WBC had parasitically attached themselves to the underside of boxing in the early sixties. By 1978, they had begun to suffocate boxing with their favoritism of promoters, countries, and matchmakers, taking money under the table—around the table, over the table, and, in some cases, even taking the table—for rating fighters and dispensing championships in the same cavalier manner a party girl hands out her phone number to everyone with the right connections. One of those with the right connections to the WBC was promoter Don King.

WHAT KING HAD WAS AN OPTION ON A Muhammad Ali-Ken Norton rematch. What he didn't have was a contract for the upcoming Leon Spinks-Ali rematch, Spinks having beaten the memory of Ali the previous February.

Undoubtedly, there are a few traditionalists remaining who are committed to the romantic and honorable notion that championships are won and lost in the ring. However, WBC president Jose Sulaiman was not amongst their number. In Star Chamber proceedings held in a smoke-filled room, Sulaiman defrocked Spinks of his hard-won mantle and conferred it on Ken Norton—only because Warren Harding was unavailable—coronating him the WBC Heavyweight Champion. Without a title fight.

Promoter King, still in possession of an option on "Champion" Norton's services, with the blessings of the WBC, set up a "title" defense for Norton against Larry Holmes, a loyal member of the King's court.

Larry Holmes was boxing's version of the "Forgotten Man." Even with 26

straight wins and 19 KOs, the only way he could have gotten recognition would have been if he had walked into a masquerade party backwards wearing his birthday suit and posing as a burnt Parkerhouse roll. His only TV exposure had been an eight-round decision win over Tom Prater as part of Don King's ill-fated U. S. Boxing Tournament. In the shower of heavyweight gold all around him, Holmes had nothing to hold but a pitchfork. And his connection with Don King.

Soon he would serve as the witting catalyst for King's territorial ambitions as he finally moved into prominence with an easy win over Earnie Shavers, he of the power to knock down tall buildings with a single swat. Now Holmes was to "challenge" Norton for the WBC heavyweight championship. And their chintzy belt, which one writer described as "looking like it was made up of broken Coke bottles found along the San Diego Freeway."

But if the WBC heavyweight title was ersatz and the belt fool's gold, the Holmes-Norton fight was pure gold,

one of the best in the history of heavyweight title fights.

For 14 rounds, the two men threw punches with no letup. Or interest in their own physical well-being. First it was Norton, slamming his vaunted right into Holmes' jaw; then it was Holmes, using his piston-like left, stabbing apart Norton's face with layer-after-layer of jabs thrown with metronomic frequency. And when his left hand had sufficiently mesmerized Norton, Holmes, fighting sideways like a man hiding behind a tree, would whip his serpentine right through Norton's crossed-arms defense.

Gathering up all their chips and piling them on red, both fighters came out for the fifteenth determined to win the WBC "championship" with their final three-minute roll. Skill and finesse were irrelevent. Both fighters were too weary and too damaged to do anything but stand in the center of the ring and take turns using each other's head as a fungo ball. Which is what they did for the full three minutes. Time and again Norton exploded his right-hand bombs off Holmes' jaw—the same rights that had destroyed Duane Bobick in record time a year earlier; the same Duane Bobick who had forced Holmes to throw up his hands in surrender at the 1972 Olympic Box-Offs. But there was to be no surrender this time. This time he was a man possessed. And in their

Born 11/3/49, in Cuthbert, GA . . . Began boxing as professional, 1973, in Scranton, PA . . . Won only 2 of first 6 by knockout . . . Undefeated but unheralded by 1977, entered in ill-fated U.S. championship tournament . . . Won WBC world heavyweight championship over Ken Norton via 15-round decision, did not receive wide recognition since Muhammad Ali still recognized by most as champion . . . First 8 defenses by knockout, a record for most consecutive heavyweight title defenses by knockout. Championship claim finally accepted after eleventh-round TKO victory over Muhammad Ali, 10/2/80 . . . Next defense, 4/11/81, decisioned Trevor Berbick in 15 rounds . . . Knocked out Leon Spinks in 3 rounds, 6/2/81 . . . Nearly lost to Renaldo Snipes, 11/6/83, but came off canvas to stop Snipes in eleventh round . . . Much ballyhooed bout with Gerry Cooney, 6/11/82, resulted in thirteenth-round victory for Holmes . . . No knockouts in next 2 defenses but near shutout performances in decision victories over Randall "Tex" Cobb, 11/26/82, 15 rounds; and Lucien Rodriguez, 3/27/83, 12 rounds . . . Close 12-round decision over Tim Witherspoon, 5/20/83 . . . Knockout victories over Scott Frank, fifth round, 9/10/83, and Marvis Frazier, first round, 11/25/83 . . . Complete record: 41 bouts, 41 won, 0 lost, 30 knockouts.

Top right: Holmes scores with right to head of Mike Weaver, June 22, 1979. Right: Holmes comes back to knock out Earnie Shavers in 11th round, Sept. 28, 1979.

146

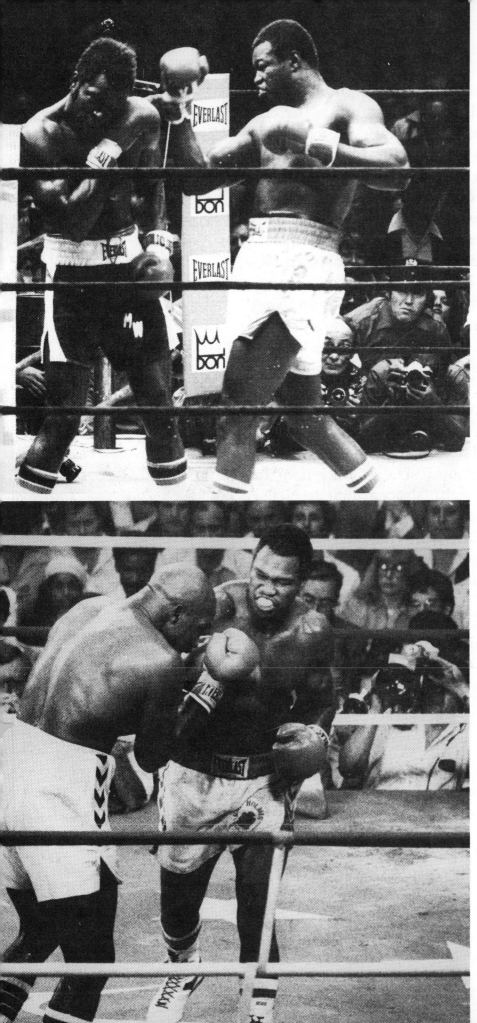

battle of wills, Holmes' was strongest as he tapped something deep inside and found the strength for a final rally at the bell. It was enough to win the round, to win the fight—by one point in a split decision—and to win the belt.

But if Holmes had won the "championship" and the belt, he still hadn't won the one thing that belonged to Ali, who had come back to beat Spinks: recognition. For the better part of two years, it didn't matter to the boxing cognescenti that Larry Holmes was the best in the heavyweight division. He still stood in the legendary shadow of Muhammad Ali.

And then, on the night of October 2, 1980, in something called "The Last Hurrah," he was to face the specter of greatness past, Muhammad Ali. And finally have a chance to escape Ali's substantial shadow. As a packed house of fans posing as cordwood watched, expecting the miracle that never happened, a merciful Holmes lambasted the tired, pathetic body of what-once-was for 10 long rounds until finally even Ali's corner had had enough. It was to be Larry Holmes' eighth straight knockout in defense of his title, tying the all-time heavyweight record. And, just as importantly, he had "been released from walking in Ali's shadow."

Still, Holmes didn't win acceptance from his critics, many of whom found his opponents—like Alfredo Evangelista, Osvaldo Ocasio, Lorenzo Zanon, Leroy Jones, and Scott LeDeux—ill-qualified for membership in Louis' "Bum of the Month" club. And that Larry was merely disproving the old theory that you can't beat a dead horse by actually fighting one. Or two. Or more. Granted, he was beating them handily, even one-handedly, with what one writer called "the best left jab in the history of the division . . . " or that his right hand was described as "a power-packed punch," the good catchwords were obscuring an appreciation.

Holmes, as a self-tribute, took to calling himself "baaaad," as in the "baaaadest Nigger around," almost like the Islamic lords who built their domed tombs for future interment before they died because they foresaw that no one would think well enough of them to do so afterward. Maybe he, like his critics, was waiting for the final chapter in the biography of Larry Holmes to be written so that he could be granted a twilight of begrudging acceptance as a great.

CARMEN BASILIO

It has been said that "honest labor bears a lovely face." But, in the case of Carmen Basilio, honest labor bore a face that made him a prime prospect for selling pencils on a street corner. The result of his honest efforts was a face that bore more stitches than a baseball, an eyebrow that carried a scar worthy of a graduate of a Heidelberg dueling academy, and occasional lumps and bumps the size of Goodyear blimps. And yet, all these welts and marks gave meaning and insight into the warrior known as Carmen Basilio, one of the most fearless and ferocious fighters of his day. Or any day. Basilio fought with the soul of a warrior, not so much fighting his opponents, as warring against them. He would walk through mine fields to get at his foes with dogged, indomitable courage and then, once inside, would throw every round of ammunition in his bandillero, sparing no bullet in his short-armed arsenal as he tried to break off his opponents like sticks of sealing wax. In the proud cliche of the manly trade, he ate leather, his face a magnet for every punch thrown as he prowled at close quarters ready to do damage. His style, if he had any, was a combination bob and weave that gave him a crab-like look. But while his fights were no place for those whose sensitivity came out like hair on a comb, the fight fans loved them. And they loved Carmen Basilio.

THE SON OF A NEW YORK STATE ONION farmer, Basilio toiled among the onions of the field until one day he finally decided he had "had enough." Throwing his handful of onions down, he hollered to his father, "I'm telling you, Pa, I'm all done workin' on onions." His father, according to Basilio's recollection to writer Bill Heinz, asked, "So then what you gonna do?" "I'm gonna fight professional," said the younger Basilio. "And you gonna get plenty lickin's," his father counseled. "Yeah, and I'll give plenty, too," Carmen remembered saying.

Basilio's big chance came on September 18, 1953, against world welterweight champion Kid Gavilan for the world's title, in his own backyard of Syracuse. Basilio gave the cocky Cuban more than he bargained for, flooring

him for the first time in his long career with a power-packed left hook in the second round and carrying the fight to the champ throughout. At the end of 15 hard-fought rounds, Gavilan barely retained his crown on a split decision—a decision Basilio regarded as "a victory in disguise . . . he keeps the title and I get the publicity. What's to be sad about? There'll be another chance."

And there was, 21 months later, against Tony DeMarco, again in his backyard. In a fight that could have been held in a phone booth, the two predatory sluggers took turns using each other as punching bags. It was Basilio's turn last and he made the most of it, stopping DeMarco in the twelfth and winning the title. Rematched five

Bottom: Basilio's face reflects more than resolute determination as he beats Sugar Ray Robinson for middleweight title, 1957.

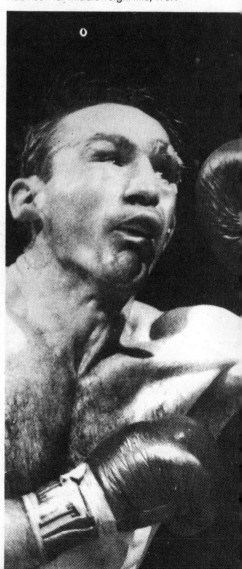

Born 4/2/27, in Canastota, NY . . . Began pro career, 1948 . . . 1950, got off to strong start, 18–2–2 . . . Defeated Lew Jenkins, 3/6/50, 10 rounds . . . Cooled off after Jenkins bout, won only 9 of next 18 . . . Defeated Ike Williams, 1/12/53 . . . Won New York State welterweight title, 6/6/53, with 12-round decision over Billy Graham . . . Drew with Graham in 12-round rematch, 7/25/53 . . . Challenged Kid Gavilan for world welterweight title, 9/18/53, but lost split decision . . . Won world welterweight title, 6/10/55, with twelfth-round stoppage of Tony DeMarco . . . Lost title to Johnny Saxton in 15 rounds, 3/14/56 . . . Rewon title with ninth-round TKO of Saxton, 9/12/56 . . . Rubber match ended with second-round knockout of Saxton, 2/22/57 . . . Successfully challenged for middleweight crown with 15-round decision over Sugar Ray Robinson, 9/23/57 . . . Robinson, as he always did, won title back in 15-round rematch decision, 3/25/58 . . . 3 more unsuccessful bids at regaining middleweight title: Gene Fullmer, 8/28/59, KO 14; Fullmer, 6/29/60, KO 12; Paul Pender, 4/22/61, L 15 . . . Retired 3 days after Pender bout . . . College instructor at LeMoyne University, Syracuse, NY . . . Elected to Boxing Hall of Fame, 1969 . . . Complete record: 79 bouts, 56 won, 16 lost, 7 draws, 27 knockouts.

months later, lightning struck again in the same place, as Basilio, surviving an early pounding that had him stumbling haphazardly around the ring, rallied to knock DeMarco out in a grotesque tableau—the referee holding the unconscious DeMarco by his right arm in a modern-day crucifixion scene—in just two seconds more than it had taken Basilio to win the title the first time out.

Now the craggy-faced ex-onion farmer stood atop the welterweight hill, king of all he surveyed. But what the straight-forward Basilio, who thought as he fought—without subtleties or nuances—hadn't surveyed or foreseen were the possibilities of shenanigans. In his next fight against the well-connected Johnny Saxton, who had already stolen the title once, from Kid Gavilan, Basilio started out like a house afire, catching Saxton several times with his sleep-inducing left hook, and then planted one solidly on Saxton's exposed jaw. Saxton went limp, his eyes glazed over and his knees jellied as

he stumbled backwards into the ropes. But Basilio was over-anxious and lost Saxton in the final minute of round two, the bell mercifully coming to his rescue. When Saxton came out for the third, a small slit with padding exposed mysteriously opened up in Saxton's glove, courtesy of one of the sponsor's razor blades. The referee ordered a new glove be put on and 15 minutes were spent by Saxton's cornermen in a Marx Brothers charade of "locating" another one.

When they resumed, Saxton had fully recovered and spent the better part of the next 12-plus rounds imitating a long-distance runner at times and at others an entrant in an all-night dance contest, entwined around his tormentor in death-like embraces. At the end, everyone who had watched the spectacle came away in agreement: Basilio had won. Unfortunately, the judges didn't share that opinion and voted for Saxton.

In their rematch, aware that if he gave Saxton an inch he'd steal his cham-

pionship again, Basilio chased Saxton around the ring with resentment in his eyes. In just nine rounds, Basilio had avenged himself, burying his left hook to the midsection until Saxton came apart at the seams, his arms and legs no longer his own, and his ill-gotten crown no longer atop his head. After the referee stopped the fight, Basilio stood in his corner crying as if he had smelled the onions, "I finally got him . . . I finally got him. . . . "

Still, the cornerstone of Basilio's fame lay ahead of him: his two fights with Sugar Ray Robinson.

Moving up in weight and drinking a gallon of water in order to bring his poundage up to a respectable level for the middleweight division, Basilio took on the man called "The Greatest Pound-for-Pound Fighter" in the history of boxing. In two fights that rivaled the Zale-Graziano brawls for their intensity, both men took turns pounding the other, Robinson trying to use his five-inch reach advantage to stick Basilio, and Basilio raking Robinson's midsection with well-directed hooks of the fire-producing variety. Hurt often by punches that had decapitated Bobo Olson and Gene Fullmer, the granite-jawed Basilio fought all the harder when wounded and gave Robinson a brutal body beating. In one of their exchanges, one of Robinson's body punches strayed low and he proffered his gloves to Basilio in a sporting gesture, asking, "Hurt you, Carmen?" Basilio merely sneered, "No, but do it again and see what happens," slapping away the glove and going back to the attack. His attack was good enough to win the battle, and the title, on a split decision.

Rematched the next year, Basilio had to fight the last two-thirds of the fight with a swollen eye the size of one of his homegrown onions. Unable to see Robinson's right-hand uppercuts, the 153-pound cyclops tried to cut down the Sugarman with body shots, bobbing and weaving under Robbie's long left lead. But it wasn't enough and this time Robinson won the split decision. Afterward, Basilio insisted he "could have gone another 15"; Robinson, upon hearing of the remark, moaned inaudibly and then mumbled something that sounded like, "Maybe he could have went another 15, but he wouldn't have went them with me . . . "

That was Carmen Basilio, the man with the beaten face, but never a beaten fighter.

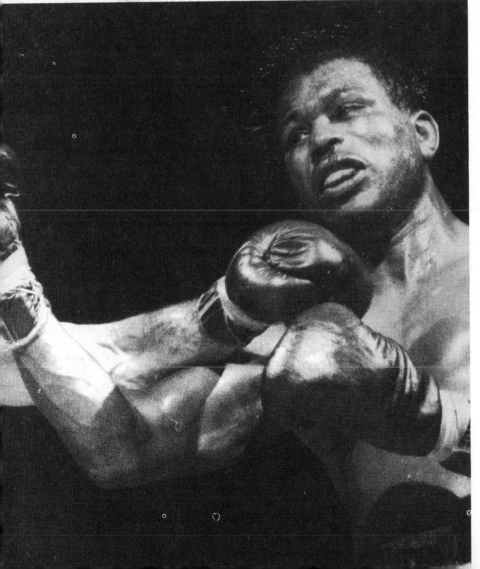

CHARLEY BURLEY

Those few boxing afficianados who know the name Charley Burley can be entered on the head of a pin with enough room left over for a choir of angels. But many in that remaining handful of boxing graybeards who saw Burley perform in the late thirties and into the forties share the opinion of venerable Eddie Futch, who says, "Charley Burley was the finest all-around fighter I ever saw. . . ." And Archie Moore, boxing's Methuselah, remembers his former ring opponent as "the toughest of them all . . . a fighter that I could identify as being slick as lard and twice as greasy." Why then is Charley Burley such a forgotten man?

THE ANSWER, MY FRIENDS, IS WRITTEN in the times, times when bigotry was a going concern and "For Whites Only" sections still abided in many areas the South having no monopoly on such prejudices. It was a time when even the name Joe Louis was anathema to many of the closet bigots behind the leather curtain, one of boxing's then-reigning landlords mentioning Louis to writer Lester Bromberg in a sneering, "Who wants him? He's just another one of those niggers!"

But, if boxing champions like Louis and Henry Armstrong were still relegated to the back of boxing's bus—for as long as possible, until talent won out and became their ticket of admission to the front—others were denied entrance to the bus entirely. These members of the rank-and-file were boxing's second-class citizens. And tragedies.

One of those second-class citizens. was Charley Burley, a dazzling young welterweight out of that fistic hotbed known as 1930s Pittsburgh. A past master of the art of boxing, Burley's style a style almost beyond appreciation, his moves purring like a sleek and well-fed cat. He could do everything: He could punch, he could box, he could adapt to his opponent's style, and he could think on his feet. The only thing he couldn't do was change his color. And so, denied access to boxing's sanctum sanctorium, Burley was reduced by his color to fighting in dubious clubs.

Still, Charley Burley might have survived the neglect fate had mandated for him because of his complexion had he

not been so good—"Too good a fighter for his own good," in the words of promoter Tex Sullivan. Everytime he was offered as an opponent, other fighters politely cough and turn their heads, remembering something else they had to do. Then and forevermore, finding it easier to stay out of the ring than to get out of it.

The fighters who turned down Burley as an opponent would make an honor roll of boxing's best. George Gainford, the manager of the peerless Sugar Ray Robinson, admitted he "bypassed"—read "ducked"—Burley "because his style was such he would have counteracted Robinson's" and asked Ray Arcel, "can't you get me someone besides Burley?" Johnny Ray, the manager of the fearless Billy Conn, who had fought such man-eaters as Fritzie Zivic, Solly Krieger, Babe Risko, and Oscar Rankins, shouted at matchmaker Art Rooney, who had proposed Burley as an opponent for the annual Dapper Dan show, "No! No! No! I don't want Burley. *You* can have him for Christmas, for New Year's, or for your Aunt Tillie's birthday. But never mention his name again." And Fritzie Zivic, who had suffered from his nearness to Burley, losing two out of three to Burley, had his manager, Luke Carney, take over Burley's contract to insure he would never have to face him again.

Heartily avoided by all, Burley was consigned to boxing's last mile, a group of Negro middleweights called by Budd Schulberg "Murderer's Row"—a den, pride, herd, and/or siege of similarly

dispossessed lions and tigers who had been denied the right to lie down amongst the lambs and, in self-defense, had to seek out each other's company. Their names, while hardly household names even in their own households, included some of the deadliest practitioners of the "Sweet Science": Lloyd Marshall, Bert Lytell, Holman Williams, Oakland Billy Smith, Charley Banks, and Joe Carter. And, of course, the clean-up hitter in the "murderer's row" line-up, Charley Burley.

Burley took them all on, not caring who, when or how much they weighed. He fought Holman Williams seven times, Bert Lytell, and Ezzard Charles twice, Jimmy Bivins and Lloyd Marshall, and even an up-and-coming oldster named Archie Moore. What he did against Moore was testimony to Burley's ring skills: They had four knockdowns between them, Moore none and Burley four as Burley won an easy ten-round decision. Unable to get fights with any welterweight or middleweight who even faintly recognized his name, Burley fought light heavyweights and heavyweights. The only ones who could beat him were bigger scientific fighters, like Ezzard Charles, who outweighed him by 15 pounds.

The closest Charley Burley ever got to the top came in 1942, when, after having been a ranked welterweight contender for four years, he came to New York as the second-ranked middleweight contender. Unable to get a fight at Madison Square Garden, he took one at St. Nicholas Arena against "Showboat" Bill McQuillan, a good journeyman. In one minute, Burley knocked out McQuillan, effectively ending two careers, that of McQuillan and his own, a victor by victory undone and now untouchable—a boxing leper.

Fame has been called a crazy old lady who hoards swatches of fabric and throws away plates of food. In Charley Burley's case, it threw away one of the great unrealized talents in the history of boxing.

Born 9/6/17, in Pittsburgh, PA . . . Began professional boxing career, 1937 . . . Fought exclusively in Pittsburgh first 2 years . . . Lost 10-round decision to Fritzie Zivic in ninth pro bout, 3/21/38, (bout was Zivic's seventy-seventh as a professional) . . . Defeated Zivic in rematch, 6/13/38, on 10-round decision—Zivic later won world welterweight championship . . . Defeated Billy Soose, 11/21/38, 10-round decision—Soose later won world middleweight title . . . Won 10-round rubber match with Zivic, 7/17/39 . . . Scored 11 knockouts in 12 bouts, 1941–42 . . . Defeated Holman Williams in 3 of 4 bouts, 1942—faced Williams 7 times in career, each winning 3, 1 bout called no contest . . . Lost twice to Ezzard Charles (future heavyweight champ) via 10-round decision, 1942 . . . Won California middleweight title with ninth-round knockout victory over Jack Chase, 4/3/44 . . . Defeated Archie Moore (future light heavyweight champion) less than 3 weeks later, on points in 10 rounds, 4/21/44 . . . Continued boxing until 1950 . . . Always a top contender (rated number-one or -two most of 1943–47) . . . Never received a title shot . . . Last pro bout, 7/22/50, Lima, Peru, won 10-round decision . . . Elected to Boxing Hall of Fame, 1983 . . . Complete record: 89 bouts, 74 won, 12 lost, 2 draws, 1 no-contest, 44 knockouts.

PHILADELPHIA JACK O'BRIEN

According to the Bible, a prophet is without honor, save in his own country. Turn-of-the-century entertainers were no different from prophets. Down through the years many have been praised and feted abroad, while still ranked as minor curiosities at home. That was the curious lot of Harry Houdini, who sailed for England in May 1900, and of the ring magician known as Philadelphia Jack O'Brien, who sailed in December of that same year, headed for the same destination in his quest for gold. And recognition. Philadelphia Jack O'Brien was to attain that recognition. And more, much more. Having come to the realization that good fighters could be found in America by shaking any tree and picking up a bountiful harvest from the fall, he determined to try his hand in England, where the pickings were better. Part Gypsy, part suitcase, he toured the British Isles, where he met—and defeated—18 of Britain's best, including the English heavyweight and middleweight champions. Always he advertised his exploits to his growing number of fans at home in those innocent days before press agentry by sending his own accounts of his fights to the Associated Press. Returning home in February of 1902, the same Jack O'Brien who had walked up the gangplank to a farewell party which consisted solely of his sisters, was greeted by ten thousand cheering Philadelphians, proud of the man who proudly carried the name "Philadelphia."

IT HAD NOT ALWAYS BEEN THUS. FOR the man called "Philadelphiaw Jawn" O'Brien in England and plain old "Philadelphia Jack" O'Brien elsewhere, had, as a wee broth of a lad, gone by the name Joseph Francis Anthony Hagen—which was only fair, it being his christened name. Like every other growing youth of Irish ancestry in the nineties, Hagen-O'Brien had tried to pattern his every move after his beau idol, the heavyweight champion of the world, "Gentleman" Jim Corbett. But his father, a contractor originally hailing from Londonderry, would have none of his son's infatuation with boxing, wanting him instead to go into the family business. In order to both pursue his love for the gentlemanly art of self-defense and to circumvent his father's disapproval, Hagen-O'Brien borrowed the name of his good friend much as he had the style of Corbett and entered the local amateur tournaments. The other part of Joseph Francis Anthony Hagen's *nom de guerre* came from the fact that there was another Jack O'Brien already fighting out of New York. And so, "Philadelphia" Jack O'Brien was born.

Starting his professional career as a lightweight, the man now known as Philadelphia Jack O'Brien continued to mature, his form finally filling out to that of a middleweight, never reaching more than 162 pounds, tops. Still, on his way up the fistic ladder he fought lightweights, middleweights, and heavyweights and just about any other weights he could find as his fame in and around the Philadelphia area became more enduring than the Liberty Bell. But Philadelphia was still just Philadelphia and Jack O'Brien sailed for Europe to prove his worth and to disprove George Bernard Shaw's line that "No Englishman is ever fairly beaten." O'Brien was to accomplish both, returning home the greatest box-office draw in boxing.

Coincidentally, it was just about that time in the fortunes of boxing that Lou Houseman, the sports editor of the Chicago *Inter-Ocean* and, not incidentally, the manager of Jack Root, a great oversized middleweight of the period, came up with the idea of inventing a division for the sole purpose of crowning his charge a champion. Of something. And that's how the division, known as the light heavyweight division, came to be.

Meanwhile, back in Philadelphia, the man now known as Philadelphia Jack O'Brien, unaware that a new division was forming that would suit him like a well-tailored outfit, was enjoying his celebrity. Inside the ring, O'Brien was now in a position to dictate his terms to the promoters, insisting on 75 percent of the gate, payable in Teddy Roosevelt dollars, a time when a 5-dollar bill represented great wealth. He also insisted on 6-round, no-decision bouts, in place of training and were not tiring, allowing him to fight 30 in nine months, almost one every week, against a veritable who's who of early twentieth-century boxing, such as Peter Maher, Marvin Hart, Joe Choynski, Tommy Ryan, Kid McCoy, Joe Wolcott, and others.

It seemed that Philadelphia Jack had everything: His rugged good lucks with the features of a Roman senator and speech pattern of a Chautauqua orator were lionized by society; his simple Irish upbringing and way of informally expressing himself, complete with the blarney and here and gone of his past, was adored by the box populi; and his classic manner of boxing, fighting almost as if he should have been wearing a tux and always giving out free boxing lessons to his opponents, was worshipped by the press. But something was missing from the picture, something which made Philadelphia Jack believe he was something less than a complete boxer: he had no championship.

When, on May 13, 1905, James J. Jeffries announced his retirement, relinquishing his crown and returning to his

they boxed 20 rounds to a draw. Rematched six months later, O'Brien lost a 20-round decision to Burns.

Jack O'Brien repaired to Philadelphia to soothe his damaged psyche and to bathe in the compliments of his bon hommes. He had boxed 40 rounds for the heavyweight championship—and would later box another 6 with Jack Johnson in a no-decision battle for the title and had come up empty in his quest. He now had to do something to regain the glory that once was his.

That "something" was to take the form of Stanley Ketchel, the man-eating middleweight champion who had left most of his opponents agonizing on the floor like a cowboy stuck in the heart with an Indian's arrow. Philadelphia Jack was aware of the chances he took, confessing to a writer after the fight, "I had heard that Ketchel's dynamic onslaught was such it could not be withstood . . . but I figured I could jab his puss off." Aided and abetted by gloves that were "broken" so that his knuckles came through, O'Brien did more than just jab Ketchel's "puss off," he damned near peeled it off. For eight and a half rounds, it was less a fight than a footrace as O'Brien would deliver a quick stinging jab, throw a right hand in the direction of Ketchel's ever-reddening face and move on, occasionally looking behind him to see if Ketchel was still in the race. The tenth was one of the most storied rounds in boxing history. Twice O'Brien was knocked head over social registry. And both times he got up, trying mightily to weather the storm named Ketchel. Finally, with scant seconds left in the tenth, and final, round, Ketchel threw his famous Ketchel left from his shift to O'Brien's solar plexus and followed with a lullaby after the baby was asleep, with a right to the jaw. O'Brien's head went back as if someone had grabbed his hair and pulled his head, his body following as he fell with his head in the resin box in Ketchel's corner. Just as the referee counted six, the final bell rang. The fight was over, the decision was a "draw."

For hours, days, months, and even years, the ending was told and retold, like so many other stories, distorted in the retelling, bent out of its honest shape by the loyalty of the person telling it. Whatever, it made a great story, which was only fitting, Philadelphia Jack O'Brien being one of the great story-tellers of all time. And one of the great boxers, as well.

alfalfa farm, even that missing piece of the puzzle seemed to fall into place for Philadelphia Jack. Leaving his beloved Philadelphia, O'Brien set his course for the Coast to challenge Bob Fitzsimmons for the vacant crown. O'Brien used his left like a pickpocket, picking Fitz clean, cutting up his face and for good measure, dancing in and out continually with an occasional right-hand counter against the quickly tiring champion. Finally, Fitz slumped over in his corner between the thirteenth and fourteenth rounds, out cold. The "championship" belonged to Philadelphia Jack O'Brien—but just which championship, the heavyweight or the light heavyweight championship, nobody knew for sure.

O'Brien laid claim to the heavyweight title. But his claim fell on some-

Born Joseph Francis Hagen, 1/17/78, in Philadelphia, PA . . . First pro bout, 1896, Philadelphia . . . Scored only 1 knockout in first 31 bouts . . . Traveled to England, 1901 and undefeated in 18 bouts . . . Fought in no-decision bouts, 1902–04 . . . Won world light heavyweight championship with thirteenth-round KO of Bob Fitzsimmons, 12/20/05 . . . Held title for 7 years, but never defended it . . . Twice challenged Tommy Burns for world heavyweight crown: 11/28/06, 20-round draw, and 5/8/07, lost 20-round decision . . . Fought 6-round no-decision bout with Jack Johnson, 5/19/09 . . . Continued boxing until 1912 . . . Fought 84 of 181 bouts in Philadelphia . . . Died, 11/12/42, in New York, NY . . . Elected to Boxing Hall of Fame, 1968 . . . Complete record: 181 bouts, 101 won, 7 lost, 16 draws, 57 no-decisions, 36 knockouts.

thing less than universal ears, especially the ears of those who backed another claimant, Tommy Burns, who had beaten Jeffries' hand-picked successor, Marvin Hart. Finally, after much equivocal negotiating, the two men were brought together, in November of 1906, to settle their disputes. Instead of settling them it merely fueled more, as

Above: O'Brien and Tommy Burns square off in heavyweight championship fight as Jim Jeffries looks on, Nov. 28, 1906.

PETER JACKSON

Had Peter Jackson been born white, there is little doubt that he would have ascended to the world's championship throne. And that he would have beaten John L. Sullivan with still greater ease than did Corbett. But back when men fought to settle a question of physical supremacy, there was something called the "color line." Peter Jackson was destined never to cross it. A finished fighter in every respect, he introduced a higher form of ring science and generalship than had ever been seen before, combining speed of hand with lightness of foot. Lean and supple as a panther, Jackson could sidestep, block or draw his head back imperceptibly, and cause his opponent to miss by inches, all the while, as the common parlance of the day would have it, "never breaking ground," and remaining in a position to counter. A thoroughbred in his movements, compared to the workhorse movements of the top pugilists of his day, Jackson replaced the almost mechanical act of sticking out the left and then shooting over the right with his own invention, a devastating one-two, thus changing the face of boxing. And the faces of his opponents as well, his punishing right, according to ring historian Nat Fleischer, "the most staggering right hand chop to the jaw of any modern heavyweight." Peter Jackson was, in short, a complete fighter for his age. Or for any age.

PETER JACKSON BEGAN HIS LONG, CIRcuitous route to greatness in the British West Indies where he gained renown for his all-around athletic prowess—particularly swimming, where he became a legendary diver for sharks and was credited with being the first to use a stroke that would later become known as the "Australian crawl." Inevitably, the swimmer would become acquainted with the clipper ships which made their ports of call in the West Indies. Older seamen, dropping off for days between trips, would tell the muscular youth of the world out beyond where his ambitions lay. Having taken up boxing as his game, he now took up Australia as his goal, and took passage aboard one of those tall-masted sailing vessels bound for the "Land Down Under" to follow his dreams.

Jackson's introduction to boxing was, at best, a rude one, his baptism coming at what was probably the roughest boxing school on earth, Australia or otherwise, Larry Foley's Hall in Sydney. At Foley's, science was hardly the order of the day, Australian fans of that rugged day favoring bull-like charges and pit-terrier ferocity, scorning anyone who merely tried boxing for points by throwing them out of the ring.

For the next two years Jackson filled the role of chopping block for the more experienced men. But gradually the intelligent and quick-thinking panther mastered the fine points of the game and soon became the past-master of the science, acknowledged as the second Jem Mace for his cleverness, speed, and science. Putting his newly acquired skills to good use, Jackson met Tom Leeds for the Australian Heavyweight Championship and when,

after 30 rounds, Leeds' strength gave way to the punishment dealt out by Jackson, the title changed hands. Jackson had come of fistic age. Unfortunately, it was an age that was somewhat less than golden for Jackson, as other Australian heavyweights suddenly feigned the headache of the unwilling and demured. Jackson fought exhibitions, meeting all comers and offering five pounds to any who could stay five rounds with him. He even offered to fight other heavyweights with his right hand "barred." But even that didn't bring out the reluctant dragons. Finally, despairing of ever fighting again, Jackson decided to try his luck in that boxing land o' plenty, America.

Taking everyone—and everything—in stride, Jackson's challenge was finally accepted by the outstanding contender for Sullivan's title, James J. Corbett. Corbett looked at Jackson as a stepping stone. But there were those who saw Jackson more a hurdle of sizeable proportions, so sizeable in fact that he was installed as a 100-to-60 favorite over the "favorite son," Corbett.

And so, on May 21, 1891, in the first bout in America ever conducted under the Marquis of Queensberry Rules, the two ranking contenders for the heavyweight crown squared off at San Francisco's California Club for a $10,000 purse, with $8,500 to go to the winner and $1,500 to go as balm to the loser. Corbett was to remember, "I soon discovered he was shifty and fast. And I thought I was fast!" For 28 rounds these two greats tried every weapon at

Born 7/3/61, in St. Croix, Virgin Islands . . . Merchant seaman as teenager—landed in Australia in 1881, and made his home there . . . First recorded bouts, 1883 . . . Early record sketchy—stopped by Bill Farnan in 3 rounds for Australian heavyweight title, 7/26/84 . . . Won Australian heavyweight title with thirtieth-round knockout of Tom Lees, 9/28/86 . . . Came to U.S. in 1888 . . . Knocked out George Godfrey in 10, 8/24/88, and knocked out Joe McAuliffe in 24, 12/27/88 . . . Won 7 other bouts in U.S. in 1889 and then sailed for London, England for exhibition tour . . . Defeated Jem Smith and Peter Maher in regular (nonexhibition) bouts in that year . . . Returned to U.S., 1890, and then to Australia . . . Returned again to U.S. for bout with James J. Corbett, 5/21/91—bout held under Queensberry rules but fought to a finish, no fixed time limit . . . After 4 hours, 5 minutes, and 61 rounds, bout was declared no contest by the referee—both fighters hurt in twenty-fifth round and could no longer throw satisfactory punches . . . Met Frank Slavin for British Empire title, 5/30/92, and won in tenth round by knockout—Slavin badly hurt and Jackson asked referee to stop bout, but referee required Jackson to "fight on" . . . Slavin unconscious at end but survived and outlived Jackson by more than 20 years—bout considered by many as one of greatest of all time . . . Jackson contracted tuberculosis and final 3 bouts in career were fought in that state, 3/22/98, stopped by Jim Jeffries in third round and 8/24/99, stopped by Jim Jeffords in fourth . . . Final bout, 12/2/99, 25-round draw with Billy Warren in Melbourne . . . Never received world title due to Sullivan's refusal to fight a black . . . Died, 7/13/01, Roma, Queensland, Australia . . . Complete record: 27 bouts, 18 won, 3 lost, 4 draws, 1 no-decision, 1 no-contest, 12 knockouts.

their disposal, Jackson trying to land his famous "Heart" punch and Corbett trying to launch his famed counterattack. In the twenty-ninth and thirtieth rounds, Corbett went on the assault, unleashing an attack that had Jackson in trouble. But Jackson weathered the storm and from then on it became a contest of sheer endurance. "Twenty . . . thirty . . . forty rounds went by as if they were nothing," recalled "Gentleman" Jim years later, "and he hadn't slowed a bit. Coming up for the sixty-first round, I was concerned, I was tiring and losing my timing. When the referee approached us and proposed we stop and call it 'No Contest,' I agreed. Believe me, it was the hardest and fastest-paced distance fight I ever

waged. . . . I shook Jackson's hand. I respected him. . . . "

With Sullivan's impenetrable "color line" uncrossable by Jackson, the title shot went to Corbett who was pleased that he "would never have to face another 61-rounder with Jackson again." Jackson, frustrated in his attempts to get a bout with John L. for the heavyweight championship, went instead to London to take on his Australian rival Frank (Paddy) Slavin for the British and Australian heavyweight championships, which he won in the most thrilling fistic encounter ever staged," according to no less an authority than Eugene Corri, British referee and boxing expert.

But Peter Jackson would never re-

cover from the battering he suffered in the Slavin fight. He also partook of the camaraderie of his newfound friends, who lionized him in song and wined him in drink. The combination of this dual dissipation made a physical wreck of the once-great form of Peter Jackson. And although he was to fight a few more times, he was living on borrowed time.

That time finally ran out on July 13, 1901, when he passed into, as it was then called, "the great majority." His epitaph sums up "The Black Prince" in just four words: "This was a man."

Above: Jackson and
James J. Corbett in famous
61-round fight, 1891.

JIMMY BARRY

67 JIMMY BARRY

Eighteen ninety-three was the year of Chicago's Columbian Exposition—or 1893 World's Fair, if you will—celebrating the four hundredth anniversary of the discovery of America by Christopher Columbus. Forget the fact that it had opened a year behind schedule. Nobody seemed to mind, especially when President Cleveland touched an ivory and gold key to start the machinery, turn on the fountains, and unfurl the flags of the "White City" on the first day of May. But by the second of May nobody was talking about the Ferris Wheel, or the Palace of Electricity, or the special display of the first locomotives or even the fleet of ships, called Columbus Caravels, that had sailed in from Spain. They were not, in the vernacular of the day, "the cat's meow." What *was* "the cat's meow" was a little 5-foot, 4-inch "hootchy-kootchy" dancer down at the Egyptian village on the midway,, a corn-fed American girl with dark eyes and a little special training, who titilated the thousands who flocked to see her with her "naughty" feline-like gyrations. Within the month, Chicago's sporting crowd was talking about another small figure—even smaller than "Little Egypt," if that were possible, at 5-feet 2 ½ inches—with gyrations all his own: Little Jimmy Barry, who was wow-ing his own following at the Star Theatre, across the Chicago River at Clark and Kinzie.

KNOWN AS "CHICAGO'S LITTLE TIGER," Barry was a good-looking Irish lad with a rakish cowlick that fell over his right eye, twinkling Irish eyes and twinkling hands as well. Looking like an under-rated bugboy who should have been wearing jockey's silks instead of column-length britches—which was only fitting considering that one of his early fights was a three-round knockout of the most celebrated jock of his day, Tod Sloane—this young spout fought like Public Energy Number-One. A prodigious worker whose quickness, aggressive infighting, and lightning-like flurries left most of his opponents to run—like a storm of rain—to get in from out of the rain, Barry also possessed a punch that was not the normal feather duster of most men his weight, but one which made most of his oppo-

nents surrender and close their eyes for a rest. In his first 27 fights, Barry performed almost as if he were trying to have his ring foes practice the old Yiddish proverb of "Sleep faster, we need the pillows . . . " knocking out 18 of them.

By 1894, with George Dixon leaving the bantamweight ranks to campaign as a featherweight, the bantamweight championship lay unclaimed, although a few claim jumpers had entered minor pretexts to the crown, like Joe McGrath, who claimed to be the champion of Ireland, and whom Barry destroyed in three rounds. Boxing, like nature, abhoring a vacuum, set up a match between Barry—whose winning streak had now reached 42 straight, 28 of those by knockout—and Caspar Leon, nicknamed "Little Italy," a sobri-

quet he proudly carried, the first of the great Italian fighters.

In the first bantamweight fight ever contested at 112 pounds, Leon gave Barry his toughest test yet, matching him in ring science, if not speed. With clever head movements, subtle side-stepping, and occasional right-hand counters, Leon minimized Barry's faster hand speed and superior infighting. For 20 rounds, the two battled evenly, Barry's all-around ring work the makeweight. Continually forcing the action, Barry moved into Leon in the twenty-first, following behind his left-hand lead with a right-hand blow that landed under Leon's heart, nearly caving him in. Throughout the next few rounds, Barry followed up his advantage, and, hands pumping like a ward heeler's, raked little Leon with several straight rights to the nose, dazing Leon and forcing him to use every defensive trick in his bag to keep on his feet. Finally, Leon collapsed in sections under the hurricane-like attack of Barry in the twenty-eighth. Barry immediately claimed the world bantamweight title, as successor to George Dixon.

A match was made at once by Bettinson between Barry and Walter Croot—who had a standing challenge to meet any man at 7 stone, 7 pounds, or 105 pounds, for 250 pounds of British sterling, or $1,250—a 20-round bout to be held December 6, 1897, at the National Sporting Club. After posting $500 as his bond, Barry had but $3 left in his pockets as "walking around" money. But he soon found two old friends, Adrian Anson, the Chicago Cubs' great "Captain," and Frank C. Ives, the world billiard champion. Together the three were able to scrape together $30,000

Born 3/7/70, in Chicago, IL . . . First pro bout, 1891, Chicago . . . Won 100lb championship (paperweight class) with knockout in the seventeenth round against Jack Levy, using skin-tight gloves . . . Knocked out Casper Leon in twenty-eighth round, 9/15/94, to claim bantamweight title . . . Rematch with Leon, 5/30/95, stopped by police in the fourteenth round . . . Fought 6-round no-decision with Leon, 7/24/96 . . . Won undisputed world bantamweight title with twentieth-round knockout of Walter Croot, London England, 12/6/97—Croot died as a result of the bout . . . Defended twice against Leon—both 20-round draws—5/30/98, and 12/29/98 . . . Retired undefeated following 6-round draw with Harry Harris, 9/1/99 . . . One of very few fighters to retire undefeated and closed career with 7 consecutive draws . . . Died 4/5/43, in Chicago, IL . . . Complete record: 70 bouts, 59 won, 0 lost, 9 draws, 2 no-decisions, 39 knockouts.

for Barry's side stake.

The National Sporting Club was an island of respectability in a day and age of when prizefighting was still considered illegal in Britain. In order to overcome the ruffian odor attached to prizefighting, the N.S.C. demanded more than decorum, it damn near demanded reverence. Evening dress was encouraged, albeit not obligatory, members only were allowed—and then only men, privileged members sat on the stage with the ring in the center of the surrounding stalls under a massive electric chandelier—and strict silence was enforced during the bouts—although, on occasion, according to author, Harry Carpenter, less high-minded members could be heard hollering between rounds such bloody encouragement as "More gore." The creed of the N.S.C. was: "Every boxer should try to overcome his adversary in a fair, manly, and generous spirit. And bear in mind that there is more honour in losing like a gentleman than in winning like a blackguard."

But cheering was excused for this one, especially from the backers of Croot, as the Brit, faster than Barry had expected, got off in front. For 19 rounds, as the contest continued at a breakneck pace, frequent outbursts of applause welled up from the stage and the stalls in appreciation of the nonstop action. And for 19 rounds, Barry's cornerman, fellow Chicago pugilist Tommy White—who shared the corner duties with two of America's sporting aristocracy, Cap Anson and jockey Tod

Sloan—had been imploring Barry to "go in and keep at him until you get him." But try as he might, Barry could not corner the elusive Croot, who pecked, pawed and piled up points.

At the call of "Time!" for the twentieth, and final, round, Barry "noticed that Tommy White, my chief second, was crying. And, although I had fought the hardest and best I could and it seemed impossible to do any more, the sight of White's tears seemed to change everything."

As Barry went out to center ring for the last round, he saw "Croot coming toward me . . . some mysterious speed and strength came from I don't know where, and I started in to do as Tommy had begged me to do." Where once he had been smoke, now he was fire, his left a honing device, his right targeted for the jugular. But Croot, who for 19 rounds had been a phantom, now determined to lock horns with Barry, and give as good as he got.

"Everybody in the place went crazy but Croot and myself. The cheers were terrific," remembered Barry some years later. At the two-minute mark, from somewhere in the supposedly austere crowd, a voice wafted up to the ring, "Come on, Walter lad . . . the bloomin' American can't win now unless he knocks you dead." Almost as if on cue, Croot stabbed out with a straight left and Barry, sidestepping, brought up a right from an angle that defied geometry. The punch landed to the heart with numbing force, and Croot wavered momentarily. That was enough for Barry and, moving with the lust of a predator, he drove inside with lefts and rights, overwhelming Croot. Then, from the windmill of punches, all aimed at Croot's head, came a pluperfect right which landed on Croot's jaw with the sound of a cannon going off. Croot fell as if shot, landing heavily on his back, his right hand folded neatly across his chest, unmoving.

Croot had been knocked as cold as a proverbial mackeral. And as dead. Before the night was out, he would expire, his skull fractured striking the canvas.

Jimmy Barry would go on fighting for two more years. But, afflicted by the memory of the lifeless form of Walter Croot, he merely went through the motions without any emotions, never again scoring—or even trying to score—a knockout. Finally, after 70 fights, the great Jimmy Barry retired. Unbeaten. And haunted.

68 CARLOS ZARATE

CARLOS ZARATE

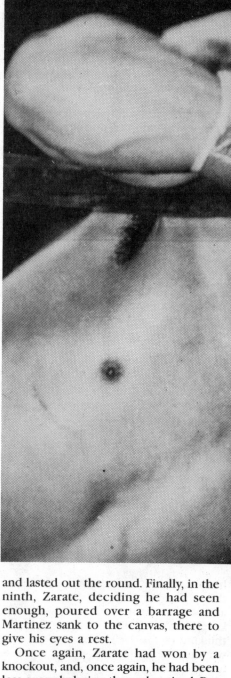

Fame creates its own standards. Carlos Zarate's standards few mortals could attain. He came close, but, in the end, the excellence demanded of him by his fame and by the proud Zarate himself were too high. From the moment the matchstick-thin Zarate emerged from one of the barrios outside Mexico City and began striking down his opponents with monotonous regularity, he struck a responsive chord in those inmates of the psychiatric wards known as Mexican fight arenas, the Mexican boxing fans. He became at once a symbol and a rarity, a ring killer in a country that loves ring killers and one with an all-perfect record for destruction—racing through his first 23 opponents like a fire extinguisher blowing out candles. Boxing's version of Evelyn Wood took less time to dispense with them than it would have taken to read their collective, or collected, names. And yet, as the legend of Carlos Zarate (pronounced Zar-rat-tay) grew, so too did the demands of his growing fame and the increasing number of fans.

AND THEN, IN HIS TWENTY-FOURTH fight, the impossible happened: Victor Ramirez stood up to the iron fists of Carlos Zarate for the entire ten rounds. Carlos Zarate won, but he was proven to be mortal. It wasn't enough that his left jab tore like a barbed fishhook, nor that his left hook to the liver made grown men cry out in pain, or that his right was always honed for the jaw. Now he was mortal and his demanding fans had demanded more of him.

But Carlos Zarate was a proud man, one who wasn't about to alter the carefully constructed alchemy of his style to suit his fans. It had gotten him where he was now and would be how he would hand-ride all the way to the finish line: his murderous eyes peering out from behind a ring-broadened nose anchored by an equally broad mustache, he thoughtfully explored his opponent in the same manner a doctor would before probing. Then, with an almost audible grinding of gears, he unlimbered his long arms—so long he could tie his shoelaces without bending over—and place a paralyzing left hook to the liver or a long, serpentine right to the jaw, all as a preamble to

smothering his foe with a barrage of blows from every conceivable angle. It was a style that had worked before and would work again, as Zarate ran off 15 more knockouts—dancing the Mexican hat dance on his opponents' heads before they had time to take off their sombreros.

Now, with 38 knockouts and 39 wins in the same number of fights, Zarate stood on the cusp of the bantamweight championship, held by fellow countryman Rudolfo Martinez. Zarate, a 3-to-1 favorite, approached Martinez as he had all his other opponents, watchful and waitful at arm's length. The first round was a typical one for Zarate, six punches in all, each thrown in the general direction of his target without any malicious intent. Pressing resolutely forward, Zarate continued to cooly stalk his smaller opponent, parrying the left-handed Martinez's quick shots to his jaw and nose, content to hold Martinez's gaze in his. Then, in the fifth, Zarate finally swarmed all over his foe, chasing him like a father chasing someone who has kept his daughter out past curfew, and drove him to the floor with a left hook. But Martinez arose at four

and lasted out the round. Finally, in the ninth, Zarate, deciding he had seen enough, poured over a barrage and Martinez sank to the canvas, there to give his eyes a rest.

Once again, Zarate had won by a knockout, and, once again, he had been less overwhelming than advertised. But it had been the standard of invincibility his fans had created. And one which Carlos Zarate had difficulty not only accepting but acquitting.

But, with nine straight knockouts in defense of his crown—including a four-round KO of WBA bantamweight champion and former stablemate, Alfonso Zamora in the action-packed "Battle of the Z's"—Zarate had begun to believe

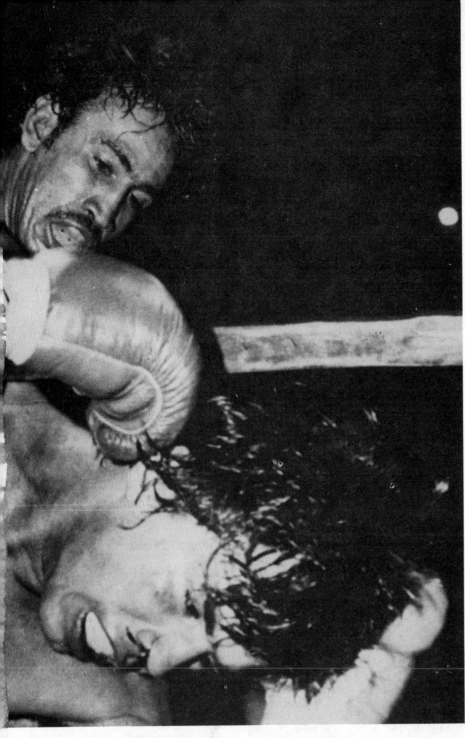

Born 5/23/51, in Tepito, Mexico . . . First pro bout, 1970, Guernavaca, Mexico . . . Fought exclusively in Mexico until November, 1974 . . . Won first 23 bouts by knockout, first 20 by knockout in second or third round . . . Went the 10-round distance with Victor Ramirez, 1/30/74, winning decision . . . Won next 28 bouts by knockout, for a total 51 of 52 victories by KO . . . Won WBC bantamweight title with nonth-round KO of Rodolfo Martinez, 5/8/76 . . . Successfully defended title 9 times, all knockouts . . . Fought WBA bantamweight titleholder, Alfonso Zamora, 4/23/77, in match neither WBA or WBC called "Title bout," though considered by all a contest bantamweight title; won by KO in fourth round . . . Fought Wilfredo Gomez for WBC junior featherweight title, 10/28/78— . . . Stopped by Gomez in fifth round . . . Retired abruptly after losing title by disputed decision to Lupe Pintor, 6/3/79 . . . Retired with one of the most incredible records of any boxer at any weight—53 knockouts in 56 bouts . . . Complete record: 56 bouts, 54 won, 2 lost, 53 knockouts.

his fans. And dream of bigger and better things. Tired of his bantamweight niche and of the rigorous grind of training to keep his weight down, Zarate was now thinking of retiring undefeated. Or of winning the junior featherweight and full-fledged featherweight crowns.

However, one roadblock prevented the accomplishment of any and/or all of the above: Wilfredo Gomez. In a fight Gomez was pressured into by the WBC powers-that-be to give Zarate an opportunity for lasting immortality rather than retirement, Gomez waited out Zarate's patient attack and then, in the fourth, unloaded on the bantamweight king, treating him to more disrespect than he had ever been shown in the

ring during his fistic lifetime—and continued with an after-the-bell assault that showed some disrespect for the Marquis of Queensberry as well. Finally, 44 seconds into the fifth round, referee Harry Gibbs signaled the end to Zarate's dreams.

Eight months later, Zarate was to be treated to some equally disrespectful treatment when he defended his bantamweight title against a former stablemate, Lupe Pintor. In one of those curious things that goes down in boxing history, Zarate's manager, Cuyo Hernandez—with whom he was on anything but speaking terms at the time—also managed Pintor. But even that wasn't the most curious thing about the

fight, which, as Alice said in wonderment, got "curiouser and curiouser. . . . "

For 15 rounds, two distinguished fighters fought a very undistinguished fight. Here was Carlos Zarate, one of the all-time great offensive fighters, fighting in reverse gear, trying to outbox the four-inch shorter Pintor. The only times Zarate stopped his backward movement came in the fourth, when he knocked down Pintor with two lefts, and in the eleventh, when he rocked the challenger with a lethal left that honed in to the jaw. Otherwise, Zarate, known for his patience, overdid a good thing. But, even so, most ringside observers, with eyesight no worse than aging owls, thought Zarate had won going away, UPI scoring it 12 rounds to three. Still, when the officials' cards were tallied the results were quixotic: one judge had it 145–133 for Zarate; the other two 143–142 for Pintor.

Afterward, a proud Zarate issued a bitter statement: "For some reason I have been robbed of my title by the officials in Nevada. I want the World Boxing Council to study a film of the fight. I should be given my title back. The decision was a terrible disgrace."

Those were to be Carlos Zarate's last boxing words. Advised by the WBC that he could have a return bout if he so desired, Zarate desired retirement instead. The proud warrior who had tried mightily to meet those demanding standards set for him had now seen boxing fail to meet his. He left, forever, his heart no longer in it, his standards still intact.

69 GEORGES CARPENTIER

GEORGES CARPENTIER

Greats come wrapped in many colors, but few have come wrapped in tricolors like France's Georges Carpentier, a fighter so good his name and deeds were spelled in the plural. Earmarked for greatness at an early age, Carpentier began his career in the noble art of *la savatte*, or foot boxing, at the age of 13. Under the tutelage of Francois Descamps, a traveling one-man performer who served as a combination midwife, clairvoyant and public-address announcer for the team, he quickly changed his style to *La Boxe Anglaise* and took on everyone who dared to put on the gloves with him. Starting as a flyweight, Carpentier won every divisional title in France—and most of those in Europe—up to, and including, the heavyweight championship.

AT 17, CARPENTIER WON HIS FIRST title, the welterweight championship of France. Four months later, he won the European welterweight title. And then the titles started falling like apples from a tree: the European middleweight title the next year, the European light heavyweight title the year after and four months later, in June of 1913, the European heavyweight title against the supposedly invincible "Bombardier" Billy Wells—a startling victory he repeated in 73 seconds 6 months thereafter when Wells assumed the legendary

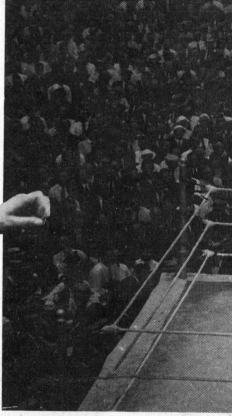

Bottom foreground: Two of France's national treasures, Maurice Chevalier (left) and Carpentier. Background: Jack Dempsey (left) and Carpentier sign for boxing's 1st "Million Dollar" gate. Below: Carpentier throws left to Dempsey's head, 1921.

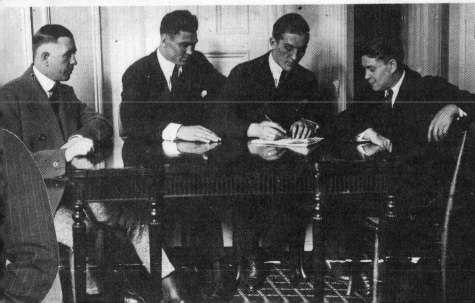

position all British heavyweights have become familiar with, supine.

In July of 1914, he won the "White" Heavyweight Championship of the World from Gunboat Smith and left the fistic wars to enlist in the French army, where he was to win the *Croix de Guerre* and the *Medaille Militaire* for heroic action in "The Great War."

By 1919, Carpentier had returned to the ring, a champion and much-decorated war hero. So great was his reputation that he became a national institution in France. And so handsome, educated, and courteous was the man now known as "The Orchid Man," that he became an international favorite of the sophisticated set. Following the trail of dollar bills, he came over to the United States to wrest the light heavyweight title from Battling Levinsky— knocking him out in the process, something only Jack Dempsey had been able to do to the venerable battler. Carpentier became the most heralded French import since the Statue of Liberty, a natural opponent for the homicidally inclined "Slacker" who held the heavyweight crown, Jack Dempsey. Carpentier would become the party of the second part in the making of boxing's first "Million-Dollar Gate."

Carpentier's style was an extension of his *Savatte* days, a form of tap dancing with gloves on, as he moved in and out like a phantom with all the grace and skill of a dancing master. (So fleet afoot was he that before the Levinsky fight he would utter one of boxing's classic lines: "Feet brought me in and feet will bring me out.") He accompanied his fistic fandango with rare handspeed, punctuating his rapid-fire flurries with a straight right to the head, a finishing blow which rendered 56 of his opponents *hors de combat*.

But his fight with Dempsey was a leap of more than faith for a light heavyweight like Carpentier; it was an impossibility. In the second round Carpentier whipped over his right at the end of a series of punches, stopping Dempsey in his tracks. Unfortunately, his hand betrayed him, broken in two places on the brine-hardened head of the champion. He gamely played out the string and went down in the fourth like an inert baby in its crib, dominant no longer.

Still Georges Carpentier was the dominant force in European boxing longer than any man in the history of the sport. And its greatest.

TONY ZALE

There have been twosomes throughout history as well paired as salt and pepper. These twosomes have sprung up in many locales and in every imaginable field: biblical, Cain and Abel; mythological, Damon and Pythias; musical, Gilbert and Sullivan; financial, Dow and Jones; comical, Weber and Fields; political, Franklin and Roosevelt. Boxing is no exception. Perhaps its most famous pairing was that of Tony Zale and Rocky Graziano. Like it says in the song, "You can't have one without the other." Any yet, there were spaces in their togetherness. For while Rocky Graziano was one of the most charismatic figures ever to come down the boxing pike, Tony Zale remains one of its all-time greats, a fighter much like other fighters. Except tougher.

RAISED WITHIN SIGHT OF THE STEEL mills of his native Gary, Indiana, Zale alternately worked in the mills between the fights of his youth, forging his toughness and earning his nickname, "The Man of Steel." Fighting around the small clubs of Chicago, those cauldrons where ingots of greatness are cast, Zale became a fighter tipped with the fine line of steel, indestructible. The only credentials the local fight crowd asked was the ability to hit hard and to take it. And Tony Zale could do both.

After an outstanding amateur career that saw the youngster with the steel-like physique take out 50 of his 95 amateur opponents inside the distance, only losing eight times, Zale embarked upon a pro career. But after nine straight wins, something went wrong. Apparently it wasn't enough just to hit hard and be able to take a hard punch in return unflinchingly, and Zale lost 9 of his next 17 fights, "retiring" to go back to the steel mills from whence he came.

Having fought just once in two years, an impatient Zale, anxious to return to the ring, listened to the overtures of Sam Pian and Art Winch—the famed Chicago manager-trainer partnership that had taken Barney Ross to the top— and returned to the ring in earnest.

Part of greatness consists of being at a strategic point in the campaign of his-

tory. Zale was fortunate to be at that point, a point where the middleweight division, the storied division of yore, was a vast wasteland, having reached the dregs of the barrel marked "talent." After two and one-half years of grafting skills onto "The Man of Steel," Pian and Winch maneuvered Zale in against the NBA middleweight champion, Al Hostak, a tough Czech from Seattle. Zale first took a 10-round, nontitle decision from Hostak and then made it two-for-two, scoring a thirteenth-round KO and winning half of the middleweight title in Hostak's backyard. Zale defended his newly won half-crown two more times, winning both by knockout, and then cemented his claim to the universal championship by outpointing Georgie Abrams in 15 rounds for all the marbles. Nine days later the United States went to war and Tony swapped his battles in the ring for the real thing, joining the Navy and leaving his title "frozen" for the four-year duration.

Upon his return to civilian life at the ripe old age of 32—and with his future now behind him—Zale found that he was the second most famous middleweight in the country, his star having been eclipsed by a Dead-End kid with dynamite in his right hand named Rocky Graziano. While Zale had spent four of his most productive years in the

service, Graziano had been fighting regularly, cleaning up on East Coast welterweights and middleweights. The two would light up the skies with their fistic fireworks and make boxing history.

In the first of their three epic encounters the supposedly ring-rusty Zale walked right into—and through— the guns of Graziano and threw his patented left hook, dropping Rocky to the floor. But Graziano, up as fast as he

went down, began clubbing Zale with his famed right hand, driving the defiantly erect Zale to the canvas at the end of the first round. Dragged to his corner, hurt and dazed, Zale emerged to take more of a battering in the second, again being toppled at the bell by four successive rights. Amazingly, he came back in the third, only to run into Graziano's persistent attack, one he would continue in the fourth with a maniacal fury. Still, Zale, his face etched

in the stale expectation of life that comes from the steel mills, came out for more, almost as if getting hit stimulated him. Early in the fifth Zale began concentrating on the body with both hands, landing the best left to the body in the history of boxing, one that had the effect of a sock with a rifle butt. And just as suddenly, Graziano leaped at the champ with a tigerish attack and drove Zale back into the ropes. But just when Tony Zale seemed to be exhausted, he

Below: Zale wins "rubber match" with Rocky Graziano by knocking out "Da Rock" in 3 rounds, June 10, 1948.

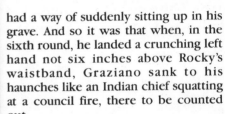

Born Anthony Florian Zaleski, 5/29/13, in Gary, IN . . . Golden Glover 1931–34, lost to Melio Bettina in Inter-city Golden Gloves final, 1934 . . . Began pro career, June 1934 . . . Won first 9 bouts in 1934 but lost 6 of last 12 . . . Lost 3 of 5 in 1935, drew in only bout in 1936 . . . Quit boxing for 1½ years, 1936–37 . . . Won 14 of 19, 1937–38; won 7 of 8 with 6 knockouts 1939 . . . Won NBA middleweight title with thirteenth-round knockout of Al Hostak, 7/19/40 . . . Defended against Steve Mamakos, 2/21/41, with fourteenth-round kayo; knocked out Hostak in second round of rematch, 5/228/41 . . . Won universal title recognition with 15-round decision victory over Georgie Abrams, 11/28/41 . . . Lost to Billy Conn in nontitle match, 12-round decision, 2/13/42 . . . In military service, 1942–45 . . . Won 6 straight by kayo after discharge, 1946 . . . Defended successfully against Rocky Graziano with sixth-round knockout in memorable bout, 9/27/46 . . . Won 5 more nontitle bouts by kayo to run streak to 12 . . . Lost middleweight title to Graziano when kayoed in sixth round, 7/16/47 . . . Scored 3 kayos in first 3 bouts in 1948, rewon title from Graziano with third-round knockout, 6/10/48 . . . Lost title to Marcel Cerdan, 9/21/48, on kayo in twelfth round . . . Retired after Cerdan bout . . . Elected to Boxing Hall of Fame, 1958 . . . Complete record: 87 bouts, 67 won, 18 lost, 2 draws, 44 knockouts.

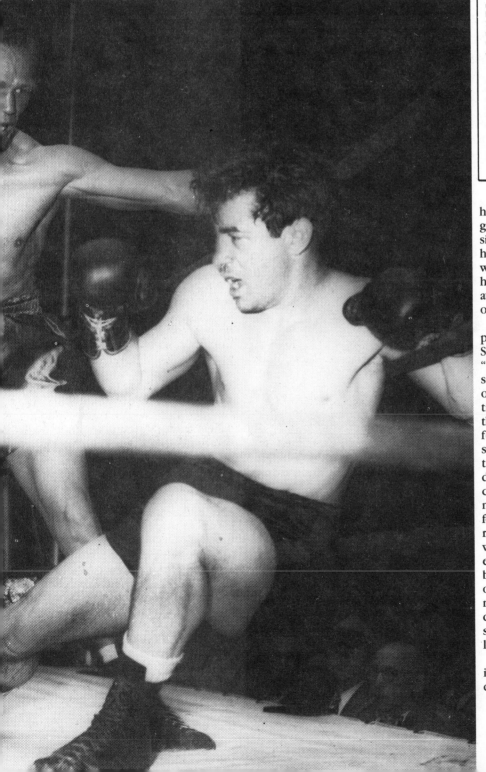

had a way of suddenly sitting up in his grave. And so it was that when, in the sixth round, he landed a crunching left hand not six inches above Rocky's waistband, Graziano sank to his haunches like an Indian chief squatting at a council fire, there to be counted out.

If Zale's light had flickered in the past, now it flamed, as "The Man of Steel" had beaten back the challenge of "The Rock" in one of boxing's most savage battles. Their rematch was more of the same, more savage than scientific, as first one then the other went on the attack. It was almost as if the performances had duplicated themselves—with one minor exception; this time Graziano, after having been on the defensive for the first four rounds, came back to defeat Zale, who had many times during the fight found the force in him fading, only to painfully rally back out of sheer will. But sheer will wasn't enough and Rocky Graziano evened the score. Zale won their rubber match with a tape-measure knockout in the third round. There had been no unconditional surrender to undeniable facts. "The Man of Steel" had shown that he was truly tipped with a line of steel.

Tony Zale was inexhaustible. And so is his legend—a man capable of being destroyed but never entirely defeated.

YOUNG GRIFFO

Young Griffo was the most multi-faceted talent in the history of boxing. The original "Will-o'-the-Wisp," he was a picture of grace in the ring, always able to outwit his opponents with his cleverness. And yet, in a day and age when the typical pugilist was as likely as not to show unmistakable signs of debauchery, Young Griffo was also the all-time champion debauchee. Part of a steady stream of foreign fighters who looked upon America as a Queensberry Golconda, Young Griffo came to the States from Australia in 1893, bringing with him as baggage a claim on the featherweight title and a record of 100 bouts without a loss. Gifted with superhuman defensive skill and an ability to make any opponent look ridiculous with his dazzling feints, his impenetrable defense, and his two-fisted attack, he quickly captured the fancy of the sporting crowd.

GRIFFO WAS, ACCORDING TO *RING* historian, Nat Fleischer, "Probably the fastest and cleverest boxer who ever performed under the Queensberry rules." His judgment of timing and sidestepping were amazing, and although he was not a hard puncher, he had an uncanny way of manipulating his gloves.

After more than holding his own against such world-class fighters as Torpedo Billy Murphy, Ike Weir, and George "Kid" Lavigne, Young Griffo was matched with the incomparable king of the lightweights, Jack McAuliffe for McAuliffe's American Lightweight Championship. For ten rounds, Griffo made a target of the title holder, peppering McAuliffe with jabs, hooks, uppercuts, and every scientific punch known to boxingkind. And yet, after ten rounds of serving as a human punching bag, the referee, Maxie More, a great friend of McAuliffe, saved the title for his friend by giving him the decision. Griffo could only say, "I beat him, but I couldn't beat the referee," as he repaired to the nearest watering hole to soothe his wounded ego.

Griffo suffered what seemed to be permanent retrogression after his "loss" to McAuliffe, spending more and more time in saloons entertaining the bar sports rather than the boxing sporting

public. Frequently, for a wager, Griffo could be found in a bar standing on a handkerchief, challenging anyone within earshot to hit him without moving from his perch. Other times he would entertain those bellied-up at the bar, catching flies on the wing or giving liquid seminars in the finer points of boxing. Too often he gave these same liquid seminars within the confines of the ropes, coming away with several ninety-eight proof wins.

Never the sort to let success go to his training—which usually consisted of a shave and a haircut—Griffo would often have to be hauled, bodily, from the bar directly to the arena. One time, matched against Tommy Tracy, a leading lightweight, Griffo, possessing a single-minded thirst and the feet to find it, "went on a bat." On the night of the fight, his managers had to send out what amounted to an all-points bulletin to find their missing fighter. "Find him," the manager told one of his go-fers, "and bring him to the [St. Louis] Coliseum. If you can't bring all of him, bring in an arm or a leg. I'll at least have some sort of evidence to prove my case." And find Young Griffo he did, in front of a pub doing a shadow dance and telling an interested crowd what he intended to do with Tracy that night. The go-fer grabbed Griffo, hired a hack and told

the driver to drive like the devil for the Coliseum, the fight being scheduled to go on in less than an hour. The hack driver obeyed too well, running into a cable car, killing the horse, and smashing the hack to pieces. By the time the totally paralyzed Griffo was delivered to the Coliseum, it was past midnight and the crowd was more than a little impatient. Pushed into the ring and all but held up by his manager, Griffo jumped out of the ring at the sight of the first blow, tore the gloves off his hands, and ran down the aisle. The an-

nouncer took the megaphone and hollered, "Mr. Griffo met with an awful accident on his way to the Coliseum and is so unnerved he is unable to go on with the fight." That was Young Griffo!

At his funeral, James J. Corbett, the man generally recognized as the greatest scientific fighter of his time, looked down at Young Griffo's bier and said, "There he is, boys, the zephyr of all time. The only one that ever hit him was the Grim Reaper. There never was one like him and there will never be another. . . . "

Born Albert Griffiths, 4/15/69, in Sofala, New South Wales, Australia . . . Began as a professional boxer, 1886 . . . First bouts bareknuckle . . . In early years, won 55-round bout from Tom Whalen . . . Had 70-round draw with Joe Pluto, 12/12/89 . . . Won Australian featherweight title via 8-round decision over Nipper Peakes, 12/27/89 . . . Won world featherweight title from New Zealander, Torpedo Billy Murphy with 15-round knockout, 9/2/90 . . . Made successful world title defense, 3/12/91, by defeating George Powell via disqualification in twentieth round . . . Fought 22-round draw with Jim Barron for Australian lightweight title, 7/25/92 . . . Abandoned claim to world featherweight title, 1892 . . . Fought exclusively in Australia until he came to the United States in mid-1893, and never fought again in Australia . . . Boxed 3 draws with world featherweight champion George Dixon, 1894–95: 20 rounds, 6/29/94; 25 rounds, 1/19/95; 10 rounds, 10/28/95 . . . Also fought draws with Kid Lavigne, 20 rounds, 10/12/95, and Joe Gans, 10 rounds, 11/18/95 . . . Fought 43 draws in career (25% of his bouts), more draws than any other world champion and more draws than 21 featherweight champions from 1968–82 combined . . . Active through 1904—made 2-bout comeback, 1911 . . . Last pro bout, 9/25/11, 6-round no-decision bout with Billy "Honey" Mellody, ex-welterweight champion . . . Died 12/7/27, New York City . . . Charter member of Boxing Hall of Fame, 1954 . . . Complete record: 173 bouts, 69 won, 12 lost, 43 draws, 48 no-decisions, 1 no contest, 20 knockouts.

Above left to right: Griffo (right in 1st picture) demonstrates the positions: left hand lead and guard; same reversed; duck and counter blow; same reversed. Opposite: Griffo and George Dixon draw, 1894.

ALEXIS ARGUELLO

In the apocrypha of boxing many of its practitioners have been known as gentlemanly, some even have been called "Gentleman," as in "Gentleman" Jim Corbett. And yet, while most of those in the busted-beak profession are, in fact, gentlemanly outside the ring, none has ever come close to that Goodwill Ambassador of Boxing, Alexis Arguello, a man who lit up the faces of his defeated opponents with postprandial grace and charm. Contrary to the belief that "Nice guys finish last," Alexis Arguello finished first, time and again, winning 76 of his 82 bouts, 62 by knockout—a better winning percentage than Leo Durocher ever dreamed of having. Arguello's looks were deceiving, not quite what the gallery gods had become used to. For here was an olive-skinned, pencil-thin body with a perfectly chiseled face and the noble bearing of a Greek god intent upon destruction. If not for his Omar Sharif mustache, he wouldn't have had any figure at all, just straight and narrow. But what he could do with that wiry, splinter-like frame—swinging his pipestem arms freely, hitting his opponents with the agonizing effect of a rifle butt and opening them up like a flowering Nicaraguan rose. And despite his elongated, washboard-like frame, with ribs sticking out like a survivor of the Bataan "Death March," the slight, but hardly brittle, Arguello could take a punch, too, his bony elbows forming a protective shield around his body. In fact, until Pryor, a fighter may as well have tried to open an oyster without a knife as get inside Arguello's defense.

THE MAN THEY CALLED "FLACO DE EXplosivo" and "Flaco bala" lost only 2 of his first 37 fights—a 6-round decision in his fourth fight and a fight in which "I broke my hand in the second round and could not use it at all. The doctor stopped the fight."—before challenging Ernesto Marcel for the featherweight title. "I thought I could beat him," Alexis said afterward, with 20-20 hindsight improved by distance. "I said so at the time. I was only twenty-one and still had things to learn." But he lost, nevertheless, and, as he would many times in the future, had nothing but nice things to say about his opponent: "Marcel was a very good champion." It was to be the last championship bout he would lose in his next 19 title appearances, as he hurdled small divisions in a single bounce, jumping more weight classes than a claim jumper and acquiring homesteading rights to the featherweight, junior lightweight, and lightweight titles on his way to immortality. Always with a good word for his vanquished foe, Arguello dealt out destruction with his razor-sharp gloves and murderous body punches—so murderous in fact that when he fetched future junior lightweight champion Cornelius Boza-Ed-

Above: Arguello knocks out Bobby Chacon, Nov. 16, 1979. Right: Two matinee idols: Clint Eastwood and winner of the Omar Shariff look-alike contest, Arguello.

Born in Managua, Nicaragua, 4/19/52 . . . Began professional boxing career, 1968 in Nicaragua . . . Boxed solely in Managua, 1968–72 . . . Won 35 of first 37 bouts, 29 by knockout, 11 in first round . . . Lost 15-round decision in Panama City to Panamanian, Ernesto Marcel in bid for WBA featherweight title, 2/16/74 . . . Won title later that year by thirteenth-round knockout of Ruben Olivares, 11/23/74 . . . Sucessfully defended title 4 times, all by knockouts, 1975–76 . . . Relinquished title, 6/20/77 . . . Won WBC super featherweight (junior lightweight) title by thirteenth-round knockout of Alfredo Escalera in Puerto Rico, 1/28/78 . . . Defended crown 8 times 1978–80, 7 by knockout, including 4 knockout victories against men who were or would be champions (Escalera, Bazooka, Limon, Bobby Chacon, Rolando Navarrette) . . . Relinquished title to move up to lightweight class in late 1980 . . . Won third world championship by decisioning Scotsman, Jim Watt in London, England, 6/20/81, in bout for WBC lightweight title . . . Defeated Ray Mancini in first defense by fourteenth-round knockout, 10/3/81—first loss for Mancini . . . Won 3 more title defenses by knockout before relinquishing third title to challenge for junior welterweight title . . . Only man to hold 3 world titles and not lose any of them in the ring . . . Became one of a select few to challenge for a fourth title, but was stopped by Aaron Pryor in fourteenth-round, 11/12/82, in WBA junior welterweight championship bout . . . Lost rematch to Pryor 9/9/83, in second attempt at fourth crown . . . Retired after that bout to devote energies to civil war in homeland . . . Fought 22 championship bouts—won 19, 17 by knockout . . . Knocked out 10 different world champions in career . . . Complete record: 84 bouts, 78 won, 6 lost, 63 knockouts.

wards a shot to *la bonza*, Boza-Edwards lost control of his bodily functions and actually soiled his trunks.

But always afterward, like a priest inviting a few friends in to hear confessional, he would have a good word to say about the ex-something-or-other he had just faced. About Alfredo Escalera, whom he beat twice in title bouts: "He said he was gonna KO me. He said it might go five rounds. But I have noth-

ing but high praise for him. I was never offended by his remarks against my person. It was his way of building up the gate by creating a degree of animosity that really didn't exist. He is a great showman. . . . " About Ray "Boom Boom" Mancini, whom he beat in 14 hard rounds, this time on national TV: "Ray, I hope I never have another fight this hard. There is no doubt in my mind you will become a champion. I know how bad you wanted to beat me and win the title for your father. But you and he have nothing to be ashamed about. You fought like a champion because, inside, you are one. . . . " And about Aaron Pryor, the whirling dervish who ended his career and his personal Everest of winning a fourth title: "I now say goodbye to my personal friend Aaron Pryor. . . . "

Here was a man who had nothing but good things to say about boxing; and about whom boxing had nothing but good things to say as in the words of one of those he beat, Ray Mancini, "[He] does everything with class. He moves with class. He is more of a champion than any man I've ever known or heard about, besides my father." That was Alexis Arguello, a champion with a capital "C".

MAX BAER

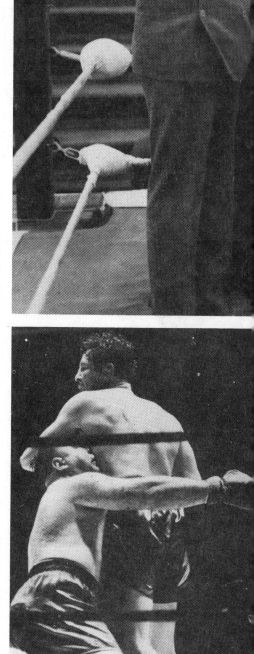

Judge Max Baer less by what he was than by what he might have been had he not possessed a self-destructiveness. When he originally burst upon the fistic scene with all the explosiveness of one of his dynamite-laden right hands—possibly the best in the history of the heavyweight division—Max Baer had all the makings of one of the all-time greats. In a career that had spanned just 15 months, the 6-foot, 210-pound Adonis had fought 26 times, winning all but 3—2 of those losses coming on fouls. His lethal right had accounted for 100 knockdowns in less than 100 rounds. With boxing on the relief roles like the rest of the nation and in dire need of a hero, it was small wonder that the boxing public would adopt this massive Puck to lift the game and their spirits at the same time.

BUT JUST HOW LETHAL A RIGHT BAER had nobody could foresee until, in two brutal fights, he killed Frankie Campbell with one blow and then destroyed Ernie Schaaf—the same Ernie Schaaf Primo Carnera would later kill as a direct result of the beating administered by Baer. Suddenly the man with the "killer punch" began holding it back for fear of fatally hurting yet another opponent, something he did in his 10-round destruction of Max Schmeling when, after repeatedly hammering his right-hand bombs to Schmeling's face and seeing that face shift like pudding, Baer called out to referee Arthur Donovan to stop the fight, saying, "This looks like the end."

Now the 21-year-old puppy-youth began to approach life with a different outlook, viewing yesterday as a canceled check and today as money on the line. He became more obsessed with his out-of-the-ring activities than those dictated by the ring. Frustrated, his manager, Ancil Hoffman, tried to implant discipline. But Baer's head rejected it. Soon his name and presence began lighting up Broadway more brightly than its famed neon signs as he set off in pursuit of wine, women, and song. Baer had become less "The Livermore Laurauper" than "The Magnificent Screwball" and "Madcap Maxie."

Still, he possessed something of his old fire when he met—and destroyed—Primo Carnera, knocking him down 12 times in 11 rounds to win the

Above: Baer drops Primo Carnero and then drops atop him, knocking out "Da Preem," 1934. Right: Baer pounds "Two Ton" Tony Galento into the canvas, 1940. Opposite left to right: Baer unleashes right hand against jaw of Pat Comiskey, 1940.

Left: The Mayor of Atlantic City presents Baer with companion of same last name, while adviser Jack Dempsey looks on. Above: Baer knocks out Max Schmeling.

those somewhat-honest Venuses, the dolls, who surrounded his every move. And so, Max Baer clowned his way out of the heavyweight championship, losing a boring 15-round decision to Braddock. He was to compound the felony by further deprecating his accomplish-

heavyweight championship of the world. Once again it seemed that Max Baer was not only leading the parade, but that he was the entire parade.

But even with the championship belt tucked safely under his massive arm, Baer was anything but a born-again fighter, and was ready to fall out of step again, this time a victim of his own arrogance. For he took the chances of challenger Jim Braddock so lightly that he barely trained for his first title defense, instead devoting his time to clowning for those dishonest ventriloquists of his greatness, the press, and

Born Maximillian Adelbert Baer, 2/11/09, in Omaha, NE . . . Began pro boxing in 1929 in CA . . . Won 24 of first 27 bouts with 20 knockouts . . . Knocked out Frankie Campbell (brother of baseball player Dolph Camilli), in fifth round, 8/25/30, Campbell died after bout . . . Next bout, 12/19/30, ironically with Ernie Schaaf, lost 10-round decision—rematch with Schaaf two years later, 8/31/32, resulted in bad beating for Schaaf that led to his death in a subsequent bout with Primo Carnera . . . Knocked out Max Schmeling in 10 rounds, 6/8/33 . . . Although outweighed by 54 pounds, won world heavyweight title, 6/14/34, by knocking down Primo Carnera 11 times in 11 rounds . . . Held title exactly 1 year, lost it in first defense, 6/13/35, to 10–1 underdog Jim Braddock on 15-round decision . . . Knocked out by Joe Louis in fourth round, 9/24/35 . . . Toured country summer of 1936, had 24 bouts in 24 towns, 6/15 to 10/19, won all but one against second-rate opposition . . . Continued bxing until 1941 . . . Became movie actor after retirement from ring . . . Starred in film "The Prizefighter and the Lady," 1933, while active contender . . . Died, 11/21/59, Hollywood, CA . . . Elected to Hall of Fame, 1968 . . . Complete record: 83 bouts, 70 won, 13 lost, 52 knockouts.

ments, or lack thereof, saying, "Braddock can use the title. He has five kids. I don't know how many I have." He had, by now, become to writers everywhere "The Man with the Million-Dollar Body and the Ten-Cent Brain."

From one viewpoint, Max Baer may well have been the greatest heavyweight champion in history at that narrow juncture in the heavyweight division between Dempsey and Louis. But from another, his career must also be viewed as a promise unkept in spite of the greatness hinted at and the awesome talent he possessed.

MARVIN HAGLER

In the early days of his career, Marvin Hagler was told by one of boxing's resident cynics that he had "three strikes against him." He was, so the naysayer said, "black, left-handed, and good." But this time the prophesy, always one of the most gratuitous forms of error, was wrong on all three counts: Marvin Hagler is more milk-chocolate than black; ambidextrous, not left-handed; and great, not good. Then again, Marvin Hagler never has been fully understood. He came from that crucible of greatness, the streets. Not just any streets, but the mean streets of Newark. Burned out of house and home when the city was trashed in 1967, his father already a memory, Marvin was bundled up by his mother with the rest of her brood and taken to Brockton, Massachusetts. There Marvin ran with the troubled and the troublesome, kids without presence or future. But Hagler had both. And he had a dream, a dream that someday he was "going to be champion," an ambition he gave voice to the first day he visited the Petronelli Brothers' Gym in downtown Brockton.

WITH HIS AMBITION UNDERLINING HIS determination to succeed, Hagler applied himself diligently to learning his newfound calling. Fighting as if he had to make up for all the deprivations of the previous years, he went on to win the 1973 AAU middleweight championship, undefeated through the first three years of his professional career—compiling a record of 25 wins with 19 KOs and one draw, against Sugar Ray Seales.

No more content to be fed the weak lemonade of steady stiffs than he had been to take the easy course in life, Hagler decided to cut his fistic eye-teeth on something more substantial. And journeyed off to that Devil's Island of boxing, Philadelphia, in quest of bigger game and bigger names. Unfortunately, he found both in Bobby "Boogaloo" Watts and Willie "The Worm" Monroe, two rated middleweights who bested Hagler in close ten-round decisions. With that innate street mentality that calls for "getting even, not mad," Hagler avenged his insults at the gloves of Watts and Monroe—together with Sugar Ray Sea-

les—knocking them out in subsequent bouts. And went through his next 20 bouts without another blemish.

By now the reputation of Marvin Hagler had come to precede him. And his style to betray him. It was a style uniquely his own, flowing like a straight line as his hands wove webs and his feet interlaced perfectly with marvelous changes of pace and splendid timing, as he crossed over from the left to the right side and back again with all the precision of a Busby Berkeley production number. At times, he would alternate this poetry in motion with the unlyrical pattern of free verse, as he interchanged his finesse for power and came boring into his opponent with a bewildering variety of punches, thrown from both sides of the plate. But his style, his record, and his appearance all served as notice to detour this one-man roadblock atop the middleweight runway. Rodrigo Valdez and Hugo Corro wanted no part of him. Neither did countless others who weren't yet ready to put their estates in order.

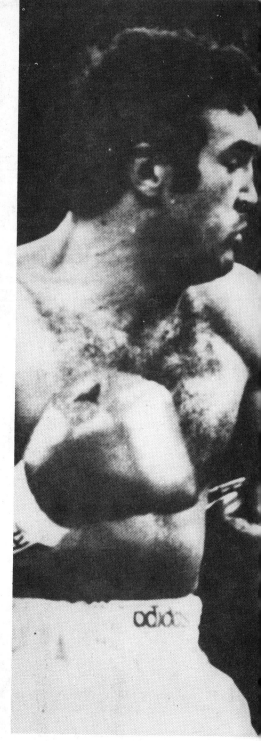

And so, Hagler contended in vain, waiting for the wheel to turn again. Finally, Vito Antuofermo won the championship and gave Hagler his chance at the title, one he was to come within a hair of winning. But, in Las Vegas, that land where the one-eyed man is a boxing official, he was to come up short, gaining only a 15-round draw for his efforts. And all the recognition of an "uncrowned champion."

His triumphant expectations giving way to bitter disillusionment, Hagler was now put into that perpetual rack

Left: Marvelous Marvin Hagler stops Juan Roldan in 10 rounds, March 30, 1984.

head and lifted him firmly out from under, picking him apart in three rounds and slicing up the Brit's eye, already heavily lidded with stitches. The reception for the new champion was underwhelming as the British fans, obviously more schooled in the split lips of the East End than the stiff lips of Eton, rained on his parade throwing more bottles on the ring than Hagler had punches on their hero, forcing him to flee without his newly-won belt.

The bullet-headed champion defended his crown with a "trespassers-will-be-prosecuted" mentality against the best the middleweight division had to offer —against Mustafa Hamsho, he set out to wipe "that shitty grin off his face"; against Wilfred Sapien, Hagler "wanted him at my feet . . . because he's got a big mouth." Translating his training champ chant of "Destroy and Destruction" into another personal credo, "When a man goes into the ring, he's going to war," the greyhound-lean and Hagler-mean champion closed the castle gate to any would-be interloper.

But still the compliments of bon hommes didn't exactly fall like summer raindrops on Hagler's shaven head, despite the grotesque latherings he handed out to one and all. If admiration of him was reluctant, it was sincere nevertheless. But only lukewarm. In order to speed up the aging process of admiration, Hagler took to calling himself "Marvelous Marvin," almost as if with the name he could make it so. Before he was to beat the "H" out of "Cave-In" Lee in a brief 67-second encounter, Hagler had insisted that he be introduced as "Marvelous Marvin." But one of those in the ABC sound truck bitingly said, "If he wants to be announced as 'Marvelous Marvin,'" let him change his name. . . . " And so, days after he had defended his title for the fourth time, Marvin Hagler officially had his name solemnized by court order to Marvelous Marvin Hagler.

But the name Marvel Marvin Hagler tends to obscure an appreciation of the skills of Marvin Hagler. It doesn't explain his phantom-like moves, his special quality of ring meanness nor his being the best switch-hitter since Pete Rose—moving from left to right, with his natural hand, the one he uses to write, eat, and throw a baseball. Another word for "Marvelous" might just be "great." And, if you have to ask what that is, then, like Louis Armstrong said when asked what jazz was, "Man, if you gotta ask, you'll never know. . . . "

Born Marvin Hagler, 5/23/54, in Newark, NJ, name legally changed to Marvelous Marvin Hagler . . . Won 1973 National AAU middleweight title . . . First pro bout, 1973, Brockton, MA . . . Undefeated in first 3 years, in 26 bouts . . . Lost 2 bouts in 2 months in 1975, Bobby Watts, 1/13/76, and Willie Monroe, 3/9/76 . . . Knocked out Monroe in 2 subsequent bouts . . . Kayoed Watts in rematch . . . Challenged Vito Antufermo for world middleweight title, held champion to draw but didn't win title, 11/30/79 . . . Won title with third-round knockout of Alan Minter, 9/27/80 . . . First 7 title defenses won by knockout, including knockout of ex-sparring partner, William "Caveman" Lee . . . Kayoed Venezuelan Fugencio Obelmejias twice in title defenses, 1/17/81, eighth round, and 10/30/82, fifth round . . . Stopped Roberto Duran's quest for a fourth championship with 15-round decision victory, 11/10/83 . . . Complete record: 60 bouts, 56 won, 2 lost, 2 draws, 47 knockouts.

called waiting. And wasting his glories fighting the Loucif Hamanis of the world in places like Portland, Maine. But then, a new champion *pro tem*, Alan Minter, replaced Antuofermo on the middleweight throne, there to momentarily hold the crown before re-routing it once again. This time to Hagler, who was given his second chance. It was an opportunity he would not waste.

This time there would be no leaving the decision in the officials' hands, as Hagler jacked the crown off Minter's

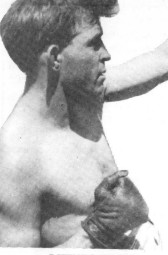

BATTLING NELSON

Prophetically christened Oscar Matthew Battling Nelson, the man more simply known as "Bat" or "The Durable Dane" held the same position in boxing as the Piltdown Man in anthropology, a genetic link joining two boxing worlds: the world of the rough-and-tumble and the world of civilized rules. Unfortunately, more often than not, the rough-and-tumble won out when it came to Battling Nelson, a man called "The Abysmal Brute" by writer Jack London. Studied by ring and social scientists alike, Nelson was found to have a head that defied both damage and definition, his skull being three times the normal thickness of any skull analyzed up to that time, all the better to absorb enormous punishment. It was a skull built to take it, and take it, it did.

NELSON'S STYLE OF FIGHTING RE-sembled a human punching bag, barreling into the wheelhouse of his opponent, ready to take three or four punches merely to land one. He could take it, although those at ringside were never quite sure he knew what to do with it. In his great battles with fighters like Terry McGovern, Young Corbett, Jimmy Britt, Aurelia Herrera, and Joe Gans, Nelson was hit flush on the underside of the jaw and in the solar

Left: Nelson (left) and Ad Wolgast before brutal fight, Feb. 22, 1910. Below: The Battler and Antone La Grave before draw, Oct. 31, 1910.

Born Oscar Matthew Battling Nelson, 6/5/82, in Copenhagen, Denmark . . . Raised in U.S. . . . First pro bouts, 1896, in Midwest . . . Undefeated in first 10 bouts—won 9, lost 7 in next 23 bouts (5 draws, 2 no decisions) . . . Scored 42 knockdowns in bout with Christy Williams, 12/26/02, Nelson down 7 times—49 total knockdowns most in boxing history . . . Lost 20-round decision to Jimmy Britt, 12/20/04—Britt claimed lightweight title after bout although Joe Gans was more widely recognized as champion . . . Nelson kayoed Britt in rematch in eighteenth round, 9/9/05, and claimed title . . . Challenged Gans to bout for undisputed title, 9/3/06, Goldfield, NE—lost on a foul in forty-second round . . . Won title in rematch with Gans, 7/4/08, with seventeenth-round knockout . . . Defended title twice in 1909: twenty-third-round kayo of Dick Hyland, 5/29/09; and fifth-round knockout of Jack Clifford, 6/22/09 . . . Lost title to Ad Wolgast in fortieth round via knockout, 2/22/10 . . . Two 40-round bouts are among the 10 longest in the twentieth century . . . Continued boxing until 1917 . . . Fought exhibitions until 1923 . . . Died, 2/7/54, in Chicago . . . Elected to Boxing Hall of Fame, 1957 . . . Complete record: 132 bouts, 59 won, 19 lost, 19 draws, 35 no-decisions, 38 knockouts.

plexus—or, rather, where the solar plexus ought to have been—only to shake the punches off and come back to win. "Terrible" Terry McGovern jammed his sturdy fists against Nelson's jaw time and again with all his strength and weight behind them, yet the blows never seemed to faze the great Dane, who kept coming in, always at the ready to implant his clublike hands into any unexposed area he could find.

As Nelson waded in, arms crossed in front of him, his widely placed eyes triangulating his prey in the piercing fire, his face assumed an almost eerie look. Once inside, he delivered his famous "Scissors" punch, a quasi-legal punch delivered in the form of a lethal left hook to the liver accompanied by a thumb and forefinger at the moment of impact delivered through the then-skintight gloves to add to his opponent's discomfort. Time and again Nelson would take everything his opponent had to offer and then, resorting to continual and often dirty in-fighting, knock out the thoroughly dispirited and discouraged fighter. It was full-scale guerilla warfare, no holds barred and no survivors taken.

Durable even beyond his nickname, "The Durable Dane" once fractured his left arm in the middle of a 15-rounder and begrudgingly admitted, "It made me somewhat cautious and kept me from winning by a knockout." And when he lost his lightweight championship to the equally tough Ad Wolgast on a knockout in the fortieth round, Nelson, with blood pouring out of his mouth, gasped, "What do you think of that dumb referee? Stopping it when I would have had him in another round. . . ."

There was nothing spectacular about Nelson. He was simply a great fighter in the truest sense of the word.

JOE JEANNETTE

The best place to hide a needle is not in a haystack, but in among other needles. Such was the sad misfortune of Joe Jeannette, a polished, steel-like heavyweight with pinpoint accurate punches, whose name and deeds were well hidden indeed by the exploits of Jack Johnson and Sam Langford for the first decade and a half of the twentieth century. And, not incidentally, denied his rightful place in boxing history by an archaic chastity belt known as the "color line." Promulgated by men whose broad minds had changed places with their small waists, the "color line" was hardly as deep as Pythagoras' theory: It was merely a sheltering line, sheltering white fighters from black, a move based on both bigotry and restraint of trade—holding that incompetent men should be helped to unearned wealth by removing them from head-to-head competition with more gifted performers. And there was no more gifted performer around in his day than Joe Jeannette, called by boxing historian, A. D. Phillips "one of the ten greatest heavyweights of modern time."

THE *CREAM* OF THE HEAVYWEIGHT crop, however, happened to be a threesome who were, also *creme de cacao:* Joe Jeannette, Sam Langford, and Sam McVey, indelicately called by Phillips, "a row of blackbirds." Together, they stood outside looking in from the other side of the "color line," one that Johnson himself now ironically invoked in search of an easier match, while the hopes and the hopeless alike were all given chances at their expense. It was a situation that the weekly British sports tabloid, *The Mirror of Life and Boxing World,* felt compelled to comment on: "It is well known that Jeannette, Langford or McVey, if unrestrained, could start out any evening after dinner and devastate almost the entire White Hope Association without having to hurry to catch the last train home. There were a few people who believe that even a White Hope should be allowed to make a living, and, as he seldom has the energy or intelligence to be a useful lumberjack, the 'color line' was invoked."

Denied the right to fight whites, Jeannette was relegated to the demi-world of black heavyweights, a sort of round-robin tournament where the outcasts regularly jousted with each other rather than with those who had conveniently ducked behind the "color line." There he met Jack Johnson 8 times *B.C.* (before championship)— Johnson confiding to Nat Fleischer that Jeannette "gave him one of the toughest battles he ever had"—Sam Langford 15, Battling Jim Johnson 7 and Sam McVey, 5, a total of 35 fights with these greats, with but eight losses to show for his efforts. However, it wasn't his losses, but his one win over Sam McVey in Paris, in 1909, that would become the cornerstone of his fame. And his greatness.

Both McVey and Jeannette were then plying their trade in Paris, effectively cut off from making a living in the States. And, while they had both been cut off before, it hadn't affected their boxing, as they proved by flourishing in French soil. Boxing—or *le boxe Anglais*—was then the craze of Paris, members of society considering it *de rigeur* to be at ringside for all the big fights. And there, none was bigger than McVey versus Jeannette.

Matched against each other in a 20-round fight, the two warriors went at each other with all the enthusiasm of someone approaching escargot for the first time—warily. After 20 disappointing rounds, the decision went to McVey. To say it was an unpopular call would do the word a disservice in any language, as a storm of protest broke out after the decision was announced, leaving papers, programs, lorgnettes, mesh bags, hatpins, hats, scarves, walking sticks, and other such mementos of good breeding washed up on the ring.

Playing the odds of controversy, the promoters quickly rematched the two. Unfortunately, rumors soon began circulating in the Paris press that the pair had not given their all in the first fight and that they had regarded it merely as "l'exhibition." The two battlers, stung by the slur on their efforts in the first fight, quickly agreed to fight the second bout to the finish just to prove that their first encounter was "on the square." However, it wasn't enough, and this time society did not attend with their lorgnettes, mesh bags, hatpins, scarves, and walking sticks. But 2,000 boxing-starved *Americans* did. And they were served a fistic feast, arguably the greatest fight in the storied history of great fights.

Shooting out of their corners, the two men joined together in the middle of the ring like bull moose in unyielding combat for their turf. McVey moved forward and from a crouch crashed a right to Jeannette's chin. Then he missed with a left, brushed Jeannette's cheek with a piledriving right, and then struck the keynote of the night when he struck Jeannette with another left and Jeannette struck the floor.

In the sixteenth, Jeannette began fighting back and missed one of his Sunday punches, a big right uppercut. McVey countered with a devastating right to the jaw and Jeannette went down again, this time oblivious to the 2,000 glassy-eyed spectators screaming at the sight of an apparent knockout. But, at the count of eight, the bell rang. Dragged to his corner like a piece of raw meat, Jeannette somehow found his way out for the seventeenth, there to meet the gloves of McVey, who, now fed by his momentum, gave Jeannette an unmerciful beating, finally driving him to the floor at the bell, the twenty-first trip he had made to the wellworn canvas.

Willie Lewis, his trainer, ran up the steps with the water bucket he had for-

his patented body shots.

After 19 rounds and 21 knockdowns, it seemed that McVey had the fight in the burlap. But he hadn't counted on Joe Jeannette and his courageous heart, more than enough to jumpstart Bert Lahr's deficient one. Between the nineteenth and twentieth rounds, Lewis turned to the private physician he posted at ringside for just such moments and had him administer a bag of oxygen he just happened to have with him. Then, as the bell rang, he hollered in Jeannette's ear, "Now, Joe, now . . . go to the head. . . . "

Like a condemned man grabbing at a reprieve, Jeannette jumped at the advice. And at McVey. All of a sudden, the fight turned over on its back. McVey, ditto. Only minutes before, outclassed and beaten beyond the vagrant glimmer of hope, Jeannette now began to wrench victory slowly from the jaw shots of defeat. And McVey, who once had almost permanent possession of Jeannette, now tired from his own exertions, wilted under his foe's steady attack to the body and head.

McVey's thunder had been impressive, but Jeannette's lightning was even more so, and by the thirty-ninth, Jeannette was rocking McVey with his heavyhanded shots. And dropping him with the same metronomic frequency he had once experienced himself. The ring was now merely a laboratory for proving Darwin's survival of the fittest theory.

For the next three rounds, Jeannette treated his former tormentor with disrespect as he worked on his face, closing McVey's right eye and reducing his left eye to a slit where the eye used to be. The forty-second saw McVey go down seven times, and seven times arise, only to absorb more punishment.

Jeannette kept at the faltering McVey, cutting him to pieces, breaking his nose in two places and pummeling him unmercifully. Finally, his knees melting, his eyes of no mortal use, and his nose unworkable, McVey sat on his stool in his corner after the forty-ninth round and moaned that he couldn't go on. The final score: McVey 27 knockdowns, Jeannette 11, with a knockout win in the forty-ninth round.

It wasn't enough that Joe Jeannette had talent. he had to have something more to deal with the rebuffs that would have discouraged a less determined man, a man no one could keep down. He had an unbeatable quality to him, one of courage. And of greatness.

Born 8/26/79, in North Bergen, NJ . . . First recorded pro bout, 1904, probably many unrecorded prior to that year . . . Limited opportunities resulted in many bouts fought against same opponents . . . Fought 14 bouts with Sam Langford, W 3, L 4, D 2, ND 5 . . . Fought Jack Johnson 10 times, only 3 went to decision, Jeannette won 1 . . . Never had title bout, all bouts with Johnson were before he won title . . . Knocked out Sam McVey in forty-ninth round, 4/17/09 . . . Longest bout in twentieth century, bout featured 38 knockdowns, Jeannette down 27 times but won bout . . . Most knockdowns by far of "bout" winner in history . . . Continued fighting until 1919, but boxed exhibition with Johnson in 1945, at age of 66 . . . Died, 7/2/58, in Weehawken, NJ . . . Elected to Boxing Hall of Fame, 1957 . . . Complete record: 154 bouts, 72 won, 9 lost, 9 draws, 64 no-decisions, 56 knockouts.

bidden others to use and tossed the entire contents on his stricken fighter, almost flooding the ring. The gendarmes rushed to the corner and tried to throw Lewis out of the building for watering down the ring, but Lewis screamed back there was nothing in the rules that prevented such revival techniques. Before anyone could make their point heard above the roaring crowd, the bell for round 18 sounded, and Jeannette was pushed out of what used to be drydock to navigate on two sea legs. He was now fighting from memory, but what a memory it was, as he began to hold McVey at arm's length, occasionally reaching him with one of

77 MYSTERIOUS BILLY SMITH

MYSTERIOUS BILLY SMITH

A boxer does not become a champion without some capacity for cruelty, no matter how subtle. "Mysterious" Billy Smith saw that capacity and raised it to the highest degree in the history of boxing. Averse to moral pressure and sporting gestures, the man known as "The Mysterious One" was one of the toughest fighters—read "dirtiest"—ever to ply his trade in a ring. More familiar with the rules of the Marquis de Sade than the Marquis of Queensberry, Smith would use anything and everything at his disposal to win, sort of an adaptation of "Each man for himself and the devil take the hindmost" school of boxing. Take his exercise in brutality against the Original Joe Walcott, for example. Not only did Smith appeal to the baser instincts of the Boston crowd to stir up the mob against his black opponent, but he also took advantage of the height disparity between the two gladiators to initiate a few base practices of his own, unheard of before.

AS THE TWO COMBATANTS STOOD TOE-to-toe, trading punches, Smith would force Walcott to duck lower than his normal 5 feet, 1½ inches and took to biting him in the scalp whenever he could maneuver "The Barbados Demon" into a position where the referee could not see his actions. Jumping back, Smith would protest to the referee that *Walcott* was biting! The crowd, already pro-Smith, was taken in. But not the referee, who told Smith to keep fighting. By now Walcott was fighting both Smith and the crowd. And, in one of the greatest nonstop fights in the history of the ring, was fortunate to come away with a draw. Many were not as fortunate, falling either to Smith's explosive fair punches or his excessive foul punishment.

"Mysterious" Billy Smith originally came to Boston from the Maritime Provinces of Canada looking for fights. But his clean-cut, rosy-cheeked appearance and the fact that Fate made him obscure by calling him "Smith", worked against his finding employment in a world overpopulated by battered specimens of unkempt appearance who proudly carried the name "pug." And when one of the newspapermen asked him what his name was and he

Born Amos Smith, 5/15/71, in Eastport, ME . . . Began pro career in California, 1890 . . . Early record sketchy . . . Won welterweight title by knocking out Danny Needham in fourteenth round, 12/14/92 . . . Defended against Tom Williams, 4/17/93, won by kayo in second round . . . Fought 2 6-round draws with Tommy Ryan, 8/29/93 and 1/9/94 . . . Lost title to Ryan, 7/26/94, on 20-round decision . . . Rematch with Ryan, 3/27/95, was stopped by police in eighteenth round and declared a draw . . . Lost to Ryan on ninth-round foul, 11/25/96, in second attempt to regain title . . . Reclaimed world welterweight crown after 25-round bout with George Green, 7/29/98 . . . Established stronger claim to title after winning 25-round decision from Matty Matthews, 8/25/98 . . . Defended title successfully 9 times, 1898–99, including 20-round decision of Joe Walcott, 12/6/98 . . . Fought Charley McKeever 4 times (W 2, D 1, ND 1) . . . Lost title to Jim "Rube" Ferns on foul in twenty-first round, 1/15/00 . . . Continued boxing until 1903 but without success—had unusual record of 5 draws in 5 bouts in 1901 . . . Fought single bout in 1911 . . . One of very few champions with more draws than victories . . . Died, 10/15/37, in Portland, ORE . . . Complete record: 82 bouts, 28 won, 19 lost, 29 draws, 6 no-decisions, 13 knockouts.

replied, "Amos Smith, of St. John, New Brunswick," it all but cinched the deal, the newsman snorting, "Amos! Amos! That's a helluva name for a fighter."

Smith stayed around the Boston area picking up a few fights here and there, but without much success, showing little ability so far as ring science was concerned, even though he could hit like a mule. With little or no prospect of getting work at a time when such stars as Doc O'Connell and Patsy Kerrigan lit up the Boston boxing scene, Smith drifted away out of sight.

The next time the name Smith sur-

faced was when a small Associated Press wire story carried the news: "Billy Smith of Boston defeated Spider in five rounds at the California A.C. last night." Nobody could place any "Billy" Smith, for none associated him with the fresh-eyed youngster who had been hanging around the hub area just a few months earlier trying to make a living with his fists. And when just one week

later another press dispatch came over the wires reading: "Billy Smith of Boston was bested last night by Frank Purcell in ten rounds at the California A.C., but the decision was a very questionable one," Boston writers wracked their memories in a frantic attempt to identify the mysterious Mr. Smith. Finally, when yet another dispatch broadcast the name "Billy Smith from Boston," one perplexed sportswriter hollered out, "Who in the hell is this mysterious Bill Smith of Boston?" and the name, by which Smith would forever after be known, stuck.

With his low-set brow, thick neck, square jaw, and sharp, penetrating eyes, "The Mysterious One" took on the look of a Dickensian tough despite his healthy complexion. He possessed quick reflexes and a hand speed some have compared to that of Jack Britton and Willie Pep. But it wasn't his reflexes or his hand speed that carried "Mysterious" Billy Smith to the top of the welterweight heap; it was his artistry in the darker side of boxing, the side known as "The Manly Art of Modified Murder."

WILFREDO GOMEZ

The bazooka, a small, portable military weapon capable of firing armor-piercing explosives at close range, came out of World War II. Wilfredo Gomez, a small, compact fighter capable of firing his own explosives close-in, came out of the gyms of Puerto Rico three decades later. It was questionable which possessed the greater fire power, the long, metal, single smoothbore tube or the double-barreled fighter known as "Bazooka" Gomez. Always fighting with the arrogance of power, Wilfredo Gomez dealt in absolutes: no nuances, no subtleties, not even a passing acquaintance with the Marquis of Queensberry.

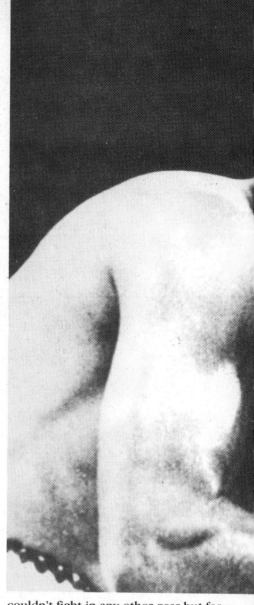

WALKING RIGHT INTO THE TEETH OF A storm to set up shop, Gomez would camp out in front of his opponent and start throwing an entire arsenal of destructive punches from every angle. And out of this threshing swirl of hand-to-hand combat, Gomez would release the trigger on one of his left-hand bombs, targeted for the ribcage. His opponent could hardly help but double over from the effect of his first strike, much as if he had just emerged from a decompression chamber, his legs begging for strength and his insides yelling for release. But Gomez, staring at his prey through coldly resolute eyes half-veiled by protruding cheek bones that gave him the appearance of a warring Aztec chieftain, would continue to slowly suffocate his opponent with body shots, finally letting loose one of his bazookas to the jaw, or the back of the head, or the beltline, or wherever. And then walk away, leaving what remained of his opponent on the canvas, another statistic in a mounting body count that nearly reached the number left at San Juan Hill. With no survivors.

Wilfredo Gomez's knockout percentage in the junior featherweight division was almost 56/100 percent better than Ivory Soap's, as he set record after record for knockout victories: most in defense of a crown, most consecutive knockouts by any champion, highest knockout percentage of any champion, etc., etc. But, truth to tell, before the "Puerto Rican Marvel" came aboard, the junior featherweight division was a non-division, almost called off for lack

of interest, its lineage and its future equally bleak.

All of that was to change on May 21, 1977, when, in his seventeenth fight, Wilfredo Gomez scored his sixteenth knockout, beating someone or something called Dong-Kyun Yum for the junior featherweight championship—or the "Super Bantamweight" championship as WBC president Jose Sulaiman prefers to call this halfway house, believing his distinction without a difference could make one. For the next six-plus years, six times longer than the division had been in existence, Gomez was to defend his title 17 times. And win all 17 by knockout.

But it was to be none of those mistaken nonentities who were to propel Gomez to greatness. It was to be Carlos Zarate who challenged Gomez for his junior featherweight title on his way to a match with Danny "Little Red" Lopez for the featherweight crown. And was to serve as the witting catalyst of his greatness. Unbeaten in 54 fights with 53 knockouts, Zarate, who had been *Ring* magazine's "Fighter of the Year" the previous year and was already being hailed by many with slightly clouded crystal balls as "The Greatest Bantamweight of All Time," went in as the slight favorite over Gomez, who had been pressured into taking the fight by the WBC intelligentsia—a contradiction in terms.

For two rounds, the 4-inch taller Zarate stalked the 5-foot, 5-inch Gomez in an attempt to defuse the bazooka. But Gomez, giving lie to the slander he

couldn't fight in any other gear but forward, fought brilliantly on the retreat, scoring effectively. Zarate found the mark in the third and tested Gomez's plimsoll line. But Gomez held firm. However, everything was to change in the fourth, one of the greatest rounds in the history of the junior featherweight division—even if it was one of the *few* rounds in the history of the junior featherweight division. With the round a little over two minutes old, Zarate finally cornered Gomez and put everything he had behind his potent right. Unfortunately for Zarate, it missed its mark. Gomez quickly countered with his power punch, a left hook, catching Zarate on the cheekbone and sending him down for the first time in his career. To add injury to injury, a hard right dropped Zarate a second time. Up at the faint sound of the bell ending the round, which went unheard by all, Zarate ran into bazookas landing left and right, all thrown by the now flat-footed Gomez who

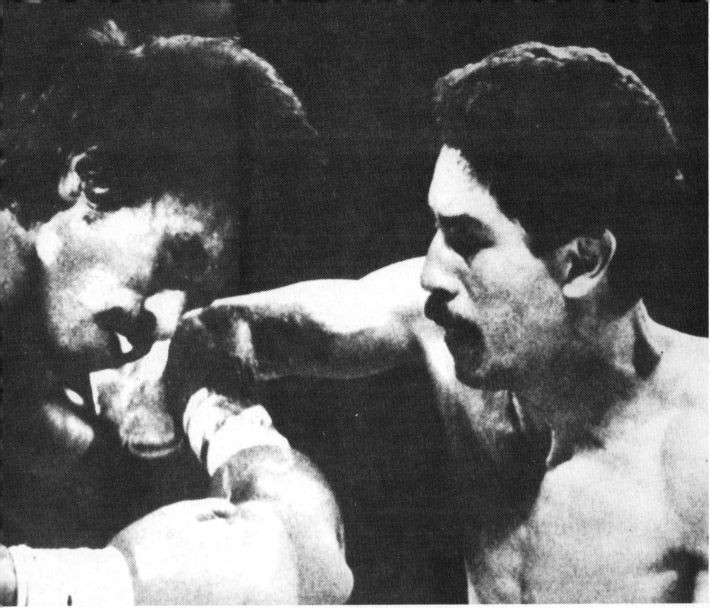

stood in front of Zarate hitting the challenger flush with everything he threw. Zarate went down again, entangled in the ropes. And Gomez, for good measure, continued to throw punches, landing a haymaker while Zarate lay on the floor. Finally, the referee jumped between the fighters, signaling the round's end after 3 minutes and 15 seconds. Zarate came out for the fifth on legs that were unwilling servants to his demands and was met by another savage barrage of blows from the two-fisted "Bazooka." Driven to the canvas once again by the shrapnel, he barely managed to wobble to his feet again. But before the "Bazooka" was unleashed yet again, Zarate's corner threw in the white towel of surrender. It was over.

As the crowd chanted "Viva Puerto Rico! Viva Gomez!," the little man who had raised himself to the status of an idol was raised to the shoulders of his countrymen, a national treasure.

Finally, tiring of the constant ordeal

to maintain his 122 pounds, Gomez challenged for the featherweight championship. And in what was billed as "The Battle of the Little Giants," lost to Salvador Sanchez in eight action-packed rounds. But even Sanchez was impressed by the little marvel, saying, "I beat him to the punch in the first round. I tried to finish him. I tried. I tried very hard. But I just could not do it. He is game and strong . . . "

The game Bazooka would come back, strong, to win the featherweight championship, this time from Juan LaPorte, Sanchez's successor. It was to be a fitting climax to the career of the double-barreled Bazooka who went by the name of Gomez, a fighter who had larceny in his heart but whose talents were honest. So honest, in fact, that if he had been hit by lightning, it was even money the lightning would have been yet another Bazooka KO victim.

Born 10/29/56, in Las Monjas, Puerto Rico . . . Represented Puerto Rico in 1972 Olympic Games, lost decision in first bout to Egyptian, Mohammed Selim in flyweight class . . . Won amateur world championship in bantamweight class, 1974 . . . First pro bout in 1974, resulted in 6-round draw with Jacinto Fuentes, 11/16/74, in Panama City—only bout that did not result in knockout victory until 1981 . . . Won WBC junior featherweight title with twelfth-round knockout of Dong-Kyun Yum, 5/21/77 . . . Defended title 13 times, 1977—1980, won all by knockout . . . Knocked out WBC bantamweight champion Carlos Zarate in fifteenth round, 10/28/78, bout matched 2 men who had scored 72 knockouts in 74 bouts (undefeated Zarate had scored 51 knockouts in 52 bouts) . . . Challenged Salvador Sanchez for WBC featherweight title, 8/21/81—suffered first career loss with eighth-round knockout . . . Defended Junior Featherweight crown 4 more times with knockout victories including fourteenth-round kayo of bantamweight champ, Lupe Pintor, 12/3/82 . . . Vacated title to compete in featherweight class, 1983 . . . Won WBC featherweight championship with 12-round decision victory over Juan LaPorte, 3/31/84, first decision victory . . . Complete record: 42 bouts, 40 won, 1 lost, 1 draw, 40 knockouts.

Above: Gomez fires "Bazooka-like" right at target, the head of Lupe Pintor, Dec. 3, 1982.

JERSEY JOE WALCOTT

To those four commendables that age cannot wither nor custom stale—old wood to burn, old wine to drink, old friends to trust, and old author is to read—can be added a fifth: Jersey Joe Walcott. Walcott's age has always been a matter of some dispute. At the time of the first Louis fight in 1947, Walcott, holding his personal life in a tight fist, admitted to being 33. But the *New York Times* labeled him as "34-year-old veteran," and many of those in the writing fraternity thought he was "33-going-on-45." Another non-authority, Jack Hearns, in one of his more puckish moments, suggested, "Anything under fifty could be right." But his skills were the skills no age could destroy. They were those of an old sand dancer who back-peddled, sidestepped, and forward-shuffled to his own rhythm in a befuddling array of moves, liberally sprinkled with decorous retreats, hyperbolic feints, and embellished shifts and sways. All designed to frustrate his opponents, disrupt their rhythm and break their concentration—and to set up his own power punch, the left hook. It was like watching a fighter in a magical mirror which never quite captures the whole boxer, or all of his sublime moves.

COMBINED WITH HIS UNIQUE FORM OF fistic hustling was a perseverance, a determination born of the breadlines of the Depression. To all who finally became aware of the man they knew as "Jersey Joe" Walcott, it seemed that he had been around since the year Zip plying his trade. But just around the time the stock market crashed with a resounding crescendo turning the roaring twenties into the ranshackle thirties, a young 14-year-old kid named Arnold Cream—adopting the surname of his late father's favorite fighter—journeyed from his rundown homestead in Camden, New Jersey, over to Jack Blackburn's Philadelphia gym at Thirteenth and Cherry Streets to see if he couldn't follow his late father's dream of his son becoming a fighter.

The well-built youngster made such an impression on the hard-bitten Blackburn that Blackburn took him under his wing and began teaching Walcott some of the tricks of the trade that had made Blackburn one of the top lightweights around the turn of the century. Now called Jersey Joe, the young welterweight made his pro debut by winning a decision over one K. O. Palmer and followed that up with a knockout over Cowboy Wallace in the first round in Vineland, New Jersey, on September 9, 1930.

Walcott went on to clock seven or eight now faceless welterweights, even though the record books don't show his exploits, and continued to train under the watchful eye of Blackburn, sharpening his rapidly-growing skills. It was about this time that two numbers kings from the Midwest, Julian Black out of Chicago and John Roxborough out of Detroit, offered Blackburn some good money to develop their amateur champion, a youngster by the name of Joe Louis. Blackburn accepted the offer with the understanding that the kid named Jersey Joe Walcott would become part of the new stable. However,

Walcott came down with typhoid the week he was to leave for Chicago and was laid up for the better part of a year. When he recovered, the men in Chicago had forgotten all about him.

The next ten years were filled with struggle, despair, disillusionment, and, above all, poverty. As the economic debacle that held America in its grip deepened with no end in sight, the word "unemployed," once a seldom-used adjective, now became an oft-used and ominous noun as every fourth worker lost his job. The American Dream was fast turning into a nightmare. But more so for the Black factory workers, always the last to be hired in good times, and now the first to be fired

as production slowed to a painful crawl. It was worse, if that were possible, for the man now known as Jersey Joe Walcott, living a hand-to-mouth existence, "It was the darkest hour of my career. I broke my arm and couldn't work because of it, if there were jobs. There was only $9.50 in weekly relief money to feed my wife and six small kids . . . I couldn't have gone any farther down, even if I had pulled the stopper," he was to tell writer John McCallum.

Walcott quit the ring on numerous occasions, supporting his family any way he could—by working in the shipyards, on road gangs, digging ditches, working in the soup plant or just taking any menial labor he could find. Always on the cusp of boxing, he would be on 24-hour call to face the likes of Tiger Jack Fox and Abe Simon for a payday. And always the story was the same: Walcott would be short-changed by those he had trusted, learning about boxing's time-honored tradition of insincerity the hard way.

From 1941 through 1945, Walcott fought two inconsequential matches, picking up some loose change to supplement the monies he made as a chipper in a Camden shipyard. But, with the end of the war and the heavyweight ranks showing more walking wounded than those returning from the front, the demand was strong for any fighter weighing more than 175 pounds who could prove he wasn't dead to fill the

arenas and the open boxing dates. Jersey Joe Walcott was a live body, although few, outside his native Camden and its environs, would have known it.

It seemed that even for Walcott to dream about returning to the active ranks was a giant leap of faith, a moat, a portcullis. But a local gambling and sports figure, Felix Bocchicchio, made it happen, opening up all the gates miraculously, restoring Walcott's New Jersey boxing license and lavishing money on him for food and essentials. Just as miraculously, within three years, Walcott had risen to the exalted position of challenger for the heavyweight championship of the world, scheduled to fight champion Joe Louis.

But Walcott had been so poorly thought of that the fight was originally scheduled as an exhibition. The New York State Athletic Commission forced the hand of promoter Mike Jacobs by holding that any bout over six rounds featuring the champion had to be for the championship. And on that December night in 1947, Joe Walcott went into the ring as a 1-10 underdog to the legendary Louis with the title on the line. In the first round, Walcott suckered Louis into a right-hand lead by turning away and walking away before pivoting back to plant his own punch on Louis' jaw. Striking Louis, Walcott struck the predominant note, putting Louis on the ground in the first and again in the fourth. Many in the audience of 18,000 began to wonder if

their confidence in Gilbaltar was misplaced. But in the final rounds, with a sharp absence of arithmetic, Walcott backpedaled his way out of the championship. A disheartened Louis started to leave the ring before the decision was announced. Restrained by cooler hands, he stood there while the microphone coughed in an ear-splitting harrumph and then announced that the decision had come down on the side of residency: Joe Louis had kept his title on a split decision.

Jersey Joe Walcott was to get more chances to win the championship than there were wrinkles in the back of his neck—of which there were several. But time and again he was turned back, first by Louis in a rematch and then twice by Charles. The talented need not believe in miracles. But Walcott was and did. His miracle came in the form of a left hook against the jaw of Ezzard Charles in the seventh round of their third fight, a punch Charles would mournfully call "a sucker punch"—but then, almost all of Walcott's punches were.

Jersey Joe Walcott was an overnight success, even if it had taken him 17-plus years to get there. A champion at the announced age of 37, when any self-respecting fighter would be home in bed, Walcott would fight three more times. One of those, against Rocky Marciano, would be one of the great fights of all time, as the cagey and cute Walcott, showing a profound contempt for the skills of Marciano, made the Brockton Blockbuster look crude and awkward. Fighting with a touch of genius, Walcott dropped Marciano with a left in the first and for 12 rounds bedeviled Marciano with his patented bag of tricks and half-tricks. And then, in the thirteenth, Walcott made a miscalculation that cost him the fight and the championship: He relaxed coming off the ropes. It was at that moment that Marciano threw his dreaded right hand, the "Suzy-Q," just 18 inches to the point of Walcott's unprotected jaw. Walcott fell into the ropes and slid down into a three-point landing, the ex-champion.

But Jersey Joe Walcott had been a champion, the type of champion the original Joe Walcott would have been proud of. Never had a namesake lived up to his adopted name so well, a name that will live through the ages—twice, thanks to the man from New Jersey named Arnold Cream.

ROCKY GRAZIANO

He was right out of the Bowery Boys, one of Jimmy Cagney's so-called "Angels with Dirty Faces." And he fit right in with the likes of Leo Gorcey and Huntz Hall, two cinematic hoodlums who were no strangers to trouble, yet who managed, in the best Hollywood tradition, to survive. He was Rocky Graziano, né Rocco Barbella, a real-life hoodlum raised on New York's Lower East Side, where both sides of the tracks were wrong. Young Barbella straddled the tracks and took the bad from both sides—along with anything else that wasn't nailed down. Enunciating his "dese" and "doze" to come out sounding something like "Toity-Toid an' Toid," Rocky recalled the days of his youth: "I never stole nothing unless it began with a 'A' . . . 'A' truck, 'A' car, 'A' payroll . . . acts of personal charity that led to his being "A" guest at "A" reform school, "A" prison, and "A" jail for most of his adolescence. Barbella was given a choice between going back to jail or serving time in the Army. Barbella opted for the Army. Unfortunately, the Army didn't opt for him, and, after he had underscored his disrespect with an extracurricular, and unrecorded, knockout win over an officer, put him away in the stockade 'till further notice. But Barbella decided he had "had enough," and took a little unauthorized "vacation," returning to New York and turning his attentions to the ring. Unable to use his real name, Barbella "went to his guy named Rocco Graziano and told him to loan me his birth certificate so I could get a license to fight. He said, 'Sure,' and I used his name to get a license. Later, I found out that the original Rocco Graziano had a bigger police record than me!"

GRAZIANO-BARBELLA HAD EIGHT fights in 56 days in and around the New York area, winning five by knockout, losing one, and drawing in the other two. Unfortunately, the minor fame Graziano-Barbella gained brought him some attention, not the least of which came from the Army, which reclaimed him as lost property and stuck him back in the stockade. Finally, after serving his "time," the Army decided it could win World War Two without Graziano-Barbella and gave him his marching papers.

With a new lease on life, Graziano turned to the ring full time, fighting 18 times in 1943 and 20 times in 1944, including two main events in the boxing mecca of the day, Madison Square Garden. The two, however, were against Harold Green, who beat him both times in ten rounds. Now at the crossroads of his career, Graziano was matched against Billy Arnold, a Phila-delphia bomber who had 28 knockouts in his 32 fights and went in as an 8-to-1 favorite. "He was beating the shit out of me, beating the crap out of me, hurting me . . . " Rocky was to tell author Peter Heller, "and I was a guy who liked to swap punches with a guy. Finally, in the third round, we started swapping punches and I hit him with my famous right hand on the chin and belted him out."

Thirty thousand fans poured through the gates at Yankee Stadium on September 27, 1946, to see "Da Rock" challenge middleweight champion Tony Zale, the "Man of Steel," for the 160-pound championship.

Zale, according to his manager, "loves boxers who move in or him. Graziano's style is made for him." And, in the first round it looked like he knew whereof he spoke, Zale catching Graziano with a hot poker in the ribs and flooring him less than a minute into the fight. But, by the second, waving his vaunted right, Graziano had leaped back to make it a two-sided

mugging, flooring Zale with one, two, three looping rights at the bell. In the third, Graziano continued to fight as if cornered, catching Zale with a Sunday full of right hands. But the "Man of Steel," true to his name, came back in the fourth to work da body of Da Rock. The fifth saw the fight turn over on its back yet another time as Rocky again turned loose his right-handed murder, wobbling the tiring Zale, who needed help finding his corner at the bell. Graziano seemed to have Zale, and the title, in his right-hand grasp. But then, in the sixth, after Graziano had rained a couple of right hands off Zale's head with a hard sound that had the resonance of a "thwackkk" heard all the way to the third row ringside, he stopped to take a breath. That was what Zale had been waiting for. A right hand landed in Graziano's stomach, up to the elbow, literally paralyzing him, followed by a left hook to the jaw that sent him to his haunches, as immense sail going limp in a change of wind. Zale had kept his championship, his crown intact, if

Born Thomas Rocco Barbella, 1/1/22, in New York, NY . . . First pro bout, 1942 . . . Won 11 of first 14 bouts, all by knockout, 1942–43 . . . Fought 20 bouts in 1944, W 15, D 3, L 2 . . . Knocked out Al "Bummy" Davis in 4 rounds, 5/25/45 . . . Stopped world welterweight champion Freddie Chochrane twice in nontitle bouts, 6/29/45 and 8/24/45 . . . Knocked out next world welterweight champion, Marty Servo in 2 rounds, 3/29/46 . . . Challenged Tony Zale for middleweight crown but was stopped in sixth round in classic bout, 9/27/46 . . . won middleweight title in rematch with Zale, 7/16/47, with 6-round kayo . . . Lost title to Zale in first defense, third-round kayo, 6/10/48 . . . 3-bout series one of boxing's all-time great series . . . Attempted to regain title from Ray Robinson, 4/16/52, but knocked out in third round . . . Retired after 10-round loss to Chuck Davey, 9/17/52 . . . Autobiography, *Somebody Up There Likes Me*, made into popular motion picture with Paul Newman . . . Became TV actor and commercial star . . . Elected to Boxing Hall of Fame, 1971 . . . Complete record: 83 bouts, 67 won, 10 lost, 6 draws, 52 knockouts.

was telling the story.

slightly askew.

Ten months later Graziano got another chance at Zale. Perhaps his last chance ever, not just at Zale, but at life—his bridges to New York rings burned behind him by his having been set down by the mental munchkins who ran the commission for not reporting a bribe-turned-joke or joke-turned-bribe, depending upon who

Zale immediately took the fight to Graziano, punishing him with a steady body barrage and closing his left eye by the end of round one. Zale switched his attack to the head in round two, but by the end of the round was in trouble himself, as Rocky connected with a long swipe to the jaw that straightened up the champion and had him so bewildered he went to the wrong corner at the bell. In round three, Zale split open Graziano's left eye and floored him for no count with another right to the head, then drove the temporarily blinded Graziano into the ropes with an unanswered volley of punches. Round four was more of the same as Graziano spent more time trying to wipe the blood out of his eye than trying to wipe out Zale. As Graziano went to his corner at the end of the fourth, he had the look of a beaten fighter, a slit where his right eye had once been and blood streaming down his face from above and below his left. From somewhere in the inner recesses of someone's pocket in Graziano's corner, a quarter piece materialized and was used to press down on his swollen eye, breaking the skin, reducing the swelling and restoring his vision. With sight again in his right eye, Graziano now gave no quarter, setting his sights again on Zale, And connecting. In the sixth, he caught Zale with a right cross, then another, sending the champion reeling. Three more rights to the head and Zale went down. When he got up, Graziano was on him like a rabid dog, biting left and right, all the time screaming to himself, "I'll kill the sonofabitch . . . " "I'll kill the bastard . . . " and putting punches to his muttered words as if he intended to fulfill his threats. Finally, referee Johnny Behr jumped in to save the helpless Zale from the frenzied mad-dog attack of Graziano.

But if it had been an improbable ending to an even more improbable fight, the aftermath would serve as an impossible Hollywood ending. For here was a beaten and battered man standing mid-ring and screaming into a microphone, "Hey, Ma, your bad boy done it . . . I told you Somebody up there likes me. . . . " It was a fitting climax for a Damon Runyon character, down to his last chance against improbable odds and somehow surviving. It was a dream come true, worthy of a romantic Hollywood potboiler without the need for a Leo Gorcey or a Huntz Hall this time around.

Left: Graziano throws "home run" hand, his right, to what passes for the features of Tony Janiro, 1950.

SONNY LISTON

Sonny Liston was an American morality play. In reverse. Giving voice to his place on the American landscape, Liston was once known to comment, "A prizefight is like a cowboy movie. There has to be a good guy and a bad guy. People pays their money to see me lose. Only, in *my* cowboy movie, the bad guy always wins." Hardly the jolly black giant of the Jack Johnson garden variety, Liston played at being a "bad guy," giving his opponents looks that could have been used to cut a tree, scowling at all those around him, and chewing up and spitting out reporters regularly. When one reporter doubted his age before his fight against the-then Cassius Clay, he roared at the cowering reporter, "My mammy says I'm thirty-four. Are you calling my mammy a fuckin' liar?" Part of it was an act; the problem was, which part?

SONNY WAS BORN INTO THE FAMILY OF an Arkansas sharecropper, a brutal drunkard who reportedly fathered 25 children. Leaving home at the age of 13 after an argument with his father, Liston went to live with an aunt in St. Louis. There he drifted into a life of juvenile delinquency, running with the hares and hounds of the streets. At 16, he was already fighting with the local constabulary, their clubs against his fists in an uneven battle—for the forces of law and order. Arrested over 20 times and working as a union goon who cracked heads with the same frequency a short-order cook cracks eggs, Liston was in constant trouble. (When the Kefauver Committee was later to ask him why he got into so much trouble, he only answered, " 'Cause I keep finding things before they get lost.") Finally, he tried his hand at armed robbery, and for his efforts was sentenced to three concurrent five-year terms in the Jefferson City penitentiary.

There, a Roman Catholic prison chaplain had the foresight to suggest to Liston that he channel his aptitude for violence into boxing. Sonny quickly blossomed into a crude, but awesome, talent. The authorities were sufficiently impressed to grant him a parole to pursue a career in the ring, a career that began with capturing the 1953 Chi-

cago Golden Gloves heavyweight championship. A few months later he turned pro.

Blinky Palermo, one of those curious creatures indigenous to boxing, took an early interest in Liston's ring career. It was to be a Svengali-Trilby relationship between the man who controlled professional boxing and the man who would come to control the heavyweight division, a relationship that was at once Sonny's making and unmaking. With Palermo's connections, Liston was given every opportunity to climb up the heavyweight ladder. Fighting every fight as if it were one step further removed from the penitentiary, he stepped over the prone bodies of his opponents, making his personal hell his foe's plague.

The heavyweight division had never seen another man quite like this chocolate-colored version of what had stood at the top of the beanstalk. He was that giant, albeit one compressed into a 6-foot, 1-inch frame whose picture, it was rumored, weighed 14 pounds. His fists, which expressed his tormented will, were 15 inches in circumference, bigger than even Carnera's or Willard's. He had an 84-inch reach, 16 inches longer than Marciano's. And he strengthened the muscles in his 17½-inch neck by standing on his head for a couple of

hours a day, listening to his favorite song, "Night Train." It was as if some futuristic geneticist had bred him in a test tube for the singular purpose of beating up other men. His left jab knocked men out, a battering ram that was in a class with Joe Louis's. His left hook was a lethal weapon, comparable to Joe Frazier's. He could go to the body with the ferocity of a Dempsey and launch a man toward the roof with an uppercut as powerful as George

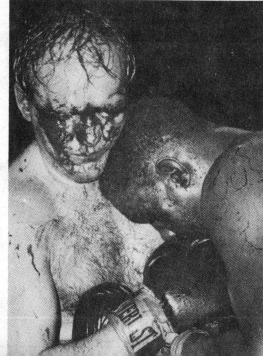

Foreman's. His right cross was a bit awkward, but he eventually perfected it into a deadly club, capable of decapitating a man with a single blow.

But for all his raw power and size, Liston's most remarkable attribute was psychological rather than physical. He made a science out of inspiring fear in the hearts and minds of his opponents, scoring knockout after knockout as if by will alone. He sought to break his opponents' wills with a stoney glower during the referee's prefight instructions, his enormous physique made to look all the more awesome by the padding of towels stuffed beneath his robe. During a bout, he would turn his icy, deep brown eyes on his opponents, looking through them rather than at them, almost as if his blink could cause seismic shock waves. In short, he was the meanest "Mutha" on the block, and wanted everyone to know it.

Liston's carefully crafted techniques of intimidation were never more in evidence than they were against Floyd Patterson on September 25, 1962, when Liston finally got his chance to fight for the heavyweight title after two long years of pursuing his goal. In just two minutes and six seconds, Liston's right, that mighty somnambulist of vanished dreams, brought Patterson's dream to an end, turning it into a nightmare and Liston into the heavyweight champion. And when, in their return bout some ten months later, moving like a dancing bear drawn to a honey pot, Liston took just four seconds longer to repeat his mugging, he became more than the heavyweight champ—he became, in the words of the press, "invincible."

But that mantle of invincibility unceremoniously fell from his shoulders in two bouts—one with Cassius Marcellus Clay and the other with his religious alter ego, Muhammed Ali—two bouts that will never be fully understood. It was to be a sad ending for the man once called "invincible" and "indestructible," one which almost canceled out everything he had ever done. But not quite. For, while it might offend our residual sense of memory to call Sonny Liston a "great," he was one, a reverse American morality play—like the Indians, when he won it was a massacre, but when he lost it was a great victory, for someone else.

Born Charles Liston, 5/8/32, in St. Francis County, AK . . . Fought as amateur in Golden Gloves—won 1953 Intercity Golden Gloves heavyweight title . . . Began pro career, 1953 . . . Only scored 2 knockouts in first 9 bouts . . . Suffered broken jaw in 8-round loss to Marty Marshall, 9/7/54, defeated Marshall twice in rematches, 4/21/55, sixth-round knockout and 3/6/56, 10-round decision . . . Won 26 straight after defeat by Marshall, 21 by knockout . . . Won world heavyweight title with first-round knockout of Floyd Patterson, 9/25/62 . . . First man to win heavyweight crown on a first-round knockout . . . Defended against Patterson, 7/22/63, and again won with first-round kayo . . . Lost title to Cassius Clay (later Muhammad Ali) on bout scored as seventh-round knockout when he failed to answer bell for seventh round . . . Lost rematch to Ali, 5/25/65, on first-round knockout . . . Only man in history to win and lose heavyweight title bouts in first round . . . Fought fewer than 8 rounds in 4 heavyweight title bouts—lowest average rounds of any heavyweight champion . . . Made comeback, 1966, won 11 straight by knockout thru 1968 . . . Won 3 more in 1969 and then was kayoed by Leotis Martin, 12/6/69, bout was Martin's last, suffered a detached retina in bout and was forced to retire . . . Knocked out Chuck Wepner in final bout, 6/29/70 . . . Died, 12/30/70, in Las Vegas, Nevada . . . Complete record: 54 bouts, 50 won, 4 lost, 39 knockouts.

Opposite top: Liston destroys Floyd Patterson in one round, 1963. Opposite bottom: Liston's last fight with bloodied but unbowed Chuck Wepner, June 29, 1970.

HARRY WILLS

Harry Wills was clearly a man born too soon. Nicknamed the "Brown Panther," Wills was a formidable heavyweight who just happened to be the wrong color and was held accountable by society for the wrongs, real and imagined, that Jack Johnson had visited on it. But they had as much chance of denying his greatness as they had of denying his very existence—which they tried to do. When Nat Fleischer first "borrowed" the concept of rating fighters back in 19-aught-24 from Walter Camp's football rankings, he also "borrowed" the name of promoter Tex Rickard to give his newfound *Ring* ratings some sorely needed credibility. Ironically, those very first yearly ratings listed the number-one contender to Jack Dempsey's heavyweight title as Harry Wills. But Harry Wills was destined to sit on a curb and clap as the parade passed him by, the aforementioned Mr. Rickard determining that Wills would never get a place in the passing parade.

ACTUALLY, WILLS HAD STARTED HIS CAreer in boxing as a promoter. Of sorts. Seems that he "had a few pennies in a bout in New Orleans between John Tholmer, the colored champion of the South, and Nat Dewey, from Denver, Colorado, the 'Wonder of the West.' Well, Johnny took sick and I'd been fighting some on ships, so I said I'd go in as a substitute for him so's we wouldn't lose the promotion money. I beat Dewey. That's how it started."

Back in those days of the color line, the existence of which is beyond modern understanding, mixed matches were outlawed in New Orleans, the theory behind such a law being that meeting a black in the ring conferred instantaneous equality on the black— and worse, if the black were to win. And so, Wills was relegated to the back of boxing's bus, fighting in black boxing circles. He made the most of the small arena, beating most of the other good southern black heavyweights over the next two years, most of his bouts held in the New Orleans Northside A. C. Jeff Clarke, the famed "Joplin Ghost," was then imported to the Northside for Harry on June 18, 1913, but the fast-improving Wills, drawing on his size-

able attributes, a 6-foot 4-inch frame and the 220 pounds that went with it, held Clarke to a draw. Less than two weeks later, the great Joe Jeannette was also taken ten rounds by the still-green Wills, and the result was, once again, a draw. Wills was now a major figure to be reckoned with in black boxing circles.

Knockouts over Roughhouse Ware, Kid Cotton, Soldier Elder, and Mexican Pete Everett were followed by a trip to the Coast, where Wills met the great Sam Langford in a 20-rounder. Harry had his way in the early going, knocking down the "Boston Tarbaby" three times but "Old Tham" finally knocked him kicking in the fourteenth. Wills and Langford would ultimately fight a total of 23 times—the greatest rivalry in the history of boxing. Langford was to win 2 in the early going, 15 were to go to that abomination of medieval boxing, the "No Decision," and Wills was to win six, most of those one-sided affairs in later years, as Langford got older. And blinder.

But if Wills was a major figure in black boxing circles, he was still a minor character in the far larger circles. He stood at the threshold of great-

ness needing someone to pull him through. That "someone" came in the strange trappings of Fred Fulton, the same Fred Fulton who himself had been the top-rated contender before Dempsey knocked him out in one round. On July 26, 1920, Wills became the top-rated contender for Dempsey's title when he demolished the big "Minneapolis Plasterer" in three rounds in Newark, New Jersey. It was a position he would hold—and be entombed in—for the first half of "The Golden Age of Sports," as challenger after challenger took shots at Dempsey's title, leaving Wills to look in from the outside, his nose pressed against the heavyweight glass.

Wills would never get his title shot. Every time he got close, pressure, coming from many sides, political as well as boxing, forced everyone to back down.

Above: Wills and Luis "Angel" Firpo before 12-round "No Decision" fight, Sept. 2, 1924.

Dempsey, like all champions before him, had drawn the color line in his public statement after he won the heavyweight title from Willard. Tex Rickard, the promoter behind the first "Fight of the Century," was unwilling to ever again be associated with a black-white confrontation such as he had in Reno in 1910. And then there were the politicians, those creatures with low license plates and I.Q.s to match. For every public pronunciamento, there were as many off-the-record denials, with everyone, from Governor Al Smith down to New York State Athletic Commissioner William Muldoon, publicly looking as if they wanted the fight when, in fact, they were maneuvering against it. Finally, Dempsey recanted; he would fight Wills, even going so far as to affix his signature to a contract to fight the "Brown Panther" and post for-

feit moneys. But with Rickard quashed the fight.

Wills was thus cast aside, caught in the groundswell created by Jack Johnson a decade earlier. Having come so close to his goal while remaining so far from being accepted, Wills was soon to be removed forever from the forefront of the ranks of heavyweight challengers by Jack Sharkey on October 12, 1926—ironically, less than one month after Dempsey lost his title to Tunney. No longer the sleek panther whose moves were once lyrical, Wills was treated as an imposter and easily beaten by the youthful Sharkey, youth having no memories of greatness.

It was a shame boxing had been denied an opportunity to witness one of the finest artisans in the history of the heavyweight division, a boxer who was clever and could feint and sidestep

with the best of all time, down to, and including, lightweights. In his prime, Wills could handle anyone. And what he didn't know about the art of boxing may not have been worth knowing in the first place.

Harry Wills, who merely tried the ancient democratic prerogative of rising higher than his source and in the end was pilloried for it, didn't lose as much as boxing did.

Born 5/15/89, in New Orleans, LA . . . First recorded pro bout, 1910 . . . Many unrecorded bouts . . . Had the misfortune of fighting during a difficult era . . . Never had a title bout although career spanned 6 heavyweight champions . . . Fought most of his bouts with other great black heavyweights—Sam McVey, Sam Langford, and Joe Jeannette . . . Fought Langford 23 times—W 6, L 2, ND 15 . . . Met Luis Angel Firpo in 12-round no-decision bout, 9/1/24 . . . Lost on foul in thirteenth round to Jack Sharkey, future heavyweight champion . . . Kayoed by Paolino Uzcudun in fourth round, 7/13/27 . . . Continued boxing until 1932 . . . Died 12/21/58, in New York City . . . Elected to Boxing Hall of Fame, 1970 . . . Complete record: 102 bouts, 62 won, 8 lost, 2 draws, 27 no-decisions, 3 no-contests, 5 knockouts.

AD WOLGAST

Ad Wolgast, appropriately known as the "Michigan Wildcat," fought like an alley cat in its ninth life, always as if cornered. There was nothing sublime about his style, a mongrelized cross between an accident on its way to happening and a bird-dog on the scent of its prey. Full of cannonade, fiber, and acid Wolgast would bare his teeth in his famous wolf's smile, his face contorted in an exaggerated grimace, fix his opponents in a cruel stare fairly crackling with electric ferocity, and, translating that ferocity to his limbs, move into them with a frenzied orgy of punches, all the while thrusting his chin out at his opponents and silently calling to them, "Hit me . . . hit me . . . . " Wolgast's face bore the marks of his profession, so much so that it looked like he hit with his face, and in one respect he did, his best punch being a left jaw to the right glove, so willing was he to accept any punishment as the cost of admission for getting inside his opponent's guard. Fighting with a feral joy and a relentless attack, he toured Michigan, Wisconsin, and then California, leaving the walking wounded in his wake.

SO UNAFRAID OF ANYTHING WAS Wolgast that he would fight anyone, anywhere, at any time. His manager, Tom Jones, once said of his warrior, "He would fight anybody. Once I decided to have a bit of fun with him. I rang up his hotel room and told him I'd just signed him up as a substitute boxer for several matches that night. I told him he had to be ready to go in three hours. 'All right,' he said. 'Wake me up in a few hours, and I'll get ready to go with you.' I said, 'But, Ad, you haven't even asked me who it is that you're going to fight.' And he said, 'Naw, and I don't care. Just wake me up so that I won't be late getting into the ring.' He was that way all the time. He'd say, 'Get me anybody for any time, and I'll fight him any time you say.' He did, too." It was almost as though Jones threw prospective opponents for Wolgast against a brick wall and the ones that got up were viewed as suitable cannon fodder for his tiger.

But all of his first 70 fights would merely serve as a table setting for his 40-round championship battle with Battling Nelson, one of history's bloodiest brawls, a two-sided fight that substituted savagery for any pretense to skill. Nelson, who always seemed to be beaten up but seldom beaten, was viewed as indestructible, so tough it did not seem as if any man his weight could ever batter him down. But, he hadn't taken into account "The Michigan Wildcat." Nor the fact that to him the championship was not a mere matter of life or death; it was much more important.

And so, in a fight that in a more civilized day and age would have been forced closed by the SPCA on the grounds of unnecessary cruelty, the two men hurled themselves at each other, their attacks unappeasable, their ferocity primitive, their wills determined beyond the frailties of boxingkind. In the twenty-third round Nelson caught the on-rushing Wolgast, flooring the man who had never been knocked out before. As the champion turned and raised his arms over his head, shouting out "twenty-three skidoo!", he felt something strange around his legs: Ad Wolgast. For there was Wolgast, still in the after-effects of a punch-induced fog, hauling himself erect by climbing hand-over-hand up the champion's body trying to get at his head. It was the turning point in the fight.

By the fortieth round, strength pouring from every hollow in his body, Wolgast had begun to impose his will upon Nelson, each new attack impressing upon the soon-to-be ex-champ the urgency of the situation. As writer W. O. McGeehan reported it, "Nelson was pressing feebly forward while Wolgast's gloves were hurling crimson splashes around the ring every time they struck Nelson's battered face. Still Nelson would not yield an inch, but it became so cruel that the most hardened ringsiders were calling upon the referee to

stop the fight." Finally, the referee had had enough, even if Nelson hadn't, and pushed Nelson away, ending the fight and making Wolgast the new lightweight champion of the world.

In his first title defense, the man alternately called "The Michigan Wildcat" and "The Dutchman," took on a fast-punching boxer with a faultless, deadly left hand, "Mexican" Joe Rivers. The result was that rarest of boxing rarities: a double knockout. In the thirteenth, Wolgast, tired and arm-weary, his small 5-foot, 4½-inch frame in a stance that suggested he was crouching under a 4-foot ceiling, brought up a left into the only area visible to him, directly over Rivers' groin. At that exact instant, Rivers let fly with a picture-perfect, left-right combination to Wolgast's jaw. Incredibly, the two bodies hit the deck with one resounding thud, Rivers falling first and Wolgast heaped atop the contender. Referee Jack Welch picked up Wolgast's prostrate body and counted out Rivers, later explaining that Wolgast had landed on top of him, and that Rivers had been knocked down first.

The Nelson and Rivers fights were to be the high-water mark of Ad Wolgast's fistic career. In his next title fight he would lose his championship to Willie Ritchie on one vagrant swing which caught him flush on the jaw. Still, with that rattlesnake instinct he had honed in over 90 fights, he managed to drive two punches south of Ritchie's border just before collapsing, losing the fight not on a knockout, but on a foul—and, not incidentally, saving the bets of all his followers.

Now on the downside of the mountain, Wolgast continued to fight every-one and everywhere, sticking to his guns, loaded or no. Still, the converted southpaw heard echoes of an earlier day and continued to campaign against the best in the lightweight division—a division that was leaking from the top with talent.

But Ad Wolgast himself was leaking from the top, the constant punishment he continued to absorb finally french-frying the last of his gray cells, causing him to hallucinate gently. Finally, his hardness of heart matched by his softness of head, he was committed to a sanitarium in Camarillo, California, where he spent the last days of his life, locked in the reason-proof room of his mind, training for a comeback fight against Battling Nelson. A sad ending to a great career. And proof positive that early-day boxing devoured its young and ate its talent.

Born Adolph Wolgast, 2/8/88, in Cadillac, MI . . . First pro bout, 1906 in Midwest . . . Lost third pro bout . . . Defeated Frankie Neil in 10 rounds, 5/6/08 . . . Fought 10-round no-decision fight with Abe Attell, 12/11/08 . . . Won world lightweight title with fortieth-round KO of Battling Nelson, 2/22/10 . . . Defended title successfully 6 times, 1910–12: 3/17/11, George Memsic, KO 9; 3/31/11, Anton Lagrave, KO 5, 4/26/11, One-round Hogan, KO 2; 5/27/11, Frankie Burns, KO 17; 7/4/11, Owen Moran, KO 13; and 7/4/12, Joe Rivers, KO 13 . . . Lost title on foul in sixteenth round to Willie Ritchie, 11/28/12 . . . Suffered broken arm in bout with Freddie Welsh, 11/2/14 . . . Challenged Welsh for lightweight title, but lost on eleventh-round foul, 7/4/16 . . . Fought only 2 bouts after 1916 . . . Final bout, 1920 . . . Died, 4/14/55, Camarillo, CA . . . Elected to Boxing Hall of Fame, 1958 . . . Complete record: 135 bouts, 60 won, 12 lost, 14 draws, 49 no-decisions, 38 knockouts.

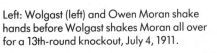

Left: Wolgast (left) and Owen Moran shake hands before Wolgast shakes Moran all over for a 13th-round knockout, July 4, 1911.

THOMAS HEARNS

Thomas Hearns looks like a fighter built by committee. From the wrists to the shoulders, the committee has dictated he be heavily muscled, possessing the physical build of a wide receiver and, with a 78-inch wingspan, the look of a basketball center. They gave him huge ham-hock hands, wide shoulders, and big biceps. But this quasi-heavyweight upper body sits atop a slender 30-inch waist poised on spindly, praying mantis-like legs, giving him the appearance of someone who could work in an olive factory dragging the pimentos through. But to his opponents, this 6-foot, 1-inch string bean—his shadow lengthened by his achievements—looked like the man Jack met at the top of the beanstalk. And just about as dangerous.

AS AN AMATEUR, HEARNS SHOWED none of the power that would later make him "The Hit Man," winning 155 of his 163 amateur bouts, only 12 by knockout. According to his manager-trainer, Emanuel Steward, "He'd jab, jab, jab . . . fire his right . . . then dance away. He didn't know what leverage was."

But under Steward's tutelage, Hearns began to grow, both in weight and in work. Soon he knew how to use that leverage, with devastating effect. And if his early opponents entered the ring laboring under the delusion that the thin, somewhat anorexic-looking fighter in front of them couldn't generate power, they didn't labor long, lasting only long enough for a quick cup of coffee and leaving with less sense than they brought in. Starting with his first professional fight—a 2-round KO—Hearns ran off 17 straight knockouts, his average encounter lasting only three-plus rounds. He so decimated them that all that was missing was a note from their mothers attempting to explain their emotional absence.

The crowds in his hometown of Detroit soon became familiar with the Hearns pattern: a veil dropping over his doleful eyes of a somewhat cruel gray, boring into his opponent with his long 78-inch reach—longer than almost all heavyweight champs, excepting the super dreadnaughts—triangulating his foes, his left swinging back and forth like a crane measuring them between pinpoint jabs and driving them in to the line of fire for his power hand, his straight right. Then, almost as quick as you could say rat-a-tat, Tommy's big guns exploded and his opponents were left with nothing to hold onto but thin air on their way to the canvas, their final resting place.

With time out for two decision wins—one over Alfonso Hayman, whom he fought with an injured right hand for the last five rounds and the other over Mike Colbert, whom he floored four times and whose jaw he broke in the meantime—Hearns ran up a streak of 28 straight wins, 26 by knockout. And became known, appropriately, as "The Hit Man."

In his twenty-ninth fight, he achieved instant immortality by destroying the legendary Pipino Cuevas in two rounds, two awesome right hands in the second driving Cuevas to the canvas like a hammer where he lay inert like an infant in its crib, face down. He was now the WBA welterweight champion. And viewed by some as an "all-time great," his demolition of Cuevas unseen by the boxing world since Sonny Liston's victories over Floyd Patterson.

But he was enshrined in the pantheon of greats with a mortgage—the mortgage of invincibility. For those whom the boxing writers destroy, they first call invincible. And soon the name of Thomas Hearns was hyphenated with the word invincible. It was a heavy burden to carry, one which Sonny Liston and George Foreman, before him, had carried, and stumbled while carrying.

Hearns carried his mantle of invincibility into a fight labeled "The Showdown" against Sugar Ray Leonard, for the unification of the welterweight title. And in 14 hard rounds, Hearns astounded the fight experts by becoming the boxer, while the boxer Leonard turned puncher. It was a classic, albeit out-of-synch match with Hearns ahead on all three judges' scorecards after 13 rounds. Then, with more than a disquieting feeling that he was fighting in the last ditch, Leonard poured it on in the fourteenth, ending Hearns' valiant comeback. There were those who felt

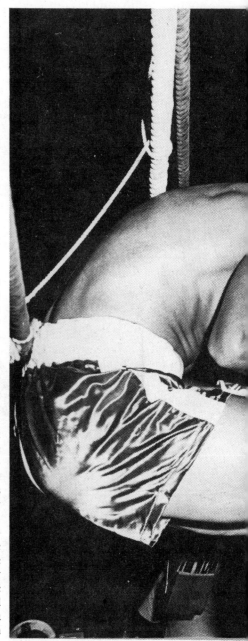

that Hearns had not really lost, but that time merely had run out on him. But whatever the case, Thomas Hearns was no longer invincible.

But Tommy Hearns is, to use a Red Smith line, as "soft-bitten" outside the ring as he was heavy-handed inside. Never uttering a word of complaint, the soft-spoken Hearns merely asked for a rematch against his conqueror—something none of his opponents had ever asked from him. When such a rematch was not forthcoming, Hearns decided to go back to business, testing the waters in the middleweight and junior middleweight divisions. Successfully. So successfully, in fact, that he beat the title holder in the junior middleweight

division, Wilfred Benitez, in a fight in which he reinjured his power hand, his right, in the fifth round. Proving that the art of boxing is not so much holding a good hand as playing a poor hand well, Hearns reverted to his amateur form, as he had in the Leonard fight, and outboxed the supposedly masterboxer.

But there were still those "Doubting Thomases" who pointed out that whereas Hearns had knocked out 30 of his first 32 opponents—for the best slugging average in welterweight history—he had been able to knock out only 2 of his next 7. Somehow, somewhere, some way, the man they once called "The Hit Man" no longer existed.

He was now merely "The Motor City Cobra." However, Hearns would dispel all of that in his junior middleweight matchup (mismatch would be more like it) with the legendary Roberto Duran. For in two rounds, Thomas Hearns did something no one had ever done to the fabled Duran before: he knocked him down twice with rights and then knocked him out. Cold.

It was the end of one era and the beginning of another as Hearns announced to all that " 'The Hit Man' is Back." And, as he begins his historic and ambitious drive toward his goal of four titles, no one would ever question his greatness again.

Born 10/18/58, in Memphis, TN . . . Known as "The Hit Man" and "The Motor City Cobra" . . . Began pro boxing career, 1977, in Detroit, MI . . . Won first 17 bouts by knockout . . . Knocked out future champ Bruce Curry, in 3 rounds, 6/28/79 . . . Kayoed ex-champ Saensak Muangsurin also in 3 rounds, 10/18/79 . . . Scored first-round knockout of ex-champ Eddie Gazo, 5/3/80 . . . Won WBA welterweight title with devasting 2-round knockout of Pipino Cuevas, 8/2/80, . . . Defended crown against: Luis Primera, 12/6/80, KO 6; Randy Shields, 4/25/81, KO 13; Pablo Baez, 6/25/81, KO 4—criticized for choice of Baez as unworthy opponent . . . No criticism of next opponent, Ray Leonard, WBC welterweight champion . . . Close bout with Leonard ended in fourteenth round with Hearns the loser, and Leonard became undisputed world champion . . . Rematch with Leonard never occurred due to Leonard's eye injury and subsequent retirement . . . Moved to junior middleweight class—defeated Wilfred Benitez for WBC title, 12/3/82, in 15-round tactical battle . . . Destroyed Roberto Duran in 4 minutes and 6 seconds with right hand, first knockout loss WCR for Duran . . . Complete record: 40 bouts, 39 won, 1 lost, 33 knockouts.

Left: True to his name, "The Hitman" swats out Pedro Rojas in one round, Oct. 26, 1978.

MANUEL ORTIZ

85 MANUEL ORTIZ

Manuel Ortiz always fought like he wanted to sit in the audience and watch himself fight. Which was only fair, considering how his career started. Unlike most boys who had their first fight in the gym, Ortiz had never had a glove on when he was plucked right out of a Brawley, California, audience to fight for the first time. On the night in question, Ortiz, then a young 20-year-old truck driver who had gotten in free for hanging up the weekly cards advertising the local show, was seated somewhere in the midst of a crowd which surrounded him in clouds of instant bronchitis. Still, he was visible to the local promoter, a man named "Ice" Brown—who honestly acquired the name while working in an ice plant during the day and staging amateur bouts on the side at night. Brown had just found out that one of his fighters in the four-round main event was a "no show," and he ran over to Ortiz shouting, without so much as a "please," "You're fighting the main event." Ortiz's opponent that night was Bobby Hager, an outstanding amateur. Less hardy souls wouldn't have taken the challenge, but the fearless Ortiz floored Hager 17 times.

ORTIZ DECIDED TO SKATE ON THICKER ice than Brown could provide and went into intensive training. Two months later he scaled 108 pounds and began his amateur career by beating the Olympic alternate, Chief Lopez. In the winter of 1937, Ortiz captured the Southern California amateur flyweight title, the Golden Gloves crown, and went on to Boston to win the national title.

Turning pro in 1938, he lost his first fight to a young southpaw out of Detroit named Benny Goldberg—whom Ortiz would subsequently defeat in a bantamweight title bout. For the first three years of his career, his record stood at just 23-10-1, with but ten KOs. But Ortiz would not allow poor fights to impede his progress and, taking on a new manager in Tommy Farmer, began his climb up the ladder of fistic greatness with a three-round knockout over Rush Dalma, the Filipino battler who had registered 31 straight wins. From that point in his career, Ortiz was virtually unbeatable.

At the time of his ascension the bantamweight division was in chaos, everyone but the Singer midgets, several of whom qualified, advancing claims to the championship. Ortiz made order out of chaos—and mincemeat out of the contenders—by scoring victory after victory. He beat Tony Olivera for the California State version of the ban-

Born 7/2/16, Corona, CA . . . First pro bout, 1938 . . . Spotty early record—lost 9 bouts in first 2 years against top-competition, losing to world champions Small Montana and Lou Salica, and title claimant Jackie Jurich . . . Won world bantamweight title from Lou Salica on 12-round decision, 8/7/42 . . . successfully defended title 8 times in 1943, to become most active champion of his era . . . Made 4 more title defenses in 1944 . . . Lost 10-round non-title fight to featherweight champion, Willie Pep, 7/17/44 . . . After 3 more successful defenses, 1946, lost title to Harold Dade on 15-round decision, 1/6/47 . . . Re-won title by decision from Dade 2 months later, 3/11/47 . . . Made 4 successful defenses, 1947–49 . . . Lost title, 5/31/50, to South African, Vic Toweel in 15-round decision in Johannesburg . . . Continued boxing through 1955 . . . Had total of 23 bantamweight championship bouts—won 21, lost 2 . . . Last U.S.-born bantamweight champion until Jeff Chandler, 1980 . . . Died 5/31/70, in San Diego, CA . . . Complete record: 128 bouts, 97 won, 28 lost, 3 draws, 49 knockouts.

tamweight championship, followed up with a 12-round victory over Lou Salica, then recognized as the New York State champion, and, when New York would not recognize his claim because he had won in a 12-round fight, perfected his claim by knocking out Salica in 11 rounds the following year—the only time Salica was ever knocked out.

This throwback to the old school of boxing took on anyone and everyone, venturing up to the featherweights and lightweights for extracurricular activity between title defenses. In 1943, Ortiz put his crown on the line no less than

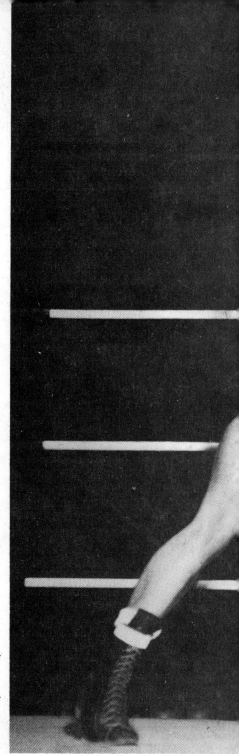

192

eight times, a record. In addition, the fighting champion won five nontitle contests. In 1944, while most of boxing's other crowns were put in cold storage for the "duration," Ortiz defended his four times and won five other bouts, losing only once, to featherweight champion Willie Pep.

Ortiz served ten months in the service in 1945 and went on to defend his title three more times in 1946, making a total of 15 consecutive defenses. Ortiz was now considered invincible. So it was one of the year's—if not decade's—big upsets when 12-1 underdog Harold

Dade outpointed Ortiz in January of 1947. But Ortiz proved that *only* a mediocre boxer is always at his best, when, two months later, he regained a touch of his previous greatness and outpointed Dade to reclaim his crown.

However, the touches of greatness were becoming fewer and fewer. His constant battles with weight were sapping his incredible strength, and his constant bouts with the good life, where it was always three o'clock in the morning of his soul, were sapping his body. Soon there was very little left of the legendary Manuel Ortiz. And

whatever there was, he left in a ring in Johannesburg, South Africa, when he lost a 15-round decision, and his belt, to Vic Toweel.

But the truck driver-turned-boxer had given his career a helluva ride since he first stepped into the ring back at "Ice" Brown's amateur show, a ride to destinations few bantamweights had ever dreamed of. Maybe that's why such greats as Willie Ritchie, Tommy Ryan, Jim Jeffries, and Joe Rivers all claimed that Manuel Ortiz was the hardest-hitting bantamweight since the days of Pete Herman.

Above: Ortiz successfully defends his bantamweight championship for the 19th and last time against Dado Marino, March 1, 1949.

86 SALVADOR SANCHEZ

SALVADOR SANCHEZ

With all the gravity of someone delivering an inaugural address, TV commentator Howard Cosell would describe all Mexican fighters as "tough little fighters" who "really can take it." But no matter how many times he used the cliche to describe those fighters who looked insulted if someone missed them, it was a cliche that would never apply to one of the greatest Mexican fighters of them all, Salvador Sanchez. For Salvador Sanchez was not reducible to mere cliches. His style and his looks were unique, his own. Facially, he combined the innocent looks of a choirboy with a striking resemblance to Popeye, complete with blown-up jaw, almost as if he had a toothache. Like Popeye, he had two uneven eyes of incurious nature, one beaming calculation and the other devastation. Etched across that jaw was a small half-smile, playing mischievously around his lips, making his entire countenance look like a cat which had just eaten cheese and sat in front of a mouse hole with bated breath. He fought that way, too, baiting his opponents, catching them with well-articulated counters after they had committed themselves, often rerouting the entire course of battle. Fighting with total detachment, this thinking fighter could maintain control of his emotions, the bout, and his opponent at all times.

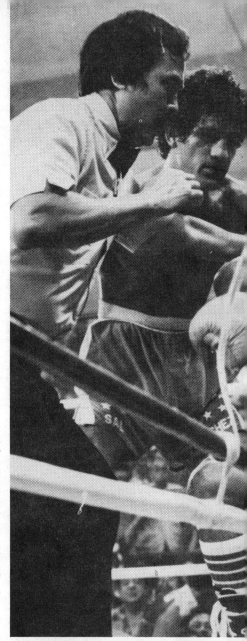

BUT FOR ALL THAT, SALVADOR SANCHEZ was hardly viewed as championship caliber before he met Danny "Little Red" Lopez. Many American sportswriters, who thought Sanchez's only chance of coming away with the belt was by breaking into Lopez's dressing room, called the bout "Little Red versus Little Known." And the majority of his own countrymen thought he had a date less with destiny than with the canvas. One of Mexico's leading sportswriters predicted, "Sanchez will go down as soon as Danny finds his big jaw, which should take, at the most, four rounds."

But the young 21-year-old kid who had lived on the raw illusions and untried dreams of out-of-the-way arenas throughout Mexico—those same creaky, hallowed old halls where dreams are made—had greater dreams. Dreams of conquest. Forgotten were

his previous disappointments, his loss to Antonio Becerra for Mexico's most cherished and important title, the bantamweight title, or his American debut, when an overpriced underdog dropped him twice and held him to a draw. Gone, too, where his self-doubts. Now all he could think of was the championship. And "how nice it would be to drive beautiful cars and wear nice suits and expensive jewelry."

Early in the fight Lopez tested that chin with one of his right-hand triphammers. To everyone's surprise, Sanchez barely blinked. And Lopez loaded up. And again Sanchez took it, countering with a well-articulated punch. "The first two right hands to my chin helped me a lot," Sanchez was to say later. "I said, 'Hey, he's not as strong as I thought. Let's keep fighting hard and giving him more and more

194

speed.' '' And he did, moving and punching, his hands Indian clubs, his eyes razor-sharp, taking in all the deliciousness of his big moment. And his opponent's jaw. By the thirteenth, he had rattled enough rights off Lopez's by-now red face for the referee to enthusiastically call a halt to the one-sided slaughter. Salvador Sanchez was now "Campeon Mundial," and, more importantly, could afford those beautiful cars, nice suits, and expensive jewelry that went with the turf.

Four months later, in what looked like a watering of last year's crops, Salvador Sanchez repeated his mistreatment of Lopez, stopping him in the fourteenth. He now stood first in the hearts of his countrymen.

But if Sanchez was first among his countrymen, he wasn't first among the Latino community, who had embraced another, Wilfredo Gomez, as their idol. And so, it was only natural that these two little giants would lock horns in what was trumpeted as "The Battle of the Little Giants."

With the density of expectancy heavy in the air and the air heavier still with the sounds of a salsa orchestra imported from Puerto Rico and a mariachi band brought in from Mexico, the two little warriors met in a ring in the Nevada desert to do battle. But while Lopez wasn't exactly hostile to the facts of his opponent's record—32-0-1, with 32 KOs—he was totally unmoved, feeling that "I'm the champion. I know I am a better boxer than Gomez, a sharper puncher with better speed and reflexes . . . . I'm not going to fall with the first punch he hits me with. I'll be there to counter every time he throws

one." And so it was, when, early in round one, as Gomez pressed Sanchez into the ropes and threw one of his patented "Bazooka" rights that Sanchez beat him to the punch, countering with a latent left of his own, flooring Gomez. Sanchez stalked his hurt prey, but couldn't put him away, try as he might. For the next seven rounds, he played the eagle to Gomez's snake as he hurt him time and again with his power punch, his straight right, finally driving him into the ropes, and out, in the eighth.

Now even the Gringos, long caught up in their own mental underwear known as heavyweights, took note of Sanchez and began to think of him in terms of the best pound-for-pound, inch-for-inch fighter in the world. It was a tribute the fight crowd paid to the ring genius of this stout Cortez.

Tragically, less than one year after the greatest fight in Hispanic history, Salvador Sanchez was dead, killed behind the wheel of his new Porsche 928 on a San Luis de Potosi highway. The effects of the crash had demolished the 5-foot 7-inch frame and shattered the face of this once-great fighter beyond recognition. The only identification were the papers found in the car and the jewelry he wore, the jewelry he had yearned for that night two years before when he became "Campeon Mundial."

To be martyred guarantees eternal greatness in the fistic heavens. But Salvador Sanchez needed no such mawkish sentiments or cliched epitaphs. He had achieved that greatness in life too many people must wait for death to gain. And he had gained it without being a cliche.

Above left: In famous "Battle of the Little Giants," Sanchez batters junior featherweight champion Wilfredo Gomez into the ropes, Aug. 21, 1981.
Left: Sanchez makes Danny Lopez see "Red" as he knock out "Little Red" to win featherweight title, Feb. 2, 1980.

FIGHTING HARADA

87 FIGHTING HARADA

Fighting Harada fought like he was sired and dam'd by a typhoon. The little 5-foot-4-inch battler would rain a cyclonic variety of punches to his opponents' unexposed landscapes, leaving them precious little protection—nothing more than an umbrella to shield them against those severe tropical storms that occasionally buffets Harada's home country of Japan. Built like a fireplug, and just about as powerful with the pressure on, this short, squat, little warrior with the legs of tree boles and the body of a small chopping block, fought as if wars stimulated him. With little respect for his own safety, except for a bobbing-and-weaving crouch that made his frame even smaller—if that were possible—Harada would come into his opponent like a tom cat whose mind was made up, underlining his determination with punches thrown from a bewildering variety of places in a never-ceasing, ever-relentless attack. The sum total of his efforts was usually the gradual erosion of his opponent, who took on the look of one of those little inflated toy ducks from which the air has been let out.

WINNER OF 26 OF HIS FIRST 27 FIGHTS, Harada signed to fight the flyweight champion of the world, Thailand's Pone Kingpetch in the fall of 1962. But the WBA, in its infinite nonwisdom unable to distinguish chicken teriyaki from chicken droppings, viewed the 19-year-old Harada as an "unworthy" challenger to Kingpetch's title. Harada proved the WBA wrong as he came out in the first round and took the fight directly to the champion, throwing a dazzling array of punches—right-hand leads, straight left jabs, and just about anything else that could be launched from a foreign object—all the while keeping the pressure on Kingpetch. By the fifth, Harada's constant abuse had begun to wilt Kingpetch, who was leaking blood from a cut over his left eye. And by the eighth, observers could see Kingpetch's cornermen trying mightily to thumb circulation back into his arms, legs, and eyelids, all numbed by Harada's nonstop attack. Finally, in the eleventh, Harada dispensed with the

tiring champion, sending his wilting frame to the floor with a devastating left and right to the head.

Three months later Harada took his title to Bangkok to defend it against the ex-champion. And left it there, despite a whirlwind attack that saw him knock down Kingpetch in the eighth with a lightning chain of punches that culminated in a right to the jaw. Still, Kingpetch got up to outbox Harada, getting two out of the three officials' votes.

Experiencing difficulty in making 112 pounds, Harada abandoned the flyweight division for the bantamweight class. But what Harada hadn't abandoned was his typhoon-like attack. Proving that he could carry his punch and his whirlwind style upstairs with him, Harada raced through the 118-pound division, winning 10 of 11, and established himself as the class of the class.

Now he stood on the doorstep of his second championship. However, there was one small, 118-pound problem:

The champion was the undefeated Eder Jofre, rightfully called by most experts "The Greatest Fighter, Pound-for-Pound" in modern boxing. But those with values plucked from the prevailing winds had not considered the typhoon named Harada. Nor his aggressive style, the perfect antidote to Jofre's pinpoint-perfect punches. Hardly had the echo of the opening bell died down before Harada was across the ring, coming in low under his patented bob and weave, driving the champion back to the ropes, there to be pinned like an impaled butterfly by his tormentor's incessant pressure. For 15 rounds, Fighting Harada never

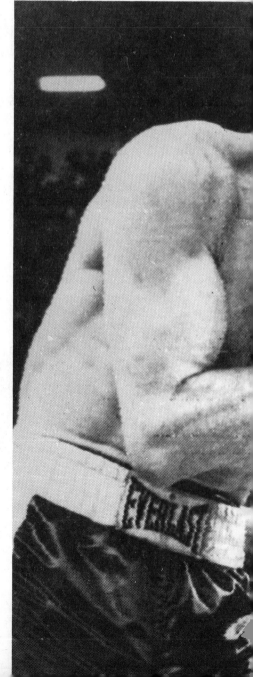

Right: Harada overwhelms the great Eder Jofre to win bantamweight championship, May 17, 1965.

Born Masahiko Harada, 4/5/43, in Setagaya Ward, Tokyo, Japan ... First pro bout, 1960, Tokyo, Japan ... Undefeated in first 25 bouts, including victory over future flyweight champion, Hiroyuki Ebihara, 12/24/60 ...

Suffered first defeat at hands of Edmundo Esparza, 6/15/62, in 10-round decision ... Won world flyweight title with eleventh-round knockout of Pone Kingpetch in Tokyo, 10/10/62 ... Lost rematch to Kingpetch by decision in Bangkok, 1/12/63 ... Won world bantamweight title, 5/17/65, with 15-round decision over Eder Jofre ... Defended title successfully 4 times including rematch with Jofre, 6/1/66—only 2 losses in 78 bouts for Jofre ... Lost title to Lionel Rose on 15-round decision, 2/26/68 ... Challenged Australian Johnny Famechon for featherweight title ... Lost disputed decision, 7/28/69 ... Stopped by Famechon in fourteenth round of rematch in Tokyo, 1/6/70 ... Retired after bout ... First man to win flyweight and bantamweight titles ... Complete record: 62 bouts, 55 won, 7 lost, 0 draws, 22 knockouts.

let up, harrassing, hammering, and hacking away at the stationary Jofre. weaving underneath Jofre's bombs,

causing them to go over his constantly moving head like well-oiled hair tonic and burst harmlessly in air. At the end of 15 rounds, Fighting Harada had added a second championship belt to his rapidly growing collection. For the next three years, Harada battled to keep both that bantamweight belt and his growing beltline in hand. Finally, the combination of weight and Lionel Rose conspired to reduce him to the less than exalted position of ex-champion.

Bowing to the inevitable, Harada advanced into the ranks of the featherweight division in search of his third belt—something that only Bob Fitzsimmons and Henry Armstrong had done before him, not counting those no-ac-

count halfway houses of the junior variety. Against Johnny Famechon in Australia, Fighting Harada almost made it a trio with brio, losing on a hairline decision when referee Willie Pep "recast" his scorecard to give Famechon the victory by one point. Harada was to get another chance to pull off boxing's versions of the hat trick. But, after 11 years the typhoon had finally blown itself out, and Harada lost not so much to Famechon as he did to that most inexorable of all foes, Father Time.

But, ah, his friends, and, oh, his foes, the typhoon known as Fighting Harada, while it lasted, feeding on its own momentum and doing great damage in its sweep over boxing, had given a lovely fight.

WILLIE RITCHIE

Willie Ritchie was boxing's equivalent of the Broadway understudy, the stand-in who substitutes for the star and, in the classic cliche, goes on to stardom. The story of future-great Willie Ritchie begins with a 15-year-old Western Union messenger boy named Gerhardt Steffan delivering cables in that city of cable cars, San Francisco. Like any other boy growing up in that early turn-of-the-century era, Steffan was influenced by the heroes of his day—men like Joe Gans, Abe Attell, Battling Nelson, Jimmy Britt, and, of course, Jim Corbett, all of whom fought in and around what was then the boxing capital of the world. And like any other boy with resin in his veins, he jumped at the chance to help out a friend who had taken up "The Manly Art of Self-Defense," serving as his timekeeper and trainer. One night Steffan accompanied his boxer-friend over to West Oakland to work his corner in the scheduled main event. Another friend, Willie Richardson, scheduled to fight that night in his first fight, was supposed to have accompanied the twosome, but somehow failed to show. When the matchmaker came looking for the missing Richardson to open the show, Steffan was volunteered by his friend to fill in, despite Steffan's argument that he had never been in a ring before. Asked by the announcer what his name was, the flustered Steffan merely said, "It's on the program." And so, he was announced as "Willie Richardson," or rather, a garbled version—"Willie Ritchie."

IT WOULD BE NICE TO NOTE THAT THE career of Willie Ritchie began with a win. However, such was not the case, the bout being more a farce than a fight and lasting just one and a half rounds. But, Steffan-Ritchie had enjoyed the pretense of being a boxer. So much so that he now dedicated himself to learning everything he could about the game, the short straw he had drawn merely becoming the first straw in the dream he was to spin, the dream of becoming a champion.

For the next five years, Ritchie applied himself with dogged determination to the development of his growing skills. It was a determination that was something more than a conscious will; it was an insight, a pattern, an overview into the character of this highly dedicated man. Through constant training, Ritchie soon became an ambidextrous hitter, capable of using either hand to advantage. Patterning his left after the left of the Old Master, Joe Gans, Ritchie developed a fast left that kept working back and forth in metronomic fashion, tantalizing an opponent while keeping him at a distance at the same time.

If that were all there were to Willie Ritchie, however, he would have presented few, if any problems, to his foes. But together with that left, which he used primarily as a feeler, was a decep-

tive right hand that was dangerous. When it started out, the right seemed to have neither speed nor force. And even looked like it might be a feint or a blow about to be withdrawn. But just as suddenly, his ambiguous right could be contradicted in mid-flight and come shooting in with great force to find its final resting place with a jolt that shook and hurt an opponent.

If Ritchie's work in the gymnasia around San Francisco and in four-round fights in and about the Bay area were his basic schooling, his graduate work was to come as the sparring partner of the unbeatable Packey McFarland, who taught him how to mix power with finesse, an unbeatable combination. Soon he was meeting, and beating, the likes of Jack Britton. And clambering up into the ring after any lightweight contest to challenge any and all worthies within the sound of his voice, including the ring announcer, to a fight.

Willie Ritchie was to get his big chance not because of a challenge, however, but because of Packey McFarland. And fate.

McFarland had come to California to meet Harlem Tommy Murphy in San Francisco on Thanksgiving Day, 1911. On the same day, down in Los Angeles, lightweight champion Ad Wolgast was

Left: Ritchie successfully defends lightweight title vs. Joe Rivers, 1913.

Ritchie fetched the onrushing "Michigan Wildcat" with a right that suddenly materialized from nowhere and stuck deep into his body. Wolgast went limp and fell into a clinch. Coming out of his corner in the sixteenth, Ritchie said to his trainer, "Say a prayer, because I think I can nail him with a good right to the chin." And, true to his word, he feinted at Wolgast's body and crossed over with a right to the chin. Wolgast went down, hard. Getting up on unsteady legs Wolgast, true to his nickname, raced into Ritchie like a wildcat, throwing everything at his disposal— and some not, like shoulders, elbows and head. He capped off his maelstrom with a blow about six inches south of the border. While Ritchie held his cup and the snarling Wolgast tottered in front of him, the referee came over and warned Wolgast that if he did that again, he would be disqualified. Even Wolgast, operating in a punch-induced fog, got the hint. Bam! He threw another right, right into the groin, thereby losing the fight. And saving his backers their money on the foul.

Suddenly, Willie Ritchie was a stock that had trebled in value. With a voice that dripped money, Ritchie asked for, and received, a guarantee of over $20,000, a record at the time, to risk his title in London against the man who had bested him when he substituted for Wolgast: Freddie Welsh. This time it would be different, Ritchie cautioned; the last time he was "little more than a novice." Five years younger than his challenger, Ritchie was convinced that "Welsh doesn't hurt when he hits; I do."

But even though Ritchie did not go over to London with the intention of leaving behind his championship belt, that is exactly what happened. The story was a number four, standard size: if you go into someone's backyard to fight, you had better win; anything less is second place. And Ritchie finished in second place as Welsh fought a smart, defensive fight—or, as Ritchie called it, "a negative fight"—moving away from Ritchie's right hand, stabbing him in the face with his left and out-distancing him to the 20-round wire with a little finishing canter to take his belt.

For 15 years, the man who had started as Gerhardt Steffan and ended as the lightweight champion of the world, had made the art of substitution a fine art. He was boxing's version of the designated hitter, gaining stardom and greatness as a stand-in.

scheduled to defend his title against Freddie Welsh. On the Tuesday before Thanksgiving, the injury-prone Wolgast was stricken with an appendicitis attack. When word reached McFarland that Wolgast had pulled out of the fight, he immediately recommended that his sparring partner, Ritchie, hurry down to Los Angeles to challenge Welsh. Ritchie, who always had his hand up as if he were trying to hail a passing cab, or a passing chance, hailed the first train to Los Angeles and went directly to the Vernon Arena, where he had to pay his way in. During the semi-final, promoter "Uncle" Tom McCarey finally

Born Gerhardt A. Steffen, 2/13/91, San Francisco, CA . . . First pro bout, 1907, California . . . Early record incomplete . . . Lost 20-round decision to Matty Baldwin in first important fight, 8/30/11 . . . Defeated future welterweight champion, Jack Britton, in 4-round bout, 10/6/11 . . . As a last-minute substitute, lost 20-round decision to future world lightweight champion, Freddie Welsh 11/30/11 . . . Another substitution, 6-round no-decision bout with Young Erne, 2/7/12 . . . Won world lightweight championship on foul in sixteenth round from Ad Wolgast, 11/28/12 . . . Defended successfully against Joe Rivers with eleventh-round KO, 7/4/13 . . . Won 20-round decision from Harlem Tommy Murphy, 4/17/14, in second title defense . . . Lost title to Freddie Welsh in London, England, on 20-round decision, 7/7/14 . . . Had 4-round no-decision bout with Benny Leonard, 2/21/19. Stopped by Leonard in eighth round, 4/28/19 . . . Had one other bout in 1924 and 3 more in 1927 . . . Scored only 8 knockouts in entire career . . . Elected to Boxing Hall of Fame, 1962 . . . Died, 3/24/75, in Burlingame, CA . . . Complete record: 71 bouts, 36 won, 9 lost, 4 draws, 22 no-decisions, 8 knockouts.

selected Ritchie from a long laundry list of aspirants and finalized the financial arrangements. Once again, Ritchie, the perennial understudy, went into the ring as a substitute. And while this time he performed better than he had the first time around—extending Welsh throughout and knocking him down the only time Welsh ever tried to "mix it"—he still lost a 20-round decision. But he had taken any hand at the table knowing the cards would be re-dealt. And they would be. Soon.

After beating the leading contender Joe Mandot, Ritchie got his chance, for the title, a 20-round fight on Thanksgiving Day, 1912, against Ad Wolgast for the lightweight championship of the world. Ritchie, who normally used his right hand to the body, decided that Wolgast's peculiar methods, which included checking his copy of the Marquis of Queensberry rules at the front gate, made it too risky to go to the body. Instead, Ritchie decided to use his superiority in height and reach and "sting him around the head at every opportunity."

For the first ten rounds, Ritchie moved away from Wolgast's garrison charges, content to stick the champion with his talented left and tie him up. In the fifteenth, switching his tactics,

JAMES J. JEFFRIES

If strength alone made for greatness, Jim Jeffries would have stood as king of the mountain called "Greatness." This giant of a sequoia stood 6 feet, 2½ inches and scaled 220 pounds, giving him the look of a brick boiler-maker, which is what he had been in his previous life. Although Jeffries was viewed as a lumbering ox by many, a throwback to primitive man, he was a magnificent athlete, fast and agile for his size. The man called "The California Grizzly" could run 100 yards in 11 seconds and high-jump 5 feet, 10 inches, both exceptional feats in a day and age when the standard was far more modest than it is today. Still, Jeffries was anything but agile in the ring. After three knockouts, he was employed by James J. Corbett as a sparring partner before his ill-fated fight with Bob Fitzsimmons, where he performed the task of a human punching bag—although story-tellers throughout the ages would have you believe he man-handled the champ.

SOON AFTER HE WAS DISMISSED BY CORbett, Jeff's theatrical backers put him in against two seasoned performers, Gus Ruhlin and Joe Choynski, who taught the big, raw-boned youth a few of the subtleties of the ring. And then some.

For it was in the second of his two draws against these two old pros, that Jeffries changed from a stand-up style, à la John L. Sullivan, into his famous "Jeffries Crouch," courtesy of a Joe Choynski chop to the mouth which broke his nose and crumbled his teeth. The "Jeffries Crouch" was a wholly defensive position, one that saw Jeff hunched over, his left arm extended in a wide swinging movement, all the better to deliver his left in a poleaxe manner, impaling his opponent, while shielding his chin behind an armor of muscle. No one knew if Jeff could jab and no one ever found out, his every punch predestined to take off his opponent's head.

Brought to New York, where reputations were built larger than the buildings, Jeffries reneged on his promise to finish off two men in one night, breaking his hands on heavyweight contender Bob Armstrong's head and pull-

Above: Jeffries (right) with trainers Tommy Ryan and Bill Delaney (seated).
Right: Jeffries and Bob Fitzsimmons, the man he won heavyweight title from.

Left: Jeffries (right) poses with Jack Munroe, his last fight before "retirement," 1904.

ing the first "No Mas" in history, calling off the second part of the double header. The New York press, typically cynical, gave Jeff anything but rave notices, scoffing, "Jeffries' manager asked us to believe that his California savage was twice as durable as any of our fighters. After last night's cancellation of the second half of the advertised program, we must conclude that Jeffries' hands are much more frail than his manager's boasts."

Ironically, it was this inauspicious debut of a man thought to have no ring past and less presence that served as a table-setting for Jeffries to challenge Bob Fitzsimmons for the heavyweight championship, Fitz seeking an "easy" opponent for his first title defense. And so, on June 9, 1899, in the first heavyweight title fight in New York history, after Fitzsimmons had broken his hands on Jeffries' jaw in the early rounds, Jeff beat down Fitz with his poleaxe left to legitimate his claim of being "The Strongest Man in the World."

Jeff would defend his title seven times before retiring to his alfalfa farm in California. But six years later, responding to the siren calls of white supremacists Jeffries tried a comeback. It was destined to be a failure. Jeffries, a hollow frame of what once had been, disappointed all with his performance, surrendering to Johnson and the inevitable in 15 rounds, a sad ending to one of boxing's most magnificent legends.

Born James Jackson Jeffries, 4/15/75, in Carroll, OH . . . Began pro career, 1896, on West Coast . . . Drew with Gus Ruhlin, 7/17/97, and Joe Choynski, 11/30/97, in 20-round bouts . . . Knocked out Peter Jackson in third round, 3/22/98 . . . Defeated Tom Sharkey in 20-round bout, 5/6/98 . . . Challenged Bob Fitzsimmons for world heavyweight title in only thirteenth pro bout, 6/9/99, won title on eleventh-round knockout—outweighted Fitzsimmons by 39 pounds . . . Defended against Tom Sharkey, 11/3/99, 25-round decision—longest heavyweight title bout to be won by a decision . . . Next bout was shortest heavyweight title bout in history—55 second-knockout of Jack Finnegan, 4/6/00 . . . Defeated ex-champion Jim Corbett on twenty-third-round kayo, 5/11/00, in next title defense . . . Knocked out Gus Ruhlin in fifth round, 11/15/01 . . . Knocked out Bob Fitzsimmons in eighth round, 7/25/02, this time outweighing him by 47 pounds—largest weight difference in title bout until Carnera era . . . Knocked out Corbett in rematch, 8/14/03, in tenth round . . . Kayoed Jack Munroe in second round, 8/26/04 . . . Retired, 5/13/05, as undefeated champion with record of 18 wins and 2 draws in 20 bouts . . . Named Marvin Hart and Jack Root to fight for title and acted as referee for that bout, 7/3/05 . . . Subsequently refereed two of Tommy Burns title defenses—only heavyweight champion to referee more than 1 heavyweight title bout . . . Came out of retirement in futile bid to reclaim heavyweight title after Jack Johnson had won it . . . Knocked out by Johnson in fifteenth round, 7/4/10 . . . Had largest percentage of heavyweight championship bouts to total bouts of anyone—9 of 21 bouts were for title (43%) . . . had ranch in California after retirement . . . Died, 3/3/53, in Burbank, California . . . Elected to Boxing Hall of Fame as charter member, 1954 . . . Complete record: 21 bouts, 18 won, 1 lost, 2 draws, 15 knockouts.

JOHNNY KILBANE

In the realm of physics, it was Sir Isaac Newton who propounded the law of motion which held that for every action there was an equal and opposite reaction; in the realm of fistiana, his disciple was Johnny Kilbane. Johnny Kilbane fought each fight as if he were afraid an apple might fall on his head, swaying back when an opponent swung, moving round and round his approaching opponent in an outer circle and doing just about everything humanly possible to avoid physical contact. And he used the same reverse dynamics to avoid risking his precious featherweight championship belt, backing away from any serious challenge for 11 years. Kilbane was one of the finest ring generals of his era. Or any other. For here was a boxer who could skillfully roll the sting out of any punch while a knowing smile flickered around his lips, and make his opponents hang on his feint, ducking the punch that never comes, while his hazel eyes twinkled; or he could play it safe with the frustrating movements of a moth coming close to a flame, but never too close. Rarely, if ever, did he mix it up, prefering instead to combine his excellent footwork with lightning-like punches and well-defined moves that made it seem as if his opponent was shoveling smoke.

JOHNNY KILBANE FIRST STEPPED INTO the ring at the LaSalle Club's annual smoker in downtown Cleveland one wintry night back in 1907, a frail, but smiling youth. Fighting a three-rounder against a rugged West Sider named Paddy Kilbane, no relative, Johnny displayed the natural speed that would later carry him to the top, landing blows and getting away in a surprising manner for such a novice.

Determined to pick up some of the finer points of the science, Johnny approached Jimmy Dunn, then a known featherweight, and asked for a chance to work with him. Dunn had no one to train with the day Kilbane came to his training headquarters, so he asked Johnny if he would like to work out with him. Dunn found that the youngster had speed and courage, enough for him to take the fledgling under his managerial wing.

Slowly and deliberately, the two climbed the stairs to the pinnacle of the profession, fighting first those ring ornaments charitably known as "opponents," and then graduating into world-class opponents, beating the likes of Joe Rivers, Patsy Kline, and Frankie Conley. By year three, Kilbane was fighting the reigning champion, Abe Attell, in a ten-round bout. But like 18 other challengers before him, he lost. However, that and a four-rounder the following year, in which Attell was forced to retire with a broken arm in a nontitle fight, were merely wet runs for his challenge to Attell's featherweight title on February 22, 1912.

For 20 rounds, Kilbane clearly outfought the supposedly peerless Attell, tattooing the "Little Champ" with his talented left jab, closing his left eye as easily as if he had pulled down a window shade, and thoroughly frustrating the fading champion with his footwork. Attell became so thwarted in his attempts to get at the fleet and fleeing Kilbane that he translated his pent-up frustrations into all the black arts of boxing: heeling, butting, and elbowing, with an occasional twisting of his opponent's arms in the clinches. But, in the end, it was Kilbane's arm that was held aloft by the referee as the new featherweight champion of the world.

For the next 11 years and 4 months, Johnny Kilbane was to reign as the featherweight champion, practicing on-the-job retirement. He defended it three times in the first year of his reign and three times in the second. But one

Above: Kilbane loses featherweight title to Eugene Criqui, June 2, 1923.

of those few times was against tough Johnny Dundee, from whom he barely escaped with a face-saving draw. Rather than face Dundee again, Kilbane put his title in cold storage and feathered his featherweight nest with no-decision fights and nontitle fights against lightweights like Benny Leonard, Joe Mandot, Artie O'Leary, Freddie Welsh,

Rocky Kansas, and Benny Valgar.

By 1922, like a man holding his breath underwater for nine years, Johnny Dundee was still waiting for his return bout. But it was not forthcoming. Dundee even went so far as petitioning those Caesars of boxing, the New York Athletic Commission, who handed down an ultimatum to Kilbane: "Defend or we'll take away your title!"

Johnny Kilbane had run out of tomorrows. Where seven years before he had been able to call his shot in a fight against Willie Jackson, he was now merely chasing memories of his greatness, fighting in his spare time, his once-substantial talents half-shot.

Caught between a rock and a hard place, Kilbane chose the hard place, accepting the challenge of European featherweight champion Eugene Criqui, thus avoiding the challenge of Dundee.

But Kilbane was finished before he started, an old fistic crone fighting as if there was safety in experience alone.

Criqui, who had been wounded at the Battle of Verdun and had had his jawbone rebuilt into a gargoyle-like chin with a perpetual half-smile etched across his face, presented an eerie sight as he came at Kilbane intent on finding out what Kilbane had left after two years of inactivity. He soon found out: nothing. After raking Kilbane with lefts and rights for five rounds, Criqui caught the floundering champion with a long right in the sixth. Kilbane reeled backwards and dropped to the canvas where he was counted out. In a sad finale to the career of Johnny Kilbane, sportswriter W. O. McGeehan was to comment: "It is now clear Kilbane should have been matched with the Mademoiselle from Armentieres . . ."

Called by Benny Leonard, "just yellow enough to be a great fighter," Kilbane put on the "dog," and enough of it, to be one of the past masters of the "Art of Self-Defense." And all played with a grin of friendly confidence on his smiling Irish face.

BOB FOSTER

As we deal in that limbo of memories that comprise the whole of boxing, there are very few moments that stay with us. But there is one. It was an instance when time was separated and unified at the same time. A left hook thrown by Bob Foster that was in the air and in *The Ring Record Book* at the same time, a picture-perfect punch the likes of which had never been seen before. Or since. Close your eyes and you can almost see it now: a left hook to the chin knocking the soon-to-be ex-champion Dick Tiger off his feet and onto the seat of his baby-blue satin trunks. Tiger sprawls over backwards, his legs contorted, the back of his head laying on the canvas. Then, as the referee's hand tolls the fatal ten seconds, his head raises a little, the whites of his eyes showing. And only the whites. Unable to gain leverage with his arms to control his compact body, he sits there, his nerves deadened, the former light heavyweight champion of the world. And a jubilant Bob Foster leaps up in the air with all the force of a Cape Kennedy space shot, his splinter-like body hurtling into space. It is one of boxing's most complete moments. And the one moment which catapulted Bob Foster into the pantheon of the greats as well.

AT 6 FEET 3 INCHES, BOB FOSTER WAS SO big it almost seemed as if some conjurer had rubbed a three-piece set of matching willow-branch luggage to create the illusion of this hyperpituitary willow stalk. But it was no illusion, the punches coming out of this 75 inches made up of gaunt body, gangly elbows, and knobby shoulders possessed the real force of a mechanized calvary unit, dispatching opponents to destinations unknown. However, if his long sleep-inducing hook was his meal ticket to greatness, it was his even longer left jab—not the normal pecking left jab, but one that hurts with skin-tearing, fire-searing ferocity, sending heads back atilting and fighters back on their heels areeling—that was to be his passport.

This big man with an even bigger stick started out as a light heavyweight, throwing tranquilizers from his 79-inch dart guns. But, after nine wins, he was

rushed in where angels feared to box, to face ranking heavyweight Doug Jones on just two days' notice—the same Doug Jones who would give a young Cassius Clay life and death in ten hotly-contested rounds in a few short months. The result was predictable: an eighth-round knockout at the gloves of Jones, Foster's first loss. And his first fight in the heavier weight class.

Throughout the first five years of his career, Foster made the light heavyweight ring less his castle than his shark-infested moat. And woe betide any 175-pounder who tried to cross it to get at him. But once he left the safe confines of his own fortifications and masochistically tried to scale the walls of the heavyweight division, he would be hurled back, the barrier too great. Finally, caught in a fistic *cul de sac*— light heavyweights not inclined to risk being in the same ring with him and Foster disinclined to cross the frontier

and suicidally climb into the ring with top-rated heavyweights—he surrendered to the obvious and retired, unable to get bouts or support his growing family. His record read: 25 bouts, 21 wins, 16 by knockout, and 4 losses, 3 of them to top heavyweights Doug Jones, Ernie Terrell, and Zora Folley.

Discouraged, disgusted, and disaffected with the world of boxing, Fos-

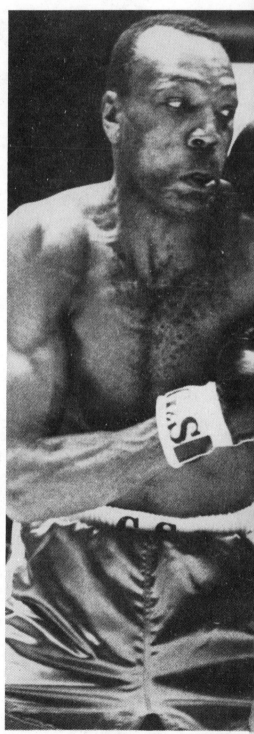

ter took a job in a munitions plant assembling explosives. But, within the year, he had an opportunity to explode his own homemade bombs in mid-ring, coming back under the tutelage of trainer Billy Edwards. It was Edwards who realized that Foster's extremely long 79-inch reach should not be used to overreach into the heavyweight class, but should instead be used as a battering ram to break down the doors to the light heavyweight division's upper strata. Even into the throne room. Running off eight straight victories before his opponents even had a chance to stock up on smelling salts, this born-again light heavyweight now stood at the threshhold of the light heavyweight title, then held by Dick Tiger.

But even Foster's elongated reach couldn't reach a title shot without some assistance. For Tiger's managerial brain trust—the same brain trust which had left a deposit check for $10,000 for his middleweight defense against Joey Giardello in Nat Fleischer's safe for safekeeping and promptly forgot about it—now demanded $100,000, cold quid. To raise the mother's milk of boxing, Edwards went

Left: Foster sets up Dick Tiger, wins light heavyweight title, May 24, 1968.

Born 12/15/38, in Alburquerque, NM . . . Silver medalist, 1959 Pan-Am Games, lost in final round to Brazilian, Abrao de Souza . . . First pro bout, 1961, Washington, DC . . . Won first 8 bouts and then stopped by Doug Jones in 8 rounds, 10/20/62 . . . Stopped by Ernie Terrell in seventh round, 7/10/64 . . . Knocked out Eddie Cotton in 3 rounds, 5/8/67 . . . Scored 23 knockouts in first 33 bouts . . . Won world light heavyweight title with fourth-round knockout of Dick Tiger—only knockout of Tiger's career . . . Stopped Frankie DePaula in first round of first title defense . . . Had streak of 19 kayoes in 20 bouts, 1966–70, including 3 other title defenses . . . Challenged Joe Frazier for world heavyweight championship, but was kayoed in second round, 11/18/70 . . . Defended title 10 times in next 4 years—scored 7 kayoes . . . Knocked out Muhammad Ali in eighth round, 11/21/72 . . . Retired 9/16/74, shortly after boxing 15-round draw with Jorge Ahumada in title defense . . . Retirement lasted less than 1 year . . . Continued boxing until 1978, but with limited success . . . Scored more knockouts (11) in light heavyweight championship bouts than any other fighter . . . Elected to Boxing Hall of Fame, 1983 . . . Complete record: 65 bouts, 56 won, 8 lost, 1 draw, 46 knockouts.

to two old friends from his Managers Guild days, Mushky Solo and Joe Nesline, who, together with wrestling promoter Vince McMahon, advanced the monies to Billy for an interest in Foster's contract.

Champagne flowed like molasses in the Foster camp until Solo, Nesline, and company backed their warrior with big bucks, hoping to recoup their losses on the guarantee by "scoring" with a big win. Foster justified their confidence, and the 12—to—5 odds in his favor, by landing the big left hook with a short and sweet trajectory to the point of Tiger's jaw, a picture-perfect punch that belonged to the ages.

For the remainder of his long career—with a few ill-fated forays into the heavyweight ranks which merely proved the rule that a champion's place is in his own division—Bob Foster would hold onto his light heavyweight title, defending it 14 times with most of his opponents giving themselves up to study astrology on their backs.

But his place in boxing history was secured with one pluperfect left hook, one worthy more of autopsy than analysis.

205

MIKE GIBBONS

It was early 1919, and Gene Tunney had yet to return from "Over There" to resume his ring career. His every fiber obsessed with what he would do in his next movie, he not only constantly thought about boxing, but asked anyone and everyone what was going on back on the home front. One morning the A.E.F. champion was doing his obligatory roadwork in the company of a corporal, who, in civilian life, had been a Midwest newspaperman. As they trotted past the castles lining one of the tributaries of the Rhine, Tunney brought the conversation around to his favorite subject, boxing, and his new fascination, the man-tiger out of the West, Jack Dempsey, then challenging Willard for the heavyweight championship. The ex-newspaperman was not only a boxing fan, but had actually seen Dempsey in action. "What's he like?" asked Tunney, pumping the corporal as he pumped his arms. "He's a big Jack Dillon," the corporal answered, evoking a complete mental picture in Tunney's mind's eye. For Jack Dillon was a compact, scrappy 5-foot, 7-inch middleweight, nicknamed "Jack the Giant Killer" for his ability to crouch and move in on any light heavyweight or heavyweight alive and throw hard, fast punches until his opponent caved in, dead to the world. But this description also conjured up the picture of another fighter in Tunney's mind, one completely different—Mike Gibbons, the clever master of self-defense, a cunning ring general who knew how to sidestep and take advantage of every inch of the ring, making Jack Dillon look foolish.

MIKE GIBBONS' STYLE WAS PROTEAN, susceptible to elegant and ingenious interpretation by all who saw him. To boxing critics, like Nat Fleischer, he was the keeper of boxing's scientific flame, the "nearest approach to the superb artistry of Tommy Ryan that the middleweight division ever boasted." To his fans, none of whom were more fervid in their appreciation of Mike than his younger brother Tommy— who fought Dempsey to a standstill in Shelby—he was "grand opera in the ring." And to his opponents, among whom could be numbered such greats

as Harry Greb, Packey McFarland, Jack Dillon, Ted "Kid" Lewis, Eddie McGoorty, and Mike O'Dowd, he was the most damnably frustrating opponent in the ring one could find, driving grown men to tears and Greb to scream at his manager during the course of one of their fights, "You sonofabitch, from now on match me with one guy at a time!"

With the death of Stanley Ketchel, claimant and claimant-toid alike, all dressed up in champion's clothing, laid claim to the title, including—but hardly limited to—Billy Papke, Frank

Klaus, Willie Lewis, George Chip, Jack Dillon, Eddie McGoorty, and Jimmy Clabby. And there, on the rim of vision, was Mike Gibbons, the 23-year-old youngster who had been fighting only four years and had 39 fights to his credit, with only one loss—that to the more experienced Clabby in his eighteenth fight. Creeping into New York on petty feet, the unheralded Gibbons punched his way quietly to the forefront, gaining the newspaper decisions—the only decisions possible in those days of "No Decisions"—in fights against what was then called the class of the division. Half-hearted recognition was now given by New York boxing officials to the claims of McGoorty and Gibbons, and the pair were matched on December 4, 1912, for what was billed as "the undisputed middleweight championship."

For ten rounds, the man of whom Nat Fleischer once wrote, "had a pretty left hook which, when unhooked, could drop an opponent," decided not to un-

Born 7/20/87, in St. Paul, Mn . . . Began boxing professionally, 1908, St. Paul . . . Claimant to middleweight title after death of Stanley Ketchel, but claim not widely recognized . . . Known as the "St. Paul Phantom" and "The Wizard" . . . Never fought for a world championship although fought more than a dozen bouts with world champions . . . Lost 10-round decision to welterweight championship claimant, Jimmy Clabby, 3/12/10 . . . Did not lose another bout for 12 years, although fought mostly no-decisions . . . Fought 2 no-decision rematches with Clabby, 9/1/11, and 1/21/15 . . . Also fought no-decision bouts with world champions Al McCoy, 2/23/14; Ted Kid Lewis, 5/18/16; Jack Dillon, 11/10/16, and 9/3/17; Harry Greb, 2/10/17, and 6/23/19; George Chip, 7/4/17, and 1/31/19; and Mike O'Dowd, 11/21/19 . . . Defeated world champion Dave Rosenberg, 5/30/21, in 12 rounds . . . Lost final bout of career to O'Dowd in 12-round decision, 5/6/22 . . . Retired due to failing eyesight . . . Died 8/31/56, St. Paul . . . Elected to Boxing Hall of Fame, 1958 . . . Complete record: 114 bouts, 54 won, 2 lost, 4 draws, 54 no-decisions, 35 knockouts.

Left: Two great past masters of the art of self-defense, Gibbons (right) and Packey McFarland, 1915.

it was the McGoorty fight all over again, this time with both fighting as if they were two porcupines making love, each carefully standing their ground, feinting, parrying, and weaving in anticipation of the other's punches, which never came.

If Mike Gibbons' career had ended with the McFarland fight, he would merely have been relegated to the slag heap of fistic memories, a successful two-hand tag player in boxer's clothing. But the next year, in front of his hometown fans, Gibbons put on the fight of his life against the aforementioned Jack Dillon, bringing him to national—and Gene Tunney's—attention. For ten rounds, against the man reputed to have the strongest punch in the division, if not in all of boxing, Gibbons was never out of position, weaving in front of Dillon with a waistline swivel and then, after Dillon had swatted the air with his best Babe Ruth swing, coming back to counter him. It was pure artistry, every one of Gibbons' movements having a meaning all its own. And leaving Dillon with the feeling he had just tilted with a windmill and come out second best.

From that one fight, Mike Gibbons made his reputation. And established his greatness. And, although he would continue fighting for the next six years—with time out for the service in 1918 and a year out to watch his bones mend after breaking his hand against Mike O'Dowd in a title bout—the Dillon fight was the centerpiece of this artistic performer's career. But it was a highlight that only the most discriminating boxing fan could appreciate, like Gene Tunney who learned the "book" on Jack Dempsey by reading up on one of boxing's greatest defensive artisans.

hook it.   Instead, Gibbons contented himself with practicing reverse polarity, staying at arm's length from his opponent and putting on a baffling display of footwork that rivaled that of Vernon Castle. In a bout about as exciting as Groundhog's Day, they went ten rounds to a no-decision.

After the McGoorty fight, Gibbons was drawn and quoted, one writer even suggesting, "to call him a fighter is a contradiction in terms." But Hype Igoe, wanting to get the reasoning behind Gibbons' curious and cautious tactics, sought him out and asked him. Gibbons thought about it a minute and then replied, carefully, "You and every other writer said McGoorty would knock my brains out. I was supposed to have gotten killed in there. But I fooled you and all the other writers. I never let him hit me. . . . Not once. . . . He never laid a glove on me. . . . I wanted to show you guys how wrong you were."

Self-preservation was not only the first law of nature, but also the first rule

in Gibbons' book. And he fought by the book, a book of his own making he was to reveal in a newspaper interview some three years later. "My brother Tom and I keep books. In it we have a careful resume of every fighter in the business either of us is apt to be called upon to fight as well as those we have already fought and are liable to meet again." Every fighter was an open book to Gibbons and "every bit of strength that a fighter is known to have is jotted down, along with his weaknesses, temperamental aspects, habits and how they are liable to affect his ring work."

Proving you couldn't tell a book—or a fighter—by its cover, Gibbons' book held that "The tough fellow, the slugger who is willing to tear at you, must be made to back up. The clever fellow who is anxious to stand at long-range and exchange his 'Long Toms' with you, must be made to come to you. . . . "

Gibbons would finally be matched with that other peerless purveyor of the sweet science, Packey McFarland. And

BENNY LYNCH

If all the opinions of Benny Lynch's greatness were laid end to end, they wouldn't reach a conclusion. But they would be united in one respect: he was proof-positive that great fighters rarely can be beaten; they either beat themselves or time beats them. In Benny Lynch's case, it was both. Lynch was a fighter of enormous talent despite his mere 65 inches and 112 pounds. The near sight of the mere size of him would have made any grandmother worth her birthright want to take this oversized cuddly doll, with the dark, slicked-down hair and deep, soulful eyes, in her arms and hug him to her bosom. And, for a while, all of Scotland did, as Lynch, with no hand or foot movement more out of place than a hair on his brilliantined head, provided them with dazzling displays of boxing virtuosity. With a wee touch of genius, Lynch fought with concentration in his every move, yet made each move with unconscious effort, almost as if there were tiny little men inside his arms, moving them independent of his body. The total sum of his style was both eloquent and susceptible to ingenious interpretation, that of the boxing booths of England.

FOR IT WAS IN THE BOXING BOOTHS OF Scotland that Lynch first got his introduction to boxing. Encouraged by his father to take up the noble calling, Lynch joined the ranks of the L.M.S. Rovers Club in Glasgow, where he won something he boastfully called the "four-stone championship" of Scotland and went on to carry the colours of his club in amateur competition.

However, it wasn't in amateur competition that young Benny learned the ropes, but in his extracurricular activities after school—or "after four," as he called it. Taking over a coffinmaker's shop near his home, Lynch promoted his own fights, collecting a penny per head at the door and then taking on all comers with his "bare 'uns." When attendance and potential victims petered out, he returned to his first remembered sight, the boxing booth, to continue his education, spending the summers touring with a booth throughout the northern counties.

After winning 35 of 37 amateur bouts and more than holding his own at Watson's Booth in the Saltmarket, where he gave away weight but never talent, Lynch decided to " 'ave a go of it" in the professional ranks. But even then, Lynch knew enough to know he didn't know enough, and, seeking out Len Johnson, who ran a gym in Ardwick, placed his future in the competent coach's hands. Lynch's entire programme of training consisted of fighting one Arthur Burke, a Manchester bantamweight, three times a week for eight weeks—with wages paid only to the lad who won inside the 15-round distance. Lynch, who had cut his "aye" teeth on booth boxing, agreed to the conditions and made them pay off, winning every time.

Now a ring "veteran" at the tender young age of 18, well-schooled in almost every nuance of the sweet science and his last ghosts of self-doubt vanquished, Lynch set out on the path leading to the Scottish flyweight championship. Sixty-two bouts—and less than three years—later, Lynch outpointed Jim Campbell at Glasgow's

Olympic Stadium in a close 15-round decision for the championship. When Campbell expressed less than complete satisfaction with the decision, Lynch agreed to give him a second chance. Six weeks later, at the same venue, Campbell got his second chance, and his second boxing lesson, losing this time by a wide margin in 15 rounds.

At that magic moment in fistic history, the flyweight state of affairs was only slightly less involved than the heavyweight wrestling situation. Everyone under 112 pounds, including the Seven Dwarfs, was advancing his claim to the title. Determined to stake out his claim and to partake of a little cleaning up of the 112-pound landscape, Lynch took on the best little men in Europe, meeting, and beating, Carlo Cavagnoli, the Italian champion; Valentin Angelmann, the French champion; Pedrito Ruiz, the Spanish champion; and a couple of other pretenders to the throne. Now, in a manner of speaking, there were only two "Little Indians" left—or, to be more exact, one little Scot and one little Englishman, Jackie Brown, the recognized British NBA and IBU flyweight titles.

Lynch inveigled Brown to come to his home turf of Glasgow to meet him in a 12-round nontitle fight. And even though the most ardent Glaswegian had high hopes for their local hero, Lynch surprised even them by outcunning, outcutting, and outcuffing Brown for the entire 12 rounds. But the referee, Johnny Summers, didn't quite see it that way, calling the fight a draw, a decision that flattered Brown. It was only a matter of time before Lynch got a return bout—at the weight.

In what was ballyhooed by the promoters of the match at Manchester's Belle Vue Stadium as a "British, European, and World's Flyweight Title Bout," Lynch combined his speed of foot with an awesome display of his dreaded left hook to drive the soon-to-be-ex-champion to the floor no fewer than ten times before Brown flung up his hands in a token of surrender halfway through the second round.

Most of boxing now believed, along with Oscar Wilde, that "three addresses always inspire confidence, even in tradesmen. . . . " and accepted Benny Lynch, the honest tradesman who held three addresses—the Scottish, British, and European championships—as *the* world champion. Still, there were some, like *Ring* magazine, which held that a Filipino named Small Montana

Left: Lynch falls into the ropes, losing to Kayo Morgan, Sept. 28, 1938.

Lynch has the world at his feet. . . . "

But if the seeds of greatness were there, Lynch had acquired a disquieting tendency to wash them down with a liberal dose of whatever went down—scotch, bubbly, whatever.

Within the year, although his obesity was not widespread, the rumors about Lynch's inability to make 112 were. Drained by excessive weight-making, Lynch turned to drink, and, his last linchpin gone, turned into a drunkard. Signed to fight Jackie Jurich, the man called by Jack Dempsey, "the sweetest flyweight seen since Fidel LaBarba," Lynch tried mightily to make 112. But despite refusing water for an entire week before the fight, still scaled 118½ pounds at weigh-in, and was stripped of his title by the British board. Nevertheless, the "nontitle" fight went on, with Lynch treating Jurich like an imposter—giving him a severe drubbing and flooring him five times before a right to the body ended the fight in the twelfth round.

The public learned the truth about Lynch's condition a week after the Jurich bout when the now-former champ was fined 22 pounds for drunk driving and had his license suspended for a year. The arresting officer, in solemn tones, told Lynch, "Sports and spirits do not go well together. There is nothing worse for a man in your calling than drink."

But sound advice or no, it was too late to help Lynch, now a helpless alcoholic. His talents all dried up even if he hadn't, three months after the Jurich bout-cum-non-bout Lynch lost to one Kayo Morgan—a fighter who wouldn't have been good enough to carry Lynch's gumshield just a short time before. Then, five days later, October 3, 1938, drained to the dregs like one of his bar glasses, Lynch suffered a third-round knockout at the hands of a second-rate Rumanian—the only knockout loss in his 102-bout career, and his last fight.

Through at the age of 25, Benny Lynch returned to the boxing booths of his youth, a memory of his once greatness. Drifting from job to job and bar to bar, leaving little pieces of himself at each stop, Lynch continued to go downhill until that final day when his dying form would be lifted out of a Glasgow gutter and taken to a hospital where he would die of acute alcoholism and debilitation at the age of 33—a great fighter who had beaten himself.

was "the best," ergo, the champion. *Ring* threw down the gauntlet when they wrote: "In this country we labor under the impression, correct or otherwise, that the best fly in the universe is one Small Montana. We recognize the abilities of Maister Lench, but we seem to believe that if Small met Maister Lench, there would be nothing much for Lench to carry oot of the reng."

After much agitation from both sides of the Great Pond, Lynch and Small Montana finally climbed into London's Wembley Arena on January 19, 1937, to decide *the* world's flyweight champion—without caveats, conditions or challenges. In what was called a "classic battle of skills," the two little warriors went at each other in what may well have been one of boxing's classic showcases of self-defense. Weathering furious attacks in the two opening rounds by Small, Lynch boxed superbly, and was, in the words of Reuters' correspondent A. Frank Tinsley, "Quicker to take advantage of every opportunity that came to him," using his rapier left hand and dazzling footwork to constantly interrupt his opponent's flow and concentration. The arena rose as one to acclaim Lynch when the inevitable decision came down in his favor.

Now Benny Lynch's claim was accepted, he was *the* universally recognized flyweight champion—the first since Fidel LaBarba retired in 1927. But he also had another claim, and that, too, was gaining acceptance: a claim to greatness, best given voice by Euan Wellwood of the Glasgow *Evening Times*, "At twenty-three years of age,

Born 4/2/13, Clydesdale, Scotland . . . First pro bout, 1931, Glasgow, Scotland . . . Fought 28 bouts in 1932, lost only 2 . . . Won Scottish flyweight title, 5/16/34, 15-round decision over Jim Campbell . . . Won British and world flyweight title, 9/9/35, with second-round kayo of Jackie Brown . . . Defended titles successfully with eighth-round stoppage of Pat Palmer, 9/16/36 . . . Won undisputed recognition as world flyweight champion with 15-round decision over Small Montana, 1/19/37 . . . Knocked out Peter Kane in 13 rounds, 10/13/37 in successful title defense . . . Rematch with Kane ended in 15-round draw, 3/24/38 . . . Fought scheduled title bout with Jackie Jurich, 6/29/38, but failed to make the weight and forfeited title at weigh-in even though previously he had knocked out Jurich in 12 rounds . . . Lost next 2 bouts, 1938, and then retired . . . Never fought outside the British Isles . . . Died 8/6/46, in Glasgow, Scotland . . . Complete record: 102 bouts, 77 won, 10 lost, 15 draws, 32 knockouts.

GEORGE "KID" LAVIGNE

Kid Lavigne was boxing's toughest man, a man who would try to gnaw off his leg in an effort to escape a trap and get at his opponent. His raw, red courage and fearless assaults in the face of disaster gave new meaning to the word carnage. "The Saginaw Kid" stood only 5 feet, 3½ inches in height, and during his fighting days never weighed more than 133 pounds. And yet, time and again, he went out of his class to meet men who towered above him head and shoulders and outweighed him anywhere from 5 to 25 pounds. As soft in appearance as he was small in stature, Lavigne was deceptively tough, able to absorb enormous punishment, possessed of superhuman courage, and so powerful his punches often broke bones. John L. Sullivan said of Lavigne, "Of all the fighters of the present day, Kid Lavigne is the one I most admire. He is the grandest little man of our time."

LIKE SULLIVAN, LAVIGNE'S "TIME" WAS that of two worlds—the old and the new. He began his career as a bare-knuckle fighter back when fights were called on account of daylight, fighting 77- and 55-round draws with George Siddons as a peach-faced teenager with little more than 8-round bouts under his belt. And when custom ended the age of bare knuckles and dictated that he switch to skin-tight gloves, he did so grudgingly, not losing any of his power, as he proved in his fight with Andy Bowen—the same Andy Bowen who fought in the longest glove fight in boxing history, 110 rounds, and in 3 fights in 1893 that went a total of 217 rounds—dealing him a brutal beating and knocking him out in the eighteenth round, a knockout resulting in Bowen's death.

But Lavigne's most brutal encounter was with "The Barbados Demon," the Original Joe Walcott, one of the greatest welterweights the ring has ever known. Considered unbeatable and unable to find welterweights who would risk their lives and limbs fighting him, Walcott agreed to a challenge from Lavigne's manager that they would fight at 133 pounds, then the lightweight limit. Moreover, one additional codicil was agreed to: that Walcott would knock out Lavigne or lose.

In the most grueling fight in boxing history, neither man asked for nor gave a quarter, as they waged a war with first one, then the other gaining the upper glove. By the ninth round, Walcott got his second wind. The Kid's trainer, Buddy Bishop, remembered years later, "It was in this round that Lavigne's ear began to swell up to the size of a lemon. It was an ugly sight. But the worst was yet to come. A right-hand smash burst the ear and splattered blood all over both of them. Then another right tore the loose part of the ear away until it hung by a shred of a shred. God, it was horrible!" Blood-spattered and arm-weary, Lavigne ignored the obvious call to retreat and attacked Walcott. When Lavigne returned to his corner, Bishop asked him if he "wanted to quit." But Lavigne merely cursed at him and told him to "let it hang. I'm going to kill that black. . . ." He damned near did, dealing out more punishment than Walcott ever took in his life. The decision—as foreordained by the terms of Walcott's challenge—was a win for Lavigne. Two years later Lavigne was to repeat his win, this time as lightweight champion. And this time without any advance agreement.

Born 12/6/69, in Bay City, MI . . . Began boxing pro, in 1885, Saginaw, MI, known as "The Saginaw Kid" . . . Fought 77-round draw with George Siddons, 3/1/87, rematch, 4/26/87, was 55-round draw . . . Knocked out Andy Bowen in eighteenth round, 12/14/94 . . . Bowen died following bout (Bowen best known for his 110-round bout, 4/6/93) . . . Defeated Joe Walcott, 12/2/95 . . . Won vacant world lightweight title with seventeenth-round knock-out of Dick Burge in London, 6/1/96 . . . Stopped Jack Everhardt in twenty-fourth round of first title defense, 10/27/96 . . . Made 6 additional successful defenses: Kid McPartland, W 25, 2/8/97; Eddie Connolly, KO 11, 4/28/97; Joe Walcott, W 12, 10/29/97; Jack Daly, D 20, 3/17/98; Frank Erne, D 20, 9/28/98; Tom Tracey, W 20, 11/25/98 . . . Lost title to Frank Erne via 20-round decision, 7/3/99 . . . Continued boxing until 1910, but not more than 1 or 2 bouts per year and mostly exhibitions . . . Died, 3/9/28, in Detroit, MI . . . Elected to Boxing Hall of Fame, 1959 . . . Complete record: 56 bouts, 35 won, 6 lost, 8 draws, 7 no-decisions.

Left: Lavigne (center) poses with manager Sam Fitzgerald, trainer Buddy Bishop (right) and ever-present medicine ball.

The following year Lavigne went to England to fight for what authorities on both sides of the Atlantic agreed would be the newly-minted lightweight championship. His opponent was Dick Burge, a big, burly 156-pounder masquerading as a lightweight, a fighter who was known for his rugbylike toughness. It had been said that no man, even one of his size or larger, had ever been able to hit him hard enough to stagger him. For ten rounds Burge cut Lavigne up, making the Kid's baby-face a look-alike for Quasimoto's. But in the eleventh and twelfth Lavigne began hewing Burge down to size with body shots, and in the seventeenth landed two lefts, one to the wind and the second to the chin, to fell the giant and become the first lightweight champion of the world.

It has been said that truly great fighters can't be beaten, that they can only beat themselves. And so it was with Kid Lavigne, who, even while at the top of his profession, began to spend more time in gin mills than gymnasia. Soon the smell of liniment wasn't the only smell emanating from Lavigne's corner as his victories, all bottled-in-bond, became fewer and fewer. After 13 undefeated years, Lavigne, as drained to the dregs as his drinking glasses, began to fight on borrowed time, losing more often than winning. But no matter how much he indulged in the wages of gin at the end of his career, he remains one of the all-time greats. In the eyes of some, like old-time fight observer Ed Dickerson, "The Kid was the greatest lightweight champion of all time."

AARON PRYOR

Like the blind men who tried to describe an elephant by researching different parts of its anatomy, Aaron Pryor is almost as capable of as many different descriptions by as many blind journalists. He is either, depending upon whom you listen to: (a) a man who just took a four-way cold tablet and realized he had three more ways to go to catch up with it; (b) perpetual motion; (c) a practitioner of the "wham-bam-thank-you-Ma'am" school of boxing; (d) a lineal descendant of Henry Armstrong; (e) a lineal descendant of Lord Greystoke; (f) a pinwheel out of control; (g) a man who fights with total abandon three minutes of every round, with the confidence that repels bullets; or (h) all of the above. In fact, Aaron Pryor is all and none of these at the same time. He is one of the most complex human beings to come upon the boxing scene in years. And one of the most unusual.

COMING FROM THE MEAN STREETS AND hard times of Cincinnati, Pryor was determined to make something of himself, rather than face a grave uncheered by any glamour of promise. That "something" took the form of boxing. "A guy hit me and I hit him back two times," remembered Pryor. "He would start crying because his nose was bleeding. So I became pretty good." Even then his own man, Pryor never had his mother sign his permission slip. "In every fight they gave you a certificate to have your mother sign before you were able to fight. My mother never signed for me. I think I must have signed about three hundred of those. . . . " He had 220 amateur bouts, winning all but 16, including more than 100 in succession. But then, as the top amateur light-weight in the country, he lost twice to Howard Davis in the Olympic trials. It seemed that his dream was at an end.

Unable to accept defeat, Pryor persevered, supplying his own divine spark of fire. Turning pro, he found his only peace in the ring, where he ran up a string of knockouts in front of his hometown fans. He supplied his own form of fistic entertainment, a sort of "In-your-face" style of boxing, constantly moving and giving the impression his gloves were caught in a revolving door.

Having been shut out of the light-weight division by contenders and champions who would "fight anybody *but* Aaron Pryor," he trained his "Hawk"-like sights on the junior welter-weight division and its champion, the legendary Antonio (Kid Pambele) Cervantes, believing any championship in the storm that raged within was better than none. From the moment he stepped into the ring against Cervantes, pointing at his opponent like a dog that sees a pheasant, "The Hawk" owned the fight and the legend, not to mention the championship. Fighting as if he were an endangered species in fear of his life, Pryor swarmed all over the aging legend, hitting him with everything but the ring post. Momentarily arrested in the first round when the overwhelmed Cervantes held out his right hand in self-defense and caught an off-balance Pryor on the end of it, "The Hawk" jumped up, whirled his right hand in a windmill spin, and went back to the attack. By the fourth round, Cervantes had had enough and, practicing his own form of on-the-job retirement, nodded his head at the referee from his kneeling position as he gave up the ghost. And his title. The proud Pryor was now the cock of the walk, even if the walk was in that halfway house known as the junior welterweight division.

Aaron Pryor was as unpredictable outside the ring as he was unbeatable inside. Outside the ring he looked like a man trying to remember the night before, constantly battling with members of his family, his management, and his entourage. But inside he could find the peace that eluded him in the outside world, escaping between the four ring posts to breach the right of peaceable assembly without worrying about the consequences. There he could ride his particular hobbyhorse to his heart's delight. And only there.

Born 10/20/55, in Cincinnati, OH . . . Won 1973 National AAU lightweight championship . . . Won silver medal in 1975 Pan-American Games (lost in final to Canadian, Chris Clarke) . . . Began pro career, 1976, in Cincinnati . . . Won all 8 bouts in 1977, but only 6 by knockout, won all subsequent bouts by kayo from 1978 until 1984 . . . Knocked out Alfonso Frazer, ex-junior welterweight champion, in fifth round, 10/20/79 . . . Won WBA junior welterweight title with fourth-round knockout of Antonio Cervantes, 8/2/80 . . . Defended successfully against: Gaetan Hart, 11/22/80, KO 6; Lennox Blackmoore, 6/27/81, KO 2; Dujuan Johnson, 11/14/81, KO 7; Miguel Montilla, 3/21/81, KO 12; Akio Kameda, 7/4/82, KO 6 . . . Stopped Alexis Arguello in his bid to become the first 4-time champion in fourteenth round of memorable bout . . . Knocked out Sang-Hyn Kim, in third round, 4/2/83 . . . Stopped Arguello in tenth round of rematch, 9/9/83—both boxers retired after that bout, Pryor's retirement only temporary . . . Forced to go 15-round distance in first bout in comeback against Nick Furlano—stopped 26-bout knockout streak . . . One of greatest kayo percentages of all time . . . Complete record: 35 bouts, 35 won, 0 lost, 32 knockouts.

As the freshly baptized junior welterweight champion of the world, Aaron Pryor scored psychological knockout after psychological knockout, performing a fistic version of prefontal lobotomy on his opponents, up to, and including, tap dancing on their chests. Still, he got no respect, being only—or so the reasoning went—the junior welterweight champion. But there are no secrets better kept than the secrets everybody knows. And everybody knew that Aaron Pryor now stood on the cusp of greatness. With a need to slay the doubters and more dragons, Pryor took on Alexis Arguello, who was in pursuit of his fourth title, and permanent greatness.

Instead, their fights would become the whetstone for Aaron Pryor's skills.

And his own greatness.

In what was called "The Ring of Fire"—all of the centuries through that of Buck Rogers already having been preempted with fights pretentiously called "The Fight of the Century"—Alexis Arguello and Aaron Pryor squared off, giving the junior welterweight division its greatest moment in boxing history. Arguello had dedicated the fight to Henry Armstrong, but, in fact, Armstrong's legacy was Pryor, whose style most mirrored that of boxing's hurricane. And for 13 rounds he proved it, coming at the three-time champion with all the energy of a frisky pup, fighting as if every moment was life and death. Still, Arguello was able to get in his fabled one-two several times, driving Pryor backward. But Pryor, who fights like a man with his nerves extracted, merely took the punches, stumbling haphazardly back one step and over two, his footwork taking on the look of a Ray Bolger with St. Vitas. And then came right back at the amazed Arguello with a lead right or a right off a right. Finally, in round 14, after trading punches in mid-ring, Arguello left an opening. Pryor filled it with an overhand right. Then, with a fusillade of punches too quick to follow, the now predatory "Hawk" drove the defenseless Arguello to the ropes, rendering him insensible.

He was to fight Arguello one more time. But Arguello, haunted by visions of the first fight and drugged by the scent of reconstituted past, merely went through the motions as his legs betrayed him. He finally resigned himself to his fate, giving up the ghost in the tenth round rather than getting back up and facing the whirlwind named Aaron Pryor again.

The "Hawk," marching to his own drummer, had finally achieved a greatness with which even he could cope.

Opposite: Pryor shows "Rocky" Sylvester Stallone, his rocks. Left: Destroys Alexis Arguello's dreams of a 4th title, Nov. 12, 1982.

LEW JENKINS

A great martini must be the correct mating of gin and vermouth at precisely the correct moment. Not a second too late. Like the proper making of a great punch. Lew Jenkins knew the secret of making both, even if he did get the two occasionally mixed up. Jenkins was one of the most irresistible, irrepressible, irresponsible whackos ever to come down the boxing pike. An American tintype who combined the looks of an Olive Oyl with the power of a Popeye, he possessed the biggest right-hand punch this side of the heavyweight division. The only trouble was that his form of spinach was of the 98-proof variety, making one of the brightest aspects of his fistic career the dazzling uncertainty of it.

BACK IN THE DEPRESSION WHEN THE line between hunger and anger was a thin one, Jenkins tightrope-walked it all the way across Texas, finally deciding to turn both into a career, of sorts: that of a carnival boxer, taking on all comers. It wasn't that this tall drink of water would rather fight than eat, it just looked that way, as in hundreds of small-town carneys in nameless destinations, he performed between one and four times a night.

For three years hard, Jenkins was to learn all there was about fighting. The hard way. He learned the art of swaying back from the swings of some of life's assorted losers, slipping their punches by the narrowest of margins and making it seem that they had missed him more by chance than by skill. The trick, he soon found out, was in not making them miss too far; the closer they got, the closer into range they got. On those few occasions when the rubes got lucky, Jenkins learned to turtle his chin between his massive shoulders so that it presented the hardest target. Then, in a practiced move, he would throw out his left to rake in his prey, bringing him into his line of fire for his power-laden right. After that, it was only a matter of a little stiff-fingered push to send the stiffs dreams are made of reeling backwards into the sawdust.

By 1938, he had graduated from the carney shows into the professional rings in and around Dallas where he got his M.A. in the Manly Arts. Sportsmen who lay great store in such things gave him half-hearted recognition as "a great puncher, who ain't got no condition." In other words, if he didn't get his opponent out quickly, he would fall over soon enough himself from the exertion.

Jenkins was, at best, a third-rate fighter, making, at most, fifty bucks a fight. (In fact, by his own admission, "I fought fights for five dollars . . . even less, on a regular fight card in Dallas.") But, then again, maybe that's all he was worth, losing almost as many times as he won to assorted pieces de resistance. Wesley Ramey, never known for being a puncher, had him on the floor several times during one of his two winning efforts over Jenkins and the hardly splendid splinter was knocked out by Bobby Britton and Chino Alvarez and beaten by Lew Feldman and Ramey twice.

Sometime in 1939—between two side trips to Chicago and Mexico City, where he kept his streak intact, winning just three of nine fights—Jenkins contacted the former manager of Maxie Rosenbloom, one Frank Bachman, giving permission to represent him. Bachman forwarded transportation money to Jenkins and, in June of 1939, Jenkins and his comely bride, Katie, arrived in a jalopy of dubious ancestry. But if it weren't for the latter, Katie, the former, Jenkins, might have never had a fight in

New York. For shortly after she arrived, she informed Bachman that she worked in her husband's corner. "Do you wear slacks?" was all the old-time fight manager could think of saying to this early-day women's libber. "Oh, yes," the de-

B orn Verlin Jenkins, 12/4/16, in Milburn, TX . . . First pro bout, 1934, Southwestern U.S. . . . Many early bouts unrecorded . . . Kayoed 3 times, 1937–38, but scored 7 straight knockouts himself . . . Hot and cold fighter, won only 4 of 12, 11/9/38–3/24/39, then won 14 straight including 8 straight by knockout . . . Won world lightweight championship with third-round knockout of Lou Ambers . . . Knocked out by welterweight champion, Henry Armstrong, in sixth round of nontitle fight between 2 champions . . . Defended title successfully with second-round knockout of Pete Lello, 11/22/40 . . . Fought 10-round draw with welterweight champion Fritzie Zivic, 12/20/40 . . . Lost 10-round decision to Freddie "Red" Cochrane, 10/6/41, in nontitle bout . . . Lost title to Sammy Angott on 15-round decision, 12/19/41 . . . Career went downhill afterwards, lost 9 of 10 bouts in 1942 . . . Served in U.S. Coast Guard 1943–45 . . . Continued boxing until 1950 . . . Lost final bout to Beau Jack 4/14/50 on sixth-round knockout . . . Had unusual feat of fighting 3 nontitle fights with 3 different welterweight champions while lightweight champion . . . Died, 10/30/81, in Oakland, CA . . . Elected to Boxing Hall of Fame, 1977 . . . Complete record: 109 bouts, 65 won, 39 lost, 5 draws, 47 knockouts.

mure Miss Katie answered. "Good," replied Bachman, "now we can get a fight."

Two weeks later Bachman had his new charge in against Baby Breese at the Queensboro Arena. And even though Jenkins shook up Breese more than a few times, he "died in there," according to his manager. It was then that Jenkins told his manager he had slept in his jalopy and had not eaten a full meal since he arrived in the Big City. That small oversight corrected, Bachman now got Jenkins fights on the average of once a month, stepping Jenkins up in class with almost every fight, until finally, with five straight-wins, he was matched with Mike Belloise in the Garden.

But if Jenkins was moving up, he was also moving out, shoveling the latest consignment of purse monies into the pockets of friendly barkeeps. Never one to let fighting get in the way of a good time, he stayed out all night, ca-

roused with everyone he could find, sparred a few rounds with Canadian Club, and did his road work on his new "motorsickle." Lew Jenkins had the sweet smell of success, one you could almost smell on his breath. It became a standing joke that even Alcoholics Anonymous wouldn't let their members come to a Lew Jenkins fight. But still, he could climb into a ring dead drunk and beat Mike Belloise, merely by aiming his power-packed right at the head in the middle. Or, in a return bout against the same Chino Alvarez who had taken him out in seven rounds just two years before, he could stagger off his stool and throw a right by memory which landed to the windpipe and then put a second right behind Alvarez's left ear, ending the fight in just 3 seconds of the first round. And give Jenkins enough time to get back to the bar to pick up the second round.

Brought back to New York for a main event in the Garden against top-rated Tippy Larkin, Jenkins found a resting place for his right in the first round and dispatched Larkin with his first well-placed punch. Suddenly, this human thermometer, who performed according to the anti-freeze he contained, was worthy of attention. And writers like Dan Parker took note of Jenkins' 12 straight wins and 7 straight knockouts by writing, "Certainly no lightweight within the memory of this present generation of fans could hit like this bag of bones."

Jenkins was now the natural contender for Lou Ambers' recently-won lightweight title. The books made Ambers 2½–1 and jumped the price to 16–5 when Jenkins showed up at the weigh-in french-fried to the gills. But hangover or no, Jenkins, standing with his hands held low in a classic John L. Sullivan stance, caught Ambers with his right one minute into the fight and decked the man who had been down only once before in 99 fights. Up at five, Ambers lasted the round. In the second, looking "like one of Frank Buck's famished leopards," in the words of Caswell Adams, Jenkins awaited his chance and bounced Ambers off the floor again. And again for a count of five. In the third, weary of watching his adversary get back up on melting legs, Jenkins dropped Ambers two more times to end the fight.

America's newest hero was the most unlikely candidate for canonization since the surly aviator of James Thurber's short story who was done away with because his values didn't reflect apple pie and motherhood. But Lew Jenkins didn't have to worry about someone doing away with him, he was doing it single-handedly, burning his candle at both ends—and in the middle, too. Picking his way through his pile of banknotes, the lusty tippler found every waterhole known to mankind, and some not. Putting the quart before the hearse, he took to riding his "motorsickle" at all hours, in any condition, once even doing a "wheelie" in front of Garden promoter Mike Jacobs and hollering, "Hey Mike! Look, no hands!," and then screeching off into the traffic, leaving the ashen-faced Jacobs to clutch at his heart, undoubtedly in search of his wallet.

Jenkins left little pieces of himself all over the highways and byways of the Northeast, losing decisions to trees, trucks, and trestles. But instead of sitting at home and watching his bones mend, he brought them into the ring with him. He fought Henry Armstrong coming off an accident on the George Washington Bridge with a truck; he fought Bob Montgomery with 16 stitches in his right hand, a battle scar he said came from falling down drunk with a beer bottle in hand, although no one had ever seen him with a beer bottle in hand; he fought Red Cochrane with three broken vertebrae in his neck, a souvenir of a motorcycle wreck in New Jersey at 90 miles per hour, and he fought Fritzie Zivic after having been beaten up by the local police in a drunk tank. It got so he could have used corks instead of catgut for his stitches.

But, sooner or later, even Jenkins could see the handwriting on the canvas. And when, after knocking out Ambers again, he lost his title to a cloying lightweight named Sammy Angott, who hung all over him like a cheap pair of coveralls for 15 rounds, Jenkins' career went downhill faster than his "motorsickle," as he hit all the bumps on the bottom of the long road at the end of his career—a career that saw this overblown featherweight fight 10 champions, and give them all hell, accidents notwithstanding.

The career of Lew Jenkins was fun while it lasted, even though it lasted for but a few years. But it was to leave us with the memory of one of the hardest punchers in the history of boxing. And one of the hardest livers in the history of the sport as well.

CARLOS ORTIZ

Jose Torres, the fighter-turned-writer, recorded the accomplishments of Sixto Escobar, the first Puerto Rican champion, by writing, "He was the very first Puerto Rican to reach the pinnacle in a most competitive sport. But his much larger conquest rested in his capacity to overcome the socio-economic conditions of his time . . . and make it easier to try harder, because it was possible for a Puerto Rican to become champion of the world . . . .He opened the doors!" Just nine days after Escobar became the undisputed bantamweight champion of the world, one of those he opened the door for, a little green-eyed *Puertorriqueño bambino* destined to become Puerto Rico's second world champion—and her first double champion—would be born in Ponce. His name: Carlos Ortiz. He was sent to the States when he was eight years old to live in in New York with his six-year-old sister for a year until his family joined them. There Ortiz took basic training in street survival techniques. "Kids in the neighborhood were pretty rough. They used to pick on me and call me bad names because I was Puerto Rican. I tried to tell them I was just as American as they were. But kids don't listen." The only thing they would listen to were his fists. And just as previous generations of beleaguered first-generation Irish, Italian, and Jewish kids had done before him, he answered their taunts "by fighting back."

WITH THE STUBBORNNESS BORN OF poverty, Ortiz learned to fight. And fight well. From the streets it was but a short hop, skip, and right cross to the Madison Square Boys Club where he fought under the banner of the Police Athletic League. Winner of 33 of his 34 amateur bouts, Ortiz found the door opened by Escobar still slightly ajar, and, determined to use his fists as his passport out of the ghetto, turned pro.

Approaching even his ordinary fights with out-of-the-ordinary performances, Ortiz ran through his first 27 fights without a blemish, confusing most of his foes with his fists, and those he couldn't confuse, covincing with his fists. In his twenty-eighth fight, he lost to veteran Johnny Busso in ten rounds.

It was a decision he would reverse three months later. Then, after beating top-rated lightweight contender Dave Charnley in his backyard of London, he faced cutey Kenny Lane, the southpaw scourge of the lightweight division. "I punched the hell out of him," Ortiz remembered. "They must have been blind to give it to Kenny . . . ." But give it to Kenny they did for Ortiz's second loss.

Ortiz next took on Len Matthews, a brawler who "could knock your head off." Fighting in Matthews' hometown of Philadelphia, Ortiz went in as the 3-to-1 underdog, so certain were the local sports that Matthews' right hand would fell Ortiz as it had so many of his previous opponents. But Ortiz, confi-

dent that Matthews "couldn't hit me with a handful of right hands all together," took the fight to Matthews, outsmarting him by outpacing him. Then, in the sixth, after working over Matthews in a workman-like fashion for the first five rounds, Ortiz threw a left hook that caromed off Matthews' stomach onto the point of his jaw, driving Matthews into the ropes, defenseless. His green eyes flashing with Latin fire, Ortiz became an out-of-control Water Pik, spewing deadly punches from everywhere at the slumping form of what used to be Matthews. Finally, the referee pulled Ortiz off the remains of his opponent to raise his hand in victory.

Ortiz's smashing victory was rewarded with a championship fight. Not the championship he coveted, the lightweight championship—then owned by Joe Brown, who was practicing on-the-job retirement with his crown—but something called the junior welterweight championship, a title that had been put in moth balls by boxing many years ago and was trotted out for ceremonial occasions only, like the Royal Family's crown jewels.

At that magic moment in time, 1959, boxing was among the walking wounded. The fighters who ruled the eight weight classes were relatively nondescript battlers, with the exception of two all-time greats, Archie Moore and Sugar Ray Robinson, both of whom were getting long in the tooth and more than a little wearisome to the National Boxing Association, which was in the process of stripping them of their crowns for inactivity. The others were in the process of retiring on their own. And Jim Norris, head of the IBC, had run boxing's fortunes into a shoestring, giving away the fights free on TV. From his first full year, 1950, into 1959, attendance at an average Garden show had fallen from 8,849 to just 2,371, the smorgasbord of mediocrity in the ring driving away the paying fans, who were now outnumbered by the ushers. Something had to be done to save the endangered species known as boxing from becoming totally extinct. Those smothers of invention, the New York State Athletic Commission, ran to the rescue with a band-aid, coming forth with an idea rivaling the Edsel for its imagination: resuscitate the junior divisions, starting with the junior welterweight class.

But even though Ortiz stopped the

Left: Ortiz lays claim to the junior welterweight championship by laying on Kenny Lane.

Born 9/9/36, Ponce, Puerto Rico . . . First pro bout, 1955, NYC . . . Won 27 of first 28 pro bouts, other one ruled "No Contest" . . . Became first junior welterweight champion in 13 years with second-round stoppage of Kenny Lane for vacant title . . . Successfully defended title twice: Battling Torres, 2/4/60, KO 10; Dulio Loi, 6/15/60, W 15 . . . Lost title to Loi, 9/1/60, in 15-round decision . . . Unsuccessful with Loi in attempt to regain title, 5/10/61 . . . Won world lightweight championship from Joe Brown, 4/21/62, on 15-round decision . . . Defended title successfully 4 times, 1962–64 . . . Lost title to Panamanian, Ismael Laguna on 15-round decision in Panama City, 4/10/65 . . . Regained title to rematch with Laguna, in San Juan, 11/13/65, 15-round decision . . . Made 5 successful title defenses, 1965–67 . . . Lost title to Dominican, Carlos Teo Cruz, 6/29/68, 15-round decision . . . Retired, 1970 . . . Brief comeback, 1971–72, winning 9 straight, 8 by KO . . . Retired permanently after sixth-round KO by Ken Buchanan, 9/20/72 . . . Engaged in 18 title bouts in career, winning 14, losing 4 . . . Complete record: 70 bouts, 61 won, 7 lost, 1 draw, 1 no-contest, 30 knockouts.

bothersome Lane in two quick rounds—opening up his eye like an overripe fruit with one explosive right hand—to win the junior welterweight title, he knew, as all boxing fans knew, that it was merely a paper title. And that he was nothing more than an answer to a sports trivia question.

For two years, Ortiz massaged the junior welterweight title for all it was worth. Which wasn't much, considering. And wrestled with his new manager-advisor, "Honest" Bill Daly—so nicknamed for the same reason one of those characters who haunted the darkened cauliflower alleys of yesteryear had been named "The Honest Brakeman," because he never pilfered a train. A charmingly disarming rogue, Daly was the sort who could go into a revolving door behind you and come out in front, wearing your pants. For Ortiz, it was like being a lion tamer working two cages simultaneously, having to battle both his opponents and "Honest" Bill. And trying to keep his back away from both. But, in that strange and mysterious way boxing worked in the early sixties, "Honest" Bill finally delivered on his promise: a

shot at the lightweight title and Joe Brown in the bargain.

Brown, appropriately known as "Old Bones," in deference to his advancing age, was a cagey veteran who looked "to go in and get him" when his opponent tired or "if I spotted a cut, to open it up big." But Ortiz—who had risen to the exalted position of challenging for the title with a symmetrical style, his potent left and powerful right leaving his opponents nowhere to turn—had devised a strategy to "outfox" the champ. "When, after a long wait," explaining the rationale behind his strategy, "you finally get a shot at a title, you don't say to yourself, 'Get the fans hollering for you. Make it spectacular. Go after him, excite the customers.' You fight the way you have to fight to win."

For 15 rounds, Carlos Ortiz fought the fight he had to fight to win, a thinking man's fight. Cool, detached, and deliberate, he kept his temper in check and the fight in control as he kept up a sustained attack of left jabs and left hooks in Brown's face, keeping Brown off balance, unable to get untracked.

At the end of 15 one-sided, and one-handed, rounds, Carlos Ortiz had become Puerto Rico's second world champion—not counting the junior welterweight championship, which nobody was counting—joining Escobar on the other side of the door.

It was Six-to and even that this one, Carlos Ortiz, would be remembered as one of Puerto Rico's, if not boxing's, best.

JACK DELANEY

Nineteen twenty was the first full year of the Volstead Act and Prohibition. It was also the first year of legalized boxing in New York State under the Walker Law. Together, the products of these two statutes were to become two-thirds of the three B's of the hedonistic Twenties: Booze, Broads, and Boxing. So intertwined were the three that the Club Gallant, one of those underground drinking places in New York known as a speakeasy, or "speak," even had a set of rules promulgated to cover the conduct of its patrons, one which mated the three: "Please do not offer to escort the cloakroom girl home. Her husband, who is an ex-prizefighter, is there for that purpose." One of those who made the so-called "Roaring Twenties" roar a little louder was Jack Delaney, a three-letter man who dedicated himself to following the national pastime of "making whoopee." It was always midnight in the soul of Delaney, a handsome French-Canadian version of Harry Greb, who could see Greb and raise him one, every place but in the ring. A bouser and carouser of the first water, Delaney rarely missed a watering well or a well put-together chorine or cloakroom attendant—a group called by the press, "Delaney's Screaming Mamies," in testimony to their unbridaled pre-Sinatra vocal support for him at fights. He responded with performances in the ring that fluctuated like a thermometer, going up and down in quality depending upon how much anti-freeze he contained.

HIS FIRST MANAGER, FINALLY TIRING O the task of trying to tame this Canadiaı outdoorsman with more than enough insolence and insouciance to try the patience of Job, sold the homesteading rights to Delaney for $900 to Brooklyn sportsman Pete Reilly. Reilly, a little man with the sharp, darting eyes of a fox, was appropriately known as the "Silver Fox"—so named by columnist Joe Williams who wrote, "They did not nickname him for his interest in animal life." The owner of a racing stable, Reilly not only looked upon Delaney, the start of his boxing stable, as his personal reclamation project, but also, in the parlance of the trade, as "a good long shot."

Delaney looked better than a long shot in his fights under Reilly's colors, ors, his rapier-like left and precision right cross soon leaving most of his opponents pillowing the canvas. And then, on February 17, 1924, Delaney began paying dividends as he out-mastered the ring master Tommy Loughran, his superb ring grace, uncanny judgment of distance, and artistic performance far outdistancing the man Nat Fleischer called "one of the cleverest boxers in modern ring history."

From that one performance, Jack Delaney made his name. And an invitation by Madison Square Garden to fight their newest ring sensation, Paul

Berlenbach, the former AAU wrestling and heavyweight boxing champion who had scored ten straight knockouts with his bear-like left hook. The Garden had a draw in the match they billed as "The Wrestler versus the Boxer," even going so far as to advertise the match with the taunt, "Can a wrestler beat a puncher?" And the public responded, packing the old-old Garden to the rafters and setting a new gate record of $50,000 to see the hulking Cromagnum known as "The Astoria Assassin" or "Der Paulie" or "Punch-'em Paul" do battle with the man known merely as Jack Delaney.

Fast out of the starting gate, Delaney kept Berlenbach from getting near him in the opening round, moving and gliding away, all the while keeping his left in Berlenbach's swarthy, expressionless face and occasionally firing over his whip-like right through any and every opening, right on target. Berlenbach, his bull-like rushes thwarted, would take a little reviving hop and skip to get back into the rhythm of his attack, much like a singer who has to repeat the first line to remember the second, and then, undaunted, hurl himself back at Delaney again.

By the second, figuring the lion was sleeping because he didn't hear its roar, Delaney went through his entire bag of tricks, with feints and hints that made Der Paulie look more like a wrestler

Left: Delaney (right) beats Paul Berlenbach to recapture light heavyweight championship, July 16, 1926.

with a lethal right, dropping Berlie like an immense sail going limp in a changing wind. Up at three, Berlenbach met the over-anxious Delaney, coming in for the kill, and dropped him with one of his rights. Delaney jumped up as if he had never been down and met the onrushing Berlenbach with a right hand that almost tore off Der Paulie's head. For the rest of the round, Delaney drove Berlenbach around the ring under the duress of his cumulative rights, leaving him so confused he couldn't find his corner at the bell.

By the fourth, the end was in sight. And, after two more knockdowns of the by-now reeling bear, referee Jack O'Sullivan mercifully called a halt to what had become a bear-baiting, waving off Delaney and engulfing the remains of "The Astoria Assassin," "Der Paulie" and "Punch-'em Paulie" in his arms.

Jack Delaney would go on to meet Paul Berlenbach again. And again. And again. Four times these two light heavyweight greats would meet, becoming a boxing "item." And three times Delaney would win, including the time he won the light heavyweight championship from Berlenbach in front of 49,186 paying customers at that little bandbox of a ballpark known as Ebbetts Field—for which they coughed up a whopping $461,789, a record gate for a light heavyweight title fight.

Jack Delaney was now the most popular fighter in New York, a handsome, happy-go-lucky warrior who personified the cocky confidence of the 1920s. Before his fight with the great Tiger Flowers, he mirrored that confidence by boasting, "If Flowers says he's going to beat me, tell him he's fulla crap and that Jack Delaney is picking himself by a knockout in an early round." And, sure enough, picking his spots like a dry cleaner, Delaney caught Flowers with a picture-perfect right in the second and dropped him. As Flowers tried to arise, his movements chained to Morpheus' slow carriage, Delaney marched around the ring with hands held aloft acknowledging the roars bellowing up from the cavernous old Garden. Two months later, as if to confirm his superiority, he repeated his mastery of Flowers, knocking him out in four.

Delaney employed his strategy against ex-light heavyweight champion Mike McTigue. For three rounds, McTigue kept throwing up his right glove to ward off Delaney's prying left. In the fourth, Delaney let go with another left and McTigue once again shot up his guard. With his left hand halfway to the mark, Delaney suddenly lashed out with his right and McTigue was found shortly thereafter crumpled on the ropes.

It was at that magic moment in time that Gene Tunney stepped down from the heavyweight throne. The venerable William Muldoon, the New York State Athletic Commissioner, came forward with a plan to stage an elimination tournament for the vacant championship, the winner to get a trophy emblematic of the title—not surprisingly called "The Muldoon-Tunney Trophy." All manner of men seeking to become a permanent part of the trophy rushed into print with their expression of willingness to enter the tournament. One of those was Jack Delaney, who relinquished his light heavyweight title without ever having defended it to pursue the megabucks in the heavyweight division.

Making his bow as a heavyweight, Delaney met Bud Gorman, who had acquired considerable fame and stature as the sparring partner who had made Tunney look bad during his training for his rematch with Dempsey. Delaney collapsed Gorman in two. Now he was ready for any and all heavyweights that could be thrown at his head despite the fact that he weighed only 175 pounds. After losing to Jimmy Maloney in ten, Delaney was matched with the Basque Woodchopper, Paolino Uzcudun, the man who had already beaten Knute Hansen, Tom Heeney, and Harry Wills. Despite being a 2-to-1 favorite, Delaney was doing little or nothing with Uzcudun until the seventh, when he suddenly grabbed his lap and fell to the canvas claiming "foul" on a punch nobody could swear they saw. Referee Jim Crowley, of Four Horseman fame, called a foul, awarding the fight to Delaney.

After one more attempt at the big boys—against Jack Sharkey, when Delaney, looking a little green around the bills, flopped on the floor without having thrown a punch and was counted out in the first round—Jack Delaney retired, his dreams now more of pink elephants than elephantine heavyweights.

But if Jack Delaney was a base alloy as a heavyweight attempting to masquerade skim milk as cream, he was pure gold as a light heavyweight, the cream of the crop. For here was a man who could fight with a touch of genius. When he wanted to.

than a boxer. Then it happened, a sweep of Berlenbach's paw and Delaney was deposited on the floor. Heavily. As Delaney groggily regained his footing and the apparition of Berlenbach appeared before him, he sank back down to the canvas without being hit, there to await another count—a move that today would beget him a disqualification for his efforts, but not back in the twenties when the rules were somewhat looser, as befitted the times. He finally arose, his resolve more than his chin carrying him through the rest of the round.

In the third, Delaney hooked his left to Berlenbach's stomach and crossed

Born Ovila Chapdelaine, 3/18/00, St. Francis, Quebec, Canada . . . Began pro career, 1919, Bridgeport, Ct. . . . Fought primarily in New England, 1919–22 . . . Defeated Tommy Loughran, 2/19/24, 10-round decision . . . Knocked out Paul Berlenbach in fourth round, 3/14/24—first kayo loss for Berlenback . . . Lost to Jimmy Slattery, 6-round decision, 10/3/24 . . . Knocked out Tiger Flowers twice in 1925, 1/16/25, 2 rounds; 2/26/25, 4 rounds . . . Lost second decision to Slattery, 2/13/25 . . . Drew with Tommy Loughran, 10 rounds, 7/16/25 . . . Challenged Paul Berlenbach for world light heaveyweight title, 12/11/25, but lost 15-round decision . . . Knocked out Mike McTigue in fourth round, 3/15/26; one week later defeated Maxie Rosenbloom in 10-round decision . . . Won world light heavyweight title from Paul Berlenbach, 7/16/26, by decision in 15 rounds . . . Never defended title . . . Abandoned claim to title, 1927 . . . Competed unsuccessfully as heavyweight, 1927–28 . . . Knocked out Berlenbach again but lost to Jimmy Maloney, Johnny Risko, Tom Heeney and was kayoed in first round by Jack Sharkey, 4/30/28 . . . Inactive 1929—31 . . . Won 3 bouts by knockout in 1932 and then retired . . . Died 11/27/48, Katonah, NY . . . Elected to Boxing Hall of Fame, 1973 . . . Completed record: 94 bouts, 79 won, 10 lost, 2 draws, 1 no-decision, 2 no-contests, 44 knockouts.

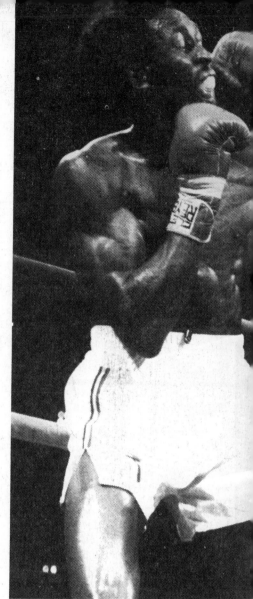

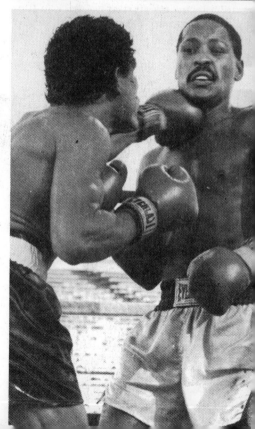

99 WILFRED BENITEZ

WILFRED BENITEZ

If boxing is, as Budd Schulberg says, "Chess played on bodies instead of boards," then Wilfred Benitez is its Capablanca, its Spassky, its Fischer, complete with opening gambits and end games. A disingenuous fighter, insincere in his moves, Benitez would mislead, deceive, trick, and lie to his opponents to coerce them to make their moves first, all the better to counter with. With a slick and sleek style designed to entrap his foe, Benitez practiced a form of boxing which emulated that of a spider trying to draw a fly into its web. He would offer his head as bait, all the while bobbing it up and down like a cork caught under a faucet. And then, almost as if by radar, he would move it at the last split second and, springing the trap, would come back with his own sneaky right, the web slowly encircling his foe. With a genius for backing into a corner and making that little patch of canvas his battleground, Benitez, in his cool and calculating way, could counter with catlike springiness or leave his opponent's imagination to fill in what they couldn't see. And couldn't reach.

WILFRED BENITEZ TOOK HIS FIRST STEP toward fistic greatness on March 6, 1976, when—in a masterful display—the then-17-year-old boy, his face yet to receive its first shave, gave the legendary Junior Welterweight champion, Antonio (Kid Pambele) Cervantes a free boxing lesson. And the feeling he was shoveling smoke as well. It was to be the first of three world titles for Benitez.

But problems were already beginning to erupt like the boils that dot Wilfred's young, handsome face—together with a long, inartistic scar that goes from the end of the nose to the jawbone, a vestigial remainder of a childhood accident when "My face got tangled up in barbed wires." For Benitez's out-of-the-ring exploits, which would have tried the patience of Job, were trying the patience of his manager-trainer, who, not incidentally, was also his father. These estranged bedfellows did more warring than training as Benitez's routine consisted of training in San Juan discotheques from ten at night until five or six in the

morning. "To be honest," Wilfred once told fighter-writer Jose Torres, "I haven't trained more than two weeks for any fight since I beat Kid Pambele."

But, as with all exceptions, Benitez proved the rule as he continued on his merry way, drawing with Harold Weston (twelve days training), narrowly beating Bruce Curry (seven days), the Curry return bout (ten days), and Carlos Palamino for the World welterweight title (fifteen days). It was enough to make a grown man, like his father, cry, but Wilfred proved a genius to his lunacy by continually piling up victory after victory with an economy of effort—both in and out of the ring. It got so you couldn't gauge his performance by taking a cursory look at his extracurricular exploits; somewhat like jumping to a conclusion when your daughter comes home at three in the morning bearing a Gideon Bible.

Finally, though, his candle-burning caught up with Benitez when he put his welterweight title on the line against Sugar Ray Leonard after only nine days in training. His legs gave way in the

220

Born 9/12/58, in the Bronx, NY . . . Raised in Puerto Rico . . . began pro career at age of 15 in Puerto Rico . . . Scored 18 knockouts in first 23 bouts, 1973–75 . . . Defeated Antonio Cervantes in 15-round decision to win world junior welterweight title . . . Youngest boxer to win world championship—17 years, 5 months, 23 days . . . Defended title successfully 3 times, 1976–77 . . . Fought 10-round draw in nontitle bout with Harold Weston, 2/2/77 . . . Vacated crown to move to welterweight class, 1978 . . . Decisioned Carlos Palomino to win world welterweight title, 1/14/79 . . . Defended successfully against Weston, 3/25/79 . . . Lost title to Ray Leonard in bout stopped with only 6 seconds left in final round . . . Became one of very few who have won 3 world titles when he defeated Maurice Hope via twelfth-round kayo, 5/23/81 to win WBC junior middleweight title . . . Defended against Carlos Santos, 11/13/81 . . . Became one of few men to defeat Roberto Duran, 1/30/82, in 15-round decision title defense . . . Lost title to Thomas Hearns, 12/3/82 . . . Complete record: 49 bouts, 44 won, 4 lost, 1 draw, 26 knockouts.

Left: Benitez catches Tommy Hearns with a long left in losing effort, Dec. 3, 1982.

third round and finally gave out in the fifteenth, and Benitez, who had entered the ring with a proud strut, was reduced to looking like a tearful little boy who had lost his mittens, his unblemished record, and title as well.

Believing, like Oscar Wilde, that "Three addresses always inspire confidence . . . even in tradesmen . . . " Wilfred and his new manager, Jimmy Jacobs, set their sights on the junior middleweight champion of the world, Maurice Hope. And Wilfred's third title. In that by-now familiar style of his, so cocky he could strut sitting down, Benitez kept Hope and the fight in control, his defense his offense, until the twelfth round when he implanted the bandolero, a hard right cross. Hope went down. Hard. And out. Suddenly, Wilfred Benitez had become the fifth three-time champion.

After defending his crown twice, Benitez put it on the line against Tommy Hearns in the last 15-round fight sanctioned by the knee-jerk-offs known as the WBC. And for 15 rounds it was almost as if Benitez, who had had his hands dealt to him, fought as if he were the king and Hearns had led the ace, as Hearns would have no part of the traps Benitez set to ensnare him and won, going away.

Wilfred Benitez will be remembered years from now as one of the most talented defensive fighters of all time; a master strategist who fought to a fault—that of his opponents, as he used their mistakes to entrap them. And, in the end, was entrapped by his own fault of not training, a fault-line which demeaned his greatness and cost him dearly.

Far left: Benitez fights Mustaffa Hamsho, fails to move into middleweight class. Left: Benitez fires at head of Sugar Ray Leonard, 1979.

221

GENE FULLMER

Gene Fullmer was not just another pretty face in boxing's passing parade. In fact, he looked like his head had been halved and put back together like an apple, only a mite off-center. With a toothache thrown in for good measure. But, then again, Gene Fullmer wasn't a lot of other things, as well. For this middleweight, who looked like he stepped right out of the pages of a Hans Christian Andersen fairy tale gone wrong, had a pitiable left jab, movements that looked like they were choreographed by Sabu—including the barreling into his opponent with his head down as if he were checking to see if his zipper was open—and a general all around style that gave the words "ring science" a bad name. To further add to his laundry list of non-assets, Fullmer did not have a devastating power punch, threw his punches from far back of the shoulder, like Bob Feller, could be hit by anyone within hailing distance. But damn, could he fight.

WHEN TEDDY BRENNER, THEN THE matchmaker at Brooklyn's Eastern Parkway Arena, and a pretty good judge of boxing flesh, to boot, first laid eyes on Gene Fullmer in the gym, he couldn't believe what he was seeing. Calling over Fullmer's manager, Marv Jensen, Brenner offered him a sound piece of advice, or something that passed for same. "Marv," Brenner solemnly intoned, "do me a favor, will ya? . . . I don't care if your boy's had 24 straight wins and 19 knockouts, just get him out of here. . . . Take him home and keep him home. . . . And, forget the train fare, this one's on me. Just get that guy out of here before he falls over his own two feet and breaks his damn fool neck!" Despite all his fistic shortcomings, Fullmer possessed an intangible something that neither Brenner nor anyone else could see: guts, a rare commodity on which he almost cornered the market.

In the fifties, Fullmer soon became standard television fare as he fought for Teddy Brenner and everybody else. And most of them were winning efforts, as this fireplug with square muscular shoulders—and muscular everything else—and an apparent death wish swarmed all over his opponents like a seven year locust, giving them little or no chance to move, catch their breath or check the license plate of who or what had just run over them.

Fullmer continued his climb up the fistic ladder until, one week after Sugar Ray Robinson successfully defended his title against Bobo Olson, he moved to the head of the middleweight class with a convincing win over the number one contender, Charley Humez. But Robinson, as crafty outside the ring as in, put Fullmer and company over the barrel, and, in the proverbial "no tickee, no laundry" threat, insisted that his contractual demands be satisfied or he would take his title and defend it elsewhere. Finally, Fullmer and company succumbed to the sweat of Robinson's brow beating and took the barrel—which, translated, came to 12½ percent of the gate and none of the television monies.

But Fullmer was satisfied with his part of the purse, even if it was so small Because, by agreeing to Robinson's demands, he had also gotten Robinson to agree to fight him. And Fullmer was more than satisfied he could whip the man who, "was recognized as the greatest thing since popcorn.

And, on the night of January 2, 1957, in front of a packed house at Madison Square Garden, Fullmer proved to be right, taking handfuls of Robinson, like freshly popped corn, as he won a 15 rounder with ease, roughing up the aging champion's body and probing at his head—or anything else that was available—with his right.

One hundred nineteen days later the two met again in Chicago. For the first four rounds it merely looked like an extension of their previous 15 as Fullmer, fighting as if the best way out was straight through, constantly moved forward and raked Robinson's body with murderous thunderclaps, delivered with malice aforethought. Robinson, who had thrown everything, including his pomade, at the advancing troglodyte, momentarily entertained notions of retiring in his corner between the fourth and fifth rounds. But fleeting thoughts to the contrary, the fleet-footed Sugarman came out for the fifth, one of the most remembered rounds in modern boxing history. As history would record it, during one of Fullmer's out-of-control forward lunges, Robinson crashed his left hand straight to the point of Fullmer's totally exposed jaw, dropping Fullmer in a manner similar to his look-alike, King Kong, there to be counted out for the first, and only, time in his career.

After the Robinson fight, Gene Fullmer was relegated to boxing's sidelines, the sport's "Forgotten Man." But Gene Fullmer would no more be forgotten than he was forgettable, and, given another chance to prove there was life in the lion yet, came back to knock out the supposedly indestructible Carmen Basilio for the NBA middleweight title.

Born 7/21/31, in West Jordan, UT . . . Began boxing professionally, 1951 . . . Won first 11 bouts by knockout and 6 in first round . . . Won first 29 bouts with 19 KOs, though only scored 5 knockouts in next 35 bouts . . . Won world middleweight championship, 1/2/57, with 15-round decision over Sugar Ray Robinson . . . Lost title to Robinson on fifth-round KO, 5/1/57 . . . Won vacant NBA middleweight championship stopping Carmen Basilio in fourteenth round, 8/28/58 . . . Again stopped Basilio in twelfth round of rematch, 6/29/60, only 2 knockouts in Basilio's career . . . Defended NBA crown successfully 7 times, including 2 championship draws in single year—Joey Giardello, 4/20/60, and Sugar Ray Robinson, 12/3/60 . . . Defeated Robinson in fourth bout of series, 3/4/61, in 15-round decision . . . Lost title to Dick Tiger, 10/23/62, 15-round decision . . . Fought draw in title rematch with Tiger, 2/23/63 . . . Stopped by Tiger in seventh round of rematch for title, 8/28/63, in Ibadan, Nigeria . . . Only champion to fight his last bout in Nigeria . . . Elected to Boxing Hall of Fame, 1974 . . . Complete record: 64 bouts, 55 won, 6 lost, 3 draws, 24 knockouts.

Those bettors known collectively as "smart money": will lay you 6-5 that if Mike Tyson were hit by lightning, the lightning would have to be towed away for repairs. His own thunder, in fact, is so impressive that this young warrior with the square torso, heavily muscled arms, and granite jaw has risen to the cusp of greatness in just three short years.

Coming out of Catskill, New York, by way of the mean streets of New York's Brownsville section, the youngster, who called himself, "a poor black heading in a direction... I don't know where," was sent, courtesy of the State, to a penal institute in upstate Johnstown. There he was to fall under the tutelage of his boxing Svengali, the fabled Cus D'Amato, who had led Floyd Patterson and Jose Torres to world titles many years earlier. Taking Tyson under his crusty old wing, D'Amato, who possessed a cauliflower tongue given equally to lessons on history, manners, and phobias, began filling the empty 5'11", 200-pound vessel with his values and philosophies, serving as a surrogate father-cum-manager.

SATISFIED WITH TYSON'S APPRENticeship in the amateur ranks, D'Amato took Tyson pro in March of 1985. Starting with Hector Mercedes—not even a household name in his own household, but a name that would go down in boxing history as Tyson's first knockout victim, and go down himself in the first round—Tyson dispensed opponent-after-opponent asfastasyoucanreadthis. Suddenly the dues-paying fan, who had watched the knockout puncher all but disappear from the heavyweight ranks, began to sit up and take notice of the growing presence on the heavyweight scene of the 19-year-old youngster.

Unfortunately, D'Amato was not there to share in Tyson's growing celebrity, passing away late in 1985. But his torch was picked up by his long-time disciple, Jimmy Jacobs, who, not incidentally, owned—in tandem with his partner, Bill Cayton—the largest collections of boxing films ever captured on celluloid. Those films were to play an important role in the ongoing development of Mike Tyson, both as a fighter and as a student of "The Sweet Science." For if one were to parse the style of Tyson, it would be part that of Floyd Patterson and Jose Torres, courtesy of Mr. D'Amato's tutelage, and part that of Jack

Dempsey and Battling Nelson, courtesy of Mr. Edison's invention. Professional Tyson-watchers, of whom there are many, claim they can see in his style both the fearsome body shots of a Patterson and a Torres and the intimidating looks of a Dempsey—from his snarling grimace that would cause burnt toast to curl up around the edges, and his ice cream-cold stare down to his soup-bowl haircut and lack of the traditional paraphernalia of boxers, coming into the ring wearing no robe, no socks, only clothed in sweat—as well as the ferocious postering of a Nelson.

Coupled with these throwbacks to greatness was his packaging. Jacobs, picking up where D'Amato had left off, continued Tyson on his "Bum of the Month" tour, one reminiscent of Joe Louis' early march through the heavyweight ranks. 19 times Tyson became a repeating decimel as he dispatched, in an average of less than two rounds, a pile of assorted millstones, all of whom came into the ring looking for corners to lie down in. Had there been an investiture for the heavyweight crown at that point, Tyson would have been named its king, gloves down.

Just when the boxing community was beginning to brush off its catchall

Born Michael Gerald Tyson, 6/30/66, in Brooklyn, N.Y....Nickname: "Iron Mike"...Began pro career 3/6/85, with 107-second knockout of Hector Mercedes in Albany, N.Y....Had 15 fights in 1985, all knockouts...Won next four fights by knockout for best knockout streak at start of career for any heavyweight in boxing history...Streak ended 5/3/86 when James "Quick" Tillis extended Tyson in 10-round decision...Followed with another 10-round win over Mitch "Blood" Green, 5/20/86, at Madison Square Garden, then knocked out next six opponents for a record of 27-0 with 25 KO's...Fought Trevor Berbick for WBC heavyweight title, 11/22/86, winning crown with second-round KO...Won WBA portion of championship in next fight with a boring 12-round decision over James "Bonehugger" Smith, 3/7/86...Defended two titles 5/30/87 against Pinklon Thomas, scoring a 6th-round KO...Consolidated heavyweight championship with a 12-round unanimous decision over IBF titleist Tony Tucker, 8/1/87...Defended unified heavyweight title three times...Knocked out Tyrell Biggs, 10/16/87, Larry Holmes, 1/22/88, and Tony Tubbs, 3/21/88, the Tubbs fight only the second heavyweight title bout in the Orient...Knocked out Michael Spinks in 91 seconds in bout advertised as "once and For All", 6/27/88, to solidify claim as undisputed heavyweight champion...Complete record: 35 bouts, 35 won, 0 lost, 31 knockouts.

phrases like "Great" and "Invincible," the ungraspable happened: James "Quick" Tillis and Mitch "Blood" Green both extended the man-boy now known as "Iron Mike" to the 10-round limit. Boxing fans began to wonder if their faith in Gilbraltar had been shaken. But Tyson preserved his negotiability with six more knockouts, and all of a sudden stood on the threshhold of the heavy-weight title. Or at least a third of it. For the sport of boxing had three heavy-weight champs in November of 1986: Trevor Berbick, recognized by the WBC; Tim Witherspoon, by the WBA; and Michael Spinks, by the IBF.

Just when it seemed that nothing short of a divining rod would be needed to find out who was who, into the vac-uum came HBO, willing to spend mega-bucks to sponsor something called "The Heavyweight Unification Tournament," a sort of a box-off for the undisputed heavyweight championship. HBO sensed that it needed a new young star to try to make chicken salad out of the chicken droppings being held out to the boxing fan as heavyweight crowns. That new star was Mike Tyson. Matched against the WBC titleholder, Trevor Ber-bick, Tyson frescoed him in two to be-come the youngest heavyweight champ in history. Then he added the WBA belt by beating "Bonecrusher" Smith in a fight about as exciting as Monday morn-ing. And, finally, solidified his claim to the undisputed title—and harmonic convergence to the heavyweight divi-sion—with a decision win over the IBF titleist Tony Tucker. And, in so doing, became the first undisputed champion since Leon Spinks briefly ruled the roost back in 1978.

However, there was a body of opinion which held that Michael Spinks, who had beaten former champion Larry Holmes, was the true champion, his lin-eage, according to Jimmy Jacobs, "tracing back to John L. Sullivan." It was, therefore, only natural, that the two claimants should settle the matter, "Once and For All"—as the fight was billed. But the fight was really no fight at all. If was fungo practice for Tyson as he smote Spinks with two wrecker's balls, driving his left hand to the head and his right to the body after faking Spinks out of his shoes, and driving Spinks to the canvas as well. Getting up from his unfamiliar perch, Spinks deter-mined to on a suicidal course: to go back into the teeth of the storm, and

threw an overhand right. But it was a right that would never land. For Tyson threw a roundhouse left to bring Spinks into range and then followed through, full timber and pallette, with a right up-percut that landed on the crouching Spinks with the sound of surf slapping shore. It was all over in just 91 seconds, the fourth quickest knockout in heavy-weight championship history.

As the referee tolled off the final sec-onds, the triumphant Mike Tyson calmly looked down at the ringside press and

told some of the assembled, "I'm the best fighter in the world and you can print that."

That you are, Mike. And one of the best of all time as well. Just how far you'll go depends entirely on you. But as of this writing we can confidently call you one of our "Greatest," and if push came to shove, rate you somewhere around number 27 on our all-time hit list. With a bullet, like they do on the music charts, to show that you're still on the rise.